Lille

the Bradt City Guide

Laurence Phillips

www.bradtguides.com

Bradt Travel Guides Ltd, UK
The Globe Pequot Press Inc, USA

edition
4

LILLE: DON'T MISS

You cannot separate the city from its people. The centuries-old buildings may be spectacular, but it is the energy of the Lillois that gives the place its unique buzz. Lille is a place where youth meets history, and the past is best viewed through the prism of a lively weekend in the present.

1 A Sunday night tango in the Renaissance cloisters of the Vieille Bourse. 2 Mooch among the menus on place Rihour. 3 Bargain hunting at the Braderie. 4 La Déesse, goddess and symbol of the city, lords over all on Grand' Place. 5 Get your culture fix at the Palais des Beaux-Arts where Napoleon's looted artwork collection is now a national treasure.

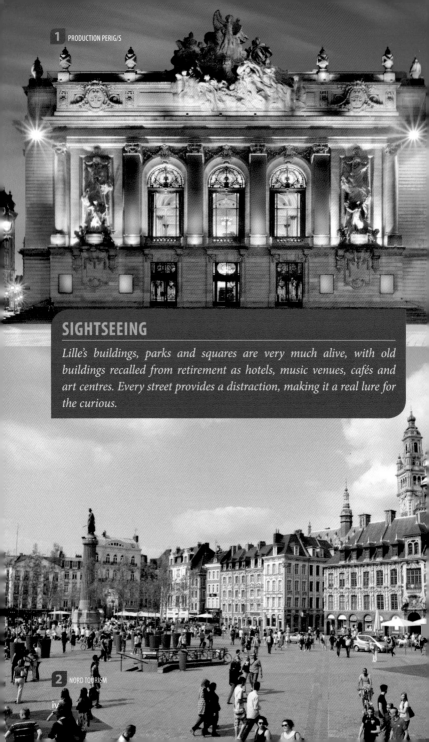

SIGHTSEEING

Lille's buildings, parks and squares are very much alive, with old buildings recalled from retirement as hotels, music venues, cafés and art centres. Every street provides a distraction, making it a real lure for the curious.

1 White and gold lights launch a night at the opera. **2** All roads lead to Grand' Place – the heart of the city. **3** The jewel-box beauty of Vieille Bourse is the perfect backdrop for a civilised book market. **4** President Mitterand's statue by Gare Lille Europe welcomes Eurostar arrivals to the new Parc Matisse. **5** Sew on a sequin at La Droguerie – Vieux Lille has eccentric boutiques for every taste. **6** Louis XIV's royal gate at the Citadelle leads to a working army garrison.

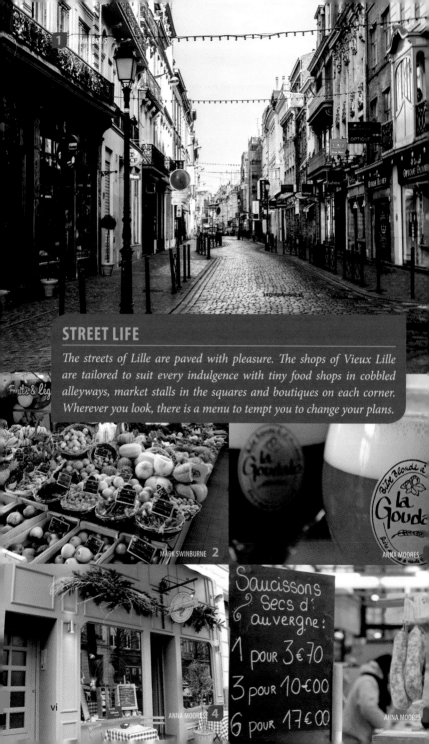

The streets of Lille are paved with pleasure. The shops of Vieux Lille are tailored to suit every indulgence with tiny food shops in cobbled alleyways, market stalls in the squares and boutiques on each corner. Wherever you look, there is a menu to tempt you to change your plans.

MARK SWINBURNE 2

ANNA MOORES

ANNA MOORES 4

ANNA MOORES

Saucissons Secs d' auvergne:
1 pour 3€70
3 pour 10€00
6 pour 17€00

vi

6   **7**   **8**

1 Meert's tea shop on rue Esquermoise is a great first step into historic Vieux Lille. **2** Fresh produce at Wazemmes market. **3** La Goudale takes its name from the English for 'a good ale'. **4** Mix passions for food and people watching at one of Lille's *estaminets*. **5** Sausages from every corner of France can be found in the market halls. **6, 7 & 8** Traditional signs abound. **9** You are always just a knight's move away from a game of chess at the Vieille Bourse.

MEDIANBAO

1

FESTIVE LILLE

The best view of Lille is only available for a few weeks each year. From early December, the city celebrates winter with the big wheel on Grand' Place and the legendary Christmas market on place Rihour.

1&2 Ride the Ferris wheel for great views over the squares. **3 & 4** Indulge in mulled wine or be inspired to upgrade your own festive decorations with ideas from the craft stalls.

2

3

4

ANNA MOORES

ANNA MOORES

MARK SWINBURNE

AUTHOR

Laurence Phillips (www.laurencephillips.com) has been escaping to France since boyhood and has written many and varied guides to the country, most recently the *Lazy France* guide to Marseillan and a Lot of Languedoc and companion to Robert Louis Stevenson's classic *Travels With a Donkey in the Cevennes*. He has been described by the French press as a charming *bon vivant* and by British critics as a witty and entertaining enthusiast. His passion for all things French has fuelled countless BBC radio broadcasts, including Radio 4's *Allez Lille*, and his is a familiar voice on travel and arts programmes. His 2009 collection of short stories, *Garson Lazarre's Paris Confidential*, is a satirical appraisal of the capital's expatriate celebrity circuit. In France, he has been honoured as a Commander of the Order of St Nectaire cheese and a Squire of the Confrérie des Sacres de la Champagne (although for the latter citation he was inscribed as Madame Laurence Phillips, which possibly makes him a Dame). Three-times winner of the prestigious Guide Book of the Year award from the British Guild of Travel Writers, for this book and the *Bradt Guide to Eurostar Cities*, he combines wanderlust with a love for theatre and work as a critic, playwright and songwriter, and has written for the Royal Shakespeare Company. His stage work has clocked up more travel miles than the author, being performed on four continents, from the West End to the South Pacific.

Fourth edition published May 2015
First published 2004
Bradt Travel Guides Ltd
IDC House, The Vale, Chalfont St Peter, Bucks SL9 9RZ, England
www.bradtguides.com
Print edition published in the USA by The Globe Pequot Press Inc, PO Box
480, Guilford, Connecticut 06437-0480

Text copyright © 2015 Laurence Phillips
Maps copyright © 2015 Bradt Travel Guides Ltd
Metro map copyright © 2014 Urbanrail.net (R Schwandl)
Photographs copyright © 2015 Individual photographers (see below)
Project Manager: Laura Pidgley
Cover research: Pepi Bluck, Perfect Picture

British Library Cataloguing in Publication Data
A catalogue record for this book is available from the British Library

ISBN-13: 978 1 84162 911 7 (print)
e-ISBN: 978 1 78477 123 2 (Epub)
e-ISBN: 978 1 78477 223 9 (mobi)

Photographs
© individual photographers credited beside images; those from image libraries credited
as follows: Alamy (A); Shutterstock (S)

Front cover Inside the famous Meert pâtisserie (Hemis/A)
Back cover The belfry on Grand' Place (Production Perig/S)
Title page Façade of the Brasserie de la Cloche (Nord Tourism); The big wheel and belfry
on Grand' Place (Anna Moores); Cakes on sale in Paul (Laurence Phillips)

Maps David McCutcheon FBCart.S

Typeset by Ian Spick, Bradt Travel Guides
Production managed by Jellyfish Print Solutions; printed in India
Digital conversion by www.dataworks.co.in

AUTHOR'S STORY

Nobody was more surprised than I when Bradt decided to back my project to write a guidebook to Lille. On reflection, it made a certain sense. Bradt has a global reputation for revealing the charms of places often overlooked, and when first I began broadcasting and writing about Lille, even the French raised an eyebrow or two. On the original publication, as part of a guide to all the Eurostar cities, Bradt determined not to launch the title in Paris, London or even Brussels, but in Lille's Palais Rihour, imperial seat of the city's heyday well before its rediscovery as Europe's cultural capital.

To the outside world, the outside France even, Lille was a slag-heap, a monochrome reminder of a failed industrial past. Echoes of Emile Zola's *Germinal* and simple metropolitan snobbery regarding northerners helped perpetuate the prejudices. I'd personally broken through the barrier when hitchhiking from the ferry ports in the rain – I found myself in a contemporary Brigadoon, where bright lights and pulsating partying punctuated the midnight hour and positively punctured the propaganda. People were vivacious, generous and fun. Next morning, in the dazzling sunlight of day, the glowing beauty of gabled cobbled Flanders lay before me, a true European jewel in a contemporary cosmopolitan pleasure-ground.

Since opening and sharing my no-longer-secret address book, each new edition, each reprint, has chronicled the blossoming of a metropolis coming of age at the heart of Europe. No more need to explain. This once unmentionable city has become a point of reference for the rest of the Continent, with style magazines and travel gurus ever hailing the next discovery destination as 'the New Lille'.

FEEDBACK REQUEST AND UPDATES WEBSITE

At Bradt Travel Guides we're aware that guidebooks start to go out of date on the day they're published – and that you, our readers, are out there in the field doing research of your own. You'll find out before us when a fine new family-run hotel opens or a favourite restaurant changes hands and goes downhill. So why not write and tell us about your experiences? Contact us on ☎ 01753 893444 or e info@bradtguides.com. We will forward emails to the author who may post updates on the Bradt website at 🖰 www.bradtupdates.com/lille. Alternatively you can add a review of the book to 🖰 www.bradtguides.com or Amazon.

© Bradt Travel Guides Ltd

Citadelle

ZOO
pages 193–4
In the grounds of the Citadelle, the zoo is an ideal (and free) family treat, and a charming digression from a country walk in the Bois de Boulogne.

Eglise Ste Cathérine

Zoo

Jardin Vauban

BOULEVARD DE LA LIBERTÉ

RUE NATIONALE

CITADELLE
pages 174–5
Louis XIV's classic five-sided fortress, built and governed by royal military architect Vauban, remains a working garrison standing in the city-centre park and woodland.

Eglise Sacré Cœur

RUE NATIONALE

Palais

BOULEVARD DE LA LIBERTÉ

RUE NATIONALE

RUE SOLFÉRINO

WAZEMMES MARKET
page 161
If you miss the annual Braderie, then make sure you visit the Sunday flea market in a lively, up-and-coming quarter.

Palais des Beaux-Arts

Marché de Wazemmes

RUE SOLFÉRINO

Eglise St Pierre et St Paul

PALAIS DES BEAUX-ARTS
pages 169–71
France's second museum after the Paris Louvre with Flemish, Renaissance and Impressionist galleries.

GRAND' PLACE
pages 177–80
The main hub and social rendezvous where Vieux Lille opens out to the modern shopping district. The square is overlooked by a statue of the city's goddess.

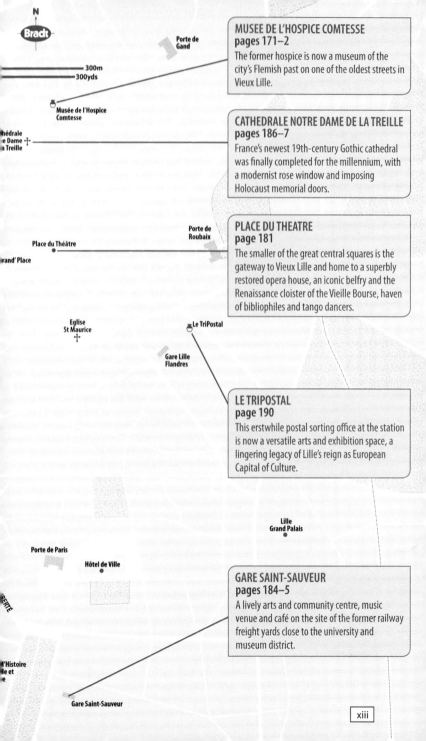

N

Bradt

300m
300yds

Porte de
Gand

Musée de l'Hospice
Comtesse

MUSEE DE L'HOSPICE COMTESSE
pages 171–2
The former hospice is now a museum of the
city's Flemish past on one of the oldest streets in
Vieux Lille.

Cathédrale
e Dame
a Treille

CATHEDRALE NOTRE DAME DE LA TREILLE
pages 186–7
France's newest 19th-century Gothic cathedral
was finally completed for the millennium, with
a modernist rose window and imposing
Holocaust memorial doors.

Place du Théâtre

Porte de
Roubaix

rand' Place

PLACE DU THEATRE
page 181
The smaller of the great central squares is the
gateway to Vieux Lille and home to a superbly
restored opera house, an iconic belfry and the
Renaissance cloister of the Vieille Bourse, haven
of bibliophiles and tango dancers.

Eglise
St Maurice

Le TriPostal

Gare Lille
Flandres

LE TRIPOSTAL
page 190
This erstwhile postal sorting office at the station
is now a versatile arts and exhibition space, a
lingering legacy of Lille's reign as European
Capital of Culture.

Lille
Grand Palais

Porte de Paris

Hôtel de Ville

GARE SAINT-SAUVEUR
pages 184–5
A lively arts and community centre, music
venue and café on the site of the former railway
freight yards close to the university and
museum district.

BERTÉ

'Histoire
le et
e

Gare Saint-Sauveur

Contents

ACKNOWLEDGEMENTS

Special thanks to my dining partners in Lille for letting me reveal their secret tourist-free tables; to those generous readers who emailed me with their own stories of this special city; to Vera Dupuis, her heirs and successors, especially Bruno Cappelle (now at the Louvre-Lens) and Audrey Chaix, for their unstinting support; and to Delphine Bartier, of the CDT Nord and her colleagues in the wider region and the Pas de Calais; to the editorial team at Bradt for reining in my ramblings, airbrushing my grammar and granting me the illusion of fluency; to my family and friends for bearing with me as I disappeared on yet another culinary and cultural expedition; and of course to my parents, Di and Ronald Phillips, for getting out the car and ferrying me from table to table, and wallowing in cholesterol when, as usual, the clock and the calendar said we'd never finish the infinite mealtime of summer.

DEDICATION
To Stéphane Fichet
who has had to endure my lyrical appreciation of so many fine meals,
without the joy of actually passing a fork from plate to palate!

LIST OF MAPS

PREFACE

How can you fail to fall in love with a city that erects a statue to a lullaby? Although the *Internationale* was composed in Lille, the song the townsfolk took to their hearts was *Le P'tit Quinquin*, a sentimental patois melodrama of a poor lacemaker and her weeping baby. The statue, ravaged by a million scrambled cuddles and kisses, is a working-class *Madonna and Child* to melt the hardest of hearts. The town clocks still chime the tune each day at noon.

For years, Lille was France's best-kept secret. Despite charming cobbled streets, broad Flemish squares and the richest art gallery outside Paris, Lille was tucked away in a coal-mining region, scorned by Parisians and ignored by tourists. Then came Channel Tunnel trains linking Europe's key capitals, and the city was reborn. Lille may have a population of barely 227,000 but, with literally millions of people now living within an hour of the city, it is an unofficial capital in its own right, deservedly chosen as the European Capital of Culture for 2004.

Lille2004 was just the excuse Lille needed to kick-start another renaissance: a dozen brand new and wonderfully inventive arts centres set up in remarkable buildings in towns around the city itself; the reopening of one of France's most beautiful opera houses; a calendar packed with reasons to dine and dance until dawn; and a programme of performance, from Shakespeare to tango, to rival any capital city in the world.

Proof came with the very first street party. We all wore white as exotic images were projected on to the milling throng. Organisers had expected around 200,000 people to take to the streets and were quite frankly astounded when the best part of a million good-natured revellers managed to squeeze into central Lille. I tried to surf the human tide to see a thousand musicians perform the opening concert (Berlioz's *Chant des Chemins de Fer*, composed for the arrival of the first Paris–Lille train in 1846), but was swept away towards the main squares where artificial snow accompanied partygoers en route to the magnificent firework display by the Esplanade. *Les showgirls* and boys of the lamented Folies de Paris performed in the Chamber of Commerce, and the rest of us danced 'til dawn around the flames of square Foch, in the pink light of the Gare Lille Flandres and to the sound of *chansons* at the Hôtel de Ville.

The year was punctuated with many such explosions of high-octane bonhomie and the theme-party tradition is now confirmed as an essential part of city life in the 21st century. Like the Maisons Folies, the new TriPostal centre, the now reinvented Saint-Sauveur goods yard, beautifully restored churches, and the promise of more new urban parks, weekends of merrymaking are the long-term legacy of an unforgettable year. Eight million party animals can't be wrong! 2004 certainly pulled in the punters to the last, with a respectable 300,000 filling the squares and beyond for November's final knees-up.

Then came the decision – the party was not over. Cue Lille3000, a biennial mini-me to the original festival. From an opening season in 2007 that brought India to Flanders – with the rue Faidherbe most memorably lined with elephants – bringing a million visitors to the city, and the 2011 and 2013 events wooing two million sensation seekers. The autumn/winter of 2015/16 is predicted to bring even more people to Lille as the city declares the launch of a new global Renaissance era open from September.

A glance at the free listings magazine *Sortir* promises hundreds of events any Saturday night, from the national theatres and concert halls to smoky dives, film festivals and rock happenings. As for art, Lille can barely contain its national and international treasures: the city's cultural map embraces towns for miles around, and not just the new Louvre in Lens. For years Picassos and Braques have packed out the Musée d'Art Moderne at the Villeneuve d'Ascq campus; Roubaix's Piscine is home to a truly eclectic and thrilling art collection, worth a day or two of anyone's life; and Matisse's private pictures are an essential drive away at Le Cateau-Cambrésis. In the city itself, museums include the Palais des Beaux Arts, France's second collection after the Louvre, with its wickedly wonderful Goyas and splendid Renaissance treats, its deep-red walls and high ceilings being the perfect backdrop to a veritable banquet of masterpieces from the 17th century to the Impressionists. The Capital of Culture drew 387,000 art lovers to a prestigious Rubens exhibition, yet visitors at any time may see the artist's majestic *Descent from the Cross* in the Palais, or while away a weekend hour in a natural history museum so quaintly dated with suspended skeletons and tableaux of taxidermy as to provide other-worldly diversions from the vibrant good-time city.

Elsewhere this might be the stuff of stuffiness, but in such a youthful and exuberant university town there is always a definite buzz in the air, the vitality of youth amid improbably quaint 17th- and 18th-century elegance.

Whether you are in Lille to meet up with friends, or just to celebrate your own special weekend; whether you are lifting a *bière blanche* in an *estaminet* or raising your fork in a Michelin-starred restaurant; whether you are admiring Old Masters in a museum or breaking bread with a young artist in his studio; whether you are among the crowds packing Grand' Place on a midsummer night's free rock concert or listening to a chamber recital in a baroque salon: wander, wonder and wallow in a corner of the world that has always been a capital city of culture. Let music follow your footsteps into history, let your taste buds tempt you from your chosen path. Let lunch segue into dinner, Art Deco streets lead you to the talents of tomorrow and the sounds of a lone midnight saxophone from an open window in the lamplight blend into a bedtime serenade in a city that, more than any other, knows the value of a great lullaby.

Laurence Phillips
e lolly@laurencephillips.com
@LazyFrance

HOW TO USE THIS BOOK

SYMBOLS These indicate the location of venues/sites/sights listed in the book (see pages 9–14 for more information):

- **VL** Vieux Lille
- **GP** Grand' Place to République
- **M** Markets
- **S** Stations/Hôtel de Ville
- 🚊 Closest métro or tram stop
- **E★** Suggests the most direct route from the Eurostar terminus, using métro, tram and bus services.
- 💰 Entrance fee
- 📍 Grid reference

MAPS *Find the city maps on pages 234–8.*
Keys Alphabetical keys cover the locations of places to eat and drink featured in the book. These can be found on page 235 for the overview map, and on the inside back cover for the Vieux Lille/Grand' Place and Gambetta and Solférino maps.

Grids and grid references Map grid references are listed in brackets after the name of the place or sight of interest in the text, with page number followed by grid number, eg: (📍 236 C3). In the eating and drinking listings in *Chapter 7*, the map page number, grid reference and number of listing in the key is given as follows: 📍 238 G4 ❶.

PRICES

Restaurants The price range included in this guide indicates options ranging from a basic set menu to indulgent à la carte. Where applicable, listings have a price code based on the average price of a three-course meal. All menu prices were verified within a few months of each other, so use them as a comparative guide. See page 74 for price codes.

Hotels Hotel room prices are based on the walk-in rate for a double room in high season. Prices quoted in the text were correct at the time of going to press. See page 55 for price codes.

LILLE AT A GLANCE

Location Northwest France, 45 minutes' drive from the Channel coast. By rail it is 35 minutes from Brussels, 1 hour from Paris and 1 hour 40 minutes from London.

Climate Average temperatures: winter 6°C; spring and autumn 14°C; summer 23°C. For weather forecasts, check online weather services or dial ☎ 08 92 68 02 59

Population 225,784 in the city; 1,108,991 in the greater metropolitan area

Language Predominantly French; also some Flemish. A composite patois *Ch'ti* may also be heard (page 3)

Religion Principally Roman Catholic; also Protestant, Muslim and Jewish (page 41)

Currency Euro

Exchange rate £1 = €1.37, $1 = €0.89 (March 2015)

Time GMT/BST +1 hour

International telephone code +33

Public holidays 1 January, 1 May, 8 May, Pentecost Monday, 14 July (national day), 15 August, 1 November, 11 November, 25 December

School holidays One week at the end of October, two weeks at Christmas, two weeks in February, two in spring, the whole of July and August

SEND US YOUR SNAPS!

We'd love to follow your adventures using our Lille guide – why not send us your photos and stories via Twitter (@BradtGuides) and Instagram (@bradtguides) using the hashtag #lille. Alternatively, you can upload your photos directly to the gallery on the Lille destination page via our website (☎ www.bradtguides.com).

1

Contexts

INTRODUCTION TO THE CITY

When French mayors go to French Mayor School, they all learn several key buzzwords. By far the most popular is the phrase '*Carrefour de l'Europe*' ('The Crossroads of Europe'). The crossroads of the silk route, the wine route, the tin route, even, I presume, the beetroot route. Almost every town in the country claims to have been, at some stage in its history, at the crossroads of Europe. A well-known resort on the Atlantic coast once seized the honour in a triumph of civic pride over orienteering. With so many mayors declaring crossroad status, the historic map of the Continent must have resembled a particularly virulent tartan.

Pierre Mauroy, unique among his mayoral colleagues, claimed the rank as a goal rather than mere heritage. Lille's mayor for 29 years, until handing his flaming torch in 2001 to Martine Aubry, Mauroy was most famously President Mitterand's first prime minister. Like Mitterand, Thatcher and Reagan, his was an iron will, and so, when the Channel Tunnel rail link was agreed, Pierre Mauroy persuaded the world that the shortest distance between two points was a right angle. Thus the Eurostar route was swung in an arc to create a new European hub. With a flourish of the presidential and prime-ministerial pens, Lille was transformed, Cinderella-like, from the depressed centre of a mining district with 40% unemployment to France's third most powerful financial, commercial and industrial centre by the turn of the millennium.

Mauroy's successor is equally worthy of the mantle that she inherited. Aubry's socialist credentials are unquestionable: the blood of Jacques Delors courses through her veins; she was the firebrand who seared the cause of women's rights on the national consciousness; and she is still cheered to the gables during gay pride parties and cultural events alike. By managing to cobble together a left and centre coalition, she survived the political minefields of the 2014 local elections and retained control of the city.

But this corner of France, birthplace of the legendary Charles de Gaulle, has a tradition of social-reforming politicians. Jean Lebas, whose name

1

▲ City rooftops beyond Gare Lille Flandres with the spire of Eglise St Maurice (see page 186)
(Meiqianbao/S)

graces the principal street of nearby Roubaix, was a much-loved mayor of that town, whose valour in two world wars is still spoken of with reverence, as is his institution of paid holidays for factory workers, introduced when he served as minister of works in the pioneering government of Léon Blum. Lebas died a hero, deported by the Nazis.

Politically, Lille may be French, but it was most famously the old capital of Flanders. Perhaps the town's heritage, being variously and successively Flemish, Burgundian, Spanish, Dutch, French, German, French, German and French again, might have inspired Mayor Mauroy's ambitious vision to create the future of Europe in a town that had long been dismissed as a broken yesterday, arguing that in an era of Eurostar, Thalys and TGV, geography should no longer be determined by distance but by time. These days, Paris, Brussels, Amsterdam and even London might be legitimately classed as the suburbs.

And so Lille, the best-kept secret in the world, with a current population of 225,784, became one of the great capital cities of Europe. She may not be the capital of any nation-state, but a morning, weekend or lifetime in her company proves without doubt that Lille is the capital city of life. With its high-flying business community and university campus, Lille is where Europe comes to party. A former director of the Opéra de Lille once told me how he would nip between Germany and Britain to arrange meetings with soloists and musicians during the working day, and how he mixed and matched choruses, soloists and orchestras from around Europe. After all, he argued, the audiences pop over from Cologne, Brittany and Kent; why not the performers? His successor doubtless agreed, and the first opera to be staged after the house's renovation was a co-production with the Théâtre de la Monnaie, Brussels's famous opera house.

The opera is not the only lure in town. With the legendary Goyas, Impressionists and Dutch masters at the Palais des Beaux-Arts, a national

2

theatre, ballet company and orchestra, not to mention scores of smaller theatres and music venues, Lille can offer the Saturday night sensation-seeker as much as any town ten times the size. Serious shopping, from Hermès and Chanel to the flea markets, pulls in bargain hunters and the money-no-object fraternity alike. Good food, great beers, cider and locally distilled *genièvre* are the recipe for a legendary good-natured northern welcome. The introduction of city-centre stewards (recognise them by their colourful sweaters, jackets and caps), whose sole function is to offer help and advice to visitors, is merely the official recognition of a long-time trait. I was not the first stranger to find myself lost in the old town, ask for advice in a bar and be personally escorted by the locals to my destination, with handshakes and good wishes all round.

Perhaps this attitude is born of Lille having discovered the secret of eternal youth. With over 150,000 students living in both the town and the dormitory suburbs of the campus of Villeneuve d'Ascq, 42% of the local population is younger than 25 (27% under 20). Every year brings a new influx of first-time residents to be wowed by the city, youngsters from all over France, and from Europe and beyond, studying at the business, arts, journalism and engineering faculties. Lille hands over to these same *arrivistes* the responsibility of producing the annual *Ch'ti* guide. The *Ch'ti* (named for the local patois) is produced by the business school and is the most comprehensive local directory you will ever find anywhere. Each year a fresh editorial team spends 12 months visiting every establishment in town. With honest, often witty reviews of every shop, photocopy bureau, bar, club and restaurant in Lille and the metropolitan area, the *Ch'ti* is a veritable bible. Until political correctness set in during the mid-1990s, the guide even rated local red-light streets with details of nearest cash and condom dispensers. In the 21st century, the spring launch of the *Ch'ti* comes with a free music festival in the centre of the city – a two-day party. Check out the number of 'C' symbols on the stickers in each restaurant window for an indication of the *Ch'ti* rating (C–CCCCC).

As such an international melting pot, it is sometimes easy to forget that Lille is also a real modern-day capital city. It is capital of a metropolitan area that embraces the former manufacturing towns of Roubaix and Tourcoing and urban areas straddling the Belgian border. It is also capital of the Nord-Pas de Calais region, home to a brand new Louvre museum at Lens, the Canadian memorial at Vimy Ridge, Montreuil, and the floating market gardens of St-Omer, with the Channel ports and tunnel only an hour's drive away.

Although the heritage of the region is generously displayed on the tables of Lille, this is also a country of tomorrows, with wonderfully ambitious projects breathing new life into the old mining district. Perhaps no more so than in Lille, where the uncompromisingly modern Euralille stands comfortably next to the Flemish squares and Art Deco shopping streets. In other cities the grafting of a new high-tech glass-and-chrome futurescape on to a historical

1

landscape would jar like UPVC double glazing on a thatched cottage or ill-fitting dentures in a favourite smile. Lille's newest quarter, from the old railway station to the *périphérique* ring road, settles easily by its classical neighbour. Architect Rem Koolhaas was given free rein over the transformation of 70 hectares of city-centre wasteland reclaimed from the army. His brief: to create a city of the 21st century to greet the high-speed trains. This continues to mutate into new business, administrative and conference districts with contemporary residential projects emerging each season in the hinterland beyond Euralille and the casino. Glass and chrome do not define all new architecture in the city, as, since the Maisons Folies projects and Lille3000 adventures (see pages 188–9), abandoned industrial and historic buildings are being redefined as exciting new public spaces.

This new Lille Europe quarter is just one of the many welcomes that Lille showers on its visitors. If the Grand' Place is forever on the verge of a party, Vieux Lille is a portal to times past, the Citadelle and Bois de Boulogne are a living legacy of the Sun King, and the marketplaces of Wazemmes and Solférino are the pulse of modern life.

Walk back towards your hotel in the late evening, tripping down the *pavé* of the old town towards the magnificent belfry, passing the illuminated ornate scrollwork and carvings over the shopfronts. Look around you at the crystal lights reflecting a hundred diners, families, friends and lovers. Then surrender to temptation and head to the brasserie tables or jazz cellars to steal another hour or two of the perfect weekend.

Lille, capital of the past and beacon of the future, has found her time. As any self-respecting mayor would say, 'Welcome to the crossroads of Europe.'

HISTORY

Lille is a European capital of culture. In its time it has also been capital of Flanders, belonged to the Austrians, Spanish and Dutch, been governed by the royal families of Portugal and Constantinople, and served as the ducal seat of Burgundy, 500km due south. As this guide went to press, it was French.

Nestling in a loop of the River Deûle and its canals, and cornered by Belgium, Lille, in the administrative department of Nord, is capital of the Nord-Pas de Calais region. The region takes in the Côte d'Opale sweep of the Channel coast from the Belgian border, via the ports of Dunkerque, Calais and Boulogne, past the resort of Le Touquet down to the mouth of the Somme, and includes the ancient areas of Artois, Hainaut and French Flanders. Always at the front row of history, this is home to Henry V's Agincourt, Henry VIII's Field of the Cloth of Gold and, more recently, those Flanders fields of World War I. Vimy Ridge lies beside the town of Arras and Hitler's V2 rocket bunker, now a museum of war and space, outside St-Omer. Napoleon stood on the cliffs and planned an invasion of Britain (which never happened) and Louis Blériot looked across the same expanse of sea and planned his historic flight across the Channel. Lille has mattered since at least 1066, when l'Isle (The Island) was mentioned in a charter listing a charitable donation by Baudoin V, Count of Flanders, who owned a fortified stronghold on the site of the present Notre Dame de la Treille. At this time, Grand' Place was already a forum. In 1205, at the time of the Crusades, Count Baudoin IX was crowned king of Constantinople, and his daughters were raised under the protection of the French king, Philippe Auguste. The eldest, Jeanne, married Ferrand of Portugal. As the English and the Holy Roman Empire united with Flanders against France, the French captured Lille after the Battle of Bouvines, in 1214, and the city was given to Jeanne.

Throughout this time Lille had been earning its living through trade. The upper and lower Deûle rivers did not meet, so merchants from Bruges and Ghent, en route to major fairs in Champagne and beyond, were obliged to unload their barges and push carts through the town centre in order to continue their journeys. This staging post evolved into a market town, and textiles and fabrics changed hands, the city even giving its name to some products: Lisle socks – ever wondered where that name came from?

"Lille, capital of the past and beacon of the future, has found her time. Welcome to the crossroads of Europe."

In 1369, Marguerite of Flanders married the Burgundian duke Philippe le Temoin. His ducal successor Philippe le Bon moved the Burgundy court to Lille in 1453 with the construction of the Palais Rihour. Less than a quarter of a century later, in 1477, Lille was handed over to the Hapsburgs when Marie de Bourgogne married Maximilien of Austria. Since the Hapsburgs were as pan-European as you can get, the Spanish King Charles V took on the mantle of emperor and therefore Lille and the Low Countries were considered part of Spain.

Of course, it wasn't too long before France came back into the picture – a couple of centuries after the Hapsburgs first got their hands on the city. In 1663 Maria-Theresa of Spain married Louis XIV, France's Sun King, who, claiming his wife's possessions in northern Europe, set about protecting the dowry, with the great architect Vauban building the fortifications that we know today. The famous five-pointed star-shaped Citadelle and the residential Quartier Royal that dominate Vieux Lille were created during the golden era of construction that began in 1667. During its seasons of favour as a Royal Town, the garrison was governed by both Vauban himself and another swashbuckling hero, d'Artagnan.

This was not the end of the shuttlecock identity saga. From 1708 to 1713, Lille was occupied by the Dutch in a war over the Spanish succession and, in

1792, 35,000 Austrian troops laid siege to the town. However, Lille remained in French hands and took its rightful place in the agriculture and education revolutions of the mid-19th century, with the completion of the main railway line to Paris in 1846 and Louis Pasteur becoming first dean of the Faculty of Science in 1854.

In July 1888, a local wood-turner, Pierre Degeyter, embodied Lille's spirit of social reform and revolution when, in the long-demolished Bar La Liberté in the old St-Sauveur district, he sang for the very first time the music that he had composed for Eugène Pottier's socialist anthem *L'Internationale*, a song that in the coming century would change the world forever.

In the two world wars Lille held out against the invading German armies for three days, both in 1914 and in 1940. Nine hundred houses were destroyed during World War I. During the Nazi occupation, the city's most famous son, Charles de Gaulle, famously led Free France from London.

In 1966 the Communauté Urbaine made Lille the capital of a cluster of towns in the wider region, and in 1981 Mayor Pierre Mauroy became prime minister, laying the seeds of a public transport renaissance. The world's first driverless, fully automated public transport system, the VAL métro, was inaugurated in 1983; ten years later the TGV brought Paris within an hour of the city. In 1994, the Channel Tunnel Eurostar service enabled the new Europe quarter to become a continental hub. The 20th century ended with the reopening of the Palais des Beaux-Arts, France's second national gallery, and the completion (a century behind schedule) of the cathedral.

The 21st century began with Mauroy handing over the city to Martine Aubry and Lille becoming European Capital of Culture in 2004. With characteristic forward planning and boundless optimism, the decision was made to continue the celebrations long past the date that Lille relinquished the European title. Lille3000, a programme of biennial culture festivals, hit the ground running, with world-class arts events and grand gestures, lining the streets with exotic elephants for an Indian-themed season one year, dressing boulevards in filigree canopies another time. The party is over, so long live the party.

MODERN LILLE

France's fourth-largest city and third financial centre, river port, medical research centre and industrial zone is an unlikely success story. The area was crippled by unemployment during the 1960s and 1970s when traditional mining and manufacturing industries declined, yet revived its fortunes in the age of the TGV. The capital of the vast Nord-Pas de Calais region, Lille is at the heart of an extensive metropolitan area of 118 communes crossing national borders into Belgium.

A legacy of centuries of textile manufacturing is the city's current status as the centre of Europe's mail-order industry. Lille is also the principal textile-trading area in France. There are more law companies based here than anywhere else outside Paris, and it is the second city for insurance companies.

By contrast, the city's huge transient student population, coupled with the region's socialist heritage, means that, unusually in a city with such a large business community, left-wing causes are very much to the fore. Even during the most recent European elections, with some creative alliances with the moderate-centre parties, Lille managed to avoid the swing to the far right that affected many other towns and cities in France. Regular good-natured marches, protests and rallies criss-cross the city, from Hôtel de Ville to Grand' Place and the stations, with a carnival air about them.

THE FUTURE

A green park for the centre of Lille itself and the reinvention of an abandoned railway yard brought a breath of fresh air to a former city car park, and the Maisons Folies (pages 190–3) continue to rejuvenate towns across the region. Most recently the slag-heaps of the old mining communities took on a near Parisian cachet as the nearby town of Lens, previously only really known for its *Sang et Or* football team, was plucked from obscurity to open France's second Louvre museum (pages 210–12). This satellite of the world's most famous museum now houses up to 700 of the nation's greatest art treasures in a rule-breaking exhibition space folded into the landscape of the former Théodore Barrois pit-head: the northern talent for reinvention continues apace. In Lille itself, the neglected southern quarters behind the conference and casino district are currently being revived with new open spaces and attractions. The next new public space to emerge in the heart of town will probably be the stunning Chamber of Commerce building under the iconic belfry by the main squares – signature venue of the 2015/16 arts festivals. The *Gault Millau* gastro guides are predicting that the next generation of great chefs will emerge from the cobbles of Vieux Lille.

For whom the lunch bell tolls;
the sign outside the Brasserie
de la Cloche (pages 86–7)
(Nord Tourism)

8

2

Planning

THE CITY: A PRACTICAL OVERVIEW

Lille has grown somewhat since its early years when it was clustered around the site of today's Notre Dame de la Treille. First, Louis XIV built his fortress on a virtual island in the River Deûle and commissioned a residential quarter next to the old trading district. As it sprawled in all directions, the city swallowed up neighbouring districts – those quarters that still bear the names associated with their own histories. On maps you will see **Lille Centre** around the main squares, with the university-lined boulevards known as **Vauban Esquermes** stretching westward; to the south are **Wazemmes**, **Moulins** and **Lille Sud**; eastward is the **Fives** district; and to the north are **Vieux Lille** and **St-Maurice Pellevoisin**. The neighbouring communes of **Lomme**, **Lambersart**, **La Madeleine** and **Hellemmes** are now very much part of Lille itself.

Lille is surprisingly compact and very easy to explore on foot – that is, if you are wearing your sturdiest walking shoes rather than the stylish footwear sold in a dozen exclusive emporia in the hilly and cobbled old town. Even without using the excellent public transport system, you can cross from one side of the central area to another in 15 minutes. To make life even easier for readers, we have divided the centre of Lille into four easily distinguished zones:

VIEUX LILLE ⓥ   Vieux Lille is a very special place. Looming gables, cobbled streets, intoxicatingly wonderful street names promising golden lions, hunchbacked cats or freshly minted coins at every turn. Since the principal roads were laid out in sweeping arcs to protect the long-forgotten castle on the site of the old castrum fortified camp, and many other streets were reclaimed from canals, no map will ever satisfactorily convey the geography of the place.

The first-, second- or fifth-time visitor should be prepared to surrender to fate and banish any dreams of short cuts. Getting lost is among the greatest pleasures that Lille has to offer its visitors, with so many entrancing little shops selling antiques, fragrant soaps and sumptuous linens that every

9

journey brings its own diversions. Don't try to second-guess the map: turning left, left, left and left again, may not bring you back to where you started. Vieux Lille is hilly, and with some streets reclaimed from canals, you may actually end up on a road 20m below the pavement you were expecting!

From central Lille it seems that all roads lead to the old quarter. The Parc Matisse may be the short cut from the station, and the Alcide archway on Grand' Place might seem an obvious entrance. However, the most comfortable introduction is from the rue de la Bourse by the distinctive belfry on place du Théâtre. A few paces lead to rue de la Grande Chaussée; an iron arm above the corner shop will point you in the right direction. Charles, Comte d'Artagnan, lived at numbers 20 and 26; you can see the old walls from La Botte Chantilly, the shoe shop on the ground floor. Turn right along rue des Chats Bossus and admire the fabulous Breton Art Deco mosaic frontage of L'Huîtrière restaurant. Continue across the place du Lion d'Or to the 17th-century rue de la Monnaie. Named after the royal mint, this is the oldest street and has many of the original traders' emblems above the regimented shopfronts. Like the rues Royale and Basse, it wraps around the cathedral, following the line of the moat. Houses of red Armentières brick and white Lezennes stone have doorways adorned with cherubs, cornucopia and wheatsheaves, all painstakingly restored in the 1960s.

Rue de la Monnaie links the market square of place du Concert with the main hub of the old town, place du Lion d'Or and the adjacent place Louise de Bettignies. The latter was named for a local heroine, a spy who died at the hands of the Germans in 1915. Number 29 is the Demeure Gilles de la Boë, a handsome baroque house dating from 1636 that once overlooked the inland port. Lille's name derives from its original position as an island between the upper and lower Deûle rivers, and the wealth of Vieux Lille comes from the thriving trade between merchants plying the two routes between Paris and the Low Countries.

Furthest from the town centre is the Quartier Royal, an elegant residential district commissioned by King Louis XIV, who fell in love with the town when the Citadelle was built. These roads were built to link the marketplaces of the centre with the fortress in the woods of the Bois de Boulogne.

The quaint narrow streets of Vieux Lille today feel wonderfully safe, with cheery groups of students in animated discussion, well-dressed couples window-shopping arm-in-arm on the narrow pavements, and traffic insinuating turns at a snail's pace, ensuring that the quarter's refined charm never slips into stuffiness. Mind you, the indiscreet working girls by the old Porte de Gand are a reminder that any town with a military presence can never become too prissy! Three decades ago, the kerbside trade was the only truly thriving *métier* of the old town, but as Lille reclaimed its streets, art dealers and restaurateurs moved into the renovated buildings to create the enchanting realm of refinement that we know today.

Carnality on the plate and in the boudoir are not the only tastes catered for in this other world of 17th- and 18th-century houses and shops. No-one should miss the pretty pleasures of saying 'I wish' to the latest fashions on the rue des Chats Bossus, and 'I will', 'I do', 'I can't help myself' to the unrivalled confections of the Pâtisserie Meert on rue Esquermoise, just a whim and drop of the willpower away from the Grand' Place.

GRAND' PLACE TO REPUBLIQUE ⏍ Absolutely everything that matters in Lille

begins on Grand' Place, from sunrise over the Vieille Bourse's morning market selling cut flowers and uncut antiquarian books, to shirtsleeved lunchtimes on the terrace of the Coq Hardi. You will not find the name Grand' Place on any map nor street sign – the square is now officially called the Place du Général de Gaulle, but the locals still refer to the place by its old, familiar name. The central column is a virtual sundial of life in the city. Carrier bags from FNAC and the Furet du Nord rest on tables during the 'any time, coffee time' of a contented shopper. Afternoon rendezvous by the fountains flow into evenings at the Théâtre du Nord, its posters proudly proclaiming a new season of Shakespeare, Pinter and Molière. Bars, beers and bonhomie beckon from all directions, but the goddess standing on the central column draws everyone back for a dawn onion-soup breakfast at a late-night restaurant.

The square is bounded by the performing arts, with the theatre dominating the south side and, to the east, the picture-book opera house on the place du Théâtre; westward, the circular Nouveau Siècle building is home to the Orchestre Nationale. Many weekends see displays or entertainment on the Grand' Place itself. Perhaps a bandstand will have been erected for a concert, or a marquee set up to house an exhibition sponsored by the local paper, *La Voix du Nord*, whose elegant building dominates the square.

The main commercial districts of Lille fan out from the Grand' Place, a giant compass where all roads lead to shopping: chain stores, multiplex cinemas and boutiques line the rues de Béthune and Neuve. Since traffic was barred from these streets in 1973, visitors have been able to admire the Art Deco architecture above the shopfronts in the pedestrianised triangle between the stations, place République and the city squares. Along the rue Faidherbe, formerly home to inexpensive shoe and clothes shops, including the diminished Tati (pages 146–7), you will now find grand pharmacies, an inevitable supermarket and chain restaurants; the wide rue Nationale has Printemps (pages 162–3) and the glitzier Parisian stores; and northward, beyond the once-upon-a-time perpendicular-style belfry of the Chambre de Commerce, are hidden the picture-perfect boutiques and galleries of Vieux Lille.

But walk along the wide, traffic-free shopping streets south of the square to reach the Palais des Beaux-Arts – the very magnet that pulls the world to the place République, providing an abundance of inspiration and fulfilment. How many visitors realise that the museum is but a gateway to the one-time Latin

Quarter of Lille, a 19th-century haven of culture and learning? The boulevard de la Liberté was laid out when the original city walls came tumbling down in the mid-19th century. Named for the Empress Eugénie, this was the essential address for well-to-do families enriched by the industrial revolution. Textile barons and their ilk competed to build grander and grander mansions with grand staircases for grand gestures and grander entertaining, many with their own private theatres for after-dinner opera at home.

The place République itself is poised between the museum and the equally grand Préfecture, which was based on the design of the Paris Louvre. Notice the emblems on each wing: an eagle for the Second Empire, the letter N for Napoleon III. At the centre of the gardens is a stepped arena, providing a stage for musicians and a well of natural light for the métro station.

MARKETS: GAMBETTA TO SOLFERINO Ⓜ

Lille is a market town, never more so than during the **Braderie** of the first weekend in September. For 48 hours non stop, the entire city sets out its stalls on doorsteps, pavements, trestles and pitches. Recycle your children's clothes for a few pence, rediscover stolen goods from that break-in in May and swap Deco uplighters for 1960s lava lamps in a tradition that dates back to the city fathers granting servants the right to earn money by selling their master's cast-off clothing once a year. A hundred kilometres of stalls appear every year, the métro runs all night long, and every hotel room for miles around is booked months in advance. The Braderie never sleeps and brasseries compete to sell the most *moules* and create the highest pile of shells on the pavement outside the front door. A special map-guide is published and may be picked up at the tourist office.

Since the event is held only once a year, a happy alternative takes place every week in the **Wazemmes** quarter, 15 minutes' walk or two métro stops from the town centre. This is the market of markets and a Sunday morning institution (page 161). A smaller market is held each Wednesday and Saturday at place Sébastopol, where the Théâtre Sébastopol dominates the square. An entertaining explosion of architectural styles – Renaissance, Moorish, classical and sheer pantomime – this people's playhouse provides popular boulevard entertainment. From populist playtime one can turn to intellectual reflection, as roads south lead to the former Faculté des Lettres, once a centre of study, reflection and tolerance. The Protestant temple and the synagogue may be seen on rue Angellier. While the secular university is now based outside the town centre to the north, boulevard Vauban is home to the Catholic university campus.

Between the two city-centre seats of learning, rue Solférino, the centre of Lille's student nightlife, is the starting point for any serious partying (see box, pages 120–1).

STATIONS/HÔTEL DE VILLE Ⓢ

Not one station but two. The modern Europe station welcomes the TGV and Eurostar and looks like the airports of tomorrow. Dominated by the boot-shaped Crédit Lyonnais building, this is the heartland of the new international business community. Constructed on land hived off by the military, there are hints of early fortifications scattered in the emerging Parc Matisse. The vast paved piazza of the parvis Mitterand is gradually being claimed by a generation of skateboarders, microscooter aces and mountain bikers.

Across the square is the Euralille shopping centre, an indoor alternative to the rest of the city. A few yards along avenue le Corbusier is the public transport hive: underground are two métro stations, and the tramway to Roubaix and Tourcoing; while at street level one finds the bus station, taxi ranks and the original 19th-century station serving all points local and beyond, and all speeds under *très grandes*.

The older Gare Lille Flandres was Paris's original Gare du Nord, moved brick by brick and stone by stone for the railway line's royal opening. The town elders, not wishing to appear satisfied with secondhand goods, insisted on building an extra storey on to the station façade to create an even more imposing frontage. The first train to arrive at the station was greeted by the Bishop of Douai, who blessed the locomotive, and by Hector Berlioz conducting the town band in a specially composed concerto, an event nearly recreated on the launch night of the Capital of Culture celebrations (sheer crowd numbers led to it being abandoned). Today, the place seems less grand, just the typical terminus hive of bars, cafés and eateries clustered around the fountains at the front of the station. Weekends see soldiers from the Citadelle flirting with students from the universities. After a while, the incongruous sight of a young lad with a sub-machine gun at his belt, composing text messages on his mobile phone, seems perfectly normal. At the side of the station, on rue de Tournai, eating is cheap with *frites* stands and burgers. Seamier services are available behind the line of brasseries facing the station, with flesh offered shrink-wrapped in cellophane in shops and in lycra on the pavements around the rues de Roubaix and Ponts de Comines (page 137). The Flandres station itself is being remodelled as a contemporary commuter hub, and the underground métro concourse has hairdressers and snack bars for the passing rush-hour trade.

Close to the motorway intersections of the ring road, Lille Grand Palais is a huge exhibition arena. The Zenith auditorium hosts major rock concerts and lavish musicals, and is the place to see international superstars such as David Bowie or Elton John. Linking the Grand Palais to Euralille is a fresh new residential quarter being built at a bewildering pace around the big, brash, glass casino.

Below the stations is the successor to the long-demolished St-Sauveur district, home to the early 20th-century Hôtel de Ville. Further out to the east and across the railway lines is the district of Lille-Fives, which grew up as a town in its own right. Fives has its own brass bands, festivals and

Planning   THE CITY: A PRACTICAL OVERVIEW   2

customs, including a wine harvest festival every autumn, when the little local vineyards produce *vin de Fives*.

Cutting a swathe from the *gares* to the République is the only slightly seedy rue Molinel, the broad street a boulevard wide in its aspiration, an un-grand ribbon of otherness and improbable neighbours: Catholic schools rubbing shoulders with kebaberies; travel agencies selling weeks in north Africa alongside artistic florists selling miniature topiary in galvanised pots opposite nail bars and religious bookshops; the long-forgotten *schmutter* trade recalled by long-closed textile traders and thriving bespoke tailors and wedding couturiers. The fluctuating fortunes of the Molinel are told by many regeneration attempts on the thwarted Monoprix supermarket at the station end of the road, and the new generation Tanneurs shopping mall where rue de Paris bisects the main road and the pedestrianised quarter spills down to the border. This is also where a modern reinterpretation of the Monoprix lives anew.

The other walk, along the avenue le Corbusier from Lille Europe past the old station, then along the rue Faidherbe to the Grand' Place and the old town, is a gentle turning back of the clock as the architecture rewinds through 21st, 20th and 19th centuries to the 18th and 17th; 400 years of optimism, confidence and faith in the future, respecting the past.

WHEN TO VISIT

Lille2004 was merely a shop window for a city with a talent for late-night partying. Some themed weekends inaugurated for the festivities have become regular events, and each year sees a string of *incontournables* – the unmissable happenings that are the perfect excuse for a trip to Lille.

JANUARY
The big wheel turns on Grand' Place
A lingering legacy of the Christmas market.
January sales Mid-Jan–mid-Feb. Dates & authorised discounts announced by the government.

FEBRUARY
Tourissima   Early Feb 🖱 www.salons-du-tourisme.com/Lille. Huge holiday exhibition at Grand Palais.

MARCH
Craft fair   Villeneuve d'Ascq

APRIL
Paris–Roubaix cycle race 🖱 www.letour.com/paris-roubaix
Fortified towns open day   Late April. Lille's Citadelle & other walled towns of the region open their doors to the public.

MAY
La Louche d'Or Soup festival in Wazemmes
The Montgolfiades Hot-air balloon meeting
Wazemmes International Accordion Festival
Flower market on Grand' Place
Independent Cinema Festival

Nuit des Musées Late-night museum weekend.

JUNE

Lille Piano Festival Mid-June 🎹 www.lillepianosfestival.fr
Gay Pride Weekend 🎹 www.lillepride.fr. Fun across the city with free concerts.
Fête de la Musique 21 June. Musical events take place throughout Lille.

JULY

Bastille Day 14 July. Much partying in the streets as summer holidays officially begin with fireworks & dancing for the French National Day.

AUGUST

Sunday evening tango at Vieille Bourse See pages 178–9.

SEPTEMBER

The Braderie First weekend. Europe's biggest market – see page 12.
Lille Half Marathon Early Sep 🎹 www.semimarathon-lille.fr
Lille Short Film Festival Mid-Sep–early

Oct 🎹 www.festivalducourt-lille.com
National Heritage Days Third weekend. Across France, private buildings open their doors to visitors for a celebration of history & heritage.

OCTOBER

Great Circus Festival 🎹 www.lagrandefetelilloiseducirque.com. Troupes & performers from all over the world come to Lille.

NOVEMBER

Tourcoing Jazz Festival 🎹 www.tourcoing-jazz-festival.com

DECEMBER

Christmas market Browse the craft stalls on place Rihour or take a ride on the big wheel on the Grand' Place.
Braderie de l'Art Roubaix 🎹 www.labraderiedelart.com. For 24hrs non stop, artists come together to breathe new life into old objects – recycled wares can sell for anything between €1 & €300!
New Year's Eve Fireworks and partying on the Grand' Place.

SUGGESTED ITINERARIES
If you are staying one day

- Walk through Vieux Lille
- Have a coffee or meal on the main squares
- Treat yourself to an excellent lunch
- Spend at least an hour at the Palais des Beaux-Arts
- Stroll round the Vieille Bourse
- Go shopping: the old town for something special; the streets around Grand' Place or Euralille for more practical purchases
- Taste a selection of freshly brewed beers at Les Trois Brasseurs before catching the train home

If you are staying two days
Day one
- Vieux Lille – and the Musée de l'Hospice Comtesse
- The Palais des Beaux-Arts

- Browse the bookstalls at the Vieille Bourse
- Wander through the magnificent churches
- Start your evening on Grand' Place and enjoy a performance at the opera, theatre or jazz club before hitting the late-night bars
- Have at least one bistro or brasserie meal with a local beer, and indulge yourself with a gastronomic treat at one of the gourmet restaurants

Day two
- Start the second day with breakfast at Paul or a walk in the Bois de Boulogne
- Shop for bargains: midweek at Roubaix bargain outlets; Sunday morning at Wazemmes market
- Explore the wider district for half a day: take the train to Lens for the amazing new Louvre, or tram to Roubaix and La Piscine, or perhaps the modern art collection at Villeneuve d'Ascq
- Or simply visit the smaller museums back in Lille itself or catch an event or exhibition at one of the Maisons Folies

If you are staying three days or more Do all of the above, but give yourself a full day away from central Lille to discover the attractions of the Métropole. Perhaps you might hire a car to visit Le Cateau-Cambrésis to see Matisse's own art collection and home movies. Or walk through the trenches and see the Canadian National Memorial at Vimy Ridge. If your French is up to it, do take yourself to the theatre or a cabaret show.

And, if you are here on a summer Sunday, do not miss the tango at the Vieille Bourse (pages 178–9).

TOURIST INFORMATION

Before leaving home, visit 📱 http://rendezvousenfrance.com, the French national tourist office in your own country (email via contact form on the website). There are also a number of regional tourist offices with information on the departments of Nord and Pas-de-Calais (see below), so do check these if you are looking to explore Lille's surroundings. For details of the tourist offices in Lille itself, see page 35.

From 2015, the Maison du Tourisme, a one-stop shop opposite the Palais Rihour, will have a walk-in reception area for information on travel, attractions and accommodation across the department and the region.

🛈 Comité Départemental du Tourisme Nord 3 rue du Palais Rihour 📍 237 G6 📞 03 20 57 59 59 e resa@cdt-nord.fr 📱 www. cdt-nord.fr. 🚊 Rihour 🚇 Métro 2 to Gare Lille Flandres, then line 1 to Rihour. For information on tourism & travel in the department of Nord (including themed package breaks & battlefield tours).

ℹ Comité Régional du Tourisme Nord-Pas de Calais 3 rue du Palais Rihour ♀ 237 G5 ✆ 03 20 14 57 57 🖥 www.tourisme-nordpasdecalais.fr 🚇 Rihour ⓜ Métro 2 to Gare Lille Flandres & line 1 to Rihour. Info on the Nord-Pas de Calais region, from the Channel ports & the coastal resorts to the inland cities.

ℹ Comité Départemental du Tourisme Pas de Calais La Trésorie, Wimille, 62930 Wimereux ✆ 03 21 10 34 60 e promotion@pas-de-calais.com 🖥 www.pas-de-calais.com. For information on tourism & travel in the neighbouring department of Pas-de-Calais.

TOUR OPERATORS

Check with Rendezvous en France in your own country for a full list of tour operators offering inclusive packages to Lille. Visit 🖥 www.franceguide.com and click on your country of residence. Alternatively you may contact the local office directly.

UK & IRELAND

Atout France Lincoln House, 300 High Holborn, London WC1V 7JH ✆ 0906 824 4123 (premium rate) e info.uk@atout-france.fr 🖥 www.rendezvousenfrance.com ⏰ 10.00–16.00 Mon–Fri. An excellent one-stop shop for buying guidebooks, booking tickets for events & picking up the free *Traveller in France* reference guides, as well as plenty of advice.

The Association of British Tour Operators to France 🖥 www.holidayfrance.org.uk. Includes scores of companies offering holidays, travel & short breaks in Lille.

USA

Maison de la France *New York* 825 3rd Av, 29th floor (entrance on 50th St), NY 10022 ✆ 514 288 1904 e info.us@atout-france.fr

🖥 www.rendezvousenfrance.com; *Los Angeles* 9454 Wilshire Bd, Suite 210, Beverly Hills, CA 90212 ✆ 310 271 6665; *Chicago* Consulate General of France, 205 N Michigan Av, Suite 3770, Chicago, IL 60601 ✆ 312 327 0290

CANADA

Maison de la France 1981 Av McGill, College Suite 490, H3A 2WP Montreal ✆ 514 288 2026 e canada@atout-france.fr 🖥 ca.rendezvousenfrance.com

AUSTRALIA & NEW ZEALAND

Maison de la France Level 13, 25 Bligh St, 2000 NSW, Sydney, Australia ✆ +61 (0)2 92 10 54 00 e info.au@atout-france.com 🖥 au.rendezvousenfrance.com

RED TAPE

European Union (EU) nationals need carry only a valid identity card or passport. For nationals of non-EU countries, passports are required. Nationals of some countries require visas. Check with the local embassy or consulate when planning your trip (taking into account the time it may take for visas to be issued).

For customs advice in France telephone ✆ 01 53 24 68 24 and in the UK ✆ 0300 200 3700. Within the EU there is officially no limitation for purchases destined for personal consumption by EU citizens, although there are recommended limits for cigarettes (800) and alcohol (90 litres of wine and 10 litres of spirits). Travellers from countries outside the EU must take heed of duty-free regulations and make a customs declaration and pay duty on items with a value of over €220. However, they may also claim approximately 15% tax discount on their purchases (page 162).

Narcotics, some pornographic material, illegal drugs, weapons, live plants and ivory may not be carried across borders.

If you lose your passport, contact your consulate immediately. Most of these are to be found in Paris, although the UK and Canada have consular officials based in Lille (page 36). Replacement passports may be reissued in France. However, if you are travelling within the EU (even if you are not an EU national) you may, under certain circumstances, be allowed to travel without your passport, subject to the discretion of the airline or carrier and immigration authorities, should you have acceptable alternative photo ID.

TIME

From the end of March through to the end of October, Continental European Time changes from GMT+1 to GMT+2.

GETTING THERE AND AWAY

BY TRAIN Eurostar, from the UK, is a fabulous way to travel to Lille: 80 minutes from London St Pancras International, 70 minutes from the station at Ebbsfleet and an hour from Ashford International. Each 400m-long Eurostar train can carry up to 560 standard-class and 206 first-class passengers from London to the heart of Lille in 18 air-conditioned carriages. Two train managers and teams of uniformed stewards look after passengers, welcoming arrivals and reminding would-be smokers that the entire train is ciggie-free. Two bar-buffet carriages, modelled on TGV bars, have space to stand and chat over a drink. Baby-changing rooms are at each end of the train, and there are toilets in all carriages. Pricier seats are spaced three abreast, one single, one pair; in standard class, two pairs. Groups of four passengers should request seats around a table. The more expensive compartments have several business seating configurations, including a semiprivate area for four or six passengers at the end of each carriage. Be warned, not all standard-class tickets sold as 'window' seats are actually next to a window: around four places in each carriage are in fact against a solid wall. Regular passengers with a good book may not mind, but first-timers and anyone who thrills to a view will be disappointed, so do insist when booking that your window seat actually has a window, if only for the thrill of arriving back at the new London terminus.

ST PANCRAS

Returning to St Pancras is always an occasion. As the train pulls out of the tunnel that sweeps under the Thames and the city itself, the view across the regeneration lands of the King's Cross goods yards is a feast of promise. Note the Grand Union Canal with its basin at the new Kings Place concert venue, the protected wildlife reserve at Canley Street, the British Library compound and the barcoded skyline of London, from the old Post Office Tower to the new Gherkin of the City and the plinthed pyramids of Docklands. Reigning supreme are the gothic spires of St Pancras itself. Glide through the new glass box of the station's extension to the splendid archway of the original Barlow Shed, the ironwork now picked out in a British sky blue, the magnificent span perched on the warm red-brick and white-stone walls. For some passengers, the centrepiece is the lumbering statue of snogging giants looming over the platforms in chunky impersonation of a cinematic farewell. For me, the station clock itself is the more potent symbol of the timeless thrill of arrival and departure, of the tender kiss of parting and the balmy embrace of return. And sculpture-wise, the more modest John Betjeman statue by the Champagne Bar is the true spirit of the place.

Flexible fares are available in all carriages, but non-transferable tickets offer sensational value, with return tickets often costing less than single fares. Self-print and ticket-on-departure options for online reservations save on postage charges when booking. Standard Premier and Business Premier passengers enjoy more spacious accommodation and a meal served at their seats during the journey. For Standard Premier passengers, this will usually be a light main course and dessert served with wine; Business Premier travellers may indulge in a three-course menu designed by restaurateur Raymond Blanc, with a welcome glass of champagne and a choice of wines served with the meal. The quality of onboard food is pretty good – an improvement on previous years. Vegetarian and other dietary requests should be made at least 48 hours in advance. For an inexpensive upgrade from standard class, consider travelling with a tour operator (page 24), since deals usually include hotel accommodation. You may also upgrade in one direction or find day-trip and weekend promotional rates. A relatively new bargain is the £34.50 lead-in one-way fare – since single fares are now half the return price.

A make-over, courtesy of France's pet designer Philippe Starck, restyled the carriages before the move from Waterloo to St Pancras. Initially, train crews were also kitted out with a dress-down look that somewhat muted the glamour that marked out Eurostar as special. This was later modified to a

DINING AT ST PANCRAS

St Pancras International is a true destination station in its own right. It lives up to its dramatic architecture and, appropriately for the UK's premier link to mainland Europe, this is a continental-style *Grande Gare*. Just as Paris's Gare de Lyon has its celebrated *belle époque* Train Bleu restaurant, so St Pancras has three flagship dining places – the Gilbert Scott in the revived and reopened St Pancras Hotel itself and, on the station, the St Pancras Grand Brasserie and the already legendary Champagne Bar. The latter encompasses around 100m of fizz, with a breathtaking selection of champagnes, from a glass of Grande Tradition brut for £9.50 to a Dom Pérignon White Gold 1995 at £6,500 a jeroboam. For the quality of some of the wines the prices are certainly not excessive, and of course the setting, along a stretch of platform, is impressive. The spectacular railway-cathedral architecture soaring above the Barlow Shed, restored in all its 19th-century glory, is a perfect place to toast a journey and turn travel into an occasion. An all-day menu features the obvious indulgent accompaniments to bubbly.

Here, even if you have not opted for an onboard upgrade, you may start your trip to Lille with flair: whether the full English afternoon tea of sandwiches, scones, cake and nice pot of Darjeeling with a glass of bubbly for around £20, or a smoked salmon, scrambled egg and champagne breakfast for £20 per person. Should you really want to greet the dawn in style, splash out on scrambled eggs, black truffle and chives on toasted sourdough, tea or coffee, freshly squeezed juice and a half-bottle of Krug Grand Cuvée at £97.50 for two.

While the Champagne Bar has its all-day menu, the St Pancras Grand is the choice for hearty appetites, with full menus starting around £20. Kedgeree has always been my breakfast weakness, but all foodie vices are catered for. Romantics might opt for the Aphrodisiac menu with the requisite oysters, chocolate and bubbly at £45 (although the proffered parsnips would never be my choice of asparagus substitute!). Sunday options range from brunch to jazz in the evenings.

Now that the main Gilbert Scott-designed building has been returned to its majestic splendour as one of Britain's greatest ever railway hotels, the St Pancras Hotel restaurant is named after its architect and is an address for special occasions. While the à la carte has prices to make you blink (the Galloway rib of beef at £66 a couple for instance), but then it does include the very best of British, a £25 set weekday menu is affordable for

more formal outfit evoking the original classy image. Whatever the whims of fashion, onboard staff remain as professional, helpful and charming as ever. From late 2015, the newly designed e320 trains will be introduced into most travellers launching themselves on a Eurostar trip to Lille. If money is no object you may hire the Kitchen Table for a *plongeur's*-eye view of the action at around £1,000 for the whole party, wine extra!

For a flavour of the quarter itself, rather than the anticipation of travel (remember, St Pancras has always been the blurred boundary of King's Cross and Bloomsbury), the original station pub from the terminus's humbler days still has a local feel. Now known as the Betjeman Arms (after the poet, Sir John, who long campaigned for the station's preservation), this pub, serving British gastro-pub grub, hosts Monday quiz nights, Tuesday sing-along sessions around the piano, offers pie and mash on a Wednesday and has live music on Friday evenings and even a midweek life-drawing art class. The food is pretty good. Delicious quality ingredients prepared just-so and an extraordinarily good wine list chosen by a shrewd sommelier. I come here even if I've no train to catch. Just around the corner (by the Champagne Bar), Martin Jennings' statue of Sir John is for me far more evocative of the spirit of the place than the Brobdingnagian lovers along the way.

Elsewhere on the station, you can find branches of Carluccio's Italian restaurant under the famous statue of the lovers kissing; Yo Sushi, the Japanese conveyor-belt eatery in The Circle shopping area; and two branches of coffee shops familiar from the streets of Lille: Le Pain Quotidien (by Eurostar Arrivals) and Paul (opposite the sushi bar).

At least a dozen other cafés and food outlets, including The Fine Burger Company, Peyton and Byrne British patisserie and most of the main international chains can be found on the station.

And now that the neighbouring King's Cross Station is complete, a range of superb eateries from the station hotel brasserie to pizza chains can be found in a vast and impressive food court, just across the road.

✖ **Betjeman Arms** Upper Concourse 📞020 7923 5440 🕐 09.00–23.00 daily
✖ **Gilbert Scott Brasserie St Pancras Renaissance Hotel** 📞0207 278 3888
🌐www.thegilbertscott.co.uk 🕐restaurant 12.00–15.00 & 17.30–23.00 Mon–Fri, 12.00–23.00 Sat, 12.00–22.00 Sun; bar from 11.00 Mon–Fri, from 10.00 Sat & Sun
✖ **Searcys St Pancras Grand Brasserie & Champagne Bar** Upper Concourse
📞0207 870 9900 🌐www.searcys.co.uk/stpancrasgrand 🕐Grand Brasserie 07.00–23.00 Mon–Sat, 08.00–20.00 Sun; Champagne Bar 08.00–23.00 Mon–Thu, 07.00–23.00 Fri–Sat, 08.00–20.30 Sun

the fleet. These will have extra facilities for travellers with disabilities (pages 30–1), a contemporary décor and varied seat pitches (even in standard class) to make journeys more comfortable for pregnant and elderly passengers.

From the regions, Ebbsfleet Station is easiest to reach by car (off junction two of the M25 near Bluewater shopping centre) and has a car park like a medium-sized continent. Ashford station, the original Eurostar base in Kent, has inexplicably been downgraded to a mere one Lille train per day. Through-rail tickets from 68 key UK cities, including Birmingham, Cambridge, Leeds and Manchester, are now available, changing at St Pancras. TGV, Thalys and Eurostar services from Paris, Brussels, Amsterdam, Cologne and other key European cities arrive at Lille Europe station, with some additional Paris services arriving at nearby Lille Flandres. SNCF, the French rail company, has online booking facilities (🖰 *www.voyages-sncf.com*). Within France, click the link for *prems* deals: discount advance-purchase tickets you can print from your own PC. UK-based travellers should go to the same site for similar discount fares for travel within France. On any non-Eurostar service, remember to validate any ticket (except e-tickets) in the red machines at the entrance to the platforms. Rail Europe's UK and US offices sell all tickets, and Interail, Eurail and EuroDomino offer passes for unlimited rail travel across Europe. French trains have dedicated compartments banning mobile phones.

Onboard meals Standard Premier and Business Premier passengers meals are served at your seat (page 19) and, for all passengers, the buffet bar offers a range of hot and cold snacks. An alternative to the trek to the buffet compartment for those encumbered with luggage, small children or delicious lethargy is an onboard picnic. St Pancras boasts a fresh food market as well as two Marks & Spencer food stores, offering a range of salads, snacks, sandwiches and sushi. A tip: when the branch opposite the Eurostar check-in is busy, nip along to the larger M&S store (next to Boots the Chemist) at The Circle by the domestic section of the station. A smaller selection of snacks is available from Boots the Chemist. For a similar treat on the return journey, Lille's Carrefour hypermarket (page 162) is located just across the parvis François Mitterand from the station. As well as the obvious pâtés, cheeses, breads and sandwiches, this store has platters of prepared crudités and dips as a healthy option – at the back of the food hall, by the fresh veg. Otherwise, pick up sandwiches, sushi and snacks from any of the myriad metro-mini-supermarkets in the city. Do make sure that food complies with international regulations. During the UK foot and mouth outbreak, meat products were banned.

Cash and carry St Pancras International sites most of its facilities before Eurostar check-in, so left luggage and bureau de change should be checked out in the main station, where a bigger range of shops includes Fortnum & Mason, John Lewis, Hatchards and Hamleys, as well as a wide range of perfume, fashion and high street outlets, from Boots and WHSmith to Marks & Spencer. Europe's longest champagne bar, more than a dozen restaurants (pages 20–1) and pub grub are also 'landside'.

Eurostar's terminal is housed in the exquisitely reconceived undercroft of the splendid Victorian Gothic station. The restoration work is simply stunning, especially to we former 'locals' who recall this area as the province of taxi repair shops and earthy greasy spoon caffs. The departure lounge area has its café and restaurant-bar. There is free Wi-Fi available and a bank of workstations in the lounge. Some fun interactive screens on coffee tables and in brick alcoves on the walls allow exploration of Britain's national art treasures. There is also a mail box at the information desk for posting those last minute letters, cards and bills. An impressive selection of international newspapers is available at the WHSmith bookshop and newsagent. You may also print up a copy of any of scores of other daily newspapers from around the world.

Holders of the Eurostar frequent traveller card have an excellent private lounge with complimentary refreshments, bar, newspapers and mobile phone chargers for first-class passengers as well as Wi-Fi access.

Passport control, customs and security Eurostar terminals run passenger security screening similar to that found at airports. The original plans for onboard passport inspections have been overtaken by more traditional checks by the appropriate authorities at arrivals as well as departures. Check-in is 30 minutes before departure (often less for Eurostar Carte Blanche holders), subject to changing security regulations. Standard class ticket holders should allow an extra half-hour, or even longer during peak travel periods. Two cases and one extra piece of hand luggage are allowed per person. Knives and other restricted items have to be registered before travel. So do allow extra time to check in.

Tickets Tickets may be purchased directly from Eurostar, as well as at Voyages-SNCF (formerly known as Rail Europe in the UK) which also offers internal European tickets for Thalys, TGV and regional trains. Some UK travel agents offer Eurostar tickets but, unless you are buying a package deal, it is easier to purchase your own directly by phone or online.

Eurostar
UK Travel Centre, St Pancras International, Pancras Rd, London ✆ call centre 03432 186 186 (+44 1233 617 575 if calling from outside the UK) 🖱 www.eurostar.co.uk ⏰ 09.00–19.00 Mon–Fri, 08.00–19.00 Sat, 09.00–17.00 Sun & UK bank holidays
France ✆ 08 36 35 35 39

Voyages-SNCF
Canada ✆ 1 800 361 7245 🖱 www.

raileurope.com ⏰ 09.00–19.30 Mon–Fri, until 17.00 Sat
UK Voyages-SNCF Travel Centre, 193 Piccadilly, London W1J 9EU ⏰ 10.00–18.00 Mon–Fri, 10.00–17.00 Sat ✆ call centre 0844 848 5848 (⏰ 08.00–20.00 Mon–Fri, 09.00–17.00 Sat, Jun–Aug 10.00–16.00 Sun) 🖱 www.voyages-sncf.co.uk
USA 44 South Broadway, White Plains, NY 10601 ✆ 1 800 622 8600 🖱 www.raileurope. com ⏰ 09.00–19.30 Mon–Fri, until 17.00 Sat

Rail information

SNCF ☎ 08 36 35 35 35 (from France)
🖱 www.sncf.com. In all other countries

contact Rail Europe (page 23).
St Pancras Station 🖱 www.stpancras.com

BY CAR From the UK you have to cross the Channel or the North Sea, either by boat or through the Channel Tunnel. Most ferries ply the busy route from Dover to Calais, with journey times averaging 90 minutes; the tunnel claims a 35-minute crossing on the same route. However, you must also allow for check-in times, queuing and visits to the terminal buildings. Slower overnight services operate from Hull.

Best value is often to be found with package deals from tour operators, but an excellent place to shop for bargain cross-Channel fares is 🖱 www.aferry.to.

Cross-Channel operators

Eurotunnel ☎ 0844 335 3535 (UK), 08 10 63 03 04 (France) 🖱 www.eurotunnel.com. Eurotunnel operates the Channel Tunnel service for motorists. At the terminal near Folkestone, motorists are directed to drive aboard the special trains that carry cars through the tunnel. It is easy & by far the most efficient route, since you need not even leave your vehicle. Of course, the ferries offer a wider range of entertainment, with restaurants, bars & children's play areas, but the advantage of the tunnel is in the saving of time & effort. Free Wi-Fi in the terminal & lounges. Certainly the least-stressful option if travelling with pets.

DFDS ☎ 0871 574 7235 (UK), 02 32 14 68 50 (France) 🖱 www.dfds.com. Regular crossings between Dover & Dunkerque with a journey

time of around 2 hours, & Dover & Calais at around 90 minutes.

P&O ☎ 0871 664 64 64 (UK), 03 66 74 03 25 (France) 🖱 www.poferries.com. Operate the biggest fleet crossing on the Dover–Calais route with the largest ships. A round-the-clock service means that passengers can turn up at the port & drive straight aboard. Also run a service from Hull to Zeebrugge, leaving the UK each evening & arriving at the Belgian port, just 53km from Lille, at breakfast time.

MyFerryLink ☎ 0844 2482 100 (UK), 08 25 04 40 45 (France) 🖱 www.myferrylink.com. The crew-owned & managed Dover–Calais ferry running the former SeaFrance ships is proud of its 'Continental flavour'.

After the crossing From Boulogne, Calais or Dunkerque take the A16 then A25 motorway (signposted for Lille). From Zeebrugge take the N31 (via Bruges), which leads to the A17 motorway, and then the A14 (which becomes the A22 as it crosses the French border). Remember that Belgian motorway signs may list Lille by its Flemish name, Rijsel. At Marcq-en-Baroeul, leave the motorway and follow the N356 into Lille.

BY AIR Lille Lesquin Airport, for domestic and continental European and African flights, is 8km from the town centre (page 49). However, visitors from UK regions and beyond Europe may fly direct to Paris's Roissy-

Charles de Gaulle Airport and take the 51-minute TGV train to Lille from the station at the Air France terminal. Air France (🖥 *www.airfrance.com*) sells through tickets to Lille from most international and intercontinental airports. Alternatively, flights to Brussels airport connect with a rail link to Lille in under 40 minutes. See 🖥 www.flying-to-lille.com for more details.

Airlines serving Lille Lesquin directly include:

✈ **Air France** 🖥 www.airfrance.com & **HOP** (the national flag carrier's smaller low-cost operator) 🖥 www.hop.com. From Bordeaux, Lyon, Marseille, Montpellier, Nice, Nantes, Toulouse & Strasbourg.

✈ **easyJet** 🖥 www.easyjet.com. From Basle, Bordeaux, Nice, Toulouse & Geneva.

✈ **Ryanair** 🖥 www.ryanair.com. From Marseille & Portugal.

✈ **Jetairfly** 🖥 www.jetairfly.com. From Toulon & Nice in France, plus Algeria & Morocco.

✈ **Vueling** 🖥 www.vueling.com. From Spain.

✈ **Volotea** 🖥 www.volotea.com. From Biarritz & Corsica.

✈ **Tunisair** 🖥 www.tunisair.com. From Tunisia.

✈ **Transavia** 🖥 www.transavia.com. From Venice & across north Africa.

✈ **Aigle Azur** 🖥 www.aigle-azur.com & **Air Algerie** 🖥 www.airalgerie.dz. From Algeria.

TRAVELLING WITH PETS

There are no restrictions on bringing pets into France, but in order to return to the UK, dogs and cats must have a valid UK or EU Pet Passport. Dogs must also have received worming treatment from a recognised vet one to five days before returning to Britain (see page 26 for vets in Lille). Ask at your hotel for the address of a local veterinary clinic or check out the establishments below.

Most cross-Channel ferry companies will carry your pets at a modest fee (usually between £15 and £30) on the condition that the animal stays in the car throughout the journey and does not accompany owners to the public areas of the boat.

As a pet owner, I prefer to travel on the Eurotunnel shuttle, where you must remain in the car with your pets for the entire journey. However you travel, you will need to go to a dedicated pets check-in before boarding the ferry back to the UK. In the past, some ferry firms did not charge to carry pets out of the UK; now all charge for both legs of the journey.

Check with your hotel in Lille regarding policies and prices for staying with pets, or consider a self-catering option. If you need accommodation right by the check-in for the tunnel, then the new, modern Inter-Hôtel L'Haut'Aile (*ZAC Les Terrasses, rue des Longues Pièces, 62231 Coquelles* ☎ *03 21 46 40 00* 🖥 *www.inter-hotel-calais.com*) is genuinely welcoming to animals (even providing special pet soaps in the rooms) and equally friendly to their owners, with an excellent menu of local produce.

For rules regarding pet travel, see 🖥 www.gov.uk/take-pet-abroad.

2

VETERINARY CLINICS

Clinique Vétérinaire Jeanne d'Arc 260 rue Solférino ♀ 238 F4 ☎ 03 20 40 79 82 🖰 www. cliniqueveterinairejeannedarc-lille.fr ⏲ 08.00–12.30 &14.00–19.30 Mon–Fri, 08.00–12.30 Sat 🚊 République–Beaux Arts 🚇 Métro 2 to Gare Lille Flandres changing to line 1 to République–Beaux Arts, then take rue Nicolas Leblanc to place Lebon, then rue Solférino

Clinique Vétérinaire de Lille St Maurice 112 rue du Faubourg de Roubaix ♀ 235 K3 ☎ 03 20 06 58 20 🖰 http:// cliniqueveterinairelillesaintmaurice. chezmonveto.com ⏲ 08.00–19.30 Mon–Fri, 08.00–14.30 Sat 🚊 Gare Lille Europe/St-Maurice Pellevoisin 🚇 Métro 2 to St-Maurice Pellevoisin

HEALTH

No inoculations are required to visit France. Citizens of EU countries should carry an EHIC (European Health Insurance Card), available from post offices. This enables the traveller to claim reimbursement of medical and pharmaceutical expenses in the event of illness or accident. You will need to pay up front for doctors' appointments, nurses' visits and prescriptions. Show your EHIC and request the necessary paperwork for a refund when you return home. GP consultations cost around €25 and home (or hotel) visits by nurses €8.

Nationals of other countries should arrange necessary private insurance cover before travelling. Insurance is recommended for all travellers (even from EU countries) to cover additional costs such as repatriation or extra nursing care.

See also *Useful telephone numbers* (page 40) for emergencies.

TRAVEL CLINICS AND HEALTH INFORMATION A full list of current travel clinic websites worldwide is available on 🖰 www.istm.org. For other journey preparation information, consult 🖰 www.nathnac.org/ds/map_world.aspx (UK) or 🖰 http://wwwnc.cdc.gov/travel/ (US). Information about various medications may be found on 🖰 www.netdoctor.co.uk/travel. All advice found online should be used in conjunction with expert advice received prior to or during travel.

PHARMACIES Pharmacies are an excellent resource for advice on injuries and medical conditions and can provide lists of GPs and nurses. They are easily identified by the green-cross sign and are open during usual shopping hours. Close to the stations and central area, you'll find three pharmacies along the rue Faidherbe, and a smaller shop in Euralille opposite the Carrefour supermarket. By the shops and bars of Les Halles, on the corner of the rue Solférino, the Grande Pharmacie des Halles has a dispensary open 24 hours a day, seven days a week. Nonmedical sales and services occur during regular trading hours. Out of hours, condoms may be purchased from supermarkets and vending machines. Details of out-of-hours opening are posted in pharmacy windows, and may be obtained from the police.

➕ **Grande Pharmacie de France** 12 rue Faidherbe ♀ 237 J5 ☎ 03 20 63 11 11 🕐 09.00–19.30 Mon–Sat 🚉 Gare Lille Flandres

➕ **Grande Pharmacie des Halles** 99 rue Masséna ♀ 238 D1 ☎ 03 20 54 02 74 🚉 République–Beaux Arts 🚌 Bus Citadine to Sacré Cœur then walk down rue Solférino. Pharmacy counter open 24/7.

➕ **Grande Pharmacie de Paris** 1 pl de la Gare ♀ 237 K6 ☎ 03 20 06 20 64

🕐 08.00–20.00 Mon–Sat 🚉 Gare Lille Flandres

➕ **Pharmacie Casetta** 35 rue Faidherbe ♀ 237 J5 ☎ 03 20 06 16 31 🕐 07.30–21.00 Mon–Fri, 08.00–22.00 Sat 🚉 Gare Lille Flandres

➕ **Pharmacie du Centre** Euralille shopping centre (opposite Carrefour) ♀ 235 H4 ☎ 03 28 38 18 08 🕐 09.00–20.30 Mon–Sat 🚉 Gare Lille Europe

ACCIDENT AND EMERGENCY

➕ **Emergency Department (A&E)** Centre Hospitalier Régional Universitaire de Lille, 2 av Oscar Lambret ♀ 238 B5 ☎ 03 20 44 59 62 💻 www.chru-lille.fr 🚉 CHR B-Calmette 🚌 Métro 2 to Porte des Postes & line 1 to CHR B-Calmette. The University Hospital Centre is a cluster of 9 hospitals on a large campus, with a 24hr emergency department at the Hôpital Roger Salengro within the complex.

➕ **La Maison Médicale de Garde de Lille-Métropole** 24 bd de Belfort ♀ 235 58 ☎ 03 20 87 74 33 🕐 20.00–01.00 Mon–Fri, 08.00–24.00 Sat 🚉 Porte de Valenciennes or Porte de Douai. Evening & weekend emergency GP doctor service. Close to local hospitals.

➕ **SOS Médecin 3624** ☎ 03 20 29 91 91. Out-of-hours medical assistance.

WHAT TO TAKE

Apart from Marmite (and you'll probably find that in the '*cuisines du monde*' aisle at the supermarket), there is virtually nothing essential that you could wish to take that cannot be found in Lille. Perhaps the only exception is plug adaptors. Electricity in France is 220 volts; appliances use two-pin plugs. Adaptors are freely available from airport and station shops before you travel.

MONEY AND BUDGETING

CURRENCY The euro constantly plays dynamic games of cat and mouse with Sterling and the US dollar. The single European currency, the euro, is divided into 100 cents (often referred to locally by the old French term 'centimes'). Notes are valued at €5, €10, €20, €50, €100, €200 and €500. In practice many shops may refuse to change the three largest denominations (and, considering that they are worth upwards of around €100 or £70 each, it would be foolish to carry them with you). Change higher-value notes at banks or supermarkets. Coins are worth 1, 2, 5, 10, 20 and 50 cents. A good way to get rid of too much heavy loose change is to use self-service stamp-printing machines in post offices. All notes bear uniform designs featuring architectural images, but coins carry national emblems (monarchs' heads for Spain and Belgium, the Irish harp, sundry symbols of the French Republic, Leonardo da Vinci's works for Italy). No matter what the motif, all coins, like the notes, may be used anywhere in the euro zone.

BUDGETING   As befits a student city with exclusive shops, Lille may be savoured by all budgets. But how much money should you expect to spend? Of course, these prices do not include shopping for clothes, jewellery, etc. But I have been as thrilled by an unexpected find at Wazemmes market as others have been at Bulgari and Cartier!

Rock bottom   If you really want to keep your hand from straying into your pocket you can manage on as little as €50 per day – by staying at the youth hostel, eating one inexpensive set meal at a modest bar or restaurant and making your own breakfast. Bread costs around 65c a loaf; cheese, pâté, water and beer are very cheap at markets and supermarkets. Don't use public transport – sit outside and enjoy people-watching on the squares and visit those sites that do not charge for admission.

Modest   Neither hardships nor extravagances at under €100 a day. Using 2-for-1 hotel promotions, a simple hotel room could cost you as little as €20 per person per night. Allow yourself €35 for meals, including a delicious set menu at lunchtime (when restaurants are cheapest), a *flammekeuche* (page 99) or *moules-frites* evening meal and a couple of beers or coffees around town. You'll have change for sightseeing and public transport.

Fun   A daily allowance of €150 gives you a better hotel room, and budgets for a delicious lunch and a good brasserie or bistro dinner, drinks at cafés and bars around town and a good deal of sightseeing and travel.

Indulgent   Spend €200 each day, and enjoy a good three-star hotel room, a gastronomic set menu, a hearty lunch, a good day's sightseeing and an evening out.

Extravagant   From €350 upwards you'll be able to afford a luxury hotel room, an à la carte meal at a Michelin-starred restaurant twice a day and as much shopping as the chauffeur can carry!

3

Lille for Visitors with Limited Mobility

Philanthropic may well have been the adjective that has linked the centuries of Lille but, despite a grand tradition of hospices for the poor and needy, jumble sales for servants and retirement homes for Renaissance hookers, you can't get over the sheer ubiquity of the cobbles. Just as the *pavés du nord* play havoc with the bruised bottoms of thousands of cyclists each season, so those stones and steps that line the old quarter provide a challenge for wheelchairs, walking frames and sticks. No wonder one mercifully short-lived trend in the last decade was for an oxygen bar where flavoured air was served to guests through masks.

Having myself walked the streets of the past with the zimmer frames, rollators, sturdy crutches and canes of the present, I can testify to the awkwardness of the city centre (just try crossing the place Lion d'Or without catching your wheels between the uneven cobble stones). However, the city is not entirely off-limits to disabled guests. The central pedestrianised area is easily user-friendly, parks are well laid out, there is flat access to cinemas and most restaurants around the squares and back streets have heated outdoor terraces. The shopping malls are well equipped, so a restaurant table near those or the department stores provides a practical alternative to the toilet problem.

PLANNING A TRIP

The national tourist office website (🖰 *www.rendezvousenfrance.com*) has the usual info: follow the links in the *Practical information* section. Alternatively, contact the departmental tourist office (page 35) and ask for the latest edition of the *Handi-Tourisme* brochure or listings. You can also check out the French language site 🖰 www.tourisme-handicaps.org.

GETTING THERE AND AWAY

BY RAIL Of course (as very few major organisations understand), there are many and varied limits and levels of mobility. Transport authorities often like to lump all differently-abled travellers as 'wheelchair users'. While it

29

is easy to book a train or plane for a full-time wheelchair user, a person of restricted mobility who may perhaps be able to walk a few yards on the flat with a frame or stick, but cannot climb the steep step into a railway carriage without a ramp, nor board a plane without level access, could face long interrogation and explanations as some booking clerks do not have a preordained keystroke on their reservation software that recognises any disability which does not involve a conventional wheelchair.

Eurostar St Pancras Station is well equipped to support passengers with disabilities, with lifts to all levels, and a gentle sloping travelator to platforms for those with powerful brakes! Eurostar has a special fare for wheelchair users, and a companion if required, with a designated space in each of the two central carriages. Ramps can be arranged for boarding these two carriages only, as when the platforms and trains were being designed for the move to St Pancras, no allowance was made for the width of second-class doors in relation to the company's pre-ordered ramps. With the arrival of new e320 trains from late 2015 onward, up to two extra wheelchair spaces will be made available. Onboard elevators for wheelchairs are also being introduced. Passengers whose disability will allow them to walk 200m without assistance may choose to travel anywhere in the train. Newly designed carriages will also have colour schemes and display panels for visually impaired travellers. Eurostar is, albeit gradually, getting there, but some front-of-house station staff at St Pancras are in need of some modern awareness training in dealing with differently-abled punters. And it is always essential to double-check that an ordered ramp is actually in the right place on the platform. Onboard train and platform staff, however, seem uniformly lovely, kind, helpful and not at all patronising. Contact Eurostar directly for information (page 23).

Those extra customer service lessons for those behind desks may be learnt from their counterparts at Lille Europe station, for travellers journeying from Lille to the UK or within France.

This excellent semi-privatised service **Accès Plus** (\ *0890 640 650 (then press 1) from France only* e *accesplus@sncf.fr* ☝ *www.accesplus.sncf.com* ⏱ *07.00–10.00*) is extraordinarily efficient. Cheery and intelligent young staff offer the friendliest of welcomes. Find the reception desk at **Lille Europe** station, next to the ticket office. At **Lille Flandres**, the Voyageurs Handicapés desk is slightly harder to find. Tip: do not use the main entrance to the station, as the specialist reception is at the side entrance, opposite the Euralille shopping centre on av Willy Brandt.

Contact Accès Plus an hour before travelling to arrange assistance. Advisers can also help plan your journey in advance and suggest alternative routes and facilities. A mini-boutique in the Lille Europe office offered a range of travel accessories from plasters to notebooks and condoms – how refreshing for

▲ Look for the glass lifts behind the escalators and stairs for step-free access to the concourse at Gare Lille Europe (Laurence Phillips)

disabled guests to be regarded as human! Arrive at the lounge and reception area 30 minutes before departure to be accompanied all the way to reserved seats on the train. The train manager will be informed as to your needs, and a team member will be waiting for you at your destination if you have booked onward travel in France. When travelling by TGV, make sure that you choose a duplex train if possible and ask to be put in a carriage with an elevated floor at the lower level. This mini-lift system makes for dignified and comfortable boarding in a wheelchair. If your train is delayed or journey disrupted, call the helpline from your mobile phone on ☎ 0890 640 650 (then press 2). Passengers with hearing disabilities can text on ☎ 06 10 64 06 50.

Lille Europe station Lille Europe has a good system of lifts – although be aware of two alternative exits from the station. Should the lift *down* to the parvis Mitterand and Euralille be out of order, take another lift up to viaduct level and walk/trundle back down the avenue le Corbusier.

Lille Flandres station Platforms here are at street level and there are entrances on rue Tournai, place des Buisses and av Willy Brandt. Métro and tram access and the Transpole public transport information centre are all on the lower level. Rather than take the escalator, look for the lifts from the station building or on the main road outside.

BY CAR Ferry and Channel Tunnel operators are very helpful. Explain your requirements when booking (page 24) and arrangements may be made for your car to be parked on board near a lift or flat, with wheelchair access to the passenger lounge. Just check in an hour before your crossing. Eurotunnel is the easiest option of all since you do not need to leave the car during the

35-minute crossing. On board the train the WC is not wheelchair accessible, so do use facilities at the terminal before departure.

BY AIR Let airlines know special requirements at the time of booking. Lille's airport is equipped with lifts and ramps for access to aircraft, has adapted toilets and telephone kiosks, and supplies wheelchairs. There are ten designated parking spaces near the terminal.

GETTING AROUND

METRO AND TRAMS The métro system is excellent, with level platforms and lifts from street to booking hall to platform level at every station. Brilliant. When a lift is to be taken out of order, for maintenance or other reasons, this will usually be announced on the www.transpole.fr website. Click on '*se deplacer*' then '*reseau accessible*'. **Warning:** do not try to use escalators instead of lifts if you are unable to climb conventional stairs. I was once stranded between platforms and concourse when a down escalator only took me partway to train level and there was no up escalator to return me to the ticket-office level. Two staff answered my SOS and a very slow and undignified rescue followed.

BUSES While most French buses are traditional touring coaches with several steep steps and not adapted to the needs of disabled passengers, Lille's Transpole network has done sterling work in opening up the network to all users. Ninety per cent of city buses are fitted with platforms that can be lowered for easier boarding. Signal to the driver should you require the ramp (usually at the rear or central door). Some buses even have a blue button by the adapted door for passengers to summon the ramp.

The following routes are fully accessible: Buses 10, 11, 12, 13, 14, 15, 16, 17, 18, 30, 32, 33, 35, 36, 37, 50, 51, 52, 53, 54, 55, 56, 57, 58, 59, 61, 63, 64, 65, 66, 67, 68, 75, 76, 78, 79, 80, 81, 82, 84, 86, 87 and 88, plus the Citadines and Liane routes.

Passengers and drivers are very helpful when it comes to swiping your ticket, and drivers will often call out to ask at which stop you will be descending, so that they can be sure to sort out the ramp before the other passengers use the doors.

The Navette Vieux Lille minibus is a real boon for visitors who find the cobbles of the historic centre a challenge too far. Pick up the bus at Rihour station ($\mathcal{Q}$ 237 H6), then get on and off at will, flagging down the bus anywhere along the route once you are in the oldest quarter. However, be warned: the ramps on these minibuses are notoriously unreliable and on more than half the occasions I have tried to use the buses, the ramps have not worked. Be prepared to wait around ten minutes for the next bus.

DRIVING AND PARKING Blue badges issued in any EU country may be used in France. However, you may still have to pay for parking.

OVERGROUND RAIL Accès Plus (page 30) may also be able to assist with train journeys across the region. As well as both Lille Europe and Lille Flandres, the service is also available at Arras, Boulogne Ville, Calais Frethun, Calais Ville, Douai, Dunkerque, Lens, Saint-Omer, Tourcoing and Valenciennes. Ask about accessibility at rural stations before travelling.

ACCOMMODATION

In France, the definition of accessible hotel rooms can be flexible. I know of one hotel, some 500km south of Lille, which boasts a fully adapted room with handrails in the en suite and all facilities up to international standard. The problem is that it is on the first floor and there is no lift. No independent hotels nor B&Bs in central Lille are listed in the *Handi-Tourisme* guide (page 29), just the Suite Novotel (page 66) and Hotel Barrière (page 60). Nonetheless, there are several *gîtes* and *chambre d'hôtes* suggested for the outlying metropolitan area. However, even if they have not been granted the official label, large chain hotels all have reasonably accessible rooms and most can provide properly adapted accommodation. Remember to specify your precise requirements when booking, and do not be afraid to ask for details relating to your own requirements. Many apartment and suite options have wet-room bathing options with no step to the shower. One provided a wide enough bathroom in a standard room, but the toilet was so impractical that I had to use facilities at the nearby railway station. Do check for recent changes, as most hotels in the city are undergoing a rolling programme of improvements. Be warned that some older, taller hotels may have a lift, but it may not reach the ground floor. Extra questions to ask when booking: does the lift run from street level to the room with no steps? Can it take a wheelchair? Is there flat access to the breakfast room? Some hotels, such as the Calm Appart'hôtel (pages 64–5) have inventive mobile platforms that carry disabled guests up the half-dozen steps from reception to the lift. Always phone to check on the day of arrival that this is not out of order.

EATING AND DRINKING

The annoying truth is that most seriously *gastronomique* addresses come complete with doorstep. But, if a helping hand with one or two steps can be arranged, nothing is impossible. Only the restaurant at the new Casino Hotel actually made it into the recent official *Handi-Tourisme* listings, but plenty of restaurants are worth considering (if you can cope without needing the loo). Pavement terraces abound and most listed restaurants and brasseries on

3

the squares will serve meals outdoors, many with excellent heated terraces in the winter or spring. Les Trois Brasseurs (page 90) opposite the Lille Flandres station serves meals outside – and you are just across the road from the station with its 'facilities'. A handful of out-of-town eateries are included in the official listings but, again, a phone call will tell just how accessible a restaurant, café or club may be. Sometimes there is just the one step, but more establishments are now investing in ramps. As ever, be warned: no matter how easy it is to get into an establishment in Vieux Lille, the street itself may still be the problem.

NIGHTLIFE

Underground cafés and cellar bars bring their own problems. Theatres and nightclubs often have a side entrance – as always, call in advance. The opera house promises seating for guests with all mobility restrictions at all performances (subject to availability) and has audio-described options for the visually impaired. A complex web of lifts takes patrons through the backstage and front-of-house areas for an escorted adventure between the booking office (only accessible entrance to the theatre) and your eventual seat. The main Théâtre du Nord on Grand' Place is also accessible, with a lift from the ground floor. A lift from street level and reserved seating are available at the Nouveau Siècle concert hall. The Gymnase and Verrière theatres in Lille are officially totally accessible. Most of the central multiplex cinemas around the rue Béthune are easy to use – just check the situation for the individual screen you have in mind before handing over your cash.

MUSEUMS

New spaces, Maisons Folies and recent conversions are accessible. Older museums bring their own problems, but a phone call will usually result in assistance in viewing part of a collection at least. Ask for the *parcours handicapé* itinerary for alternative routes through museums (often featuring hidden lifts). The Louvre-Lens, Forum Mitterand and Musée du Souvenir in Villeneuve d'Ascq, Manufacture des Flandres in Roubaix, Domaine Mandarine Napoléon in Seclin and the dolls museum in Wambrechies are all considered fully accessible. Visually impaired visitors should contact museums for details of tailor-made visits, often allowing hands-on exploration of exhibits.

4

Practicalities

TOURIST OFFICES

In late 2015, Lille's tourist office will move from its long-term home in the magnificent remains of the ducal Palais Rihour. The new address will be right across the road in a modern office building where the regional and departmental tourist offices have their visitor information desks (pages 16–7). The tourist office offers a friendly welcome with multilingual staff who can offer advice on sightseeing and excursions, and help with hotel bookings. Stacks of free leaflets and brochures may seem bewildering, but pick up the following essentials: a good, free, fold-out city map, an up-to-date shopping plan and guide, and the latest issue of *Sortir*, the essential listings magazine. A range of specialist guidebooks is sold here, and this is the check-in point for those taking advantage of the all-inclusive city pass and hotel deals (pages 48 and 54). You may buy public transport passes from the information desk. Various guided walking tours of the city may be booked here and depart from the building. The hour-long minibus tour of Lille (strongly recommended) also departs from outside the main entrance. Prices and information are given on page 49.

A guided tour option allows visitors to create their own itinerary, with a soundtrack delivered to smartphones, tablets or MP3 players. Historical commentary, extracts from radio interviews and documentaries are available in French or English at the Palais Rihour, Grand' Place, place du Théâtre, rue de la Grande Chaussée, rue Esquermoise, Hospice Comtesse and Notre Dame de la Treille. Other regional guides are available for Lens, Roubaix and Cassel. Simply download the ZeVisit app on to your mobile device from the App Store, Google Play or www.zevisit.com.

Lille tourist office GP Pl Rihour 237 H6 (from late 2015: 3 rue du Palais Rihour) 03 59 57 94 00 info@lilletourism.com www.lilletourism.com 09.30–18.00 Mon–Sat, 10.00–12.00 & 14.00–17.00 Sun & holidays Rihour Métro 2 to Gare Lille Flandres, then line 1 to Rihour. Additional information desks at Lille Europe station & Lille Lesquin Airport are open during peak season.

CONSULATES

ⓔ Canada 30 av Emile Zola ♀ 235 K1 ☎03 20 14 05 78

ⓔ UK 11 sq du Tilleul ♀ 236 E4 ☎03 20 12 82 72

ⓔ Australia 4 rue Jean-Rey, 75015 ☎01 40 59 33 00

ⓔ Ireland 4 rue Rude, 75016 ☎01 44 17 67 00

ⓔ New Zealand 103 rue de Grenelle, 75007 ☎01 45 01 43 41

ⓔ USA 4 av Gabriel, 75008 ☎01 43 12 22 22

BANKS AND MONEY MATTERS

BANKS Branches are all around town, with most major French banks to be found along rue Nationale. Generally open Monday–Friday 10.00–17.00 (some close 12.00–14.00); some branches will open Saturday 10.00–13.00; some may close Monday. Banks close earlier than usual on the eve of holidays. Cash can be obtained out of hours at ATMs (*distributeurs automatiques de billets*), widely available around town (there are even four within 100m of place Lion D'Or in the old town). Most ATMs will accept Visa and MasterCard, and debit cards on the Cirrus and Maestro schemes.

CURRENCY EXCHANGE Available at most banks and post offices, and also in department stores, railway stations, airports and near tourist sites. Caution: even though exchange rates are fixed, commission rates are flexible. They must therefore be clearly indicated. For more on the euro, see pages 27–8.

CREDIT CARDS Visa and MasterCard are widely accepted, and American Express and Diners may also be used in many tourist and business areas. There is often a minimum purchase requirement of around €10. Depending on the type of card, you may withdraw up to €300–400 at ATMs and banks. French credit cards contain a computer chip (*puce*), and users may be asked to key in a private PIN during transactions. The magnetic strips on old-style credit cards from other countries sometimes fail to be read by the local swipe machines. Should this be the case, ask for your card number to be typed in manually. Should you lose your card, you must notify the issuing bank as soon as possible to block fraudulent charges. Keep a note of your credit card number and call the appropriate customer service number:

American Express ☎01 47 77 70 00 (customer service) or 01 47 77 72 00 (lost or stolen cards)

Diners Club ☎08 20 82 05 36 (customer service) or 08 10 31 41 59 (lost or stolen cards)

Eurocard/MasterCard ☎08 00 90 13 87

Visa ☎08 00 90 11 79

TRAVELLERS' CHEQUES These are rarely used nowadays. Whether in euros or international currencies, these may be converted in banks, exchange outlets and selected post offices. You are insured in case of loss or theft.

VAT AND TAX REFUNDS France charges value-added tax, VAT (or TVA in French), at 20% on most purchases. Food and drink, public transport and books are taxed at just 5.5%; newspapers, as well as medical items from pharmacies, at the even lower rate of 2.1%. Non-EU residents over the age of 15 and staying less than six months in Europe can get a refund of the TVA on purchases amounting to more than €175 at any single store. Budget a reduction of 16.5% of the purchase amount, and add half an hour on to your shopping time to take advantage of the deal. Galeries Lafayette and Printemps department stores each have a department which specialises in handling this. The store staff have to complete a VAT refund form, which you then give to customs (within three months of date of purchase) when leaving France or the last EU country you visit. Therefore, you will need to add at least 30 minutes to your check-in time and have your purchases handy for inspection. Customs will stamp the form, which must then be mailed back to the shop within six months of the date of purchase. Refunds are usually simply credited back to your credit card account. A bit of a palaver, but have you seen those French wedding dresses, and that tableware? It's worth it!

TIPS AND SERVICE Restaurant bills are obliged to include service charges (15%). However, it is traditional to round up the total in restaurants and bars, leaving small change behind. Hotel porters should be tipped €2–5, and chambermaids left an appropriate gratuity. Tip taxi drivers 10–15% of the fare. Hairdressers should be left 15%. Cloakroom attendants should be given €1. Public toilet attendants usually expect around 50 cents. In cinemas and theatres, tip the usherette between 50c and €1 if escorted directly to your seat.

COMMUNICATIONS

INTERNET Discover internet access points at key métro stations for picking up emails and surfing on the move: three at Lille Flandres, three at République–Beaux Arts, another three at Roubaix-Téléport and one at Tourcoing Centre. Lille Flandres station also has free Wi-Fi. Most hotels and even B&B establishments provide cabled internet connections or Wi-Fi for travellers (check at the time of booking); otherwise Lille has been slow to offer large city-centre internet facilities, though the post office opposite the opera offers them (pages 39–40). All branches of McDonald's offer free Wi-Fi for their patrons, as do more and more bars, cafés and brasseries. If you do not have your own device, or need to print off your boarding passes, and require a cybercafé, check with the tourist office. Remember that French keyboards differ slightly from UK layout, so type slowly and carefully!

Internet cafés

Atlanteam Ⓜ 93 rue Solférino ♀236 D6 ☎03 20 10 05 15 ✉lille@atlanteam.com ⏰10.30–24.00 Mon–Sat, 14.00–22.00 Sun 🚇République–Beaux Arts 🚌Bus Citadine from Gare Lille Europe to Sacré Cœur. Popular with a young crowd. Prices start at €1 for 15 minutes, then €3 an hour, but loads of deals offer free time online – you can even take out a subscription to cover a short break in Lille. Gaming sessions from 4 hours non stop at €10 should be booked in advance.

MEDIA

Press UK daily papers are widely available, as is the *International Herald Tribune*. A selection of free daily newspapers, such as 20 Minutes (🖥 *www.20minutes.fr/lille*) and MetroNews (🖥 *www.metronews.fr*), are distributed at stations and shopping centres.

Going Out Free bimonthly arts and eating magazine. Pick up in bars and restaurants. Interviews with local restaurateurs as well as Hollywood A-listers.

La Voix du Nord Outside Paris, the French prefer to get their news from regional rather than national papers. This local daily paper gives the essential low-down on everything happening in the region, with good national and international news coverage as well. Once an underground news-sheet published by the local Resistance, it has become the key news source for the region, publishing editions for each town in the north of France from its distinctive office on Grand' Place (pages 177–80). Read it over breakfast at your hotel, or sitting in a central café or bar to look cool as you check up on listings and entertainment news. The online edition was worth checking out before travelling at 🖥www.lavoixdunord.fr. However, much of the site is now blocked by a pay-wall. There are also several daily tabloid free sheets. Pick them up outside the stations for good arts coverage.

Le Figaro Popular middle-market national daily.

Le Monde The national daily paper of record.

Libération This left-wing tabloid has never lost its cool image with students and intellectuals.

Nord Éclair Local weekly.

Sortir Grab a free copy of the weekly listings magazine for Lille and the wider region. Published each Wednesday and available at hotel receptions, most bars and the tourist office.

Radio Local news can be heard on 94.7FM and the university campus station on 106.6FM. Motorway traffic is on 107.7FM. Lille is also within the transmission area for BBC Radio 4 on 198LW.

TV Lille has its own TV channel, Grand Lille, with a good breakfast show and programming from events around the city. Catch it online before your trip at 🖳 www.grandlille.tv. The main digital rolling news station is BFM TV. Local news and weather bulletins and can be found on France 3. Tune in to France 2 in the morning for the *Télé Matin* news and arts programme. Weather reports are on at around 06.55, 07.25, 07.55 and shortly before 08.40.

French TV on mainstream channels offers loads of franchise music 'talent' contests, reality *Big Brother*-type shows, emotional food series (reality heartstring-pulling blended with recipes) and endless discussion programmes featuring people in brightly lit studios wearing strong primary colours. I was once traumatised by an hour-long debate on the psychology of underwear – this at 21.00 on the leading commercial station. TFI, France 2 and to a lesser extent France 3 churn out lots of this stuff, but all have good one-hour evening news broadcasts from around 19.00. As for daytime TV, forget it! Once upon a time, before deregulation, there were stimulating daytime shows, such as *Continentales*, Alex Taylor's round-up of news bulletins from around Europe. Now expect shopping infomercials and cartoons. The bilingual French and German arts channel Arté, is well worth watching. M6 is pop vids and imported US series dubbed into French, and Canal Plus is a subscriber cable channel mainly showing movies, often in their original language. Some hotels offer cable or international satellite TV, which usually means CNN or the BBC World news channel, and occasionally Sky News. The national state-owned rolling-news channel France24 broadcasts three streams: French, Arabic and English.

POSTCODES Most central Lille addresses use the postcode (zip code) 59000. Some roads on the edge of the centre use 59800. Since the principal code covers most of any urban area in France, GPS navigation within French towns and cities should be based on street names rather than postcodes.

POST OFFICES At the post office you may buy stamps, post letters and parcels, make phone calls, send faxes and receive your mail *poste restante*. The branch at boulevard Carnot (♀ 237 J4) offers internet access and prefranked envelopes. A great way to get rid of fiddly small change is to use the vending machines selling stamps. Many post offices accept payment by Visa and

MasterCard. Stamps may also be purchased from tobacconists, kiosks and bars displaying the red cigar *tabac* symbol. Letterboxes are painted yellow. Post offices are generally open from 08.00 to 18.30 on weekdays and from 08.00 to 12.00 on Saturdays.

TELEPHONES Call boxes in some restaurants and bars may accept coins, while most public telephones require a phonecard (*télécarte*) available from post offices, railways stations, tobacconists and news kiosks. Calls from hotels are invariably more expensive. Ask at reception for their rates per unit, and length of each unit: some hotels charge in units of 15 seconds! However, if you have free internet in your room, consider using Skype or other VOIP services to save money. Post offices offer fax services. Internet cafés may offer web phone services.

Mobile phones Most mobile phones will be able to use France Telecom's Orange or rival networks. Contact your service provider before leaving in order to set up or cancel international roaming. You should seriously consider this if your smartphone is liable to eat up data charges at international rates.

Roaming charges for calls and texts across the EU have been reduced, so using your own mobile phone from another European country is not as expensive as in the past. But if your phone is already unlocked, then consider buying a pay-as-you-go SIM card from a supermarket or the post office. Alternatively, you can pick up a basic mobile phone with local SIM card at under €30 and top it up online or at supermarkets, *tabacs* or some ATMs.

Dialling When calling France from outside the country, use the country code (33) and omit the first 0 of the listed number. To call international numbers from France, dial 00 then the country code and number (omitting the first 0). To call within France, dial the ten-digit telephone number. For operator-assisted dialling, key in 00+33+country code.

Country codes	*Useful telephone numbers*
Australia 61	**Emergency services in English** 📞112
Belgium 32	(police, fire, ambulance)
Canada 1	**Ambulance** 📞15
France 33	**Car pound** 📞03 20 50 90 14
Ireland 353	**Duty doctor** 📞36 24
New Zealand 64	**Fire** 📞18
United Kingdom 44	**Hospital & medical emergencies** 📞03 20
USA 1	44 59 62
	Lost property 📞03 20 50 55 99
	Operator 📞12
	Police (emergency) 📞17

Police (all other matters) 🞄03 20 62 47 47
SOS (English-language crisis line) 🞄01
47 23 80 80

Tourist information (anywhere in France) 🞄32 65
Weather (France) 🞄08 36 68 02 75

WORSHIP

A full list of churches and other places of worship may be obtained from the tourist office (page 35).

(Anglican) Christ Church   Rue Lydéric
♀ 238 H3 🞄03 28 52 66 36 🚇 Métro 2 to
Gare Lille Flandres, then bus 14 to Mairie de
Lille, & cross Porte de Paris to rue Lydéric.

(Muslim) Grande Mosquée de Lille 🚇 59
rue de Marquillies ♀ 238 B5 🞄03 20 53 02 65
🚇 Métro 2 to Porte d'Arras, then bus 14 to
Faubourg d'Arras, & walk along rue Henaux to
rue de Marquillies.

(Jewish) Synagogue   5 rue Angellier ♀ 238
G3 🞄03 20 52 41 59 🚇 Métro 2 to Mairie de
Lille, then bus 14 to Jeanne d'Arc & walk up
rue Jeanne d'Arc to rue Angellier.

**(Roman Catholic) Basilique Cathédrale
Notre Dame de la Treille** 🚇 ♀ 237 J3.
See pages 186–7 & other churches listed on
pages 184–7.

TRAVELLING WITH CHILDREN

Like any city, Lille can be paradise for kids, or a nightmare for parents. It is just a matter of planning your day.

PRACTICALITIES   Department stores and shopping malls have toilets and baby-changing facilities. If you've not brought the essential equipment with you (or your low-cost airline charges a fortune for extra luggage) you can hire buggies, cots, high chairs, etc. Book in advance at 🞈 www.location-de-poussette.fr and collect from Planète Mômes (see below). Most hotels and apartments can provide cots/high chairs.

Vieux Lille has cobbled streets and its shops and restaurants may have steps, so follow tips in *Chapter 3* if you will be pushing a pram or buggy during your stay. Public transport is adapted for buggies as well as wheelchairs, with lifts to platforms and ramps on buses.

Planète Mômes   133 rue Molinel ♀ 238 G1
🞄03 20 06 28 48 🞈 planetemomes-lille.com
🕐 14.00–19.00 Mon, 10.00–19.00 Tue–Sat
🚌 République–Beaux Arts 🚇 Bus Citadine
to Tanneurs & walk along rue Molinel. The all-
in-one address for shopping & lunching with
your kids. As well as finding trendy new
clothes & shoes in the fashion section, the

dépôt-vente department is a great place for
selling your own unwanted stuff & buying
secondhand goods at reasonable prices. Think
of it as a real-life version of eBay. The in-store
bar & restaurant is child friendly. Pop into a
specialist children's hair salon or check out the
school holiday & weekend workshops (from
circus skills & painting to dance classes).

4

You can hire baby equipment (carry cots, car seats, etc) or collect items you've reserved online through 🍎 www.location-de-poussette.fr.

EATING AND DRINKING Families eat together in French cities, so there are no problems with mealtimes. Most restaurants have a children's menu, and **Flam's** restaurant (page 99) offers a free child's meal with every paying adult diner on Sunday lunchtimes. If you want to avoid the ubiquitous chicken nuggets or *steak hachée* (tell the kids it's a burger), try **Brasserie André** (page 86) where youngsters are given a more gastronomic choice. Fussy eaters will enjoy the stuffed jacket potato options at **La Patatière** (pages 108–9). In the centre of Lille, if the weather is good enough, sit outside at a table on the terrace. Most child-friendly museums and attractions have a family-orientated restaurant.

ATTRACTIONS AND OUTINGS Most museums have kids' activity packs available from receptions, offering interesting and enjoyable things to do, as well as suggesting a child's itinerary and exhibits that youngsters will enjoy. Organised and supervised activities, workshops and games take place in most French museums on Wednesdays and Saturdays. Traditionally Wednesday afternoons were school-free in France; however, since 2014, many schools have stopped giving pupils the afternoon off.

On rainy days, consider the **Planetarium** at Villeneuve d'Ascq (pages 205–6), easily reached by métro. On Wednesdays and Saturdays, parent and child screenings take place at local **cinemas** (films chosen for the over-fives), such as **L'Hybride** (page 130).

Bookshops can be fun and **Le Bateau Livre** (page 143) only stocks titles that will appeal to the under-16s. So, find a picture book or easy reader for the youngest, or challenge the others to attempt a J K Rowling or Stephenie Meyer in French. There are board games to play, plus cake to eat, at **Café Livres** secondhand bookshop (pages 116–17).

In good weather, you've plenty of parks to discover (pages 193–5). The **zoo** (pages 183–4) by the Citadelle is free and always worth a visit, and is only walking distance from the puppet theatre in Jardin Vauban and **Parc des Poussins** play park, with rides for younger children. Away from town, the **Musée de Plein Air** in Villeneuve d'Ascq is great for letting off steam and keeping children entertained. If you are staying in Lille for a while, there

---

OPENING HOURS

Opening hours for specific sights are covered in the relevant chapters. For **restaurants** see pages 75–124; for **shops**, pages 143–63; for **museums**, pages 169–74.

▲ The Musée de Plein Air in Villeneuve d'Ascq offers a taste of traditional country living (Musée de Plein Air)

are regular direct trains from Lille Europe station to **Disneyland Paris**. But there's no need to drag the kids and their accessories across the capital, as the Marne La Vallée-Chessy Station is in the theme park itself. Tip: take the train from Gare Lille Europe to be there in just over an hour; trains from Gare Flandres take around 40 minutes longer.

Parc des Poussins 1 av Mathias Delobel
♀ 236 C2 ☎ 03 20 54 81 11 🖥 www.
lespoussins.fr ⏰ Feb–Oct 14.00–18.30
weekends & school holidays (brasserie
⏰ from Mar 11.30–18.30 daily) 🚍 Bus 12 to
Champ de Mars. A children's park by the zoo in
the grounds of the Citadelle. Rides for small
children include a train, carousels & a gentle
nursery-slope version of a roller-coaster. Pay
€2 for 1 ride, 8 rides for €13. There are
trampolines for bouncing off excess energy or
the side effects of too much candyfloss & fizzy
drinks.

Musée de Plein Air 143 rue Colbert,
59493 Villeneuve d'Ascq ☎ 03 20 63 11 25
🖥 www.museedepleinair-asso.org ⏰ Apr
& May Wed–Sun, Jun–Aug daily, Sep & Oct
weekends 🚇 Métro 2 to Gare Lille Flandres,
then line 1 to Pont de Bois & bus 13 to
Masséna; 10-min walk is signposted. Meet
carpenters, blacksmiths, painters, sculptors,
artists & artisans working in the traditional
manner in the heritage village & park setting.

This is not just a collection of traditional old
buildings, but a complete way of life preserved
for new generations. An old-fashioned toy
maker has a workshop here & musicians play
in the gardens & streets. Children's events at
weekends & in summer. A book of activity
ideas for youngsters is available for just €1
from the museum shop. For hours & diary of
events, visit the website.

**Théâtre de Marionnettes du Jardin de
Vauban** Jardin Vauban, 1 av Léon Jouhaux
♀ 236 C4 ☎ 03 20 42 09 95 🖥 www.
lepetitjacques.fr ⏰ Apr–Oct weekends &
school holidays 🚍 Bus 12 to Champ de Mars
then walk through the park to the theatre
🎟 €4.60 adults, €3.90 children. Generations
of children have known Monsieur Rameau's
Goat House, where today the puppet theatre
stages the many exploits of le Petit Jacques as
the marionette has countless adventures. Each
season brings a good selection of stories, so
you may come back more than once.

With around 250 stations in and around the city, bikes are a popular way of getting around Lille
(phjpix/S)

5

Local Transport

METRO, TRAMS AND BUSES

METRO A superb métro system ties in with the tramways and buses. The unmanned VAL métro is completely automated, and runs on two ever-expanding lines crossing central Lille and serving the suburbs and *métropolitan* area. Central métro platforms are sealed off from the tracks by sliding glass doors that open when the train comes to a standstill. *En route* to the suburbs, the trains swoop and soar from underground tunnels to futuristic tracks high above the countryside and motorways. Try to sit at the very front for the true fairground-attraction experience.

Métro lines in France do not have names: they are numbered and platforms indicated by the terminus. Thus, Line 1 will be marked either 4 Cantons/Stade Pierre Mauroy or CHR B-Calmette, and Line 2 CH Dron or St Philibert.

TRAMS Twin tramways run out to Roubaix and Tourcoing, passing the pretty Parc Barbieux and, on sunny days, provide a pleasant alternative to the underground. Métro and tram services run from 05.15 to midnight (from 06.20 at weekends).

BUSES The city bus network covers the areas of the old town that no métro could possibly reach, since so much of Lille is built on land reclaimed from canals and waterways. From the principal bus stops at place des Buisses, alongside Gare Lille Flandres, services fan out to the outlying districts, even crossing the Belgian border. Buses generally run from around 05.30 until 20.30.

In the evening, the late bus network meanders through the town centre, Vieux Lille and out to the satellite towns half-hourly from approx 21.30 until 00.30. Most routes out of town leave the place des Buisses and some depart from place de la République.

Line 4 will get you back from Vieux Lille after dinner. Buses go midweek every 20 minutes until 22.30 then half-hourly until 00.30, Saturdays every 20 minutes until 23.30 then half-hourly until 00.30, and Sundays hourly from 22.30–00.30.

A **weekend night bus** runs a half-hourly service on Thursday, Friday and Saturday nights from 01.00 until the full network kicks in first thing in the morning. This route from Lille Porte de Douai to Villeneuve d'Ascq takes in the bus stops at Jeanne d'Arc, Philippe Lebon, Masséna, Sacré Cœur (return route only – otherwise stops at National) to Rihour and Gare Flandres, so linking the bar and club quarters with the main hotel districts.

The **Citadine** bus route is a useful circuit, taking in the principal boulevards, the Citadelle, Zenith and both railway stations in a continuous, sweeping loop around the city. It runs from around 05.30 until 21.30.

While most bus routes merely skirt the Vieux Lille quarter, a recent addition to the public transport fleet is the **Navette Vieux Lille**. Using the discount ZAP fare (page 48) this fleet of minibuses runs èvery 10–15 minutes between 07.00 and 21.00 from outside the métro and tourist office on place Rihour. It runs on a loop taking in the squares, Vieux Lille from place Lion d'Or and looping through rue de Gand (except in summer when the road is pedestrianised), the garrison district on the edge of the city, back through the Royale and Voltaire quarters, out to the Citadelle, and back through rues de la Barre and Bouchers to the starting point. An invaluable aid to exploring the cobbled streets of the oldest part of town, the hail-and-ride service can be boarded anywhere along the route in Vieux Lille, not just the bus stops, and you may ask the driver to drop you off at a convenient point.

A road traffic calming measure has led to the removal of bus routes from the main thoroughfare between the stations, the Grand' Place and rue Nationale. Now, only the Navette Vieux Lille links place Rihour and the squares to Vieux Lille. For hotels and restaurants based in this area, I suggest either taking the métro to place Rihour and walking across the squares to the old town, or using bus route 50 to place Lion d'Or in the heart of Vieux Lille and walking from there. Otherwise use the Navette Vieux Lille.

Public transport information can be found at ☎ 03 20 40 40 40 and 🖥 www.transpole.fr. The website has an excellent journey planner; click on '*Itineraires*' to research a route by bus, tram, métro and/or rail. You can pick up a transport map from stations and tourist offices.

TICKETS AND PASS PASS Traditional tickets are now a thing of the past. All your travel, from a single journey across town, to a day pass, season ticket or *carnet* for ten journeys, now only requires a simple smart card – the Pass Pass.

Types The Pass Pass is fully rechargeable across town (sometimes even online) and is available in three forms.

Ticket Rechargeable (20c – refunded on the fifth recharge) Simplest option for visitors to Lille. This cardboard smart card is available from all outlets and can be recharged up to ten times. Download single tickets, *carnets* for multiple journeys, day passes, even ZAP tickets (page 48). Several people can travel on the same card at the same time and you may lend it to friends.

Carte Non-Personnalisée (€2) Versatile option for all ticket types, but can be used by several people travelling together or lent to a friend. Virtually unlimited recharges.

Carte Personelle (€4) A plastic smart card for one person's use. Ideal for regular users and season-ticket holders, even for those signed up for bike and car hire. Order online at 🖱 www.transpole.fr.

Where to buy Buy your Pass Pass from the vending machines at métro stations and certain bus stops, or pick one up at a *tabac* (tobacconist/ newsagent). They are also available at any Transpole travel centre or ticket office. At Gare Lille Europe, you may pick up the basic *ticket rechargeable* or *carte non-personnalisée* at the métro ticket machine on the same level as the station concourse. It is best to buy a simple *carnet* for your first purchase – that will get you and your party safely to the hotel! There are 200 ticket machines across the network and 60 recharging points at stations and key bus stops. Otherwise, pick up your first Pass Pass from any bus driver – charged for just one single journey at €1.70 (including the 20c refundable card charge).

How to use Card readers and validation screens may be found at the entrance to platforms, escalators and lifts on the métro, and close to the doors on buses and trams. Hold your Pass Pass over the screen (do not swipe, it will not register) and wait for the beep and tick symbol to appear on the screen. If a cross appears and the buzzer sounds, try again. If you have bought discount ZAP tickets (page 48) for specific journeys, press the ZAP button on the card reader before placing your Pass Pass over the screen. When travelling with friends and using just one Pass Pass, hold your card against the screen and key in the number of fellow passengers.

When transferring between bus/tram/métro, remember to present your card for each leg of the journey (no need to update numbers of passengers when travelling in a group). You will not be charged if the second or third mode of transport is a continuation of your original journey.

Failure to validate your card results in a €5 fine. Travelling without a Pass Pass or ticket incurs an immediate fine of €49.50.

Prices Tickets cost around €1.50 for any journey on the Transpole métro/ tram/bus network and allow you to travel in one direction, changing from métro to tram to bus if necessary without buying another ticket. *Carnets* of ten tickets are better value at €12.50, and one-day Pass Journée tickets are available offering unlimited travel for around €4 for one day, €7.50 for two days or €9.50 for three days (each day is a full 24 hours from the moment of first use, so if you buy your pass at 19.00 you may use it the following day until the same time).

There are also a couple of lesser-known bargains to consider: the Pass Soirée for travel after 19.00 until the night bus network stops in the morning is just €2. And, if you are taking only short trips of less than three métro or tram stops, such as the Wazemmes market, or wish to use the Navette Vieux Lille, buy the less-than-half-price ZAP ticket at just 80 cents each or 10 for €8. Should you intend to stay around the Grand' Place and Vieux Lille, the chances are you will not use much public transport, since the métro does not serve the old town (although buses manage to reach a surprising number of streets there). In that case you may be better off buying just the occasional ticket rather than day or weekend passes. Should your plans involve trips out to Roubaix, Tourcoing or Villeneuve d'Ascq, or a few cross-town trips to and from the markets, a carnet between friends or a day card would be better value. Note that regular overground SNCF rail services (such as the journey to Lens for the Louvre) are not included in regular network tickets/passes. Your Pass Pass may also be used to pay for park and ride services.

During the two days of the Braderie (page 12) a special Pass Braderie gives unlimited travel on public transport across the *métropolitan* area for €5. A similar deal may be offered from noon until the last bus, tram or métro on National Music Day (21 June).

If you are staying in Lille for a while, or are a student at the university, there are many alternative discount options to discover. See the Transpole website (🖳 *www.transpole.fr*) for details.

LOST PROPERTY If you have lost an umbrella, walking stick, wallet, sunglasses or domestic pet on any bus, tram or métro, telephone 📞 03 20 81 43 43.

LILLE CITY PASS

The Lille City Pass allows you to travel on all trams, métro and bus services, and provides unlimited access to major museums and attractions in Lille and the neighbouring towns, including the Planetarium and distillery tour. It also offers discounts on many concert, theatre, opera and ballet tickets. The pass costs €25 for one day, €35 for two days or €45 for three days, and may be bought at any local tourist office or by calling 📞 03 59 57 94 00.

▲ The City Tour Bus is a great way to explore Lille's sights (Nord Tourism)

TOUR BUS

An excellent way to see the sights in the shortest possible time is to take the one-hour minibus city tour. Buses leave every hour from outside the tourist office on place Rihour. The multilingual audio-visual commentary is first rate. Tickets cost €12 (*children and unemployed €10; free for under-6s and holders of the City Pass*) from the tourist office. It is wheelchair accessible.

AIRPORT TRANSFERS

BY BUS A shuttle-bus service links Lille Lesquin Airport (8km out of town) with the main Lille Europe TGV and Eurostar station, a few steps away from the main bus station at place des Buisses. The service runs hourly 05.00–20.00 Monday–Friday, 05.00–18.00 Saturday, 07.00–22.00 Sunday. The single fare is €8, return €10, with reductions of around 30% for under-25s or groups of three or more travellers. Buses leave from the stop 'A' outside the arrivals hall. Call ✆03 20 90 79 79 for departure times.

BY TRAIN Trains link central Lille to both Paris Charles de Gaulle Airport (the TGV train takes 51 minutes) and Brussels Airport (Thalys train in 38 minutes). Services also run from Lille Flandres and Lille Europe stations, but prices vary considerably – check online at 🖱 www.voyages-sncf.com.

TAXIS

Taxis may be found at clearly marked ranks and, if you are very lucky, hailed in the street. The main ranks are outside the two railway stations, Lille Europe (♀ *235 J3* ✆ *03 20 06 64 00*) and Lille Flandres (♀ *235 G4* ✆ *03 20 06 06 06*).

Remember: when you book a taxi, the meter starts ticking from the moment of your call, not from the time and place you board the cab.

CAR HIRE

Most international car-rental agencies have desks at Lille Europe station and the airport, and offer special discounts to the various airlines and rail companies. However, it is often cheaper to rent a car from one of the smaller companies in town. Rent a Car (*113 rue du Molinel* ♀ *238 H1* ☎ *03 20 40 20 20*), a five-minute walk from the Gare Lille Flandres, has very low rates for one- or two-day rentals. Online bargains can often be found at 🖥 www.auto-europe.co.uk.

🚗 **Avis** ☎ 03 20 51 12 31 (station) ☎ 03 20 87 59 56 (airport) 🖥 www.avis.com

🚗 **Budget** ☎ 03 28 36 50 40 (station) 🖥 www.budget.fr

🚗 **Europcar** ☎ 03 20 06 01 46 (station) ☎ 03 20 90 45 45 (airport) 🖥 www.europcar. com

🚗 **Hertz** ☎ 03 28 36 25 90 (station) ☎ 03 20 49 67 89 (airport) 🖥 www.hertz.com

🚗 **Sixt** m 08 20 00 74 98 (station) 🖥 www. sixt.fr

PARKING Lille boasts 9,000 secure parking spaces in huge underground and multi-storey car parks tucked around the central area. Check with the tourist office for current rates as prices vary from site to site – from around €2 per hour. Most car parks close at 01.00; however, the Euralille car park remains open 24/7. When shopping at Euralille, leave the supermarket trawl until last, since Carrefour checkout staff will stamp your ticket for free or reduced-rate parking. Night owls take note that if you are planning an evening on the town, best value may be found at the Rihour-Printemps (♀ 237 H5) and Nouveau Siècle (♀ 237 G5) car parks, which sometimes offer a special evening rate of €2 from 19.00 to 01.00 – check with the tourist office. If you must park in the street, seek out the nearest parking meter and display the ticket on your car dashboard. If you stay out of town and use the public transport system, park for free at Porte des Postes, CHR Calmette, St Philibert and 4 Cantons. In Lille, the car parks at Champs de Mars (just by the Citadelle) and Porte de Valenciennes cost just €2 for three hours or €4 for the whole day and include free bus transfers to any stop on the Citadine routes. For information, call ☎ 03 28 36 86 86.

CITROEN 2CV HIRE

🚗 **Tradi'balade** GP 1 rue des Trois Couronnes ♀ 237 H5 ☎ 03 20 51 10 29 🖥 www.tradibalade.com ⏲ 10.30–12.30 & 14.00–19.30 daily 🚊 Rihour ⬤ Métro 2 to Gare Lille Flandres then line 1 to Rihour. Rent a classic open-topped Citroen 2CV for the day at €159, or be chauffeured around on a personalised city tour from €28pp in the iconic French classic car. Office based just behind the Vieille Bourse between the main squares.

No matter how enjoyable the guidebook or how informative the pamphlet, nothing matches the experience of being personally escorted around somewhere new by a local. Meet les Greeters du Nord: a dozen volunteers from Lille, Roubaix and the villages and towns of the Nord département who love their county and are delighted to share their tips, secrets and stories in person. Book an hour or so with a local 'greeter' and arrange for a personalised tour, tailor-made to suit your own interests. During the week, the greeters may be university lecturers, customs officers, architects or shop workers, but they give up their time for free at weekends to introduce visitors to the area. Some specialise in museums and the arts, others enjoy cycling in the countryside or walking the cobbled streets of old villages. Go to the CDT Nord website 🖳 www.tourisme-nord.com and click on 'Meet a Greeter in the Nord', where you can contact the right person for you.

CYCLING

Hire a bike at one of the many pick-up-and-drop-off points by railway stations. You will usually be asked to leave a returnable deposit of around €300, which can be organised by credit card. Ask at the tourist office for maps of cycle routes around Lille. For itineraries outside the city, see pages 214–15.

BIKE HIRE

🚲 **V'Lille** Ⓢ Gare Lille Flandres, pl des Buisses ♀ 235 H4 🖳 www.vlille.fr ⏱ 07.30–18.30 Mon–Fri, 11.00–18.30 Sat 🚉 Gare Lille Flandres 🚇 Métro 2 or walk to Gare Lille Flandres. Bright red bikes for hire across town. Register for the first time at the V'Lille office outside Gare Flandres or the Transpole information office in the métro station downstairs. Pay €1.40/day or €7/week to access the bikes. If you hold the full Pass Pass *personnalisée*, no deposit is required, otherwise a €200 deposit is taken from your credit card & returned to you at the end of the rental period. Register at any Station V'Lille equipped with a credit card machine or sign up with your card details online. You will receive a user code & PIN which you may use to retrieve any bike from any

bike station on the network (full list can be found on the website). Choose the option VLS (V'Lille Libre Service) for casual non-residential use. Longer-stay residents have the option of monthly or annual rentals & even electric bikes. There are around 100 bike stations in Lille at métro stations & the most popular streets & squares. Another 150 may be found outside the city limits, so you will always find somewhere to dock or collect a bike. If your journey is less than 30mins, the ride is free; you just pay €1 for each extra 30mins in the saddle. So if you pick up the bike at the main station, ride down to the Palais de Beaux-Arts & park up at rue Inkerman, there's nothing extra to pay, & if after the museum you wish to head off to the old town, that can easily be done within a free 30-min cycle. You could then ride back to the brasseries on pl Rihour in a few mins. For help & advice, contact Transpole customer service.

BIKE TAXI

🚲 **Happy Moov** ☎ 06 24 16 08 18 🖥 www.happymoov.com. Rickshaw taxi service in the city centre. €1 pick-up charge + €1 per km & per person (2 people max). Optional guided city tour at €18/half-hour or €30/hour. Rickshaw ranks at pl Rihour, pl des Buisses (Gare Lille Flandres) & parvis François Mitterand (Gare Lille Europe).

SEGWAY HIRE

🚲 **Mobil'Board** ☎ 06 60 97 74 52 🖥 www.mobilboard.com/en/agency/segway/lille. Alas, since the expansion of the V'Lille bike scheme, the Segway-for-hire option offered by the Transpole public transport organisation is no more. But a private company has taken over the tradition, with 2–3 hour Segway training sessions on the Champs de Mars & around town. You can even get a licence after the €65 course. This is of course, the somewhat retro sci-fi way to travel. Sway backwards or forwards to steer while standing on what looks like a garden roller pretending to be a hovercraft. Naturally, France has decided that the universal name Segway is too Anglophone and has introduced the official noun *gyropede* instead. The name is

even less likely to catch on than the transport itself. In Lille, it has already been modified to *gyropode*. Shoppers should note that there is a Segway parking zone at the Tanneurs shopping mall (page 142). Book in advance or call to find out where the group will be meeting.

SOLOWHEEL HIRE

🚲 **Ch'ti Mobile** ⑤ 21 av le Corbusier 📍 235 H4 ☎ 03 66 72 42 20 🖥 www.lille-solowheel.com 🚉 Gare Lille Europe. Travelling by Segway is so last week; the electric pedestrian of today rides a SoloWheel. Imagine a laptop-sized hybrid of a skateboard & a unicycle that slips between your shoes. This electric wheel with two footpads fits into a briefcase, or may be carried with its integral handle to be taken out & whiz you on your way at 16kph. An hour's charge will take you 11km along the city streets (speed limit on pavements is 6kph, free range on cyclepaths though). I first encountered them during one of those free student concerts on place République as supercharged youth wove between more pedestrians mooching around the stalls. Not cheap at €45/day, €60/weekend or €100/week, but at €1,890 to buy a SoloWheel, & with accessories costing several hundred euros as well, the rental price seems more palatable.

SKATEBOARDING

The parvis François Mitterand (📍 235 H4) outside the Gare Lille Europe has been popular with skaters, both inline and on boards, since it first opened. However, the youth of Lille went a stage too far when skaters adopted guerrilla building tactics one night in 2014 and concreted ramps and half pipes on the central reservation and kerbs of a main road in the business district on the outskirts of town, turning a dual carriageway into a skate park – causing rush hour chaos.

6

Accommodation

In a city where hospitality comes as standard, stories of northern welcomes are legendary. I only regret that one offbeat gem closed its doors just too early to be included in my Bradt guides: a B&B run by a former *madame* who, after years of service to the garrison, had ultimately transferred her attentions from the bed to the breakfast. Friends told me that many men who had visited the establishment as soldiers in their youth, and partaken fully of the fleshly delights on offer, had returned in later years with their families for a more orthodox *accueil*. Nonetheless, there are still plenty of conventional treats to be discovered in and around Lille, from the home-baked *petit déjeuner* brioche in a family home to a luxurious bedroom in a distillery devoted to the memory of Napoleon.

Chambre d'hôte is a particularly Gallic twist on bed and breakfast and, as well as our choice of the most welcoming and unusual homes (pages 67–71), it is always worth checking out the latest B&B lists issued by the tourist offices. **Self-catering** is well worth considering if you are planning a longer stay. In the countryside outside Lille, consider the charms of a *gîte* (see box, pages 68–9); otherwise rent a studio or one-bedroom apartment at an **aparthotel** in the town centre. Remember that supermarkets and even some restaurants will often deliver and that Lille has some great markets for fresh food if you fancy recreating restaurant masterworks with a two-ring hob and a microwave!

Mobility-restricted guests should be aware that some of the older hotels, especially around the old Flandres station, do not have lift access from the ground floor to the bedrooms – so always check when booking if you have issues with stairs (page 33).

Should you go for the **city-centre hotel** option, take a tip from me. Unless you are staying in one of the larger hotels with a grand breakfast-buffet selection – in which case you should eat heartily and just opt for a baguette and cheese for a lunchtime picnic – forego the standard hotel breakfast, usually costing €5–10 on top of the room rate. Instead, make your way to the main Paul bakery (page 122), on the corner of rue de Paris and the place du Théâtre. In the magnificently tiled surroundings of this fabulous shop, enjoy an excellent *petit déjeuner* of fresh-baked bread, homemade jams, and superb coffee or tea, or sinfully sensational hot chocolate – all for around €4. Other good breakfast options include Le Pain Quotidien (pages 121–2) and the lobby of the Hermitage Gantois (page 59).

BON WEEKEND – BON PRIX

Loyal readers of this guide who mourn the passing of the excellent 2-for-1 Bon Weekend hotel deals may take heart. The Tourist Office still runs a series of packages for weekenders. The most practical is the **Séjour Lille Découverte** deal. From €45 per person it includes one night's hotel accommodation and a one-day or two-day City Pass for free entry to museums and public transport. Optional cycling city tours and restaurant evenings can also be added to the deal. It is available all year, except during the Braderie. In the Christmas market season, a similar deal might feature a night's hotel accommodation, the city tour bus trip, a turn on the Ferris wheel and a glass of mulled wine.

HOTELS

ALLIANCE   17 quai du Wault ♀ 236 E3 ✎ 03 20 30 62 62 www.alliance-lille.com
🚌 Bus 12 to Nationale, then a 10-min walk along the rue Nationale to sq Foch & through the square to the pond
The highest-profile hotel in the city may be found just behind the recently renovated gardens of the square Foch, in a quiet waterside street a short walk from the Citadelle. On the banks of a dock built in the mercantile age of Charles the Bold, the high walls of the Couvent de Minimes are testament to four centuries of change. The usual 4-star perks of big buffet breakfasts in the morning, AC in the summer, and minibars and muzak all year round. Service is courteous and efficient and all is as one would expect of an establishment of this quality. Continued refreshment

Walk-in rate for a double room in high season. Outside conference periods, rooms from around €40 are easily found. Do check online deals.

€€€€€	Over €200 per night
€€€€	€150–200 per night
€€€	€100–150 per night
€€	€75–100 per night
€	Under €75 per night

of the décor has made the hotel a much more attractive place than the venue I first stayed in more than ten years ago. To be honest, on that visit, had it not once been a monastery, I'd have enjoyed the place a good deal more. But the fact that the old cloister of this listed 17th-century building has been smothered in glass and chrome and muzzled by an atrium and mezzanine piano bar gave the core of what might have been a charming and tasteful conversion the air of an airport hotel. Thus the gentle strains of George Gershwin were generally muted by my murderous thoughts towards the architect or corporate philistines who conceived and executed the project. Perhaps I was being unfair or unduly sensitive. On revisiting, the personality of the building has now emerged. And in any case, the current incarnation has greater dignity than that allowed over the previous 200 years. When the religious order was disbanded by the Revolution, the Couvent de Minimes saw service as a uniform warehouse to the garrison across the water. Happily, successive make-overs have brought out much of the original charm, not least the sophisticated brick vaulting from the craftsmen who built the monastery back in 1622. The well-equipped and very comfortable bedrooms have now evolved into relaxing and aesthetically pleasing bolt holes from city life. Most of the major hotel guides wax lyrical about the place, and the Lille business community swears by it. Live jazz evenings are *très décontracté*, and the restaurant in the glazed courtyard is well respected by discerning locals. The hotel room rate rises from around €250 and *demi-pension* deals are also available. Wi-Fi. €€€€€

ART DECO EURALILLE 110 av de la République, 59110 La Madeleine 🕑 235 J1 ✎ 03 20 14 81 81 🖱 www.hotel-artdecolille.com 🚃 Tramstop Romarin 🚊 Tram to Romarin
Rechristened to name-check the district around the Gare Lille Europe, the hotel is technically in the suburbs. Although La Madeleine is officially outside central Lille, the hotel is a lot closer to the Eurostar station than many of the alternatives officially designated as town-centre establishments. A relative newcomer to the scene, this is smart, modern, and with more than a nod towards the Art Deco style of its name. The reception area, with its helpful and charming staff, is dominated by a coloured glass ceiling, and the bedrooms are neat and stylish. Internet access and radio are welcome additions to the ubiquitous cable TV and pay-per-view movies. The hotel is just five minutes' walk from Lille Europe station (turn left on to bd Pasteur and right into av de la République), or you can take any tram leaving Lille Europe heading towards Roubaix or Tourcoing. The hotel is opposite the Romarin tram station. A free shuttle-bus service runs between the hotel

and the Grand' Place (stopping at the station on request) 07.15–10.00 and 18.00–23.00. Rooms €70–140. €€

BEST WESTERN PREMIER WHY HOTEL ⓖ 7 sq Morisson Ⓠ 237 G6 ☎ 03 20 50 30 30 🛏 www.why-hotel.com 🚇 Rihour ⓔ Métro 2 to Gare Lille Flandres then line 1 to Rihour; walk past the tourist office & sq Morisson is on your left

Not just a Best Western hotel but arguably the Very Best Western. This boutique hotel converts a dull concrete office block on the wrong side of the place Rihour into a rather lovely pamper palace within walking distance of everything. The reception desk might be made from glazed-over vintage kitchen cabinets, but bottles and cases of quality champagnes feature in display cases by the lift on each floor. Facilities include a mini gym. My bedroom was a modest-sized, lozenge-shaped sanctuary with huge circular windows, top branded soaps and plenty of treats and distractions. Welcome nibbles included mini Mars, Snickers and Bounty bars, a plate of pastel-shaded macaroons and a little tub of Haribo sweets to cover all comfort food cravings and inspire sugar rushes. There is a smart Nespresso machine in the room with a selection of premium coffee blends. The Wi-Fi allows for four devices per room. The bathroom features a wooden sink (triumph of design over function) and a peek-a-boo shower with full voyeur potential, thanks to one wall being a full length window in prime line of site from the pillows on the bed – although there are venetian blinds to tease or temper exhibitionism with modesty. The firm, high-level bed itself was the most comfortable I have enjoyed in Lille. The ground floor Why Dinette restaurant spills into a glazed terrace, popular with local office workers (page 56). A professional team glides between the front-of-house zones, lounge and reception with the neo-kitsch self-awareness of the décor, reminding visitors that, despite the veneer of informality, this is still a quality deal. Breakfast at €14 in the restaurant is imaginative yet familiar. Delicious *pain au chocolat* and excellent country-grain breads are on offer from the superb modern bakery Silence Ça Cuit (page 154). Hot food on my visit included creamy mushrooms, which were simply scrumptious, with smoked salmon atop toasted brioche. The ubiquitous Nespresso machine also makes an appearance at the buffet. Great range of imaginative fruit juices. Fine jams and honeys, and a choice of quality butters. Rooms €129–390. €€€

CARLTON ⓖ 3 rue de Paris Ⓠ 237 J5 ☎ 03 20 13 33 13 or toll free 0800 181591 (UK), 800 888 4747 (USA & Canada) 🛏 www.carltonlille.com 🚇 Gare Lille Flandres ⓔ Bus 12 from Gare Lille Flandres to pl du Théâtre, or walk along av le Corbusier & right on to rue Faidherbe

As with Cliveden in the UK, no account of this hotel is complete without a breath of scandal. Until a few years ago, this was best known as a provincial grand hotel of the old school, with the usual 4-star comforts liberally dispensed. Though the Alliance (pages 54–5) has the higher profile in the package-tour brochures, the Carlton has always enjoyed an enviable location, one of the key corner sites in the very centre of town, a chime away from the belfry of the Chambre de Commerce. However, in the wake of the notorious Dominique Strauss-Kahn affair which dramatically cut through the presidential ambitions of the former head of the IMF, the next high-profile political sex scandal was set at Lille's Hotel Carlton, with tales of call girls and VIPs from top cops to politicians, and DSK himself was called in for interview among the red-faced A-listers. With Louis XV-influenced rooms from €150 and suites soaring skyward price-wise, before booking it is always worth asking for any weekend promotions (all above board, I hasten to add)

DOMAINE MANDARINE NAPOLEON 204 rue de Burgault, 59113 Seclin ☏ 03 20 32 54 93 📧 www.domainenapoleon.com 🚇 Métro 2 to Lille Porte des Postes, then bus 55 to Burgault

Want something different for the weekend? Try this *chambre d'hôte* with an emperor, spending the night in a distillery and museum. No longer available for casual visitors alas, but if you are planning a family party, wedding or other such bacchanalia in the Domaine's function rooms, here's an imperial treat to consider. Ten minutes outside town at exit 19 of the A1 is the new home of the Mandarine Napoléon distillery, with its splendid grounds and private museum dedicated to Napoleon himself (page 202). Not everyone gets to visit the old manor house at the centre of the farm. Exquisitely decorated and furnished, from the *trompe l'œil* tent of the entrance hall to the elegant dining room, there are beautifully and individually styled bedrooms and an honesty bar, where guests are trusted to pour their own drinks and settle their bills. Not a hotel as such, more a hugely upmarket *gîte* or *chambre d'hôte*. Breakfast is laid out in the kitchen each morning. The room rate is around €200, breakfast €10, with payment for any other food and drink settled privately on departure. Advance reservation is imperative. €€€€

that may easily halve the bill. An experience at any price is a stay in the panoramic rooftop cupola duplex suite, actually inside a turret dome, with arguably the best view of any building in town, overlooking the squares, the Vieille Bourse, the opera house and the first cobbled alleys of Vieux Lille. Wide picture windows on one level, quaint round windows on the other, and plasma TV should you ever tire of looking out on the city. A spa bath en suite adds to the feeling of luxury and romance – no need to mix with the lower castes in the hotel's main sauna. Mind you, we are talking around €1,000 per night here. The public areas may seem slightly stuffy, but this is what the French consider British Club and therefore the height of sophistication. If buffet breakfast at €19 is not included in the deal, then the home-baked delights *chez* Paul (page 122) are just yards away. Private parking available. Wi-Fi. €€€€

CHAGNOT 24 pl de la Gare 📍 237 K6 ☏ 03 20 74 11 87 📧 www.chagnot.com 🚉 Gare Lille Flandres 🚇 Walk along av le Corbusier (or take métro 2) to Gare Lille Flandres & pl de la Gare

Helpful service and surprisingly comfortable and quiet (if bland and compact) rooms at the side of the Gare Flandres and above the fabulous Trois Brasseurs. The slowest lift in Christendom serves an astonishing 75 bedrooms, but be warned, as with so many of the hotels around the stations, the elevator does not go all the way down to the ground floor, so there's still one flight of stairs to negotiate. Reception and rooms are stocked with local entertainment guides for visitors and the location provides for a quick getaway if you have an early train in the morning. Unexpectedly, for

Accommodation HOTELS

6

the price, the hotel can offer Ethernet cables for the laptop. Rates from around €60, not including the uninspiring breakfast. I prefer to have a quick coffee at the bar next door then amble into town for hot chocolate and fresh bread by the Grand' Place. €

CROWNE PLAZA 335 bd de Leeds ♀ 235 J3 ✆ 03 20 42 46 46 🖥 www.crowneplaza.com 🚊 Gare Lille Europe 🚇 Upstairs through station exit & cross the road

Yes, it is one of those conference-type hotels, but it is the best of the breed, stands slap on top of the Eurostar station and has superbly patient, efficient and helpful staff; and if you are in town for business and can't run to the absolute luxury of the 4-star alternatives and prefer a room more practical than quaint, you can be in the shower within 3 minutes of the train pulling into the Gare Europe. Impressive views over the city from the top floors and the multilingual front desk can even answer your queries in Serbo-Croat. Valet parking available too. A very good buffet breakfast is actually worth the extra charge (though some online discounters include breakfast in the deal). A conference-hotel-dining standard restaurant means that if train times and business commitments stop you taking the ten-minute trip to the city centre, you need never starve. Be warned, the Wi-Fi options here are tiered, with best-quality connections charged at a higher rate. If you want to do more than check a very occasional email, you may find yourself having to pay for your Wi-Fi if the very basic free version is not up to scratch. An annoying extra charge these days, when decent broadband should be considered as standard as hot water and bedlinen at any hotel – paying extra for working internet just feels wrong. Rooms are €195, suites €480, with breakfast adding an extra €16 to the bill. €€€€

GRAND 51 rue Faidherbe ♀ 237 K5 ✆ 03 20 06 31 57 🖥 www.legrandhotel.com 🚊 Gare Lille Flandres 🚇 Walk along av le Corbusier (or take métro 2) to Gare Lille Flandres, & turn right on to rue Faidherbe

Clean, modestly priced hotel on the recently restyled main thoroughfare from the stations to the squares. Each storey is decorated in a slightly different utilitarian style and rooms are bright if a teensy bit tight on space, which is fine if you intend to spend most of your time out exploring the town and saving the extra money for a special meal. Satellite TV, free Wi-Fi and soundproofed windows come as standard. Pay a little extra for the *chambre grand confort* with more room to manoeuvre and a nice big bathtub. Cheery and welcoming reception staff. Rooms €55–150. €

GRAND HOTEL BELLEVUE 🅖🅟 5 rue Jean Roisin ♀ 237 H5 ✆ 03 20 57 45 64 🖥 www.grandhotelbellevue.com 🚊 Rihour 🚇 Métro 2 to Gare Lille Flandres then line 1 to Rihour

Never mind the postal address, this hotel has double-glazed rooms on the Grand' Place itself, giving a thrilling goodnight view of a city at play. No mere onlooker, however, the hotel has long played an active role in Lille's musical heritage and not simply because the brass plaque by the entrance announcing the address as the Brazilian Consulate might inspire dreams of Latin nights and carnival costumes. Ever since the evening that the young Mozart played in one of the building's original salons (the nine-year-old prodigy stayed here for four weeks with his father Leopold when he was taken ill *en route* from England to the Netherlands), the building has enjoyed much dabbling in the arts. A function room occasionally doubles as a theatre and breakfast is served in the Vivaldi room, whatever the season. The reception area adds a hint of a flourish to the décor, and the Windsor piano bar is the place for weekend cocktails. The marbled en-suite facilities add a certain indulgence to prices that are comfortably lower 3-star (€100–200). A complimentary daily newspaper and Wi-Fi are available. €€€

L'HERMITAGE GANTOIS 224 rue de Paris ♀ 238 H2 ☏ 03 20 85 30 30
🖰 www.hotelhermitagegantois.com 🚉 Mairie de Lille 🚇 Métro 2 to Mairie de Lille, then walk westward along av du Président Kennedy & turn left on to rue de Paris

Lille's only 4-star *luxe* hotel is more than just a place to rest your weary head, it is a veritable spa for the soul. One of the best-kept secrets in the city, it's an unmissable site in its own right and architecturally a consummation devoutly to be wished. Before the turn of the 21st century, most visitors saw 224 rue de Paris as little but an imposing 15th-century gable on the walk from central Lille to the Porte de Paris remnant of the original city walls (page 182). To locals, it always had a special place in their hearts as the Hospice Gantois, a hospital and old people's home, its courtyard a peaceful haven and escape from the bustle of everyday life. The institution was founded in 1462 as the St John the Baptist Hospice by wealthy merchant Jean de la Cambe, better known as Jean Gantois. His other main claim to philanthropic fame was in establishing a rest home for retired prostitutes, but his legacy of health care for the poor (irrespective of their lifestyles) continued until 1995 when the hospice, a listed building since 1923, finally closed its doors. This cluster of religious and secular buildings has been united by architect Hubert Maes into an exciting celebration of one of the few survivors of the long-demolished St-Sauveur

"*Flop in a comfy sofa and gaze heavenward at architectural harmonies.*"

quarter. The imaginative revival of the street façades gives not a clue to the thrilling marriage within: contemporary design ties the knot with a respect for history, with beamed ceilings, panelled walls and smart tiled floors. The former dormitories and wards make way for 67 bedrooms and suites, clustered around four courtyards. Rooms are nicely equipped and bathrooms well proportioned. Even if you can't afford to stay the night or go for the full €21 breakfast, remember that the central atrium bar is open to everyone. Flop in a comfy sofa and gaze heavenward through glass at the architectural harmonies or relax in the sauna. Among the eclectic treasures housed within the hotel are sundry vintage medical instruments (including a 1926 X-ray machine) and the body of the hospice's founder, buried in the chapel. Tuesday mornings see tours of the building (a bonus since the listed building used to open to the public only two days a year), but you may sneak peeks at the courtyards, chapel and other gems of the ground floor when you take the coffee and croissant bar breakfast or afternoon tea. A lively New World wine list at around €5 a glass is the perfect way to toast the original general manager Danielle Gey, whose wit and perception in hand-picking an excellent staff showed that this lady from Biarritz was blessed with the typically Lillois wisdom to unite old walls with young minds. Raise a second glass to her successor André Grosperrin, who is overseeing the extension of the hotel with a new annex next door without losing the charm of the original buildings. One trick of discreet revisionism makes me chuckle: the principal ballroom has been renamed the Salle des Hospices, the original title being considered unsuitable for the hospitality industry. Since Jean Gantois's day it has been better known locally as the Salle des Malades! Wi-Fi. Rooms €165–545. €€€€

HOTEL BARRIERE 777 Pont de Flandres ♀ 235 J5 ✎ 03 28 14 45 00 ⚇ www.
lucienbarriere.com 🚆 Gare Lille Europe ⊕ Lift or escalator to bd Turin, then walk along the
boulevard to Pont de Flandres
One thing to say about a hotel almost completely made of glass: not much risk of a gloomy room.
So, at Lille's resort-style casino, designer Pierre-Yves Rochon makes the most of architect Jean-Paul
Viguier's glazed walls for this luxury hotel with muted colours and soft furnishings and drapes
to project the natural light. It has 125 bedrooms (four adapted for disabled guests) and several
suites, with free internet in all rooms, but top-price executive rooms see the minibar filled with
complimentary soft drinks. You will find exactly what you'd expect if you've ever stayed at one of
the chain's casino hotels at resorts anywhere else in France. A health spa, gym and sauna feature
among hotel facilities as well as the casino, its two restaurants and four bars, games tables and
show room/theatre. Rooms around €130–200, suites much pricier. €€€

HOTEL BRUEGHEL 3–5 parvis Saint-Maurice ♀ 237 J6 ✎ 03 20 06 06 69 ⚇ www.hotel-
brueghel.com 🚆 Gare Lille Flandres ⊕ Métro 2 to Gare Lille Flandres, left into rue de Priez
& walk round the church
The least-known and most charming of the central hotels, this little gem is very much a word-of-
mouth favourite. Tucked away in a quiet pedestrianised street between the old Gare Flandres and
the shops of the rue de Paris, the hotel faces the recently scrubbed and shining church of St Maurice,
which hosts some excellent classical concerts and organ recitals every summer Sunday afternoon.
Overflowing window boxes announce the hospitality guaranteed within. Inside the cosy reception
area, an authentic 1920s cage lift takes guests Noah-fashion, two-by-two, to the bedrooms. Each
year another floor is carefully restored. With impeccable taste, the rooms have been styled to
combine minimalism with elegance and comfort. Natural coir carpets and laminate floors, wrought-
iron mirrors, picture frames from salvaged wood, classic bathrooms – all proof that a modestly
priced hotel need not lack artistic inspiration. If you are planning to spend any considerable time in
your room, do pack some slippers, since coir is lovely on the eye but less so on the soles of the feet
(you can usually pick up a pair of slippers for under €4 at Tati around the corner, see pages 146–7).
Only the very smallest rooms miss the sophisticated touch but, with rates at €65–180, comfort and
a warm welcome will not break any bank and it is genuine value for money. You may want to forego
the lift just once to look at the excellent collection of paintings, prints and posters on each landing.
Pick up a leaflet advertising the hotel's luxurious sister establishment, Le Château de Mazan in
Provence, the former home of the Marquis de Sade (just imagine the room service). €€

HOTEL DE LA PAIX ⊕ 46 rue de Paris ♀ 237 J6 ✎ 03 20 54 63 93 ⚇ www.hotel-la-paix.
com 🚆 Gare Lille Flandres ⊕ Métro 2 to Gare Lille Flandres then cross to rue Faidherbe,
then left on rue des Ponts de Comines to rue de Paris
Another family-run gem, this time just around the corner from the Grand' Place. Rooms here are
devoted to great artists, and rather than merely boasting a few cheap prints in the bedrooms and
lobbies, the walls are covered with neatly framed posters from great exhibitions around the world. You
may share your room with Van Gogh, Lautrec or Magritte, or perhaps you might spend time getting to
know a less-vaunted talent. Of course, the hotel provides great inspiration to visit the many museums
and galleries in and around town. Larger rooms, at €130, have a lounge area with soft furnishings for

flopping after shopping, and each floor of the hotel boasts a residents' lounge by the lift, where one may admire the in-house exhibitions. Extremely helpful staff on duty day and night, and a room rate around the €90 mark, make this a firm favourite. To be honest the only possible reason for the hotel remaining in the 2-star category is the modest size of the bathrooms, with surely the teeniest tubs in town. Since this is one of the closest hotels to Paul's bakery, the establishment has upped its game when it comes to breakfast, with an à la carte option as well as the croissant, bread and jam standard deal. Wi-Fi. Regular rooms from around €75 at weekends, a tad higher midweek. **€€**

HOTEL DE LA TREILLE 7–9 pl Louise de Bettignies 237 J3 03 20 55 45 46 www.hoteldelatreille.com Bus 50 to Lion d'Or

What a difference a decade makes. When we first stayed here it was an anachronism, a standard, internationally smart, clean and bland hotel in the most charming historic quarter of town. Revisiting in 2014 I was seduced and won over by a delightful make-over that has turned this city-break brochure-favourite into a hideaway at last worthy of its picturesque setting. Previously, you only chose this hotel for its location in the very heart of the old-town bustle. The famous cathedral Notre Dame de la Treille is just behind the hotel, and across the way, through a doorway by a craft shop, is the unexpected treasure of the Hospice Comtesse. Now, visit for the hotel itself. The entrance and light, bright reception area are welcoming, and bedrooms, renovated in smart beiges and greys, have contemporary baroque-inspired curves and decorative swirls, neatly straddling the period setting and current lifestyle tastes. Some rooms are quite compact, but no less comfortable, others (pricier) have space for couples. Smaller single rooms are ideal for those who just use the hotel for sleeping and spend their weekend enjoying all the city has to offer. A new adapted room for disabled guests was also part of the 2014 refit programme. The architecture- and horticulture-inspired framed prints on the bedroom walls may also be seen in the breakfast room and the stylish reception lounge – a great place for welcoming friends over coffee before slipping out to hit the shops and attractions of the district. Otherwise, just looking out from a bedroom window towards the rue de Gand and down to the place du Lion d'Or provides the perfect appetiser to an evening on the town. Private parking option at €14 a day available on request. €80–200 rooms and breakfast from around €14. **€€**

HOTEL FLANDRE ANGLETERRE 15 pl de la Gare 237 K6 03 20 06 04 12 www.hotel-flandreangleterre-lille.com Gare Lille Flandres Walk along av le Corbusier (or take métro 2) to Gare Lille Flandres

OK, so the hotel is hidden behind an infinite number of gaudy restaurant signs promising *frites* with everything! But this is an unpretentious, old-fashioned railway station hotel. The current owners offer a family-style welcome to the simple yet spotlessly clean rooms. The rooms are soundproofed against late-night revellers catching the last train to Brussels and all place names Flemish. Rooms €68–100. Breakfast is reasonable at €8.50, but there are loads of coffee shops and cafés just outside the door. You may even book parking in advance at €13 when available. **€**

HOTEL LILLE EUROPE Av le Corbusier 235 H4 03 28 36 76 76 www.hotel-lille-europe.com Gare Lille Flandres Leaving Gare Lille Europe, either walk along av le Corbusier at street level or take the escalator or lift down from the station & cross the piazza to Euralille

A suitably anonymous modern hotel in a suitably anonymous modern building, the *hôtel de la gare de nos jours* has friendly, helpful staff, lots of identikit rooms and an excellent value buffet breakfast served in a fully glazed first-floor salon. The hotel is part of the Euralille tower-block shopping and business complex. The plus point for overnighters and seasoned travellers with heavy luggage or plans to strip bare the shelves of the en-suite shopping mall is its location, close to the TGV Eurostar station. But let's face it, with the Grand' Place and old town just 5 minutes away, this is unlikely to be a first choice for visitors seeking the charm of old Flanders. After a period experimenting with pay-as-you-go internet options, the hotel now offers cabled internet in the bedrooms and Wi-Fi broadband to all guests at the first-floor business centre, with views over the bustling city. Rooms €75–100. €€

HOTEL UP 17 pl des Reignaux ♀ 237 K5 ☎ 03 20 06 06 93 🖥 www.hotelup.fr 🚆 Gare Lille Flandres ⓐ Métro 2 (or walk down av le Corbusier) to Gare Lille Flandres then rue des Buisses & left towards pl des Reignaux

In the shower of 4-star and fashionable hotels that have landed in Lille since the last edition of this guide, this sprouted in the most unlikely (and convenient) of locations. The streets just behind the little row of brasseries in front of the Gare Flandres are best known for narrow and uneven pavements, sex shops, massage parlours and kebaberies. Yet, some 2- and 3-star chains have chosen the location, so it's no real surprise that the next grade up should find its way there. The Hotel UP (yet another member of the Best Western clan) is now established under the tag of a 'design' hotel. The phrase generally means canny use of space and bold use of shiny wallpapers with contemporary accessories, such as lights you'll only ever see in lifestyle shops and the inevitable branded Nespresso machine instead of an electric filter jug or kettle complete with capsuled coffees in the bedroom. Beds in standard rooms are usually queen sized, and there are king-sized mattresses in the superior rooms (which also boast a standard double sofa bed, so can cope with four guests). All the bathrooms are stocked with L'Occitane designer toiletries. Wi-Fi – of course, a good breakfast option and a bar open until midnight. Useful tip: surf the web and the discount travel sites for the best rates, then call the hotel. The establishment has a price-match guarantee, and ultra-confident guests have been known to negotiate further – since there is always the agency commission to shave as well! Rates from just under €160 to over €200. €€€

KANAÏ ⓖ 10 rue de Béthune ♀ 237 H6 ☎ 03 20 57 14 78 🖥 www.hotelkanai.com 🚆 Rihour ⓐ Métro 1 to Rihour, then walk along rue Vieille Comédie to the corner of rue de Béthune

Well known to night owls, this centrally located 2-star hotel in a noisy district has clean, modest-sized rooms smartly tinged with mauves and fresh, sharply designed shower rooms. Above the shops in the lively pedestrianised zone and with no lifts to take you up two or three flights of stairs to bed, the place is nonetheless popular with a younger crowd and presided over by very welcoming and efficient reception staff. L'Occitane freebies and the introduction of the *de rigueur* Nespresso machine give a pretty good indication that the management are aware of what is being offered by pricier and starrier establishments elsewhere. Most rooms are around €75 at weekends, up to €100 weekdays and higher during festivals and major events. The very smallest rooms are under €70 at weekends. If Wi-Fi in the reception area and broadband and flat-screen TV in the rooms are not your thing, you can always borrow a book from the shelves in the lobby. Owned by the team that runs so many of the brasseries around the place Rihour, the hotel offers guests 10% off lunch or dinner at its six popular restaurants. €€

MERCURE LILLE CENTRE   2 bd Carnot ♀ 237 J4 ✆ 03 20 14 71 47 🖥 www.accorhotels. com 🚃 Gare Lille Flandres 🚇 Métro 2 to Gare Lille Flandres then bus 86 to Lycée Pasteur

This dear old diva loitering behind the stage door of the opera house has finally dropped her maiden name and fallen in corporate line announcing herself as the Mercure. Previously known and loved as Le Royal, now she works under the colours of the Mercure brand. She had a first serious face-lift just as the Opéra itself was rejuvenated for 2004, and this, until recently, somewhat faded, slightly worn chain hotel, with its friendly provincial welcome, has been spruced up anew for the renaissance of this long-ignored corner of the city beside the place du Théâtre. With good-sized bedrooms and spacious en-suite bathrooms, this acquisition of the Accor group with its smart new look is no longer the forgotten hotel of Lille. Perfectly poised at the junction of the old and new towns, a short walk from the station and handy for the fun of a night on the town and a day at the heart of the city. Bright, AC rooms with smoke alarms, huge windows, Wi-Fi and cable TV. Rooms €103–185. €€€

NOVOTEL LILLE CENTRE GARES   🛈 49 rue de Tournai ♀ 235 H5 ✆ 03 28 38 67 00 🖥 www.novotel.com 🚃 Gare Lille Flandres 🚇 Leave station on rue de Tournai & walk along the road to the end of the platforms

There is another Novotel in the heart of Lille; however, this branch of the Accor chain is well placed between Lille proper and the conference/business district. You can walk to the exhibition centre during the day and the city at night. Just a couple of minutes further along the rue de Tournai at the other side of the Gare Flandres than you would normally want to go, the hotel is tucked at the far end of the platforms by the car-hire offices and parks, so a good choice if picking up a car for exploring further. The standard rooms and services you'd expect from one of the country's best-known business-class hotel chains, but a few surprising extras, notably the fact that it caters for children, with an electronic game zone in reception and a library of children's books to keep the kids occupied if you've bought them with you on a business trip! Room rates from €130–200 but discounts often available. €€€

SELF-CATERING

Aparthotels are a great way to enjoy the basic services of a hotel, with the freedom of your being in your own home – so you do not need to pay for each breakfast, lunch and dinner of your stay in Lille. Budget-conscious travellers can cook for themselves, saving the restaurant experience for the occasional evening, and true foodies can try to recreate a great restaurant dish for themselves with fresh produce from the local markets.

As well as the establishments listed below, and other apartment chains with branches a little farther out from the centre, you may find city-centre self-catering options in private homes from around €300 per week. See box, pages 68–9.

ADAGIO ACCESS LILLE VAUBAN 17 rue Colson ♀ 236 B5 ☎03 20 15 43 00 🖥 www.adagio-city.com 🚌 Bus Citadine to Sacré Cœur, then walk along rue Nationale & it's the first right into rue Colson

I needed a little persuasion to return to this address a few years back. When, many moons ago, the place was simply student digs, I had spent the longest of long weekends here, first abandoning the bed for the floor and finally rushing out to Tati (pages 146–7) to buy my own fresh bedlinen. Nowadays my demons are laid to rest, and I've been back several times. The place is once more under new management where decency prevails, and this is an excellent value, clean and welcoming self-catering option. Recently rebranded by latest corporate owners Accor from its interim identity as a Citéa establishment, it now serves holidaymakers and business guests as efficiently as it continues to host a cheerful student population in the heart of the halls of residence district. Behind what looks like a basic apartment block in this side street beyond the Solférino and linking the rue Nationale and the bd Vauban, is a warren of pathways linking a chain of buildings, all home to studios and one-bed apartments with decent internet access. Some accommodation is still reserved for the university, other flats designed for visitors. Good-sized rooms, kitchenettes with microwave, hob, coffee-filter machine and fridge, with sliding doors to the bedroom in larger units. The ground-floor bar serves optional breakfasts and here the student residents mingle with visitors. Very friendly and helpful reception staff, an underground car park (pay extra) and internet in the apartments. Ideally situated for night owls as the place is around a 15-min walk home from the restaurants of the old town and less than ten minutes from the bars of the Solfé. Get to know the bus network, as walking to the nearest métro is not easy. However, several bus routes from the stops on both main roads will take you to and from the République– Beaux Arts métro in five minutes or so. The distance from Lille Europe (around 15 minutes on the Citadine bus) keeps the rates surprisingly low. Rooms from around €50 per night. €

CALM APPART'HOTEL 2 rue des Buisses ♀ 237 K5 ☎03 20 15 84 15 🖥 www.appart-hotel-lille.com 🚉 Gare Lille Flandres 🚌 Walk down av le Corbusier (or take métro 2) to Gare Flandres then rue des Buisses behind the Napoleon bar

The latest of the new wave of *aparthotels* is located just yards from the Gare Flandres, behind the more traditional station hotels. A young, fun vibe with smart full-length black-and-white photos in the lobby and walls covered with those random English phrases that you might find on a French teenager's T-shirt or a souvenir mug. Reception is at street level, and each member of the team I met during my few days here was as helpful and charming as the last. A mechanical pneumatic folding platform at the side of the few steps up to the hotel lift is groaned and creaked into service for disabled guests, and a conventional elevator takes you to the bedrooms, each equipped with the standard mini kitchenette. As a more budget version of some of its trendier neighbours, here the *de rigueur* Nespresso machine is a communal affair, kept in the hallway seating areas by the lift rather than in guest rooms (and you must pay for each capsule). Since there is no coffee machine in the room/apartment itself (an oversight, since even budget hotels with horrible instant coffee sachets offer hot drink facilities by the bed) you'll need to fork out a euro each time you want to get dressed and pad along the corridor to the capsule device. Breakfast here is not served in the bedrooms, but instead delivered as a take-away in a brown bag (coffee capsules included), but this is pricey at €12. On my first morning, I walked down the road to the string of coffee shops outside the station. Dithering between American-style *grandes* with muffins and the local option, I spent a couple of euros on a take-away *café crème* and croissant from Paul's nearest sandwich stall counter. By day two, I had visited the Carrefour hypermarket around the corner and had bought a pack of ground coffee and a carton of milk for the room fridge and some brioche for the larder, as well as a plastic filter cone and a huge pint-sized coffee mug. Interestingly (perhaps this is a sign

"Interestingly, despite no official in-room coffee option, an aerosol of balsamic vinegar was provided."

of just how cutting-edge fashionable is the clientele here), despite no official in-room coffee option, an aerosol of balsamic vinegar was provided. Comfy bed, decent internet connection and pleasant grey and white décor. The most basic are a good size (better than at many posher hotels), with excellent bathrooms, and there are larger (and even larger still) bedrooms to opt for, the top being a massive 40m^2 (bigger than a flat in Paris) with both bathtub and shower. Rooms from around €100–140. €€€

CITADINES CITY CENTRE LILLE   83 av Willy Brandt ♀ 235 H4 ☎ 03 28 36 75 00
⌨ www.citadines.com 🚆 Gare Lille Flandres 🚌 Walk along av le Corbusier to Euralille, then left on to av Willy Brandt

In the Euralille building, this central self-catering option offers extremely competitively priced modern studios and larger apartments with well-equipped kitchenettes and extra facilities, from buffet breakfasts (€9.50) to an in-house launderette – wash, dry, and detergent for €10. Studios from around €95–145 per night, reductions for weekly bookings. A slightly higher rate is charged for those requiring the full hotel package, with daily maid service. Otherwise, pay the basic price and use the dishwasher, vacuum cleaner and ironing board provided. Security is pretty good, with the front doors locked and guests given private entry codes whenever the main desk is unmanned. Very helpful staff at reception, and basement parking among the bonuses. Internet connection in rooms, Wi-Fi in reception area. €€€

COSY'S LILLE VAUBAN RESIDENCE   69–71 bd Vauban ♀ 236 B5 ☎ 03 28 82 24 24
⌨ www.cosys-residences.com/fr/lille 🚌 Citadine bus from Lille Europe to Solférino, then walk along bd Vauban to number 69

Close to the parks and the Citadelle in the *Catho* student quarter, yet still an easy walk down the Solfé to nightlife. Flats sleep one to five people and are efficiently equipped. Standard two-hob and microwave kitchenette combo with separate workstation and basic cable TV channels. Brown wood veneer dominates the colour scheme with rich reds and greys. The optional breakfast is OK, but if you are staying more than one night, prepare your own in the room. A filter-coffee machine is provided. There's pretty good pizza place next door if you don't want to cook in the evening. The lower prices reflect the location away from the métro network, but the Citadine bus stops outside the reception linking the apartments to the stations and République districts. Summer studio rates often start at under €60, but regular prices from just over €90–180. €€

SEJOURS ET AFFAIRES   271 av Willy Brandt ♀ 235 H5 ☎ 03 20 04 75 51
⌨ www.sejours-affaires.fr 🚆 Gare Lille Flandres 🚌 Walk along av le Corbusier to Euralille, then left on to av Willy Brandt

6

Don't be seduced by the Franglais implication of the name; this is not a love nest, as much as a collection of self-contained studio and one-bed flats, aimed at the budget end of the business travel market, with a fair smattering of student digs as well. Less of a hotel-style complex than the neighbouring Citadines, this slightly pared-down version has its key collection during working hours from a busy office rather than a traditional reception desk. Small but well-equipped apartments in the Euralille Towers. There is a breakfast option in the mezzanine bar – but with coffee machine, crockery and fridge in the room, why bother? Situated right next door to the Carrefour entrance to the shopping mall (by the green pharmacy sign), it is very convenient for bringing in your own food and drink. Internet connection available. Sometimes appears on bargain listings as Les Estudines. Budget €60–110 per night. €

SUITE NOVOTEL LILLE EUROPE Bd de Turin 235 J4 03 20 74 70 70 www.suitenovotel.com Gare Lille Europe Cross bd de Turin from the station
A brilliant concept by the Accor chain, this *aparthotel* opposite the Credit Lyonnais tower on the edge of town is a reinvention of the concept of hotel rooms. An L-shaped space, with bedroom and bathroom at 90 degrees to the living space, the room may be divided by sliding screens. An extra divan by the table/workstation allows a friend to crash for the night. Wi-Fi and Ethernet connection are part of the multimedia kit which includes TV with movies and music on demand, free domestic phone calls within France and a computer keyboard for harvesting emails from the telly. Fridge, microwave and kettle in each room, and chill cabinets in the reception area stock salads, soups, desserts and ready meals. You may also dial out to order dinner from a score of restaurants Lille-wide, ranging from oriental and Italian take-away to gastronomic addresses such as Clément Marot (page 96). The extras are what make this place special. Free massage on Thursday evenings, nutritionally balanced breakfasts and the option of borrowing a bike, a Smart car or a digital camera from reception. Closest address to the Eurostar station – simply take the lift to street level and cross the road! Budget €120–150 per night. €€€

HOSTELS

Hostels are excellent value for travellers on a budget, with bunk beds available in shared rooms sleeping four, six or more. As well the traditional Youth Hostel close to the Hôtel de Ville (you'll need to be a member of the Youth Hostels Association or SN International Affiliate), Lille has other private hostels which cater for a wider clientele, from the backpackers willing to share dormitory accommodation to those looking for a private room. Unlike many hotels, these have washing machines available to guests and the bars often prove lively hangouts for the locals as well as guests.

AUBERGE DE JEUNESSE 12 rue Malpart 238 H2 03 20 57 08 94 www.fuaj.org
07.00–11.00 & 15.00–01.00, closed mid-Dec–Jan Mairie de Lille Métro 2 to Mairie de Lille, walk west along av Kennedy, turn left on to rue de Paris & right into rue Malpart
The best-value accommodation in Lille, if you don't mind sharing a room and have a membership card from a recognised national Youth Hostel Association. Rooms sleep two to seven people and pay €20pp per night. €

CIRQUE HOSTEL Ⓜ 139 rue des Postes ♀ 238 B5 ☎ 03 62 10 76 86 🛏 http://
lecirquehostel.fr 🚇 Wazemmes 🚌 Métro 2 to Gare Lille Flandres then line 1 to Wazemmes,
then walk east along rue d'Iéna to rue des Postes

Hooray! The 1960s lives on in this privately run independent youth hostel. Despite the sturdy brick
houses in the street, this is essentially a 15-bed wooden cabin in the Wazemmes district. €20/night
for a bed and clean sheets in the dormitory, two showers available. Breakfast starts at under €5 and
includes homemade jams; a bigger, pricier option is also available. All served in the organic/fair-trade
café-restaurant, where during the day you can get a bowl of soup for under a fiver or a decent bite
for around a tenner (page 124). You can use the kitchenette to heat up your own food, there is an arts
and crafts room for 'self-expression' and you may use the washing machines too. €

GASTAMA 109 rue Saint-André ♀ 237 G1 ☎ 03 20 06 06 80 🛏 www.gastama.com
🚌 Bus 10 from Gare Flandres to rue de Magasin, or take the Navette Vieux Lille
from pl Rihour

In most hostels, you may learn to speak French with a Scandinavian or Australian accent. After all,
these places are where we meet up with fellow backpackers from around the world. However, this
address in Vieux Lille is a bit different: you are just as likely to strike up a conversation with someone
who lives around the corner as your Norwegian or Tasmanian gap-year student halfway between
Paris and London. Think of this almost as a nightspot with beds, since the street-level bar is a seriously
popular hangout in the old town. A range of beers, from the Baltic to the Med, outnumber the *bières
de Flandres*, and some weekend nights it's the mojitos and tequila slammers that set the tone for the
evening. Accommodation-wise you have the standard dormitories with gunmetal-framed bunk beds
lined up against the red-brick walls, but this hostel also boasts a range of private and family rooms
– with en-suite facilities – to rival some local hotels. There is disabled access and you'll find laundry
facilities too. Dormitory rooms from €21–30; private rooms from around €40–100. Weekend rates are
usually one or two euros higher than midweek. The €5 breakfast is a euro less if you book it on arrival. €

BED AND BREAKFAST

Local tourist offices (page 35) have updated lists of B&B establishments.

CHEZ B&B Ⓜ 78 rue Caumartin ♀ 238 D4 ☎ 03 61 50 16 42 e chezBandB@wanadoo.fr
🚇 République–Beaux Arts 🚌 Métro 2 to Gare Lille Flandres & line 1 to République, then take
rue Nicolas Leblanc, cross pl Philippe Lebon to rue de Fleurus & turn left on to rue Caumartin

Long ago, I kicked myself for including this special address in my original guide to the Eurostar
cities, since it had previously been a secret shared only with family and friends. We have enjoyed the
hospitality of B&B, Bernard and Béatrice Quillerou, since the days that they lived in a quiet street
outside the city walls with (then) young children who contributed to the same polite and charming
welcome. After moving to their current home, more than a decade since, a five-minute walk or ten-
minute stroll from the Palais des Beaux-Arts, they continue to offer bed and breakfast *en famille*. The
welcome is heartfelt, and Béatrice speaks flawless English. The guest accommodation is tastefully
furnished and homely, and whenever I speak to Béatrice I hear of the latest *coup de décor*. Breakfast
with the family might include homemade brioches and breads. On the top floor is a single and double

Accommodation   BED AND BREAKFAST

6

room with Mansard windows, each en suite with a mini kitchenette, two-ring cooker, microwave, fridge and coffee machine. On the second floor, the large double room has a family-sized bathroom (tub and shower). Stay a minimum of two nights and explore the many restaurants nearby. A great location for pottering around away from the shopping crowds; tranquil, yet still within easy reach of lively bars and restaurants. Rooms cost around €41–50/night. €

LA MAISON DU JARDIN VAUBAN 6 rue Desmazières ♀ 236 B4 ✆ 03 20 54 74 05
🖱 http://lamaisondujardinvauban.fr 🚌 Citadine bus to Solférino, then walk north & 1st right on to rue Desmazières

Ever eclectic and confidently stylish, where you might find life-sized carved horses looming behind traditional leather armchairs in the salon, in its newest incarnation this *maison bourgeoise* by the eponymous park is a B&B with a definite style. Fairground memorabilia, stuffed birds, urban and Art Deco artworks nestle among more conventional furnishings in the living rooms. The three bedrooms offer their own brand of fantasy: from the king-sized double bed and exaggerated cream-and-gold draperies in the Chambre d'Or, to the expensively graffitied and double-height Chambre Urbane, with its '80s street art, to the exotic traveller's retreat Chambre Voyage, kitted out with African masks, exotic furnishings and the occasional Buddha. The tree-filled city garden has a teak deck for breakfasts looking out over the lawn, but this boutique B&B also offers a full

GÎTES

Self-catering *gîtes* are a great way to get to know a region, and the Département du Nord (🖱 *www.tourisme-nord.fr*) has a huge range of privately owned holiday homes in the surrounding countryside that are within easy reach of the city. It is best to drive to the car parks at the end of the métro lines and travel by public transport into the centre, or take a deep breath and drive to the city for a day or two and then explore the wider region.

You will also find self-catering apartments in the heart of the city itself, and from €400–600 per week for four people, or €300–400 for a couple, it is almost unbeatable value.

Outside the city, in villages within the greater *métropolitan* area, you may find *gîtes* in farm buildings from as little as €200 per week, with the average around €350. Consider basing yourself even further afield, at an hour or so from the city, perhaps along the Côte d'Opale, or inland around the Monts de Flandres, along the battlefield remembrance circuit or the protected natural woods and parkland of Hainaut and the Avesnois.

To be at one with the environment check out the **Gîtes Panda** brand in the protected countryside of the Avesnois or Scarpe-Escaut Natural Regional Park. Far from the city, this eco-friendly accommodation is approved by the World Wide Fund for Nature. These options include little extras to help understand the natural setting, from binoculars and suggested walks to buffet brunch as an alternative to conventional breakfast. An oriental twist to the Victorian setting comes with the optional extras. A Thai massage may also be booked. Wi-Fi. Rooms from €80 including brunch. €€

OU DORMENT LES FEES (M) 106 rue des Meuniers ♀ 238 C5 ✆ 03 20 38 3998
🚇 Porte d'Arras 🚌 Citadines bus to Meuniers, walk east along bd Victor Hugo & turn left on to rue des Meuniers

'Where the fairies sleep' is a grand mansion offering a suitably large-scale welcome, slightly off the main tourist map in the residential district around Wazemmes and Moulins. Managing to bestride the chasm between imposing and comfortable, this taste of the fine life remains homely. The spacious salons on the ground floor lead out to the delightful garden, with a table by the ornamental pond. Just the one guest room (a double) in what is still very much a family house. It is bright, with a marble washstand and a modern four-poster bed. Budget around €100–120. €€€

PENICHE LILLE FLOTTANTE Sq du Ramponneau/Champ de Mars ♀ 236 E3
✆ 03 20 07 92 38 🖥 www.lilleflottante.com 🚌 Citadine bus to Champ de Mars & walk to the waterfront

Excuse the pun (the name is a play on *île flottante*, a dessert of meringue and custard served in

jam-making or trout-fishing excursions with the property's owners! The *gîte* at **Féron**, in the Avesnes, for instance, is in a restored old village far from city living, which has developed into something of an artists' colony. Here, Florence Beaurant teaches visitors her skills as a glassblower, and her fellow artists open their studios and workshops to their work of restoring old paintings, creating unique ceramics or basket-weaving. Other artists direct their skills towards the table: village *boulanger* Mario bakes organic breads, and, in the café-bar, proprietor David serves beers brewed by the independent *brasseurs* of Flanders. Families at the *gîte* may even hire donkeys on which they can explore the parkland.

Most recommended homes will be members of the associations **Gîtes de France du Nord** (🖥 *www.gites-de-france-nord.fr*) or **CléVacances** (🖥 *www.clevacances.com*), with comfort ratings indicated by the number of ears of corn or keys (respectively). These organisations rate and inspect all properties listed. As a rule, prices do not include bedlinen and towels, which may be hired locally (reserve them in advance), as many families prefer to pack their own and save the cost for an evening out. Some *gîte* prices are exclusive of electricity, for which a supplementary charge may be payable. Others are all-inclusive. See online listings for details including accessibility, Wi-Fi and whether pets may stay at the property. Information brochures and booking details are available from the Maison du Tourisme (page 35).

AND NOT FORGETTING

As well as the very individual charms of the hotels reviewed in the guide, the international hotel chains are well represented in town and across the *métropolitan* area.

The Accor group alone (Sofitel, Novotel, Mercure, Ibis, etc) has nearly 2,000 rooms in the district. This is just a selection of chain hotels in the central areas; there are plenty more to choose from on the corporate websites of the hotel groups.

Several other budget hotels can be found in the streets around Gare Lille Flandres station. The tourist office (page 35) publishes a list of all registered hotels in and around town, and offers a booking service.

CAMPANILE
Lille Sud Rue Jean Charles Borda ♀ 238 B5 ✎ 03 20 53 30 55 ☂ www.campanile-lille-sud-chr.fr

HOLIDAY INN EXPRESS
Lille Centre Ⓜ 75 rue Léon Gambetta ♀ 238 E2 ✎ 03 20 42 90 90 ☂ www.hiexpress.com/lille

IBIS
Lille Gares Ⓢ 29 av Charles Saint-Venant ♀ 237 K7 ✎ 03 28 36 30 40
Opéra ⒼⓅ 21 rue Lepelletier ♀ 237 H4 ✎ 03 20 06 21 95
Lille Roubaix Centre 37 bd Gl Leclerc, 59100 Roubaix ✎ 03 20 45 00 00
Lille Tourcoing Centre 1 av Gustave Dron, 59200 Tourcoing ✎ 03 20 26 29 58
Lille Villeneuve d'Ascq Grand Stade rue des Victoires, 59650 Villeneuve d'Ascq ✎ 03 20 91 81 50

IBIS STYLES
Lille Centre Gare Beffroi (formerly All Seasons) 172 rue de Paris ♀ 237 J8 ✎ 03 20 30 00 54 ☂ www.ibis.com/lille

KYRIAD
Lille Centre 21 pl des Reignaux ♀ 237 K5 ✎ 03 28 36 51 18 ☂ www.kyriad.com

NOVOTEL
Lille Aeroport 55 route de Douai, 59810 Lesquin ✎ 03 20 62 53 53
Lille Centre Grand Place 116 rue de l'Hôpital Militaire ♀ 237 F5 ✎ 03 28 38 53 53
Lille Centre Gares See page 63.

▲ Once legendary, now notorious, the Coupole Suite on the roof of the Carlton (pages 57–8) has an unrivalled view of the squares (Laurence Phillips)

almost every French restaurant) – in a university town which once had a jazz club called Anglo-Saxo on the corner of the rue Angleterre, wordplay rather comes as standard. This is the most original B&B in town, a barge moored on the canal by the Citadelle. Don't expect standard barge comforts, as this houseboat is much more *luxe* than the average working vessel. The two bedrooms are bright nautical white and blue with comfy double beds, slippers and bathrobes as standard. Power shower to wake you up in the morning and a nice deck with teak tables and tubs of plants for a leisurely breakfast as the rest of the city goes to work. The leafy mooring even has its own parking space. Wi-Fi. Budget around €120. €€€

Traditional desserts in a modern style at the estaminet Au Vieux de la Vieille (page 85) (Anna Moores)

7

Eating and Drinking

Food and drink matter in Lille. The best argument of the day is deciding where to eat – a tavern serving savoury tarts with fresh-brewed beers; an old-fashioned traditional brasserie; gastronomic elegance with starched linens and eloquent menus to set the pulse racing; or a moody jazz café by the city walls.

There are so many flavours to be discovered that one mealtime is simply not enough. From one table to the next, you may segue from that which makes Lille French and that which sets it so very much apart. Regional specialities are a happy blend of the Flemish and northern French styles. Dishes may feature the cheeses of Mont des Cats and Maroilles, *genièvre* juniper gin, the famous Blanche de Lille white beer and other local brews, all tickled with local wisdom to transform the simplest of ingredients into something special.

Waterzooï, on many a menu, is a stew usually of freshwater carp, tench and pike; rabbit may be prepared with prunes; winter warmers include the *hochepot* stew of meats and market-garden vegetables, and the inevitable *carbonnade à la Flamande* stewed in beer, onions and brown sugar. Year-round favourite *potjevleesch* is a white-meat terrine, usually of chicken and rabbit. If all is reminiscent of Belgian comfort food, remember that Lille's borders have shifted almost with the tides.

Even more Belgian is that most traditional of budget meals, a pot of mussels served with a heap of chips. *Moules-frites* are an institution here, the single menu served during the Braderie (page 12), when the piles of shells outside the restaurants are the most photographed icon of the season. Sausage lovers should seek out the *Cambrai andouillette*, rated as among the best in France. *Welsh* is a peculiarly northern reinvention of Welsh rarebit, usually served in a soup bowl: cheddar-style cheese melted in beer and drenching a hidden slice of bread and (generally) ham, sometimes with an egg; always with chips. See individual brasserie or bistro reviews to discover the myriad variations on this cardiovascular white-knuckle ride.

To round off the meal, modern chefs make ice cream and sorbet with local flavourings: *fleur de bière*, gin and the ubiquitous *chicorée*. Traditional desserts include *tarte au sucre* and a local variation of bread-and-butter pudding known as *pain perdu*.

Easy to forget, with all these local flavours, that Lille is in France. Fortunately, almost every other region is represented with a restaurant or five to offer the flavours that lure most visitors across the Channel in the first place. Plenty of Breton *crêperies* to ward off summer snack attacks, and a browse through the following pages should guide you to specialities of Bordeaux and the southwest, and Lyon and the southeast. So, great steaks, *confit de canard*, truffles and foie gras are never too far away. Never forget that Lille is still a port, the third most important river port in France, and it is very close to the big fishing fleets of the Channel. The freshest fish is on every menu: Dover sole and cod among the local catches; tuna, salmon and sea bass among every chef's party pieces.

What to drink: might I suggest a beer (page 114)? Lille is a great brewing region, with some brasserie restaurants serving draught created in-house. It would be a waste to order a standard multinational brand when the breweries around Lille create such memorable ales as the local Ch'ti, La Goudale or Trois Monts. A traditional lager is known as a *bière blonde*. Be guided by your waiter or barman and go with the seasonal specialities: in March, order the Bière de Mars, for one month only, a sprightly and heady affair; at Christmas, the spicy and fruity Bière de Noël is a treat; at any time, but unbeaten as a summer cooler and quencher, the cloudy white Blanche de Lille, served with a slice of lemon, is simply heavenly. For a bit of an extra kick, try the beer brewed by the Wambrechies Genièvre distillery.

Genièvre, a Dutch-style juniper gin, is distilled in and around the city (pages 207–8) and is a popular chaser, flavouring or mid-meal *trou* (to be gulped in one to clear the digestive system for more food). The base of many a house cocktail, it was once popular 'with the ladies' as a Chuche Mourette, blended, like a kir, with *crème de cassis*.

However, in France, these ratings are not to be considered definitive. Even a €€€€ or €€€€€ designated restaurant may have a lunch deal to suit the seriously budget-conscious. In France all restaurants are obliged to display their prices outside the front door, and most will offer a set-price meal deal.

RESTAURANT PRICE CODES

Average price of a three-course meal. **Note:** not all listings have price codes as some establishments do not serve three-course meals.

€€€€€	Over €60	€€	€20–30
€€€€	€40–60	€	Under €20
€€€	€30–40		

Very expensive restaurants usually have a far cheaper *prix-fixe* menu at lunchtimes, usually featuring two, and occasionally three, courses.

Nonetheless, the inexpensive set meal may not be suitable for people with special dietary requirements. Non-meat eaters, for instance, may have to pay much more à la carte than their companions happy with the *plat du jour*! Restaurant prices include all taxes and service charges. It is customary to leave a small tip (usually loose change) to reward good service.

BUDGETING

I lingered long, mused much and pondered hard over how to categorise the restaurants of Lille. Unlike hotels, it is not really fair to classify the eateries of the town by price, since a good value set-menu lunch at even a famous gastronomic restaurant can often cost less than grazing à la carte in a bistro. So do not be hidebound by the restrictions of these listings since, should you fancy just a main course at a pricier restaurant, it may still work out cheaper than three courses at a mid-range restaurant. Nonetheless, the listings ahead also feature a reality check with the rates for a free-range food-fest.

Almost every restaurant will offer a special lunchtime deal at under €20 per person, with most having a two- or three-course suggestion for around €13–18. Be warned: the lowest-priced menu is usually served only at lunchtimes, so if you fancy good food and are worried about how far your euros will stretch, go for a big meal in the middle of the day and aim for something lighter in the evening.

Brasseries are ideal for those who would rather just have one course instead of the pricier menu, and make a lively option for kicking off or rounding out an evening on the town. Check out the bar and café options at midday for a filling sandwich or *plat du jour*.

OPENING HOURS

Most restaurants open for dinner from around 19.30 to 23.30, and lunch from 12.30 to 14.00. City-centre bars usually stay open until after midnight, generally closing between 01.00 and 02.00. Where establishments open or close later than usual, it is mentioned in the text. With the exception of late-night brasseries, it is advisable to telephone in advance to make a reservation for dinner after 22.00 or for late lunches. Gastronomic restaurants tend to close for two to four weeks in summer.

WHERE TO EAT AND DRINK

Bistro, brasserie or fine-dining room: to be fair, they are all restaurants. I have highlighted those that offer traditional bistro and brasserie fare or style, or that offer a typical Lillois, Flemish or French atmosphere. The other restaurants listed may be trendier or more traditional, but each establishment offers something different. However, in recent years the trend towards 'Bistronomie' has blurred the boundaries between bistro, brasserie and even fine dining so much that you are as likely to find a *choucroute*, *andouillette* sausage or *Welsh* in a conventional restaurant as in its traditional setting, and cross-cultural international fusion has become confusion in the other direction. So do browse through the reviews in all categories before deciding where to lunch or dine. Lille's wine bars and *estaminets*, originally intimate bars in the front or back room of a village house, are also well worth thinking about. Also consider the Maisons Folies (pages 190–3) in town and around the region for the opportunity to break bread with the artists of Lille and beyond. For typical opening hours, see page 75.

BISTROS AND ESTAMINETS

L'ARRIERE PAYS ⓥ 47 rue Basse ♀ 237 H4 ② ☏03 20 13 80 07 ✉ www.arriere-pays.com ⓜ Métro 2 to Gare Lille Flandres then line 1 to Rihour, then take the Navette Vieux Lille to rue Basse
Lovely rooms (red-brick décor upstairs, classic style downstairs) are simple and modern, respecting the period of the building, which doubles as a local grocery shop selling terrines and oils. Pause to sample the traditional fare. €7 buys a wholesome tart. Breakfast/brunch-style menus (€15) are popular at Sunday brunchtime. Budget €18 à la carte, or indulge in the soup of the day and *plat du jour* for €10. Great value *tartines* (open sandwiches) at three for €10. €

BASILIC CAFE See Urban Basilic Café, pages 84–5.

LE BARBUE D'ANVERS ⓖ 1 rue Saint-Etienne ♀ 237 H4 ⑪ ☏03 20 55 11 68 ✉ www.lebarbuedanvers.fr ⓘ closed Sun ⓡ Rihour ⓜ Métro 2 to Gare Lille Flandres then line 1 to Rihour, then walk along rue Roisin into rue de Pas & right on to rue Saint-Etienne
Tipped off about this welcome arrival on the scene, I made my way to the arched gateway tucked behind the squares back in January 2005, just weeks after the upmarket estaminet made its debut for the year-end party season. Directly opposite the crowd-pleasing Compostelle (page 97) and hidden behind a high wall, the Barbue presents classic Lillois fare to an appreciative blend of after-work colleagues, uni friends and quieter couples, and manages deftly to be both estaminet and restaurant according to appetite. For the lighter eater, the menu proposes a selection of soups 'to eat' or 'to drink' and standard dishes are tickled into a playful mood with a dash of something extra. With the duck-and-prune-based starter, the local *genièvre* gin from Wambrechies (pages 207–8) made a welcome appearance and, when I first visited, the reliable marinated herring had a clove-and-cinnamon-scented hint of Christmas spice to it. Now, fusion has made its inevitable mark on an essentially Flemish table, so a starter platter may feature Indian spiced smoked salmon with grilled dill *gambas*. But the local combos still rule the roost, namely Trois Monts beer in a gingerbread *carbonnade* and slow-cooked chicken with *spéculoos* biscuit sauce. You might not

easily find a traditional *moules-frites* on every visit, but a contemporary gastro tweaking of the classics won't be too far away and a bistro standby *steak tartare* will set you back €17. Midweek lunch menus hover around the €22 mark for two courses, €25 for three, and the evening set price meal is €39. Otherwise budget lavishly for food and indulge in the wine list, featuring the ubiquitous Chinon, fast becoming the city's house red. €€€

BERLINER ⟨VL⟩ 22 rue Royale ⚐ 237 G3 ⑬ ✆ 03 20 39 38 54 ⟨M⟩ Métro 2 to Gare Lille Flandres, then bus 10 to Voltaire & walk down rue Royale

Trusted friends love the burgers (in wholegrain buns), the décor (both streetwise and squat-style), the music (cool enough for students and the after-work crowd alike), not to mention the reinvention of the tapas concept of casual eating and the modern concept of '*le fooding*' ie: world-snacking and lazy drinking. You'll find New York bagels and cheesecakes, and warm croutons of St Marcellin cheese with crisp vegetables which fires as vegetarian indulgence. In summer, a table outdoors is prized. Spend €15 on the menu or budget ten more euros for a freer roam through the menu. €€

BISTROT DES TOQUEES Les Toquées de la Cuisine, 110 quai Géry Legrand ⚐ 236 A6 ㉙ ✆ 03 20 00 12 46 💻 www.bistrotdestoquees.com ⏰ lunch Mon–Fri, dinner Thu–Fri 🚇 Bois Blancs ⟨M⟩ Métro 2 to Bois Blancs then walk the length of the av Dormoy, bearing left on to av Butin & turning right on to the quai Géry Legrand

This is a pleasing little oddity. The bistro is part of a waterfront cookery school a good half-hour from the stations and more than a walk from the centre. Budget around €60+ for full à la carte, €45–65 for evening menus, and from €25 for two-course lunches. However, it could be the ideal choice if you couple the meal with the gift of a mini *cours de cuisine* for the wannabe chef in your life. For €55 you may study one particular dish for two to three hours, and learn how to prepare it with tips from the experts. €€€€

CAFE LIVRES See pages 116–17 for more on this unexpected café in a bookshop serving out-of-hours soups, salads and desserts. It also hosts summer barbecues among the hardbacks and thrillers.

CAFE MANU ⟨VL⟩ 5 pl du Concert ⚐ 237 H2 ㉓ ✆ 03 20 74 11 40 ⏰ closed Sun evening & all day Mon ⟨B⟩ Bus 50 to Palais de Justice, then follow rue Colas

Any chef who relays broadcasts from his kitchen to a flat screen in the dining room could never be accused of lacking in self-confidence. So Emmanuel Cauchy has made his mark at various addresses in and around the city. His latest showcase is earthy and real, and proof that substance will always triumph over style. Slap bang opposite the Conservatoire, across the thinking foodie's market square at place du Concert, the former A Côté des Arts is now renamed Café Manu with full-length windows for two-way people-watching. If you are dining alone, pull up a seat at the big communal table and make friends, or dine *à deux* at your own table. Within, all is wood, real wood: rough timber, old railway sleepers, rescued beams and salvaged chairs and tables, all designed to warm the heart of an artisan or woodsman. Food on these tables is ripe and ready crowd-pleasing stuff for the well-turned-out crowd in the know, who may have spent the last half-hour weighing up the relative merits of five varieties of *chicon* from market gardens. The

7

décor is marked by dripping wax and old Ruinart champagne bottles, but don't be fooled: there is nothing old-fashioned and lazy about the cooking. While contemporary summery vinaigrettes may season light and imaginative approaches to bream and seafood (the fresh catch laid on beds of perfectly pitched basmati), come the season when the air outside grows chilly and sharp, a late autumn/early winter menu is laden with the time-tested promise of proper lamb stews. Each forkful inspires a happy sigh. For lunchtimes budget around €20, evenings à la carte nearer €30. €€

CHEZ LA VIEILLE 60 rue de Gand ♥ 237 K2 ☺ ✆ 03 28 36 40 06 ☷ http://lavieillefrance. fr ⏰ closed Sun & Mon ☻ Bus 50 to Lion d'Or, then cross pl Louise de Bettignies to rue de Gand

Franck Delobelle may not be a grandmother, but his welcome is as warm as the old wooden tables and hop-decked beams of this cheery Flemish dining room. From the crockery on the shelves above the seats to the traditional wooden toys and games in the window, La Vieille is very much in the tradition of homely conviviality that marks out this popular estaminet from the master hosts of Cassel (see t'Rijsel on pages 79–80, and the newest successor Vieux de la Vieille on page 85) as the real McCoy rather than the fashionable reinvention that is the latest urban-rustic retro fad. Here the food is of exclusively seasonal regional standards – warm stews in winter and tasty flans in summer – all prepared to old country recipes and tasting as though stirred by a granddaughter under the watchful eyes of a matriarch. Black pudding and apple *tatin* or chicken with Maroilles cheese are among the winter warmers. The house beer is Les Sept Péchés. The two-course lunch menu comes in at around €12, three-course free-range dining at €25. €€

LE COQ HARDI ☺ 44 pl du Général de Gaulle ♥ 237 H5 ☺ ✆ 03 20 55 21 08 ☷ www. coq-hardi.fr ☷ Rihour ☻ Métro 2 to Gare Lille Flandres then line 1 to Rihour & walk to Grand' Place

An institution on the central square of Lille for donkey's years, the tables spreading out across the pavement are better known than the small restaurant behind them. In fact it was only when the winter weather grumbled ominously that I ventured to check out the restaurant itself. Small but perfectly busy, with service on two floors, the Coq Hardi is unashamedly basic and rustic. Untreated wooden ceilings, sacks of baguettes inside the front door and a constant flow of customers keen on value-for-money lunching. Huge portions are the order of the day, whether *andouillette de Cambrai avec frites* or a *tartare aux deux saumons*, served ready-mixed or with the additional ingredients on the side. Most *plats* are €7–12. In the sunshine, take a big bowl of *moules* or a huge summer salad and lunch outdoors for well under €15, indulging in good old-fashioned people-watching at this key corner between the old town and the main square. €

LA DUCASSE 95 rue Solférino ♥ 236 D6 ☺ ✆ 03 20 57 34 10 ☷ www.laducasse.fr ☷ République–Beaux Arts ☻ Bus Citadine from Gare Lille Europe to Sacré Cœur, then walk along rue Solférino to pl des Halles Centrales

Just another corner bistro with an accordionist leading a sing-along of Saturday night standards. Perhaps, yet the atmosphere is second to none: the simple local stews and platters hit the spot, the beer and wine flow freely and the local crowd are the nicest people you could ever meet.

Students passing through Lille for two or three years may choose the newest addresses along the road, but those living in apartments in the streets between the boulevards drop in here to sup with friends and neighbours rather than cook for themselves. The menu is unashamedly Flemish, and the local beers pulled from the pump. After an arduous day recording our BBC feature *Allez Lille*, my colleagues and I chose this corner for an anonymous, off-duty collapse. Hearing our English conversation, a local birthday party at the next table sent us over a bottle of wine and invited us to join them for coffee. A coin or two in the ancient pianola, and the honky-tonk piano-roll music whirred into action. Thankfully, producer Jerome Weatherald had a spare recorder in his pocket and was able to capture a few moments of that magical mood on tape. We ended the programme with a hint of our wonderful evening at the Ducasse, and shared the true spirit of Lille in a way mere words might never have managed. Have a *hochepot* or *waterzooï*, a chunk of steak and a hefty slice of *tarte*, and pour a large drink, sing along to a *chanson* from the golden age, and feel the glow for yourself. I returned a year later to celebrate the launch of the Beaujolais *nouveau* – a bottle of wine was left on our table to tempt us to try it. You might each have change from a €20 note at lunchtime and budget around €25–35 in the evenings, including a tipple or two... €€€

ESTAMINET GANTOIS   See page 100.

ESTAMINET T'RIJSEL   **25 rue de Gand** ♀ 237 K2 🕿 ✆03 20 15 01 59 ⏱ **closed Sun, Mon & for much of Aug** 🚌 **Bus 50 to Lion d'Or, then cross pl Louise de Bettignies to rue de Gand**

Rijsel is the Flemish name for Lille, so it's no surprise to find a warm corner of old Flanders in this relative newcomer to the restaurant scene. Jean-Luc Lacante, whose estaminet t'Kasteel-Hof in nearby Cassel is a long-time favourite with those who explore the countryside, brought his trademark combination of wit, style and homeliness to town at the turn of the millennium. Expect all the regional specialities here, from *potjevleesch* to sugar flans, on menus printed on old school exercise books. Late one cold winter's morning, my parents and I stopped by for a hearty bowl of homemade soup and were made very welcome, even if the kitchen was not yet officially open. Budget

▼ *Carbonnade flammande* is a classic Lillois dish (Anna Moores)

comfortably around €20, and around €13 for lunch. Check out, too, Chez La Vieille, the sister estaminet across the way at number 60 and Au Vieux de la Vieille, off rue de la Monnaie (page 85). €€

GOSPEL CAFE (M) 78 rue Léon Gambetta ♀ 238 D1 (G) ☏ 03 20 07 39 64 ⏰ 11.30–18.00 Mon–Thu, 11.30–22.30 Fri–Sat, 11.30–17.00 Sun ☒ République–Beaux Arts ⊕ Métro 2 to Gare Lille Flandres & line 1 to République–Beaux Arts, then walk down rue Gambetta, where the restaurant is on your left

Oh, happy days. The spices grab you by the eyes and heart, and lure you into this cheery Caribbean influenced eatery, café and occasional nightspot. Bright bold colours, Obama T-shirts and a morning-after-carnival atmosphere greeted us as we arrived for lunch a few days after President Obama's inauguration in Washington. Madame Boyunga welcomes visitors with spicy, ricey soul food and comforting creole savours of the south, making for lively lunches. Late-afternoon chocolate fixes are the perfect reward for hardcore shopping across the square. Closed most evenings, except the weekends, when live gospel music takes to the floor on the first and third Saturday of the month. Great on Sunday too, when brunch is served until 16.00 after a Wazemmes market moochfest. Graze rather than dine and bring a €20 note. €€

LA HOUBLONNIERE (GP) 42 pl du Général de Gaulle ♀ 237 H5 (37) ☏ 03 20 74 54 34 ✆ www.lahoublonnierelille.fr ☒ Rihour ⊕ Métro 2 to Gare Lille Flandres, then line 1 to Rihour & walk to Grand' Place

You might be forgiven for thinking that the Grand' Place was lined with restaurant tables where one could sip and sup the day away simply people-watching. In truth, most of the restaurants are to be found in the street that links Grand' Place with the place Rihour, the main square itself being given over to grand buildings and the goddess. However, the Coq Hardi (page 78) and its neighbour La Houblonnière offer that rare treat: rows of tables out on the square with the view over Lille's favourite meeting place. Admittedly tables are rather close to the traffic, but hey, you are eating and drinking in the heart of the city. Don't spend a fortune – €25 should see you all right for the full three courses. Menus start at around €17. Go for traditional foods such as *rillettes*, *andouillette*, a chunky *tartare* of smoked and raw salmon or the ubiquitous cheese dishes: *tarte au Maroilles* or *Welsh*. Not gastronomy, just hearty stomach-fillers halfway through a day's hardcore walking or before an evening's serious partying. Dine upstairs to enjoy the witty artwork. €€

L'IMAGINAIRE (VL) 5 pl Louise de Bettignies ♀ 237 J3 (39) ☏ 03 20 78 13 81 ⊕ Bus 50 to Lion d'Or

Between the better-known dining areas of the centre is a bar-brasserie whose best asset is hidden from passers-by. Next door to the Hôtel de la Treille (page 61), it overlooks one of the busiest junctions of the old town. But it is what lies behind that makes this a dinner venue to consider. The terrace at the back of the restaurant has a surprisingly excellent view of the gothic back-end of Notre Dame de la Treille on the crest of the castrum hill. An unexpectedly quiet and sunny spot for lunch or an early evening rendezvous, this is a great late-night hideaway from the busier streets. The menu is unashamedly tailored towards hardened carnivores, with steak mains averaging around €14 a plate. Choose your fillet steak of equine or bovine provenance and appease the vegetarian in the party with a salad (around €10). The place opens late as a bar and local hangout. €€

MEATBALLS 🚇 10 rue du Pont Neuf ♀ 237 H1 ☎ ✆ 03 28 36 91 33 🖥 www.meatballs-restaurant.com 🚇 Métro 2 to Gare Lille Flandres & bus 10 to Conservatoire, then walk up rue St André to rue du Pont Neuf
New look for the original Basilic Café (pages 84–5), the revamp of a long-time Lille-spun fast-food hangout is a world away from the meal you are thinking of – as served by the checkout at a well-known Swedish furniture store. The only thing the two places have in common is the number of students on a budget scoffing the signature dishes. Round food in a sauce on a plate may be the theme, but meat is a loose concept and the balls in your bowl on rue du Pont Neuf may as easily be fish or vegetarian. Prawns and falafel spheres share the menu with bacon, pork, beef and chicken, and you could even have a blend of steamed cod, ginger and coriander. Delicious. Priced depending on whether you have four, six or eight balls on the plate, you choose from a wide range of sauces (curry, creamy tomato, parmesan and mushroom, sweet and sour, satay, tzatziki, etc) and have a custom-made main course. There are salads, sides and desserts to browse, an €11 lunchtime menu as well as an all-you-can-eat evening option around €20. €

LE PASSE-PORC Ⓜ 155 rue Solférino ♀ 238 D2 ☺ ✆ 03 20 42 83 93 🕐 daily for lunch & Fri evening, closed Aug 🚇 République–Beaux Arts 🚇 Métro 2 to Gare Lille Flandres, then line 1 to République–Beaux Arts, then follow the rue Inkerman to rue Solférino
Appropriately located across the street from a cluster of butchers' vans, this is a country market town bistro on market day. Old-fashioned (as opposed to knowingly retro) velvet and brown décor and honest earthy fare. In a street where style is on the up, here is a rare survivor of the bloodline that still exists only around the old market and slaughterhouse quarters on the edge of Paris or deep in what is now designated *La France profonde*. The French, unlike their queasy neighbours *trans-manche* who take provenance of farmyard fodder no further than cellophane and polystyrene, love their meats for being meat, and a restaurant that makes free with the word abattoir is certain to find favour with hardcore carnivores. Signs in the window proudly announce the speciality (tripe) and the locally brewed La Goudale to be served with the meal. In reality the bottles that pass over the counter are as likely to be champagne or rich reds from the ever-changing wine list selected from the traditional wine regions of Bordeaux and Burgundy. My porcophile friends cannot recommend too highly. €€

LE PETIT BARBUE D'ANVERS 🚇 3 av du Peuple Belge ♀ 237 J2 ☺ ✆ 03 20 06 81 65 🖥 www.lepetitbarbue.fr 🕐 closed Sun evening 🚇 Bus 50 to Lion d'Or
Amid the confusion of the foodie heart of the old town, this relative newcomer has a prime location. Just beside the place Louise de Bettignies, this traditional estaminet boasts a little courtyard open to the green space behind the Hospice Comtesse offering the intimacy of Vieux Lille without feeling too closed in. The menus – seriously carnivorous – present plates that are redolent with the flavours and aromas of the north, that same distinctive signature scent of the main dining room down in the town centre (pages 76–7). There is a spiciness of *spéculoos* crumbs on a beef carpaccio, and the *chuche mourette* gin and *cassis* combo give a definite Lillois twist to a crème brûlée. The dining rooms are a comforting combination of neat, preserved brick and sturdy woodwork, and tables are not too close together, considering the limited space. Tall young waiters, with the air of free-range barmen let loose from behind a counter, glide from room to room taking

7

orders and explaining the menus. Lunch deals at €21 and €24 and the evening set menu at just under €30. Or graze the full *carte*, as I did, and nudge the budget towards €40. Non-meat eaters should be prepared to question their waiter for details as many fish dishes may have a hidden meat heritage somewhere in the recesses of the recipe book. €€€

LA PETITE COUR GP 17 rue du Curé Saint-Etienne 📍 237 H4 64 ☎ 03 20 51 52 81 ⚑ www.lapetitecour-lille.fr 🕐 closed Sun and Mon ⊕ Métro 2 to Gare Lille Flandres, then line 1 to Rihour, then walk to Grand' Place & under the Alcide arch to the rue des Débris Saint-Etienne before turning left on to the rue du Curé Saint-Etienne

Once merely a very busy café in a courtyard with basic seating and tables: if proof were ever needed that the average age in Lille is 25 then this place, popular with families during the day and with students at night, was textbook watertight evidence. Smartened up over the years, the days of a sleeping beauty forest of salad or basic *steak haché et frites* have mellowed into a smarter dining room and courtyard serving classic bistro dishes with a more contemporary spice rack (the salmon *tartare* is distinctly Thai these days). Menus from under €19 at lunchtime but pushing €30 in the evening; à la carte over €30. €€€

LE POT BEAUJOLAIS GP 26 rue de Paris 📍 237 J5 65 ☎ 03 20 57 38 38 ⚑ www.le-pot-beaujolais.fr 🕐 closed Sun & Mon evening 🚉 Gare Lille Flandres ⊕ Métro 2 to Gare Lille Flandres & cross to rue Faidherbe, then left on rue des Ponts de Comines to rue de Paris

Le Beaujolais ancien est arrivé! Most restaurants in town remember Beaujolais only when the *nouveau* wine is released in autumn. In this tiny bistro on the rue de Paris, the spirit of the most traditional of regions is reflected year round in the brown wood and check-cloth décor, and most of all in the menu. Outside traditional mealtimes a selection of terrines and tartines are available at all times for those who fancy staving off hunger pangs with the taste of old Lyon. A modest outlay will buy an alternative to a conventional sandwich, this time layered with *chèvre* and smoked duck breast. But at lunchtime and in the evening, tuck your napkin under your chin, take a deep breath, allow your waistline room to expand and get stuck in to the menu. This place is serious about its steaks, and the meat is treated with as much respect as wine, even to the listing of the butcher's name on the menu. Expect quality with the *onglet* or *entrecôte*, but do not even think of ordering the *côte de bœuf* if your vocabulary includes the French for 'well done' or even 'medium'. Classic comfort cooking means a steaming plate of *petit salé* with puy lentils or *andouillette* sausage in a *mâconnaise* sauce. Don't ignore the wine list. The Beaujolais classic crus are all there – and can be taken away too – so enjoy a Moulin à Vent or a Brouilly with the meal. Squeeze inside or sit on the pavement terrace and consider spending around €24 a head. Midweek lunchtimes see a menu at around €18 for two courses, and a dish of the day at €14. Keep an eye on this stretch of the rue de Paris. For years it has been the least interesting of the roads south of Grand' Place, but bars and restaurants are taking over from tired shops. Could be on the up. €€

LA RESERVE M 47 rue du Marché 📍 238 B4 10 m 09 66 91 22 49 🕐 closed evenings Mon–Wed & Sun, all day Sat 🚉 Gambetta ⊕ Métro 2 to Gare Lille Flandres & line 1 to Gambetta, then walk along rue Manuel to rue du Marché

You have heard of the concept of the *bar à vin*, but welcome to Lille's new *bar à manger*, where eating is an art and you leave your pretensions outside this little dining room where décor is a throwback to the '60s. OK, you may end up with a square plate (ie: style over substance), but the food on it will have more than enough flavour and texture to make up for the pretty colours nicely positioned. Right in the heart of Wazemmes food market so, if you want to know the provenance of any of the ingredients, just point – the restaurant buys fresh food every day from stalls just across the road and makes up the menu accordingly. There are two or three dishes to choose from for each course, and à la carte should still keep you safely below the €30 mark, but menus are very affordable from €18 to €23. Game and fowl prepared to the sticky savoury max, fish fair floats off the fork into silky sauces, vegetables are as crisp as the seasons and, in the age of the bake-off, leave room for desserts, since skills are honed to their finest here. Pavlovas, *mille-feuille* made with *beurre d'Isigny*, patisserie to tease a tear and pop a shirt button or two along the way, not to mention the crusty organic home-baked loaves of bread that banish memories of floury white baguettes forever. €€

LE RESTO DU CH'TI 61 rue d'Isly ♥ 236 A6 ⏰ ☎ 03 20 00 85 73 ⏱ lunch Mon–Sat, dinner Thu–Sat, closed Sun ☒ Cormontaigne ⏎ Métro 2 to Cormontaigne

Bienvenue chez les Ch'tis, so the cinema posters had it for the best part of a year. The tradition here, just that bit further away from the centre than most visitors would think of travelling, is less of comedy, but more of the honest northern welcome and value for money. Where else will you eat home-style cooking at these prices? Henri and Murielle Leclercq had long been mine hosts on rue St André. Now, away from the pricier centre of town they can serve classic braised chicory dishes, grandmotherly ladlings of rabbit with prunes and a hearty steaming *carbonnade*, each for under €10. *Cuisine du terroir* without paying the earth. €

LA ROYALE ⏰ 37 rue Royale ♥ 237 G2 ⏰ ☎ 03 20 42 10 11 ⏱ lunch Mon–Sat, evenings Thu–Sat ⏎ Métro 2 to Gare Lille Flandres then line 1 to Rihour before crossing Grand' Place to rue Esquermoise into rue Royale

Oh my, how the winds of Bistronomie have blown along the staid old rue Royale. For as long as I have been writing these notes from the tables of Lille this was always the genuine article. Despite the rustic mirrors and milk-churn décor, it was a real estaminet neighbourhood bar in a centuries-old building in Vieux Lille, where a simple, traditional, home-cooked lunch would be on offer at midday only. Old-fashioned *Rognons de veau* or a simple poultry dish served only until 14.30, but where you would be welcome to drink with the chatty locals into the early evening. Now, while humble origins are honoured with *œuf cocotte en meurette* and a fine Association Amicale des Amateurs d'Andouillette Authentique (AAAAA) *andouillette* sausage, the young chef Mickael Braure presents an experience closer to the trendy designer bistros of Paris than the neighbourhood bars of the north, wooing hardcore foodies with inventive reimaginings of risotto (served *en tartiflette* at the start of the meal or with squid ink and cod as a main course), an entrée beef cheek ravioli in *jus de carbonnade* followed perhaps by a couscous-style pesto-infused lamb main course, cheese from Philippe Olivier (page 156) or pineapple carpaccio with basil *mascarpone*. For more traditional lunchers the *bœuf à la moelle* (ie: with marrow bone) and *frites* is €21 and there is the €16 burger (here proffered *à l'Italienne*). So you'd need to budget closer to €35 for three courses these days. Locals tell me that if the pan-fried foie gras is on the menu when you drop in, ignore all else on offer! €€€

LE SQUARE D'ARAMIS VL 52 rue Basse ♀ 237 G4 ⑳ ✎ 03 20 74 16 17 📷 www.le-square-d-aramis.com ⏲ closed Mon evening, Sun and Aug 🚇 Métro 2 to Gare Lille Flandres & line 1 to Rihour, then take the Navette Vieux Lille to rue Basse

Big portions and no illusions of grandeur in a bustling, bistro-style café that gets packed with families at lunchtimes and youngsters in the evenings. Value for money is the lure. The menu, *midi et soir*, is €22. Whatever you choose, the service is informal, with starters big enough to eat as a main course, and local dishes full of flavour. My first food memory of the place is of a *saumon cru* marinated in *bière de garde* that proved pretty darned yummy and *andouillette-frites* was ever the popular choice. A house speciality is a brace of reinterpretations of that old stager the *steak tartare*. You'll find the raw beef classic being mixed in a dozen brasseries across Lille, but only here will you be offered the €15 dish either Thai or Mexican style! The budget-conscious tend to opt for the sizeable *salade de poulet* with feta, fruit and a sesame dressing or the pasta of the day from the small but wide-ranging menus. €€

LE TCHIOT RESTO 100 rue du Faubourg de Roubaix ♀ 235 K4 ④ ✎ 03 28 14 12 39 ⏲ closed weekday evenings & all day Sat & Sun 🚆 St-Maurice Pellevoisin 🚇 Métro 2 to St-Maurice Pellevoisin then walk down the rue du Faubourg de Roubaix towards the city centre

The name is patois for 'little' or 'littl'un', and the cooking is just as homely, but generously served. Modern estaminet lunches on the 'wrong side' of the Gare Lille Europe for tourists, but the right side for locals who come for the food and don't need centuries-old bricks and low beams to set the scene. In a tiny modern room with white walls, and a big glass shopfront, find light salads or heartier grandmotherly classic meat dishes, with heaps of unfashionably tasty home-cooked veg, and some moreish desserts. Only open midweek and for a few hours a day. The atmosphere is one of lunching with friends; the regulars who work in nearby shops and offices are fiercely loyal and devour the two or three *plats du jour* with gusto. Walking distance from the Lille Europe station too. Budget €9–15 according to appetite. €

URBAN BASILIC CAFE GP 24 rue Esquermoise ♀ 237 H4 ⑳ ✎ 03 20 31 21 47 📷 www.basilic-cafe.com 🚆 Rihour 🚇 Métro 2 to Gare Lille Flandres & line 1 to Rihour, then cross the Grand' Place to rue Esquermoise

Cool address for brunching at weekends, decent burger hangout any day of the week, with a changing programme of art exhibitions on the wall and run by a team with a finger on the pulse of trendy feeding, this address, amid some of the most traditional restaurants, is home to those who have blurred the concepts of a long snack and a light meal. Saturday and Sunday brunches are legendary, served from 11.30 to 16.00 and available in vegetarian format from €18 or fully carnivorous at €26. There is also a generous and wide-ranging buffet plus world food hot dishes prepared to order. Unashamedly stylish, from the award-winning architecture and interior design to the jam jars of salad served with your burger in lieu of chips should you wish. The place has a terrace that buzzes day and evening – the free Wi-Fi helps keep it popular. Now spawning a clutch of similarly zeitgeist-tapping dining rooms in the centre of town (latest is the self-explanatory eponymous Meatballs reinvention of the original Basilic Café on rue du Pont Neuf – see page 81). These two restaurants have managed to create a buzz since the first café opened in time for Lille's city of culture gig and continue with the adding of the word Urban to the title. Innit. Look out for original theme nights: a 2014 favourite was unlimited burgers on Thursday evenings. Menus from €13 to €17; freer grazing will run to around €25. €€

AU VIEUX DE LA VIEILLE ⓥ 2 rue des Vieux Murs ♀ 237 H2 ⑦ ✎ 03 20 13 81 64 ⓕ http://estaminetlille.fr/auvieuxdelavieille ⓛ 10.00–22.30 Mon–Sat ⓑ Bus 50 to Lion d'Or, then cross pl Louise de Bettignies to rue de la Monnaie & turn left on to rue Pétérinck

First the estaminet t'Rijsel, then came Chez la Vieille and now, inevitably, the Vieux de la Vieille: these glimpses of Flanders past in the present are the perfect antidote to the cutting-edge trendiness that never quite takes over the city. No matter how close fingers come to the pulse of the present, hearts and souls are always closest to the past. Since the boys from Cassel first brought their simple, honest country-style café concept to the big city around a decade or so ago, the sharp style of the rue de Gand has introduced a fresh generation of Lillois to the simplest pleasures known by their parents and grandparents when this part of France was still ignored by sophisticated society and was left to its own devices. An estaminet was originally a bar in a corner of someone's front room, where neighbours might drop in for a beer for an hour or two before bedtime. The t'Kasteel-Hof in the rural hinterland between the coast and Belgian border retains that feel of makeshift hospitality, and in the rue de Gand the success of the two city branches, each with its own style, has been heartening. Such is the popularity of these simple bistros, while smarter premises change hands like dancers in a reel, this third *estaminet-café* has opened at the point where the rue Pétérinck unbuckles its belts and expands into almost a square in that straggle of workshops, studios and quaint counters meandering from rue de la Monnaie to the cathedral. This traditional café-bistro concept has old-style wooden games to play with while you linger over any of a couple of dozen artisan-brewed beers and the red-brick room itself is filled with drying hops and bric-a-brac from every granny's parlour. Papi and Memère's influence is to be found on the homely *potjevleesch*-rich menus and in the spirit of their guests. Hospitality spills over from the bowls of Flemish soups and stews into the friendliness of the clientele. If you can't find a table for two, certainly don't be surprised if a group of friends in a corner decide to squeeze closer together and invite you to sit with them. The menu deal for just over €20 includes three courses and a beer. €€

BRASSERIES

BLUE MOON CAFE ⓖ 10 rue Léon Trulin ♀ 237 J5 ⑮ ⓜ 06 71 62 88 99 ⓛ closed Sun & Mon ⓡ Rihour ⓑ Métro 2 to Gare Flandres, then walk up rue Faidherbe to the squares

Behind the Opera House on the 'wrong side' of the building for tourists, and opposite the Mercure Hotel, this newcomer to the Lille restaurant scene opened in summer 2014, replacing what had been more of a stage-door bar. The bright lights of the square and sirens of Vieux Lille may be the more obvious attractions for theatre-goers or music-lovers, but this bar-brasserie attracts a youngish and cheerful crowd and is perfectly located for a pre-Mozart or post-Puccini bite. The menu is fine, but regulars turn up at lunchtimes for a very affordable *plat du jour* with a definite Lillois flavour, such as *endives gratinées au Maroilles*, a white fish *mille-feuille* or classic *carbonnade flamande*. The exception that proves the rule would be the very popular house lasagne. The daily special will cost around €9 and you can check the restaurant's Facebook page before you leave your hotel room or office for the update. Otherwise great for finger food (platters and flams) and menus at €13 and €19. Open late morning until around midnight. €€

BRASSERIE ALCIDE ⓖⓟ 5 rue des Débris Saint-Etienne ♀ 237 H4 ⑱ ✎ 03 20 12 06 95
🚈 Rihour ⓔⓥ Métro 2 to Gare Lille Flandres & line 1 to Rihour then cross Grand' Place
Just as we went to press with this edition of the guide, the future of this iconic dining room was once more in doubt. Temporarily closed, then reopened as the company went into receivership. However, Alcide has been found under the arch at the main square since the 1870s, and has gone through many identities, reinventions and make-overs, yet somehow always remained the essential address for classic Lille dining. Where better to indulge in a *carbonnade flamande* than in this most typical of brasseries? In its most recent incarnation, that which led to notices from bankers and lawyers in place of the announcements of chefs in the window, it dropped the word 'brasserie' in favour of the title 'restaurant', and contemporary décor threatened to smother the original Napoleon III style. Traditional platters heady with the *saveurs* of the brewery and laced with the scent of the centuries were eclipsed by a more 21st-century take on brasserie fare. Hopefully the commercial stability of the business will have been settled by the time this book reaches the shelves, and either the most recent owners will be back in the kitchen, or an independent chef with a sense of culinary heritage, or perhaps one of the city's serial restaurateurs with a penchant for the classics, will have stepped into the breach. If you get there before me, let me know your thoughts.

BRASSERIE ANDRE ⓖⓟ 71 rue de Béthune ♀ 238 G1 ② ✎ 03 20 54 75 51
📷 www.brasserieandre.fr 🚈 République–Beaux Arts ⓔⓥ Métro 2 to Gare Lille Flandres then line 1 to République–Beaux Arts & cross pl Richebé to rue de Béthune
A true survivor of the golden age of brasseries, this is where good *moules* go when they die. Sumptuous traditional brasserie décor, with wonderful wooden-panelled arches and dark wooden walls contrasting with white, starched napkins, tablecloths and aprons. Not cheap by brasserie standards – your meal could set you back €50 – but your lunch companions will be businessmen, bankers and people who don't mind paying a tad over the odds for a classy setting for classic favourites. For the non-mussel-eater, indulge in beefsteaks, lamb and the like served in rich *bordelaise* fashion. The menu reeks of tradition: starters featuring Burgundy *escargots* and house foie gras, or scrambled eggs with smoked salmon and the northern treat of herring with warm potato salad; mains of Breton lobster, *entrecôte*, *tournedos Rossini* and fillet steaks. The pavement terrace spills out on to the main shopping area, and service continues between mealtimes with a limited selection of dishes. The children's menu is hardly of a chicken-nugget standard, featuring fillet steak and roasted fish. Perfect for trainee gourmets.

BRASSERIE DE LA CLOCHE ⓖⓟ 13 pl du Théâtre ♀ 237 J5 ⑲ ✎ 03 20 55 35 34
🚈 Rihour ⓔⓥ Métro 2 to Gare Flandres & walk up rue Faidherbe to the squares
Having had the square pretty much to itself, the Cloche is facing up to new competition with the emergence from the shadows of a string of bars and bistros around the revived and revitalised cultural hub by the Opera House. My money says that nothing much will change here, but time will tell. The restaurant on the Rang de Beauregard is known for its distinctive sign on the wall, but even more so for its tables on the square itself, where informal and friendly waiting staff serve

unpretentious fare to an undemanding public. So the waiter's apron stains are a veritable menu for the illiterate, and the waitress's air hostess *maquillage* is rendered human by the tattoo on her shoulder; all is convivial, and the portions are the size that friends would serve you. Food is a bit of a hit-and-miss affair: my leek tart had much of the string and card about its consistency, but a fellow diner's *plat du jour* wafted the appetising aromas of home-cooked meat and two veg, and the *salade bergère* was the cheesiest double-edged platter of comfort food you could hope to risk. You might get away with spending under €20. Best of all is the wine list, with more than a dozen interesting wines served by the glass. I predict the post- (and intermission) concert and opera crowd will welcome the €15 late-night snack of smoked salmon and champagne. €€

BRASSERIE LA PAIX GP 25 pl Rihour ♥ 237 H5 ⓴ ☎03 20 54 70 41 🍎 http://paix. restaurantsdelille.com ⊕ closed Sun 🚊 Rihour ⊕ Métro 2 to Gare Lille Flandres then line 1 to Rihour

Café society '20s- and '30s-style lives on here; the décor, the welcome and the food are from the heyday of the French brasserie. Recent editions of the *Ch'ti* guide have waxed almost Proustian on the subject. Great platters of seafood, roast *canette de Challans* cooked with fresh figs, and a chicory crème brûlée are among the attractions. The period feel is strictly for diners inside the restaurant. Sit outside on the pavement and you can enjoy the very modern spectacle of shoppers trekking from boutique to boutique and commuters emerging from beneath the queasy custard-coloured waters on the pyramid fountain at Rihour métro station. Menus from €22 (except Saturday night) to €32. €€

CAFE LEFFE GP 1–5 pl Rihour ♥ 237 H5 ⓰ ☎03 20 54 67 37 🍎 www.cafeleffe.fr 🚊 Rihour ⊕ Métro 2 to Gare Lille Flandres then line 1 to Rihour

On the corner of Grand'Place and place Rihour, next to the theatre and on the threshold of the pedestrianised shopping zone, Leffe's tables prove irresistible to the laden and the early. A midweek menu adds to its popularity during shopping hours. Fast service keeps the Belgian beer flowing at the dithering point of the evening as you debate whether to go to a show or a restaurant, stay and watch the match on the big screen, head off to a local club or hop on a train to Belgium. But nowadays, this is part of a national chain of brasseries under the name of the celebrated beer, and steaks, burgers (one uses glorified potato *latkes* in place of a bun) and hearty Oktoberfest-style fare reign supreme. Big salads usually drizzled with either meaty bits or cheese (note the grilled toasts of *chèvre* are being challenged by the newly fashionable and decidedly bovine Saint-Marcellin cheese) rival classic foie gras and soup starters. I have enjoyed an excellent tuna burger here with a quality fish steak cooked to order within the bap. The onion soup now also has a healthy slosh of *bière blonde* in it! The menu does get a modernising update more often than some more conventional places. €€

LA CHICOREE GP 15 pl Rihour ♥ 237 H5 ⓴ ☎03 20 54 81 52 🍎 http://chicoree. restaurantsdelille.com 🚊 Rihour ⊕ Métro 2 to Gare Lille Flandres then line 1 to Rihour

We have all found ourselves here at some stage of a late-night session. Open from 10.00 until dawn, the old reliable brasserie on the corner is the perfect standby when an evening has just flown by at the bar, café or jazz club and nobody is ready for bed yet. Part of the family stable of brasserie-style restaurants that cluster around the corner of the place Rihour, the décor is now

Latin-block shades with strategically placed artworks. An all-day (until 22.30) midweek menu of around €12 is a bit limited; the €23 version is more varied and the full-blown and discretely updated à la carte should run to around €30. However, a steaming bowl of onion soup topped with a Gruyère-covered *croûton* should fill you up and leave the wallet relatively unscathed. Just when you start to feel that the place might have descended into a tourist spot routine, you return to find the buzz is still young and happening, the young couple at the next table find time to hold hands between releasing their fingers to text updates of their dining to other lands and the staff still lovely, happy and on top of their game. Since prices rise by around 20% after midnight, the waiters are perfectly happy to serve just a starter or one-course refuelling option in the small hours. At sunrise, the place is busy with night-shift workers, road sweepers and métro staff rounding off the night's work with a hefty steak and refreshing beer, as the rest of us follow our noses to the bakery for breakfast croissants and hot chocolate! €€

LILLE OPERA BRASSERIE GP 32 rue Lepelletier ♀ 237 H4 ⑮ ✆ 03 20 33 35 30
 www.lilleoperabrasserie.com ⏱ closed Sun Ⓜ Métro 2 to Gare Lille Flandres, then line 1 to Rihour, then cross the squares & walk under the Alcide arch to the Débris Saint-Etienne & continue to rue Lepelletier
A witty 21st-century take on the traditional brasserie-décor concept has plenty of brass and copper: here, with a battery of copper pots and pans clustered chandelier-like and suspended from the dining room ceiling. A newcomer to the local brasserie scene, it has a smart dining room and a sharply considered menu. The hand-chopped (rather than minced) *steak tartare* uses prized Aubrac beef and there is still room and respect for *sole meunière*, and frogs' legs amid modern reinterpretations of other classics; the *magret de canette* glazed with spice honey and served with puréed carrots and the *ris de veau*, here pan-fried with wild forest mushrooms. Budget €40+ to pick and choose your three courses from the full listing or opt for the midweek €19 set lunch of *plat du jour*, dessert and coffee. A wide selection of scotches on the drinks menu. €€€€

LE MEUNIER 15–17 rue de Tournai ♀ 235 G5 ❸ ✆ 03 20 04 04 90 www.restaurant-le-meunier.fr ⛟ Gare Lille Flandres Ⓜ Walk down av le Corbusier, or métro 2 to Gare Lille Flandres
Once upon a time, every provincial French railway station had a stolid, reliable railway restaurant serving basic meat, fish and chicken – standard fare to while away the two-hour delay between cross-country trains. At the side of the old Flandres station, amid the friteries and burger bars, is to be found one such old-fashioned *buffet de la gare*-style dining room, which has been fuelling weary passengers since 1946. Canteen cutlery and heavy white plates, and a respectable line in pâtés and *rillettes* are there to take away as well as to eat in. Diners will be offered such fare as *tripes à la mode de Caen*, *tête de veau* or *tournedos Rossini* rather than the pan-fried spring vegetables with steamed fruits in their *coulis* of pretension that one might expect from more fashionable eateries. One eats here to remember railway holidays chugging through a less sophisticated France in less demanding times. Lots of choice on lots of set menus at €16–30. €€€

AUX MOULES GP 34 rue de Béthune ♀ 237 H6 ❷ ✆ 03 20 57 12 46 www.auxmoules.com ⛟ Rihour Ⓜ Métro 2 to Gare Lille Flandres then line 1 to Rihour, where rue de la Vieille Comédie leads to rue de Béthune

No surprises here – the menu pays lip service to other tastes, but the speciality of the house is *moules*, either *marinières* or in beer, in big pots or small bowls, with or without *frites*. Mussels by name and mussels by the bucket load. When the establishment first opened its doors in 1930 the set menu was four francs; these days a *moules* meal will cost around €18. Famous for boasting the highest pile of mussel shells stacked up on the pavement outside the restaurant during the Braderie festivities each September, the place is dominated by a huge mural of the heyday of the *plat du jour*. Waiters are either young and chirpy or lifers who can recall prices in 'old' old money! Great for late lunches on Sunday afternoon, or mid-afternoon *crêpes* during a shopping excursion through the pedestrianised streets south of the place du Général de Gaulle. Leave room for the house rhubarb tart at lunchtime or the massive éclair for self-indulgence at any hour. €€

OMNIA 9 rue Esquermoise 237 H5 03 20 57 55 66 www.omnia-restaurant. com Rihour Métro 2 to Gare Lille Flandres & line 1 to Rihour, then walk along rue Roisin into rue de Pas
Over 150 years ago, this was a dance hall, *café-concert*. Then, the dancing girls extended a welcome that was a little too enthusiastic for the morals of the day, so the place became a brasserie. The affectionate nature of the personnel continued to enhance the reputation. It closed down for a while, to reopen as an art cinema in the 1960s, then the programming nudged way beyond the frontiers of art, and it closed once again to reopen as the flamboyant brasserie Taverne de l'Ecu, with the old music-hall stage restored to house the vats for the home-brewed beers served on tap in house. The next incarnation for Omnia ditched the brasserie cuisine and the alternative entrance through the old theatre foyer on rue de Pas, in favour of a rather garish 1980s-hairdressing-salon Formica frontage and a main entrance that looked more like a modern homage to its dodgy nightclub past. Finally, the place has found its niche as a cinema-themed brasserie with a more monochrome feel, although the movies inspiring the décor owe more to Hollywood's golden age than the skin flicks of the '70s. Look out for Charlie Chaplin, Rita Hayworth or Veronica Lake among the famous faces on the walls, and enjoy sundry famous last words inscribed on the panelling as you leave: Joe E Brown's classic 'Nobody's perfect!' The theatre and stage are still in place, serving mainly as a function room; the main day-to-day restaurant feels more like dining in the brasserie of a classy cinema during a film-fest. The food selection is standard brasserie choices of seafood and meats with additional ranges of burgers (including a very carb-heavy vegetarian potato burger with *frites*), pastas, risottos and stir-fries. Menus hover around €20–25 and a set lunch is €13. €€€

LE PAON D'OR 2 pl de Béthune 238 F1 03 20 42 83 52 République–Beaux Arts Métro 2 to Gare Lille Flandres, then line 1 to République
I had arrived on the place de Béthune looking forward to dropping into the popular Baignoire brasserie only to find it had closed down and reopened as yet another Monop' metro supermarket. I was not in the mood for fast food nor for the serious chef stuff nearby. And so it was that, a decade after I first published my list of favourite tables, I finally discovered Le Paon D'Or on the corner of the rue de l'Hôpital Militaire. This is surely the least flamboyant of the *ancien régime* of trad brasseries in the Art Deco pedestrian quarter of town. Unlike so many of its sisters, this conventional brasserie has not been tempted too far into pimping

its heritage into a glamorous version of the past. Within, textbook lines of yellowed walls, Deco glass ceilings and blue-and-white tiles on square pillars. Classic without being copycat Flo. Good, honest food is served inside and out in the traditional manner by a team of young professional waiters, who carry off the house polo shirts with the fleet-footedness of youth and the demeanour of much older men wearing starched white apron, shirt and bow tie. The clue to authenticity is the note on the menu that if you order *andouillette Saint Amande* sausage or steak *haché* you should expect to wait longer for your meal, since food is minced and prepared to order. That and the fact that the menu standards are ham on the bone and steaks both bovine and chevaline, and there are platters galore of Flemish meats. Good salads and the local favourites such as *tarte Maroilles*, with the concession to modern and international dietary requirements being egg or salmon options instead of plain ham in the *Welsh-frites*. Some pasta dishes, salads and a *parmentier* (shepherd's pie) are on a more limited menu served between mealtimes, since the restaurant stays open from morning until midnight, though the midweek's full lunch is available between 11.30 and 14.30, when the big round plates are filled with food. But the menu offers the option of double-sized portions for heartier appetites and those with concrete stents in their arteries. €€

LES TROIS BRASSEURS 22 pl de la Gare ♀ 237 K6 ⓰ ↘ 03 20 06 46 25 ⓶ www. les3brasseurs.com 🚉 Gare Lille Flandres ⓶ Walk along av le Corbusier (or take métro 2) to Gare Lille Flandres & pl de la Gare

Flanders is famed for its beers – whatever you do you must try at least one of the region's distinctive flavours. Many local *artisanales* beers are made in the traditional method, and some larger breweries offer guided tours and tastings for the public. As for me, I stay in central Lille and always pay a visit to Les Trois Brasseurs opposite the old Lille Flandres station. The director of Pelforth – the commercial brewery behind the Pelican lagers favoured by Calais trippers – created this genuine brasserie. Monsieur Bonduel decided to get back to brewing basics, and we all have cause to be grateful to him. It was the welcome I found here that first drew me to Lille, and I will never cease to be thankful. The clientele ranges from solo business types at the bar to groups of friends, locals and visitors. The bar staff are rarely less than convivial, but the waiters never less than harassed. In this always-packed bar-restaurant the only beers served are those brewed in copper vats on the premises. For €4.50 buy a *palette* – a tasting tray of four small glasses of the various home brews, the *blonde, brune, ambrée* and Blanche de Lille, the refreshing bitter-sweet thirst quencher ideally served with a slice of lemon. This tasting tray is the best way to get to know the beers of Lille. March and Christmas see special seasonal beers added to the range. The menu is excellent northern home cooking: rabbit stews, roasts and the cholesterol-packed *Welsh*: a bowl of melted cheese, ham and beer with a slice of bread and chips. If you are feeling really adventurous, try the beer tart or beer sorbet! Set-menu deals are the best value at around €14–20, as are the house *flammekeuche*, and the daily special, such as marrowbone or a *carbonnade*, is always reasonably priced. A range of promotional combinations can be found on the blackboards or in the newspaper-style menus. Otherwise budget at €25 and you won't go far wrong. The sister restaurant next door serves the same food in a more traditional bistro setting, but I like to dine among the dark wood and bright copper of this convivial and very special brewery. The house beers may be bought to take home by the bottle or *tonnelet* (mini-barrel), a useful souvenir on a Sunday when the Euralille shops are closed. €€

RESTAURANTS

L'ADRESSE 34 rue des Bouchers ♀ 237 G4 ❶ ☏ 03 59 89 66 33 🚊 Rihour ⊕ Métro 2 to Gare Lille Flandres then line 1 to Rihour, then pass the tourist office & it's right on to rue de l'Hôpital Militaire, cross pl de l'Arsenal to rue des Bouchers; alternatively, take the Navette Vieux Lille almost full circle & step off at rue des Bouchers

It stands to reason that if a burger bar were to open on rue des Bouchers, there would be no polystyrene packaging within a hundred paces. And so it is here, where a simple beef patty with a lettuce leaf, gherkin and slice of processed cheese simply would not *coupe le moutarde*. Not if punters are going to shell out €14–19 for a burger made with quality breads. The eponymous house sandwich here has cod topped with Munster cheese, asparagus, spinach and a hollandaise sauce, and the Rustique burger matches the beef with Mimolette cheese, soft fruits and roasted Mediterranean vegetables. Lunchtime sees the 'BBC' deal (this stands for Burger, Boisson, Café) with one of three burgers, cold drink and an espresso for €18. During the week, there is a

> *"A simple beef patty with a lettuce leaf, gherkin and slice of processed cheese simply would not coupe le moutarde."*

conventional side to the menu, with a bun-free fish and meat dish to choose (two starters, two mains and two desserts). But the house speciality is the gourmet burger and, on Saturdays, it reigns supreme. Do not expect the automatic 'fries with that' accompaniment. The kitchen chooses the default 'side' according to the style of the burger. Thus, a *choucroute*-based winter warmer will be served with simple steamed potato; the Parmentier comes with mashed potato; the Parisian with a honeyed and baked half-Camembert cheese; and as for the celebrated Rustique, roasted apricots and bacon. Since patron Frédéric Parois used to run a wine bar, there is an excellent selection of wine by the glass. €€€

L'ASSIETTE DU MARCHE ⓥ 61 rue de la Monnaie ♀ 237 H2 ❹ ☏ 03 20 06 83 61 🖥 www.assiettedumarche.com ⏰ closed lunchtime Sat & Mon, all day Sun & holidays ⊕ Bus 50 to Lion d'Or

Venture away from the cobbled streets around the Musée de l'Hospice Comtesse into the sedate courtyard of a townhouse that was, once upon a time, Louis XIV's royal mint in the city and the building that gave the street its name. In our time, the *maison particulière* has a more modern tradition as a restaurant and the newest incumbent is yet another scion of the Proye family who hold court at the celebrated A l'Huîtrière (pages 100–1). The cuisine *chez* Thomas Proye is something of an *assiette* from many *marchés* with talents and tricks culled from all six corners of France. If the regional or fashionable food terminology is too obscure, just ask your waiter to interpret. The *carte* wryly acknowledges the ephemeral nature of trendy menu-speak. Nothing obscure about the ingredients: hearty halibut roasted with mustard and a Valenciennes *jarret* in beer were on the weekly menu when first we checked the place out. Flavours may not always have lived up to the excellent presentation on an initial visit, but on encouragement from some readers

7

(mailbag has been evenly split on this one) we tried again and relished a starter of Camembert with black cherries and dessert of pan-fried pineapple and ginger *mille feuille*, the goal of fusion now comfortably attained. As for the wine list, it is a true *tour de France*. Pay €19 for two courses or €24 for three on the set menu, lunch and evening. Grazing free-range nudged the bill towards €35 a head before we started on the wine. €€€

LE BARBIER QUI FUME ⓥ 69 rue de la Monnaie ♥ 237 H2 ⑩ ✆ 03 20 06 99 35
🏠 www.le-barbier-lillois.com ⏰ closed Sun evening 🚌 Bus 50 to Lion d'Or

Don't let the name make your heart sink, as for once this *barbier qui fume* is not selling refills for e-ciggies. The smoking here is strictly culinary. All the meats at this butcher's dining room are smoked over beech wood. However, the wood that greets the visitor is not the well-chosen range of shavings that create the subtle fragrance and flavours of the meat, but a fine panelled salon of an elegant butcher's shop on the corner of rue de la Monnaie and the eclectic rue Pétérinck. Chandeliers hang above the grand Flemish dresser and a counter of prime cold cuts, each vacuum-wrapped to be taken home. For the visitor, the main attraction would be the main dining room (formerly known as Le Barbier Lillois), with its ostentatious woodwork against blackened brick walls and an à la carte menu for the reduction of willpower and restraint. Might you opt for *souris d'agneau* with rosemary and thyme, or may your taste in lamb run to a *carré d'agneau* with honey and cloves, ripened in the smoke house for six hours. My friends speak softly of a moist and vulnerably pink centre encased in the sweetest caramelised crust. No-one bats an eyelid at the €24 price tag. If you are among those who believe that meat is not meat unless it is scarlet and comes from a cow, then slices of 14-hour-cold-smoked beef with a roasted, unpasteurised Camembert and side dish of walnut salad might float your ark without upsetting your bank manager – a main course at less than €20. A midweek dish of the day is around €11, or served as a mini menu complete with drink and dessert for €17. Otherwise, true carnivores surrender to the wild pleasures to be found à la carte. The restaurant serves robust red wines to accompany the mains, and has a selection of sugary *cassonade*-type desserts to round off the meal. €€€€

LE BLOEMPOT ⓥ 22 rue des Bouchers ♥ 237 G4 ⑭ 🏠 www.bloempot.fr 🚊 Rihour
🚇 Métro 2 to Gare Lille Flandres & line 1 to Rihour, then pass the tourist office & it's right into rue de l'Hôpital Militaire, cross pl de l'Arsenal to rue des Bouchers; alternatively, take the Navette Vieux Lille almost full circle & step off on to rue des Bouchers

You don't phone to book a table here. You pray. Or, if your faith is not strong enough, you go to the website. Food lovers check the online reservations and cancellation pages daily in the hope of getting to dine at Lille's must-go address before the ageing process really starts to kick in. At the time of typing, there is no weekend evening table free for the next three months, though there are four chairs still going begging on a Thursday lunchtime in three weeks' time. Mind you, they could be snapped up by the time I've booked my Eurostar ticket to Lille. Yes, it is that popular. I have tried to get a last-minute (ie: a week in advance) table for two in March, April, September and October but had no luck.

This is the restaurant that turned the dining map of Lille on its head and brought the world and its dinner date to rue des Bouchers. Just about the last street to qualify as Vieux Lille, the rue des

Bouchers has been home to an eclectic range of modestly fashionable eateries over the 15 years or so that I've been idling with intent in the quarter. Just a bit farther than you'd like to walk from the métro or bus stop, the road has seen a succession of trendy dining rooms, each with smart brick walls, smart artworks and far smarter habitués, which stayed their two or three years before passing the tenancy on to the next cutting edge cook whose hairdresser's scissors were even sharper than the Sabatier knives in the kitchen. Then along came Florent Ladeyn, the chef whose main restaurant 30 minutes out of town had France's leading food writers sitting up and begging for more. Rather than set up another fine-dining *palais de gastronomie*, Ladeyn decided to follow his heart and open a simple Flemish country restaurant in the heart of the city.

A graduate of the television food-fetish generation, Florent Ladeyn followed up his success on the reality TV series *Top Chef* by opening his celebrated Auberge du Vert Mont in the Monts de Flandre. Hailed by the food bible *Gault et Milau* as France's best young chef north of Paris, in 2011 Ladeyn could have moved anywhere in the country, or even the world, to take his career to the next level. Instead, he spent two years planning the Bloempot project (the word is Flemish for flowerpot), a simple kitchen-garden canteen in Lille. All this was achieved in his mid-20s so it is no surprise that the young master chef has trained up a team even younger than himself to do the day-to-day cooking at the new restaurant – a style of cuisine he calls 'wild and creative' to be served against the industrial girders and brick backdrop of his '*Cantine Flamande!*'.

To say the scheme was successful would be an understatement. As I say, I've been able to do little more than salivate at the daily lunch menu from outside and rely on friends in town who have won the lottery of lunch to tell me about the meals that they have shared there.

The dining room is an old carpentry workshop just behind the street itself, with the outside space turned over to the essential kitchen garden for Ladeyn's young team to plunder. This is why there is no massive terrace for the dining room overspill, just the basic 40 covers that book up in the click of a mouse.

Lunch menus at €20–25 include a glass of wine, beer or soft drink and the evening sitting has three options between €35 and €50. I can't call them menus because they are not. Come here in the evening for a culinary leap into the unknown. You simply tell the waiter if there is any food you cannot stand or if you have an allergy or intolerance, then trust is handed over to the chef. The meal is tailored to your taste buds. The first time you discover what is on the menu is when the plate is placed in front of you. Expect some full-flavoured root vegetables and wonderfully ripe fruits to tickle the main attractions. A recent salt cod *brandade* came out of the kitchen with the claret hues of organic beetroot giving an unexpected sweetness to the creamed fish. If you cannot get this particular table on the rue des Bouchers, have no fear. You will not go hungry. From burger bars to a literary café to bistros galore, the street now rivals rue de Gand as a food destination in its own right. €€€€

Eating and Drinking RESTAURANTS

7

IN BOCCA AL LUPO ⑫ 1 rue des Vieux Murs ♀ 237 H3 ⑩ ☎ 03 20 06 39 98 ☗ www.in-bocca-al-lupo.com ⏲ lunch Tue–Sun, dinner Thu–Sat ⊞ Bus 50 to Lion d'Or, then from rue de la Monnaie turn left on to rue Pétérinck

Opposite the celebrated Italian deli-palace La Bottega (page 94) stands its Latin sister. Where else would the trendy place aux Oignons crowd choose to lunch? Seriously fashionable, no linens, just shiny table tops, polished floors and comfy chairs, the atmosphere suffused with orange and inky hues. Somehow this contemporary city-centre look manages to straddle the very Flemish traditions of the quarter and the reassuringly conservative classic Italian flavours from *antipasti* to *dolci*. No anachronistic modern twists here, just *scaloppa alla Milanese* and *saltimbocca* to please the most critical *nonna* in the business. No set menu, but a budget of close to €30 per healthy appetite should suffice. €€€

LA BOTTEGA ⑫ 7b rue Pétérinck ♀ 237 H2 ⑯ ✆ 03 20 74 33 12 ⌨ www.la-bottega.com ⏰ closed Sun evening, all day Mon 🚌 Bus 50 to Lion d'Or, & from rue de la Monnaie turn left on to rue Pétérinck

For the Italians, everything is about family, so no surprise that this memorable delicatessen across the way and the restaurant In Bocca al Lupo are all run by the ubiquitous Annunzio clan. But here is the place where *la familia* makes the very best pizzas in Lille. No USA-style dough-fest; here the bases are spun and stretched to perfection and all the toppings have a provenance: ham San Daniele, Gorgonzola Guffanti, salami di Napoli. Budget €10–14 per pizza. End the meal with a cherry panna cotta or a Flemish twist on tiramisu (ie: made with *spéculoos*). €€

LA CAVE AUX FIOLES ⑫ 39 rue de Gand ♀ 237 K2 ㉗ ✆ 03 20 55 18 43 ⌨ www. lacaveauxfioles.com ⏰ closed lunch Sat, all day Sun & holidays 🚌 Bus to Lion d'Or, then cross pl Louise de Bettignies to rue de Gand

Eccentric, eclectic and the warmest welcome in town, happiness comes à la carte at the top of the dear old rue de Gand. Whenever I close my eyes and think of eating out in Lille, it is La Cave aux Fioles that springs to mind and, judging from my postbag since first writing about the place, many readers feel the same. Follow the cobbles to the far end of the old town to the honey glow from the windows of a warm and friendly dining room. What looks like the front door to the restaurant remains resolutely locked, but enter the unmarked door to the side of the windows, and pass through a narrow and dark entrance hall lined with posters from legendary Lille festivals past to reach the central covered courtyard between two houses. All around are the husks of 17th- and 18th-century homes, paneless casement windows opening out to the brick, stone and cobbled court. Inside, tables are scattered through the various rooms, candlelight enhances the brickwork, and the trad jazz sounds mellow the scene further. In winter a roaring fire concentrates the cosiness even more but, whatever the season, the true warmth comes from the welcoming and hospitable staff: from the barmen who serve the house cocktail Fiole d'Amour (grapefruit, gin and grenadine), to the waitresses who patiently wait as you agonise over choices. The house *foie gras de canard* comes with a surprise tipple, but the fresh mushrooms stuffed with Roquefort sound fabulous. Then again, what about a soup of mussels with leeks? Will tonight be the night for the local *waterzooï d'homard* or should one indulge in strips of goose *magret* dripping with a honey sauce? Whichever dish wins, the garnish and vegetable accompaniment varies '*selon l'humeur du chef*'! By dessert I have usually rediscovered decisiveness, and I forego such sirens as *gâteau au chocolat de la Tante Mazo* in favour of the remarkable *délicatesse du Nord* – the bitterest ice cream I have ever tasted, blending chicory with *genièvre* gin. Although there are 20 tables here, such is the artful design that one never notices more than one's immediate neighbours and the sense of privacy is supreme. The full menu comes to €35 or €49; lunchtime *plat du jour* is just €10. If a day's shopping on the rickety paved streets has played havoc with your calf muscles, don't be daunted by the thought of the trek up the rue de Gand: the restaurant's private London taxi will collect you from your hotel. €€€

LE CHANTECLER 22 rue Nicolas Leblanc ♀ 238 F2 ➌ ❧ 03 20 57 48 19 ⓦ www.le-chantecler.com ⓒ closed lunch Sat, all day Sun & Mon 🚇 République–Beaux Arts ⓜ Métro 2 to Gare Lille Flandres, then line 1 to République–Beaux Arts, then cross the pl de la République to rue Nicolas Leblanc

Opposite the celebrated Aux Ephérites (pages 98–9) is a tiny shopfront bistro with an excellent two-course lunch menu for €15. The glorious Art Deco stained-glass window of a cock crowing at sunrise illuminates the little dining room, with a vintage radio carrying the period theme inside. Ask the locals and some will tell you they come here for the legendary *frites maison* (seriously quality fries it has to be said, uneven irregular chunks and strips, prepared with the attention to detail that the chef learnt studying under the doyen of French cuisine, Paul Bocuse). Most of the €11–14 main courses come with a choice of the *frites*, or a jacket potato, rice or the veg *du jour* (cauliflower *vinaigrette* proves a zingy, refreshing and unexpected summer choice). Starters and desserts priced at around €6 at the time of writing, so budget around €50 per couple, plus drinks if you go for the fully liberated experience. Duck is a speciality of the house and the kidneys in mustard sauce are very popular. Farm-reared chicken with a Natua sauce and the increasingly high profile *lieu noir* were on the lunch deals when I was last in town following fishy and artichoke-based starters. The apple crumble has a *spéculoos* topping, but a traditional fruit salad is a refreshingly light option. If you don't book, or turn up at the start of service, you may not get a table. Lunchtime is very popular with locals rather than visitors and the inevitable foodie guide trekkers. The young chef Philippe Nonet is no stranger to the media; his saffron twist to the traditional platter of *moules* from Mont St Michel caught the eye of local TV crews in the run up to the 2012 Braderie. In 2014, Nonet told reporters that the dish was inspired by his Lyonnais mentor Bocuse and confessed that of all the dishes he prepares at the Chantecler, the *moules au safran* were his Proustian *Madeleine* memories. €€

CLAIR DE LUNE ⓥ 50 rue de Gand ♀ 237 K2 ㉗ ❧ 03 20 51 46 55 ⓦ www.restaurant-leclairdelune.fr ⓒ closed lunch Sat, all day Tue ⓜ Bus 50 to Lion d'Or, then cross pl Louise de Bettignies to rue de Gand

Early visits opened the eyes and mouths of my friends to the potential of *mignon* of pork in an arabica coffee sauce, halibut in cider, and a somewhat scrummy *œuf cocotte* with smoked trout and leeks. Recent forays have only slightly reined in invention and concentrated on bringing to the fore the essential ingredients, whether a supreme of guinea fowl or that old standby, trout with almonds. My many months each year in the Languedoc port of Marseillan, birthplace of the king of vermouths, means I must mention the starter of *escargot* spring rolls with leek and Noilly Prat, and my family connection to Normandy leads me to pass on the news that the quail here is cooked in calvados! Desserts continue to comfort. Bread-and-butter pudding is what *pain perdu* is all about, only the bread here is brioche and the spices heartily northern – and, with that on the menu, who needs the ubiquitous tiramisu and crumbles – those parvenu puds that have all but elbowed France's native *tatins* into obscurity from Lille to Marseille. Though some have claimed the service to be brusque, I found nothing to complain about. Unpretentious staff did not bat an eyelid when I opted for a couple of starters one evening, having overindulged elsewhere at lunchtime, and paid me the same courtesies as others pigging out on the €26 or €32 menus. €€€

CLEMENT MAROT 16 rue de Pas 237 H4 03 20 57 01 10 www.clement-marot.com closed evenings Sun and Mon Rihour Métro 2 to Gare Lille Flandres then line 1 to Rihour, then walk along rue Roisin to rue de Pas

It took me four years of eating and treating in Lille before I found myself crossing the threshold of Clément Marot's dining room near the upfront terraces of his louder neighbours. I could hardly wait four weeks before returning. Suffice to say, this is the type of restaurant we all hope to stumble upon in our journeys across France. The main dining room is somewhat post-war traditional in decorative style: commemorative plates on a rack above panelled booths; heavy plate ice buckets and tureens on well-polished surfaces; certificates alongside framed paintings of favourite holiday spots; and a waitress in black skirt, white blouse and lace apron hovering by the champagne magnums and long-stemmed cut flowers. The other room next door is more modern and presumably favoured by the business-lunch brigade. In the older room, I settled down to wallow in traditional dishes and investigate the wine list. The price of the à la carte menu varies, depending on whether you choose a half-bottle of wine or Tattinger on ice. I quickly discovered that recipes as described on the menu are not written on tablets of stone. A lively chat with the waiter, chef or (if you are lucky) patron brings plenty of alternative suggestions. The signature catch of *sandre* on the menu on my first visit was intended to be prepared with sesame and a *coulis de poivrons*. I needed little persuasion to agree to an alternative version using Marot's hallmark flavour *chicorée*, a locally produced delicacy from the sandy soil of coastal Flanders that the chef uses in dishes from the main course to the *bavarois*. Inspiration! The smoky, coffee-like flavour of the sauce complemented the fish's crisp topping of sesame seed. I was equally glad to have been nudged away from my original thoughts of a terrine starter in favour of a *salade de poisson en escabèche*. This turned out to be a wonderfully old-fashioned and fabulously sharp presentation of sardines marinated in the house champagne vinegar (Marot eschews the balsamic), with a dash of lemon juice and thyme on local leaves to provide a truly kicking salad. Lovers of game should find their own nirvana here. In 2014, the menu was boasting a rum and raisin pheasant starter at €22 and the classic venison dish *carré de biche grand veneur* at just under €40. Local produce is first choice wherever possible. Thus poultry comes from the town of Licques where free-range turkeys dine on corn and grain to become the north's answer to the legendary fowl of Bresse, and where, once a year, before Christmas, the mayor and corporation, and *confrères de la dinde*, march the town's flocks to one of the great gastronomic fairs of the region. One such fowl may be found even on the €24 midday two-course menu or the evening €30 *prix-fixe* – a trio of choices offered for each starter, main and dessert. Remarkable value.

If, like me, you cannot decide on a dessert, just let the chef-patron choose for you. I may well never eat another crème brûlée as long as I live. It was pure cream, which still breathed the air of the dairy, and was quite simply the best I had tasted this side of childhood. The welcome from all the restaurant team was second to none, and hospitality seems to be the key to this place's discreet success. The 'be our guest' approach even extends to the wine list. Rather than compromise with a half-bottle of a lesser vintage, we were encouraged to buy a full bottle with the assurance that, at the end of the meal, staff will wrap up the rest of the bottle to be enjoyed – as the wine list has it – at your own table in the comfort of your own home. Cold winter evenings are ideal for indulging oneself on the grander menu at €41, or throwing budget to the wind and going à la carte. €€€€€

LE COMPOSTELLE GP 4 rue Saint-Etienne 237 H4 ⑪ 03 28 38 08 30 www. lecompostelle.fr ⚑ Rihour ⬛ Métro 2 to Gare Lille Flandres then line 1 to Rihour, then take the rue Roisin into rue de Pas & right into rue Saint-Etienne

'Make yourself at home' is the unspoken invitation at this great big popular restaurant just beside the main square of Lille. The building (a staging post on the pilgrims' route to Santiago de Compostela) may date from the 16th century and boast the only Renaissance façade in Lille, but the refurbished décor is the very model of a modern appreciation of *temps perdus*. Alain Roussiez has glassed in the open courtyard and created a warren of colourful dining rooms on each floor. The bar and the Blue Room are my favourites, being packed with real bookcases – not stuffed with imposing leather-bound tomes, but well-thumbed paperbacks stacked and piled at random. The urge to browse and dip when waiting for friends is irresistible. Other salons are Provençal pink and theatrical yellow. As to the kitchen: at best imaginative and thrilling, otherwise serviceable fare with an ambitious blend of regional and national dishes; little to offend the palate. Sometimes I've found nothing so exciting as to distract me from my conversation. At others, flavour and texture have won through and the meal itself has fuelled debate and memories. Set lunch from under €20. Menus at €30 and €36 (though with many dishes incurring a €5 supplement), but what to choose? My advice would be to stick to the *cuisine du nord*: a cold North Sea *hochepot* of fish, then the *noix de veau* prepared with melted Maroilles cheese. A refreshing sorbet made from the *genièvre* gin from nearby Houlle makes for a sparky finale to the meal. There is even an imaginative vegetarian alternative (albeit à la carte) working out at €33 for two interesting and flavoursome courses. €€€

LE COURT DEBOUT GP 24 rue du Court Debout 238 G1 ④ m 06 34 55 06 76 www. restaurant-lecourtdebout.com ① closed Sun & Mon ⚑ République–Beaux Arts ⬛ Métro 2 to Gare Lille Flandres then line 1 to République, then walk to the rear of pl de Béthune & right on to rue de l'Hôpital Militaire to pl Vieux Marché au Chevaux

Just before the shopping district decants into the more pensive arts quarter is a tiny square on the edge of rue du Molinel. Once the city's horse market, now the trade is in musical instruments. On one corner is a shop window filled with elegant violins, next door a keyboard and piano shop, across the square an array of accordions and drums. On sunny days, the one nonmusical corner sees the Café Citoyen spreading tables out on to the cobbles. This is the start of the rue du Court Debout, an unlikely setting for peaceful gastronomy, so close to so many fast-food outlets and the buskers and beggars of place Béthune. For here is the new home of Christophe Scherpereel, celebrated chef to presidents and ambassadors. Having served his time with the legendary Bernard Loiseau in Burgundy and at Paris's landmark Tour d'Argent, Scherpereel worked his flourishes at the Palais de l'Elysée before opening his discreet eatery in Lille, where he had originally started his career.

Here, the menu is determined by one factor alone: the market. The most popular formula is the *menu du marché* chalked up on a board each morning. Prices start with a simple *plat du jour* at under €20, to two courses at just under €30 and three courses for around €6 more. Also around €30, you may have the fish or meat dish of the day with a *café gourmand* – surprisingly good value. Those whose budgets are led by their taste buds should trust in the kitchen for the *menus surprises* at €60, €80 and €100 (the price reflects whether the meal is served 'dry' or with a range of wines or champagnes to suit each course). This option is for all guests at the table and it is up to your waiter and the chef himself to decide what will be presented at each of the three or five courses. Food reflects the season and the region, so in early autumn the main menu of the day includes creamed pumpkin soup with lobster ravioli; earlier in the year, sea bass with asparagus was the blackboard suggestion. The décor within is understated northern dining room, light and classic smart. Outside, the terrace garden is a virtual salon in its own right, with tables for two and four, each within a parterre of its own, surrounded by a low box hedge. Lovely on a sunny day. €€€€€

L'ECUME DES MERS ⒼⓅ 10 rue de Pas ♀ 237 H4 ⑪ ℡ 03 20 54 95 40 ⅆ www.ecume-des-mers.com ⓞ closed Sun evenings & most of Aug ⌂ Rihour ⓢ Métro 2 to Gare Lille Flandres then line 1 to Rihour, then take rue Roisin to rue de Pas

Refurbished in pleasure-port seaside blues and framed Poseidonesque mosaic, the newest aspect of the restaurant is the menu, the entire *carte* printed daily to reflect the catch of the day. There are a few non-fishy items on the menu, but one comes here to taste the sea. At L'Ecume des Mers, they do what they do and they do it well, and what they do is prepare freshly caught fish in the classic manner. Nothing too clever: a *tartare* of the oft-overlooked haddock with olive oil, raw sardine in a tarragon marinade, a cold monkfish *bouillabaisse* perhaps, as a change to the standards, but traditional favourites follow the seasons. On a grey day go for an *aïoli* of *morue* or a warming and filling *choucroute* with halibut, smoked haddock and salmon, or perhaps curried tuna with spices from the French island of La Réunion. When your credit card and whim decides to leap like a lustful salmon, push your financial boat out and order turbot or lobster. A mix of well-to-do couples and business foursomes choose to dine indoors; a younger element basks on the pavement terrace outside sharing platters of oysters from the iced counter, be they *fines claires* or *belons*. Eavesdroppers with a cultural bent might spot illustrious neighbour Jean-Claude Casadesus, director of the Orchestre National de Lille, in conversation with a world-renowned soloist. From every other table comes the reassuring clink-clank of *glaçons* in well-stocked ice buckets ringing against a crisp Chablis or a *demi* Pouilly-Fumé from the fairly priced wine list. Oh, and the worst-kept secret in town is that the reason the fish is so good here is that everything the kitchen knows it learned from A l'Huîtrière (pages 100–1). Here, it is Antoine and Elvire who uphold the good name of the legendary Proye family. Midweek-only menus are €18 at lunchtime and €25 in the evenings, otherwise make sure you've a good €60 or more in your pocket or on your credit limit. €€€€

AUX EPHERITES 17 rue Nicolas Leblanc ♀ 238 F2 ① Ⓜ 09 81 31 55 24 ⅆ www.auxepherites.com ⓞ closed evenings Mon–Wed, all day Sat & Sun ⌂ République–Beaux Arts ⓢ Métro 2 to Gare Lille Flandres and line 1 to République–Beaux Arts, then cross the pl de la République to rue Nicolas Leblanc

Since the Sébastopol restaurant closed down, on the retirement of the unmatchable genius Jean-Luc Germond, there has been a gastronomic void in the triangle between the Beaux Arts and the places Sébastopol and Philippe le Bon. No-one could leap in with the sort of plates that seduced the Michelin and *Gault et Millau* inspectors, so food lovers welcomed a modest little dining room that serves mainly lunches as an alternative to more flamboyant haute cuisine. Bistronomie is the buzzword for classy inventive dishes to be enjoyed at simple tables, far from the starched linen and polished cruets of the established addresses. Here, chef Alexandre Suergiu comes up with four starters, four mains and four desserts each day and charges just €18 for the meal, or €13–16 for a main. Chalked upon the long blackboard will be haddock, veal or *bavette* of beef and the like with mashed, crushed or creamed potatoes on the mains; crumbles, lemon meringue tart, chocolate mousse or (in strawberry season) a smackingly piquant *soupe des fraises* on the dessert list. Good comfort food, but presented with flair on Formica-style bistro tables in a narrow dining room, with bare walls and etched windows – a seriously understated address that could be taken for an insurance office by the unwary passer-by. Reservation nigh on essential. €€

LE FLAM'S   8 rue de Pas 237 H4 03 20 54 18 38 www.flams.fr Rihour
Métro 2 to Gare Lille Flandres & line 1 to Rihour, then take rue Roisin into rue de Pas

Welcome to the home of the *flammekeuche* – that not-quite-pizza, not-quite-*crêpe* adopted speciality of the city. The fad has long left its Alsatian roots to become a social must here in Flanders. We are talking about a large, thin, dough base spread with either savoury or sweet toppings; the former based around cheeses, mushrooms and ham, the latter the blend of fruit, sweets and *eau de vie* toppings that one finds in any *crêperie*. Cut out a square of your 'flam', roll it into a cigar shape and hold it with your fingers to munch over a chilled beer and a heated discussion about life, love and politics. Lunchtimes, the place is filled with office workers and shoppers taking advantage of the special deals (a savoury and a sweet *flammekeuche* with a 25cl glass of *bière blonde*) and menus starting at €12.40. Evenings, it's a regular student hangout, 50m from the Grand' Place, with groups of friends sharing a selection of flams, picnic-style. After dark, budget €20 to feel replete. In good weather, step across the road to the summer terrace; in winter stay cosy indoors among the warm brickwork. Quick snack is only €7.10 on the express menu. €€

LE FOSSILE   60 rue Saint-Etienne 237 G5 03 20 54 29 82 www.lefossile.com
 closed Sat & Sun Rihour Métro 2 to Gare Lille Flandres & line 1 to Rihour, then take rue Roisin to rue de Pas & left along rue Saint-Etienne

Many years ago, I knew a restaurant in Paris that never bothered with menus. They had only ever served one dish as long as anyone could recall and it was that or nothing! I was reminded of the old place when I came to revisit La Coquille, a favourite address of many readers of this guide, the dining room sandwiched between the Nouveau Siècle building and the back entrance to the Novotel. Alas, that last relic of the realm of the barnyard – very much the country of clucking and grain – had shut its doors for the last time and in its place stood Le Fossile – a newcomer to the city, but a restaurant with its own 35-year pedigree in Alsace and a worthy successor to the previous tenants of this fine old red-brick building.

The reminiscences were ignited by the house speciality, or perhaps that should read the house obsession. Steak is served here. Steak, steak or steak is the choice on the menu. Unlike the Parisian table of sepia-tinted memory, there is an option. Either go for *onglet* (the house cut) in any of three guises, or choose a *filet* steak (more of which follows). A friend of mine whose carnivore credentials would satisfy both Darwin and Tennyson salivated at a repast red in tooth and claw, and pronounced the house speciality of *onglet à l'echalotte* triumphant. The beef may also be served with mushrooms or on its own. The *filet* is presented in all the classic formats, *maître d'hôtel* or with Roquefort cheese, mushrooms, cognac, pepper and a choice of wild mushroom sauces. Mind you, after 22.30, these alternatives are dropped from the menu, as is the only other main course dish, *tournedos Rossini*. As you might expect, the wine list has practically adopted Bordeaux citizenship, and our first snuffling through the pages yielded a 2000 Chateau Beau Site *cru bourgeois exception* St Estèphe and a 2002 Margaux. The various steak main courses straddle the €23 boundary and the starters (very *escargot, très canard*, seriously *foie gras*) range from €8 to €17. Desserts are equally classical at around the €8 mark, but only a true trencherman will get that far. Still my wimpy *côterie* has not discovered the 'secret' pudding, the identity only revealed at the table. When pushing the boat out and loosening the belt buckle, do indulge in a glass of Armagnac. I only know one other eatery with anywhere near such a selection of *digestifs* and that is to be found over 1,000km south of Lille! The Fossile Armagnac archive ranges from 1885 to the turn of the millennium and features in the *Guinness Book of Records*. €€€€

HERMITAGE GANTOIS AND ESTAMINET GANTOIS 224 rue de Paris ♀ 238 H2 ⑤
⚲03 20 85 30 30 🚊 Mairie de Lille 🚇 Métro 2 to Mairie de Lille, then walk westward along av du Président Kennedy & turn left on to rue de Paris
Chef Sébastien Blanchet founded the showcase restaurant of the magnificently renovated Hermitage Gantois (page 58) as well as its sister Estaminet Gantois next door (entrance in rue Malpart), so you can be sure of the same sharp eyes supervising the shared kitchen whether you want to spend more than €40 in the one or less than half that amount in the other. In the flagship dining room (itself as much an occasion as a location as the rest of the gloriously refurbished building), part with €50 for the three-course menu, or €40 for just two dishes (not served at the weekend). Evening set menus with wine can nudge up to €100. Lille's fervour for fish is well served with a starter of mango-enlivened perch fillets that demonstrates a flirtatious talent for matchmaking, followed by a classically and simply presented turbot. Or you may start your meal with foie gras on a carpaccio of seasonal asparagus with a sharp citrus *coulis*. Alternatively, a braised *jarret de veau* emphasises the simplicity of prime ingredients treated with respect. Desserts head towards the comfort-food route with scintillating *clafoutis* and traditional *tatins* given good menu space and plenty of attention from pastry chefs with the lightest of touches. All this, and a sympathetically selected wine list. Next door at the Estaminet Gantois, the bill of fare reflects the history of the working-class quarter, home of this great 4-star *luxe* hotel. *Rillettes* and terrines, *flamiche au Maroilles, hochepot* and the spoils of *la chasse* are offered at €13 for a main course, €19 for two courses or €26 for three, including coffee. €€€€ and €€€ respectively.

A L'HUÎTRIERE ⚋ 3 rue des Chats Bossus ♀ 237 J3 ⑤ ⚲03 20 55 43 41 ⏚ www. huitriere.fr ⏰ closed Sun evening 🚌 Bus 10 from Gare Lille Flandres to Lion d'Or
'Absolute perfection and faultless' was the verdict of my dinner guest; I just beamed in contentment and the glow of unalloyed pleasure. The short walk past the fresh fish counters, the classic mosaics, baskets of shells and wondrous confections *en gelée* and in bottles is dappled in a maritime twilight. Once in the narrow vestibule 'twixt the domains of the fishmonger and the *maître cuisinier*, a warm welcome from the fabulously efficient and courteous staff instantly sets the standard for the evening.

In the restaurant itself all is calm, all is bright. Light wood panels; lovely wool tapestry; table appointments charming, with white and navy Limoges service atop crisp white linen. Exquisite and discreet service is attentive with no hint of intimidation. The wonders from the kitchen never fail to stimulate nor enchant. I recall an entrée of wild Scottish salmon *mi-cru mi-cuit*, lovingly prepared, briefly roasted, pan-fried and seared in spices on the outside, yet succulent and raw within and laced with a fine horseradish dressing. *Trois petites royales* revealed themselves as truffled-up seductions of leek, cabbage and petits pois: simply superb. Though this is a fish restaurant, honourable mention must go to the *escalope de foie gras de canard* in a *pot-au-feu de légumes nouveaux*. The main course varies with the catch and the season, and according to the taste of the diner. Our waiter regarded my companion's request for a variation on the menu suggestion as a challenge rather than an affront, and took a genuine delight in consulting with the kitchen to create the perfect dish to meet a customer's exacting tastes. John Dory roasted in its skin with asparagus *meunière* with *vinaigrette au beurre* was proof, if such were ever needed, that the sea is no poor relation to the pasture. The *sorbet à la fleur de bière* is the northern answer to a *trou normand* and clears the appetite for game.

Impeccable desserts – try *mi-gratin*, *mi-soufflé* of wild woodland strawberries – and pastries, chocolates and petits fours are simply heavenly. A wisely compiled wine list included a smooth and refined Château Moulin Riche *2ème cru* Bordeaux St Julienne decanted in time for the main course. Budget a good €100 per head, or €138 for a seasonally truffled or lobstered seven-course gastronomic menu. Three-course business lunch is €45. There's also a new oyster bar for more modest munching.

Since my last visit, A l'Huîtrière may have lost her Michelin star, but the place still has its loyal fans. At around 18.00, ladies who have spent the afternoon window-shopping will commandeer the two or three little tables outside the front door. Wearing pashminas or sunglasses depending on the season, they order glasses of chilled chardonnay, designer handbags on the tables, giving way to dinky little plates of oysters for the *apéro* between life as one of *les girls* and the evening role of the good wife. €€€€€

L'INTRIGUE 44 rue de la Halle ♀ 237 G1 ⑩ ☏ 03 20 74 28 60 ⊙ closed Sun ⊕ Bus 50 from Lille Europe to Les Bataliers, then from sq Grimonprez, turn into rue de la Halle & the restaurant is opposite the Halle au Sucre at the junction with rue des Archives

Intrigue is well named: darkened windows from the street, a first dining room smart and neat for a respectable public display of acquaintance, and the back room where even lunching businessmen look as though they might be having an affair. Here is low lighting, a huge parody of the sort of clock that might have been designed for trysting and, on all sides, secret staircases and arches in the brickwork to suggest forbidden rendezvous after coffee. Only the wipe-clean vinyl tablecloths in this room bring an unwelcome quasi-sordid addition to the mock-furtive feel.

With a midday menu at under €20 and à la carte at around double that, this intrigue is certainly not the exclusive preserve of sugar daddies and their gold-diggers. As befits an address where the inappropriate partnership is practically the *raison d'être*, the menu is no *mariage blanc* of inappropriate and doomed flavours – instead we encounter unexpected and unlikely bedfellows ripe with ulterior motives, and throbbing with unexpected passions: peanut and foie gras crème brûlée, mussels with lemon grass and coconut milk, sweet and sour steak, and even the North Sea's resident paragon cod here cross-dresses in banana leaves.

Staider options imply respectability. The hamburger with non-startling rosemary potatoes and guinea fowl with sage are probity *sur plat*. But maybe they are not quite as naïve as they seem. The tuna *à la plancha* with salsa and cereal turned out to be a connivance of north Africa, Latin America and a dash of what classic crooners used to call 'Old Italee'!

Since almost all my fellow diners this Monday noon had already opted for the tuna, I followed suit and was not disappointed. The side dish of creamed mashed polenta arrived first, with the main platter just a discreet moment or two later. If the mangetouts belied their promise and were too overcooked to be considered anything other than garnish, the fish itself was perfection, practically *à l'unilatérale*. The top was sprinkled with whole grain, flash-cooked to nearly a crisp, while the core and underside were moist, tender and so rare as to be collectable. Served on a bed of lightly parmesaned salad leaves with the side bowl of salsa. I was still fragile from a wonderful Saturday night some 36 hours earlier, and therefore was not as young as I might have been so I forwent wine, but neighbours quaffed the fruits of Languedoc with evident satisfaction.

Since I was that day merely putting a tentative toe into the waters of fine living, I listened to the litany of *desserts du jour* – a recital of original thought – and opted for the *écume d'agrumes*, since I thought it sounded fruity and guessed it might be a kinder oasis among so many grand chocolate ideals. Then the French dictionary of my subconscious threw up the translation of *écume* as froth and I was filled with dread that the most ghastly gift Britain has forced upon the world of cuisine these past few years might be presented to me – the hated 'foam' that trendy chefs like to inflict upon their acolytes, as pointless and unwelcome as frogspawn at a picnic.

But frabjous day, this chef has no tawdry chemistry set and what was presented was a scrumptious airy cream suffused with tangy citrus fruits – sublime, delicious, light; a triumph of flavour over substance, a dream. I toddled out from the contrived low-lit discretion of Intrigue into the bright, sunny Lille afternoon feeling deliciously guilty and content. €€€

LE JARDIN DU CLOÎTRE   17 quai du Wault ♀ 236 E3 ⊕ ⬊ 03 20 30 62 62 ⊕ Bus 12 to Nationale then walk along rue Nationale to sq Foch & through the square to the pond; the restaurant is on the right bank

In the business-park perpendicular atrium of the Alliance Hotel (pages 54–5) is to be found a restaurant that boasts professional service, a fine *filet mignon* in the inevitable *blanche* and the ubiquitous piano player. This is where business people from TGV business towns north, south and east of Lille meet up to discuss business policy over a jolly decent business lunch. Menus €29–33. €€€€

JOUR DE PECHE   ⓖ 2 rue de Pas ♀ 237 H5 ⊕ ⬊ 03 20 57 60 59 ⬚ www.jourdepeche.fr ⊕ closed Sun & Mon ⬚ Rihour ⊕ Métro 2 to Gare Lille Flandres & line 1 to Rihour, then along rue Roisin to rue de Pas

Around a quarter of a century ago, my family treated me to a special birthday lunch. My first ever lunch at a Michelin-starred restaurant was just along the seafront from the old port of Boulogne-sur-Mer and La Matelote was everything I wanted it to be (delicious food, imaginatively and delicately presented by charming staff in a room that allowed for a relaxing family occasion to be celebrated in comfort). The chef, Tony Lestienne, understood his fish as well as he did his diners, and it was no surprise when he expanded his empire to the neighbouring Nausicaä sea centre and aquarium, and gradually built up his main restaurant business into a fine hotel as well known as that flagship restaurant.

Now, close by Lille's more famous dynastic fish restaurant, l'Ecume des Mers, the Lestienne family has come to Lille, with this gem of an eatery tucked neatly beside some of the most established establishments in the city – this time under the eye of the next generation of the Matelote lineage, Stellio Lestienne, who grew up in his father's kitchens and honed his trade on both sides of the Channel at the Waterside Inn and Lenôtre. The family connection with the site goes back 45 years to when Lestienne Père worked in these very kitchens when they belonged to a long-established Russian restaurant, Chez Koff.

On a day-to-day basis, the estimable Jean-François Bride is in charge in the kitchen, while Benjamin Maczenko runs front of house; between them, clocking up a serious *resumé* of some of France's most noted restaurants. But all the cheering elements of that long-ago meal at the Matelote are echoed here in a room unencumbered by the impedimenta of an *étoile* or *macaron*. Almost 45 minutes into my sojourn, and well into my first course, the waiter reciting the daily specials for the 20th time to a later arrival, the head waiter retained the same sense of enthusiasm and occasion.

The lovely aroma of freshly roasted fish skin, luscious tomatoes being primped and pampered and a waft of vanilla proves a seductive first

> "The aroma of roasted fish skin, luscious tomatoes and a waft of vanilla proves a seductive first impression."

impression. Charming and accommodating dining-room staff welcome guests, who tend to be ordinary decent people who like their food out of the ordinary and with a heightened level of decency.

A shrewd wine list is almost exclusively French, but for a singular foray to Romania, stretches from a Terret-Chardonnay Pays d'Oc in the late €20s to a 2011 Puligny-Montrachet Bouchard in the mid-€80s. Since Diana Krall goes very well with the décor of soft linens and clean, modern glassware, a *coupe* of the Matelote's house champagne, fruity, delicious and hinting at hidden depths goes very well with Diana Krall and a lingering lolling at the *carte*. Everything a house wine should be. An excellent value €20 midweek two-course lunch menu was the universal choice on my noontide visit.

Forgoing the *encornet* with red pepper, I opted for salmon *rillettes*, served not on the usual 'bed' but here overcanopied with genuinely interesting leaves that tickled hitherto untapped flavours of the salmon, here tantalisingly creamed with finely chopped shallots, chives and the currently unfashionable, but always appropriate, dill. I was still accepting the mute thanks of my lips and taste buds for such a wise choice when the main course arrived. I can forgive even the squarest plate I have ever known for the sheer quality of this midday masterclass on how to make a simple white fish noble enough to merit a public holiday. The plaice divested itself of its skin with the expert grace of a courtesan shedding a superfluous negligee. Within a ring of pert, cracking and perfectly pitched vegetables, the three fillets lay on as excellent a risotto of *confit* tomatoes as I have tasted in many months. This kitchen does more than merely respect its local produce, it flirts and flatters and dances attention on all its fish (from the rare to the everyday), until ripe for kissing, let alone serving on a plate.

7

Since I spend the sea lion's share of my year in a French fishing port, my seduction threshold is quite high when it comes to inland fish restaurants. Jour de Pêche is already high up on my list of favourite places in France, let alone Lille. Get here early or book. €€€€

LAKSØN ⓖⓟ 21 rue du Curé Saint-Etienne ♀ 237 H4 ⓸ ☎ 03 20 31 19 96 ⓘ www.lakson.fr
ⓜ Métro 2 to Gare Flandres then line 1 to Rihour, then cross Grand' Place & walk under the Alcide arch to Saint-Etienne into rue Lepelletier

On the cusp of the squares and Vieux Lille, and in the quarter of pricey jewellers and antiquaries, discover a Scandinavian delicatessen and dining room that has been feeding blinis, smoked fish and satisfying Danish pastries to the Lillois for more than 25 years. One of the best Scandi tables between Paris and the Baltic, honours are evenly shared between the various Nordic nations from Denmark to Lapland. Menus are a veritable net load of herrings, sprats, sundry smoked fish and crabs. With smoked salmon and gravad lax given pride of place, a spicy salmon Swedish burger is pricey but appreciated and signature dishes include an *aumônière de crêpe au saumon fumé*, a distinctive Nordic wave of lobster tails, and the eponymous (and salmonised) house poached eggs. Just leave room for one of the moreish Danish cheesecake or crumble desserts. Midweek set lunches are €19–25, platters from €20 to €30 and the full Menu Copenhagen is €45. Not cheap, but if you are looking for an alternative approach to the traditional comfort food of the city, a very tasty change. €€€€

MEERT ⓖⓟ 27 rue Esquermoise ♀ 237 H4 ⓸ ☎ 03 20 57 07 44 ⓘ http://en.meert.fr
⊙ Mon–Sat lunch, Thu–Sat evenings, Sun 11.00–14.00 (brunch) ⓡ Rihour ⓜ Métro 2 to Gare Lille Flandres & line 1 to Rihour, then cross the Grand' Place to rue Esquermoise

Best known as the pâtisserie to the great and the good, the grandest tea shop in the north of France (pages 120–1) now has a restaurant behind the exquisite shopfront and the dainty *salon de thé*. Of course, as visitors to the Piscine gallery in Roubaix already knew, the house is no stranger to proper catering, so the arrival of a dining room around the courtyard at the back of the building was probably inevitable. Here, budget is not the issue, as you are as likely to part with around €35 on a main course should you choose rack of wild boar or Audreselles lobster in one season or suckling pig cooked in straw, a traditional shepherd's pie or even a grey Burgundy truffle risotto further along the calendar! But coming in closer to €20 during an early visit was Lille's take on a Brit standard and entitled (in English) 'Double Fish and Chips', here presented with skate and a langoustine risotto. You might also get away with paying €24 for a soft-boiled egg and truffle salad, and a similar price for a lobster Caesar salad. The simplest omelette is probably the truest test of a kitchen. No suspense here, trust me, it passed! To match the offerings of the newer fashionable dining rooms across town, set menus have recently been introduced at €29 for a two-course lunch and €35 for three courses, with dinner from €45 to €90 depending on whether you choose four or six courses and take the suggested accompanying wines. Otherwise, budget upwards of €65 per person. Delightful, charming and genuinely welcoming staff, as chic and special as the place itself. Dine upstairs or downstairs at courtyard level. Midweek evenings, an alternative bar-snack style menu of platters is offered, from 19.00. €€€€

MONSIEUR JEAN ⓖⓟ 12 rue de Paris ♀ 237 J5 ⓹ ☎ 03 28 07 70 72 ⓡ Rihour ⓜ Métro 2 to Gare Lille Flandres & line 1 to Rihour, then walk along rue Rihour & rue des Manneliers to the corner of rue de Paris

In this post-TV-chef and colour-magazine world, you know that you are getting gastronomy when the plate presented to you bears no relation to the reasonable assumptions inspired by the menu description. To me, a *velouté de chou-fleur, saumon fumé et caviar de hareng* suggested a smoky du Barry soup with a dotted garnish of fish eggs. I was right about the herring hundreds and thousands, but the anticipated warm cauliflower soup barely covered the bottom of a vast white bowl, and merely served as a groundsheet for lavish piles of superior-grade smoked salmon and samphire with those promised black sprinkles. It was quite lovely.

This was my first time *chez* Monsieur Jean, but by no means my debut in the dining room. In the two decades that I have been sharing my culinary tales from Lille, the restaurant at the original Paul bakery by the squares has had many personalities, for many years part of the bakery itself, a few flirtations with outside chefs, but finally it has discovered a permanent identity as Monsieur Jean, home to chef Marc Meurin, the only *maître cuisinier* in the region with two Michelin stars (for his Château de Beaulieu hotel restaurant) and the proprietor of the restaurant at the new Louvre-Lens (page 212).

The décor retains the familiar elegance, with its legendary views of the squares from the first-floor windows. The former breakfast room on the ground floor is now fully separated from the shop and is a completely accessible dining room at street level. Here, there are the limed timbers and ornate woodcarvings on plump dark beams, blue-and-white Flemish tiling and faux-Baroque chandeliers that I recall from so many extravagant breakfasts *chez* Paul, now with a few personal touches, such as lavishly upholstered bucket chairs and prints of the siege of Lille. Proper butter with excellent breads are the last echo of the staid old days; now, this is the home of clever food. The à la carte selections flirt with preconceptions just as shamelessly as my non-soup on the daily menu had played with the language of lunch. Red-fruit muesli is the twist given to pan-fried foie gras, and a mackerel bruschetta promises echoes of classroom window sills with mustard and cress. Budget above the €50 mark to marry these two to a dessert.

I opted for the set menu, with that unexpected flourish of well-garnished smoked salmon as a starter and a steamed white fish main featuring shiitake mushrooms, local baby leeks and chunky noodles. The oriental spin on my main course is atypical, as M Meurin prides himself on locally sourced seasonal vegetables, so new potatoes will be *rattes* from Le Touquet and watercress in season is no stranger to Monsieur Jean. However, the spice rack knows no geographical bars, thus North Sea fish could as easily have a tandoori dressing as French meats receive a North African dressing. At €25 for two courses and €32 for three this is sensibly priced, and to start off the lunch hour the *bouche* may be amused by an eggcup carrot and orange chorizo emulsion. At the weekend (Friday and Saturday evening or Sunday lunch), the fixed menu has a fourth course option for €39 and at any time the meal may be augmented with well-chosen drinks (*apéro*, wine and coffee) for a supplementary charge.

Orders are taken by a brace of highly professional secretary-bird waitresses and the food itself presented by an improbably perpendicular waiter. Nobody outside the imagination of L S Lowry should be quite that tall and thin: I found myself looking round for a three-brush-stroke whippet and a backdrop of the industrial chimneys of Roubaix. I saw his hands as they placed the plates in front of me and heard a voice from above describe the treats in store, but I never actually glimpsed his face, my neck not managing more than a 180-degree turn nor 45-degree tilt. Fashion is as fashion does, and I must confess that the elegant and ergonomic cutlery was actually defeated by a leek which refused to succumb to the genteel blade of the knife and so had to be peeled and looped linguine-like around the fork.

Since the original two-Michelin starlets of Lille no longer grace these pages, it is exciting to see that, as well as the top chefs who have helped revive the rue des Bouchers across town, even here by the squares, France's most decorated out-of-town cooks are bringing their talents to the budget of ordinary people enjoying a day or night out in the city. €€€€

N'AUTRE MONDE ⓖⓟ 1 rue du Curé Saint-Etienne ♀ 237 H4 ⓢ2 ☏ 03 20 15 01 31
🖳 www.nautremonde.com ⓣ closed Mon 🚇 Rihour 🚋 Métro 2 to Gare Flandres & line 1 to Rihour, then walk through the squares to rue Esquermoise & take the first left

Would-be culinary stars take note: a truly great chef does not have to be 'clever'. A maestro should be able to play his ingredients without too many theatrical flourishes. In this comfortable squeeze of a dining room between shopfronts, a stumble from Grand' Place into the old town, the weft and weave of nature does the bidding of a young virtuoso for even the simplest dish on the menu. David Bève's piece of cod that passeth all understanding was sublime, divine and delicious: speared with a vanilla pod on a bed of the most basic garden produce. The stalwart of the greyer reaches of the Atlantic proved as exotic as a conventionally nobler catch. The first lesson of the day was that garden produce does not have to be red or shiny or drizzled with oils and vinegars to be worth a second glance. The masterclass in root veg was steamed only to an awakening: each of the half-dozen winter varieties, privily spiced, attained perfection in texture and taste.

North African and Indian Ocean spices fragrance the air, testament to the world food philosophy of the place, always delightfully balanced so that the gentle scent of later arrivals' tagine in no way distracts from the playful mirabelle or pistachio lacings of your own final course. Desserts, in their turn, are gorgeous, and the option of an extra cheese course is a no-brainer, given that next door is the counter of *maître fromager* Philippe Olivier – so the provenance is impeccable. There are nine coffees to choose from, all arabica.

Coffee is not exclusively shackled to the end of the meal: a frustrating glance at a recent menu (frustration due to the fact that, by the time I get back to Lille, the dish will have been overtaken by an even fresher innovation) offered a walnuted crumble of *sandre* served with endive braised in coffee. Mild consolation for missing out on some of the dishes is David Bève's online recipe page on the website. A neighbour of mine has downloaded the secrets of rabbit thighs with sesame and Fourme d'Ambert cheese, and will one day pluck up the courage to cook the dish!

The menu changes almost with each new moon and, on the winter noon of my first visit, the prime plate among my fellow diners was a wild boar risotto. More recently it was sole *en croûte* with a creamy cauliflower sauce ennobled with vanilla and almond. You know the food is good when even business lunchers do the lovers' thing and pass forks across the table. This is not the exclusive province of expense account *divertissement*; besides a smattering of *hommes d'affaires* were a few true couples and plenty of ladies lunching *entre filles*. A sharply coiffed man in black who knew the value of skincare lunched with a tousle-haired, bluff fellow in boots who knew the value of life.

The chairs may be doll's-house-princess Baroque, but the subdued décor falls safely short of the operatic. The obligatory chandelier and solitary candelabrum do not outshine the regular lighting in the room, and spotlights are turned to photos of orchids hanging on pink walls. Not conventional Barbie-pink, but the rosy hue of an older and wiser Barbie, two marriages post-Ken and with a judicious appreciation of the muted palette being kinder to riper skin tones.

Starters cost €12–16, mains in the €20s and desserts a little over €11, so budget easily over €50 for a full-scale immersion. Discover a limited midday menu at around €20, exclusively woven from the daily specials, so that adventurous diners on a timid budget need not miss out on a taste of the future. There is usually a lighter-priced vegetarian plate, modestly couched amid the more exotic dishes on the menu.

The innate sophistication and well-tuned instinct of the young chef and his partner Harry Baclet led to the 2009 *Gault et Millau* guide singling out Bève as a new *'jeune talent'* of France. A first trophy stands among the various laurels and garlands on a table by the door. If, since the last edition of this guide, you read of a sister establishment N'Autre Bistrot, don't go looking for it. It opened. It closed. But the original restaurant goes from strength to strength. €€€€€

ORANGE BLEUE ⓖⓟ 30 rue Lepelletier ♀ 237 H4 ㉟ ☏ 03 20 55 04 70 🖥 www. restaurant-lorangebleue.com ⏱ closed Sun 🚇 Métro 2 to Gare Lille Flandres & line 1 to Rihour, then cross the squares & walk under the Alcide arch to rue des Débris Saint-Etienne & continue to rue Lepelletier

I am so glad that I took a short cut along the rue Lepelletier on the evening of signing off a previous edition of this book, or else I might have missed out on the smart, efficient and welcome treat that is this popular eatery just a matter of yards from the Grand' Place. Here, in a large airy dining room with enough space 'twixt tables for plenty of bulky carrier bags – proving it to be popular among the serious shopping set at lunchtime – celebratory portions are enjoyed with a sneak peek down into the spotless kitchens of the basement. Swift and friendly waiting staff whiz-glide through the room, managing the extraordinary feat of dashing from one end of the restaurant to another without anyone else feeling in the least bit hurried. Food-wise, expect to be assailed by savoury flavours, whether you take the Orange menu (served at all times except Saturday evening) of tapenade, pasta and dessert for less than €20, or graze à la carte for around €10 more. My *croquante* of haddock *à l'aneth* offered gossamer-fine leaves of filo, dill and smoked haddock that hit more culinary G-spots than you might expect. Pasta and salad options are served in huge quantities as are all the main courses. Cheese does not wait for the end of the meal here, appearing (as Maroilles) inside chicken in a gingerbread sauce, and (in *chèvre* guise) as stuffing to a saffron-teased salmon dish. Red meat carpaccios are generously presented and late risers looking for a kick-start to the remains of their day might even forego the *plat principal* and opt for a starter and dessert in the name of a tardy brunch. Most recently, a regional menu offered fishy *waterzooï* and rabbit thighs with sage and Maroilles cheese served with jacket potato and rounded off with a local gin-infused lemon sorbet. Don't bother with the wine list – do as the locals and go for the seasonal suggestion chalked around the room. Inevitably a red Chinon was available for just over €20 a bottle, with around half the bottle price for a jug and perhaps €5 a glass. No need to rush off after licking the platter clean: no matter how busy, the staff encourage lingering with a good choice of *digestifs* from *fleur de bière* to calvados, to keep the feel-good factor nice and high. €€€

ORIGAN 58 bd Carnot ♀ 235 G3 ⓖ ☏ 03 20 13 08 88 ⏱ closed Sun 🚉 Gare Lille Flandres 🚇 Cross the Parc Matisse to the bd Carnot

An inexpensive luncherie so painfully trendy and sharp that you'd cut yourself if you fell upon this place by accident. At Origan, the fusion concept goes far beyond the plate. New York studio-style skylights burnish an endless row of shiny black tables with individual linen runners and, to keep the place exclusively packed with the young and fit, the painted grey doorstep is obviously inspired by the north face of the Eiger. You can guess just how New European the smart guys at the next table will be merely by reading the menu: open sandwiches of foie gras with Granny Smith carpaccio and chopped hazelnut and glass of white port (I kid ye not) have optional side orders of either a *légume du jour* crumble, tomato confit salad or gratin of penne with Grana Padano. Admit it, you can already picture their homes!

But don't mock, people this hip won't be fobbed off with anything but the best when it comes to actually eating, so food is prepared with flair and talent and served with style, and flavours certainly live up to the gilded frieze that runs the length of the restaurant, an enumeration of fine herbs scrawled across panels and mirrors alike. The monochrome of the décor serves to highlight the vibrant hues on the plates. Since this is already a hit with the busy and beautiful lunch crowd, most food is the sort of thing you might enjoy while keeping your finger on the pulse and your eye on the ball, and is itself a euro-combo of mezze and tapas. The hyper-fusion theme continues through the proper main courses. Lunch menus and sandwich-based snacking at €18 and €21, weekly menu at €26 for three courses, à la carte budgets around €35. €€€

OUI ⓥ️ℓ️ 13 rue des Bouchers 📍 237 G4 🅴️ 📞 03 20 38 52 67 🖥️ www.leoui.fr 🕐 closed Sat lunch, all day Sun & Mon 🚇 Métro 2 to Gare Lille Flandres & line 1 to Rihour, then pass the tourist office & turn right on to rue de l'Hôpital Militaire, then cross pl de l'Arsenal to rue des Bouchers; alternatively, take the Navette Vieux Lille almost full circle & step off at rue des Bouchers

While Le Bloempot (pages 92–3) is the flagship of the new wave that has engulfed this street in recent years, another Michelin starlet twinkles at number 13, with Eric Delerue (whose honours were also won in another town over 30km away) as chef partner in the reinvention of a favourite venue. Here, in an 18th-century vaulted cellar, a laid-back crowd focuses on imaginative seasonal dishes, gastronomy without the stuffiness. The atmosphere was created with no Gitanes-rich fug of smoke, since ciggies were banned at number 13 long before the European ban came in; all the better to appreciate the fine flavours. Less troglodytic types may prefer the main room, with full-length windows and a hint of spindly greenery taking advantage of the natural light to grab a fix of photosynthesis as the rest of us enjoy the €22 or €29 menus. Formerly known as Oui Fooding (one of those new French hybrid noun-verbs that can depress a lexicographer at 20 paces), it challenged conventional taste pairings for seven years; now, under the whisk and skillet of M Delerue, the restaurant just says yes to a more conventional, but no less appetising, menu than its last incarnation. Intriguing combinations still prevail, such as the mango and tarragon *tartare* of sea bream starter and green tomato and coriander take on lobster as a main course. An €8 *pain perdu* is an apricot and rosemary spin on bread-and-butter pudding. Budget a good €45–50 per head, plus wine from a choice of over 250 labels. €€€€

LA PATATIÈRE 🅖️🅟️ 31 rue Saint-Etienne 📍 237 G5 🅶️🅟️ 📞 03 20 06 14 78 🖥️ www.la-patatiere.fr 🚇 Rihour 🚇 Métro 2 to Gare Lille Flandres & line 1 to Rihour, then walk along rue Roisin into rue de Pas & left along rue Saint-Etienne

After the passing of Les Charlottes en Ville in its various incarnations on rue Faidherbe (now swallowed up by a Buffalo Grill), jacket potatoes still prove filling fast-food rivals to Flam's (page 99) as this city's carb rush of preference, both at lunchtime and before surrendering to nightlife. This bistro-styled venue opposite the car park/concert hall combo of the Nouveau Siècle building serves jacket potato platters from €12 to €16. Themes range from spicy veggie options and Landais homage to the country of foie gras and smoked duck. For those who want to cut back on the carbs, the platters are available without the potato, served as a salad. Just as the original restaurant names its plates after regions of France, here you will find a mix of Camembert apples and gingerbread as tribute to Normandy, and cockles and mussels heralding Dunkerque. Expect international concepts as well, from Italy to Mexico: the triple-filling *dégustation* platter features curry from India and smoked fish from Norway. A full set menu, with coffee, for €16.50. €€

> *"Here you'll find a mix of Camembert apples and gingerbread as a tribute to Normandy."*

LES REMPARTS Logis de la Porte de Gand, rue de Gand ♀ 235 H2 ⑤ ✆ 03 20 06 74 74 📱 www.lilleremparts.fr 🚌 Bus 50 to Lion d'Or, then cross pl Louise de Bettignies to rue de Gand

Easy to find your way to and from, this, the final restaurant on the rue de Gand gastronomic thoroughfare: it is a listed landmark and marked on all the maps. Housed in the original 1620 fortifications of the old town constructed during the Spanish invasion, there can be no more dramatic setting for a restaurateur with a knack for the flamboyant and romantic gesture. My first experience of the restaurant had been pretty disappointing – a bland lunch served in a stuffy overheated function room on the day President Chirac opened the Palais des Beaux-Arts. Even when chums began nagging me to give the restaurant a second chance, saying that the cuisine had enjoyed a thorough overhaul, I was not inclined to return. When, however, a sudden summer downpour found me stranded at the foot of the steps leading to the restaurant that straddles the main road, I decided to dry out and try out the new-look Terrasse. The place was packed to capacity, the outside terrace on the fortification being *hors de combat* owing to the weather. Charming staff managed to find us a table amid the eccentric décor, which resembled the private dream life of a hyperactive department-store window dresser. We made ourselves at home among wooden sunflowers beneath huge polystyrene rabbits hibernating on mock grass and outsized daisies on the rafters overhead. Then, under new management, the design grew trendier, the bunnies replaced by discreet sheep. Now, with another proprietor, we hear that the higher standards of food remain, but the nursery kitsch has finally been abandoned in favour of more conventional restaurant décor in the conservatory on the ramparts and the dining room proper. Menus start at the €30 mark, with lunch options from €20. Poached eggs with langoustines figure among the more free-range starters and *le filet de bœuf sur toast au Roquefort* is an original alternative to turbot or pan-fried *ris de veau* mains, all in the mid-€20s price-wise. To be honest, most people have traditionally come here for the location but, in recent seasons, more have returned for the food. One tip for the new proprietors: since the restaurant is one of the few with a working lift from the street to the dining room, it might be worth considering finding a way to give access to disabled diners, since the elevator stops several stairs before the level of the dining room, so no use at all for disabled visitors who cannot climb stairs! €€€€

ROUGE BARRE
50 rue de la Halle ♀ 237 H1 ⑰ ☎ 03 20 67 08 84 🖱 www.rougebarre.fr ⏰ closed Sun & Wed 🚌 Bus 50 from Lille Europe to Les Bataliers, then from sq Grimonprez turn into rue de la Halle

This one is still on my 'to dine' list, as it was closed on my last gastro dash round town before putting the latest edition of this book to bed. My previous trip had been hijacked by the mushrooming of new restaurants across the centre in rue des Bouchers and I only made it here on a Wednesday – the chef's day off. Chef is Steven Ramon who shot to fame in France as a semi-finalist in the 2014 *Top Chef* series (France's answer to *MasterChef*). Telegenic, curly haired and wearing his heart on the sleeves of his chef's whites, he was a hit with the public. (Who could forget his emotional tearful outpourings while strapped into a harness and sitting at a dining table suspended from a crane above a city street? It was reality TV, after all.) He has a talent for working with fresh fish and vegetables, and spoke on TV of his dream of one day opening his own restaurant. This is the very restaurant. He serves menus at €21/28/52/78 – the former at lunchtime and the latter during evenings to tables of six or more. €€€€

WHY DINETTE
🄶🄿 7 sq Morisson ♀ 237 G6 ⑰ ☎ 03 20 50 30 30 ⏰ closed evenings 🚆 Rihour 🚌 Métro 2 to Gare Lille Flandres & line 1 to Rihour, then walk past the tourist office & sq Morisson is on your left

From the tourist office, walk away from the Lorelei lures of the bustling restaurants of the main squares and the shopping on rue Bethune, and make your way to the new Why Hotel (page 56). At lunchtimes, the hotel breakfast room becomes a lively restaurant for local office workers and busy business types who nip out for a classy light lunch, tailored to fit into an hour. The restaurant spills out on to a large pavement terrace. A *plat du jour* (perhaps lamb, veal or a choice chunk of cod), served on a bed of fashionable beans and pulses of *MasterChef*-styled carbs, followed by the ubiquitous *café gourmand* espresso sharing a slate with a quartet of mini dessert treats, is a pretty good deal around €15. I was particularly stuck by the fact that the selections were not uniform. At our table, a different array of sweet things was presented to each diner: one had a teeny trifle, another a shot glass of lightly whipped mousse – even the *macarons* were not identikit. Professional and welcoming service, and the glazed terrace under the trees was perfect for lunch on the first day of spring. Surprisingly close to anywhere you want to be, with a brisk buzz of other people networking, while you are off-duty. €€

WINE BARS

CHEZ MOI
🅅🄻 14 rue des Bouchers ♀ 237 G3 ㉙ m 09 83 09 77 86 🖱 www.chezmoilille.com 🚌 Métro 2 to Gare Lille Flandres & line 1 to Rihour, then pass the tourist office, turn right on to rue de l'Hôpital Militaire & cross pl de l'Arsenal to rue des Bouchers; alternatively, take the Navette Vieux Lille almost full circle & step off at rue des Bouchers

Perhaps this should be listed under estaminets rather than wine bars. Comfort food is served here on the new foodie strip of rue des Bouchers. Red-brick and purple walls plastered with hundreds of classic wine labels announce that here you choose the food to go with your wine, rather than the other way round. Classy sausages, choice cold cuts and ripe cheeses are selected to enhance a full-bodied red wine. You may choose a classic hot stew, but the regulars tend to order a platter of charcuterie for €13 or strong cheeses for €10 to go with the Burgundies and Bordeaux. Welcoming, cosy and friendly. €

LES COMPAGNONS DE LA GRAPPE ⓖ 26 rue Lepelletier ♀ 237 H4 ⓔⓓ ⬎ 03 20 21 02 79 🍴 www.lescompagnonsdelagrappe.mobi ⓘ closed Sun & Mon evening Oct–May only ⓔ⬩ Métro 2 to Gare Flandres & line 1 to Rihour, then cross Grand' Place & walk under the Alcide arch to the rue de Débris Saint-Etienne into rue Lepelletier

I stumbled across this summer terrace quite by chance: there is a gap in an alleyway, which opens out to reveal a wine bar with a delightful courtyard. Families and friends sit and chat under sunshades, sipping wines from some of the lesser-known vineyards of France. Platters of charcuterie and farmhouse cheeses are colourful and plentiful. The place positively hums with contentment. It's worth popping in to check on any special theme evenings or culinary events. No reservations taken, service can be a hit-and-miss affair and the opening hours of noon 'til midnight vary with the weather. In winter enjoy a glass of wine in front of a roaring fire. Budget €30 per person. €€€

DELASSIC FRERES ⓥⓛ 11 pl des Patiniers ♀ 237 J3 ⓔⓓ ⬎ 03 28 52 32 88 🍴 www.fromage-delassic.fr ⓘ 12.00–14.00 & 19.00–22.00 Tue–Fri, 12.00–17.00 Sat, closed Sun & Mon 🚉 Gare Lille Flandres ⓔ⬩ Bus 50 to Lion d'Or & walk back down pl des Patiniers, then take the Navette Vieux Lille along rue des Arts

They serve some very good wines here, but this is the one room where every bottle is chosen to go with a stylish goat, chic sheep or classy cow. Twins Tristan and Morgan run Lille's first cheese bar (see page 156 for the shop) where you might choose an individual cheese at this first-floor *bar à fromages*, with room for just 15 diners, but I suggest that you opt for one of the recommended platters (3–11 different cheeses) from €8 to €20, or choose the €11 lunchtime *plat du jour*. Your waiter will offer breads and salads to go with each cheese and will explain the correct order for working your way round slate or plate. Where better to taste that dietary French paradox mixing rich, ripe cheese with red, red wine? Booking advised.

AU GRE DU VIN ⓥⓛ 20 rue Pétérinck ♀ 237 H3 ⓖ ⬎ 03 20 55 42 51 ⓘ 12.00–14.20 Tue–Sat, 12.00–13.45 Sun ⓔ⬩ Bus 50 to Lion d'Or, & from rue de la Monnaie turn left on to rue Pétérinck: the shop is on your right

Go on, treat yourself. Have a nice glass of wine from the Languedoc at probably the only place in town you'll taste a tangy Picpoul de Pinet with a cold collation. Lunchtimes only, this neat little wine shop – specialising in the oft-overlooked but ne'er forgotten full-flavoured delights of Languedoc Roussillon – serves a simple platter of food with which to sample the Corbières, St Chinians, Fitous and Banyuls, or the better-known bottles of the southwest. A good place to buy exotic specialities for picnics or presents: *aubergines à la Languedocienne* or jars of salt flavoured with the spices and scents of the garrigue scrubland of the sultry south. Find change from €20. €€

MONSIEUR JACQUES ⬝Vℓ⬝ 30 rue de Gand ♀ 237 K2 ⬝50⬝ ☏ 03 20 74 85 59 ⬝◈⬝ www.
monsieurjacques.com ⓘ closed lunchtimes & all day Sun ⬝🚌⬝ Bus 50 to Lion d'Or
Besides a 300-label printed wine list, regulars check out the blackboard for an ever-changing
selection of noteworthy wines by the glass. Interesting Beaujolais and Languedocs from €5 upwards
per glass. Choose a platter of cold meats, cheeses or savouries such as tapenades to accompany your
wine choice, a peculiarly Gallic take on tapas. Pay from €5 to €15 for your choice of plate. €

LA PART DES ANGES ⬝Vℓ⬝ 50 rue de la Monnaie ♀ 237 H2 ⬝58⬝ ☏ 03 20 06 44 01 ⓘ daily
from 09.00 until at least midnight ⬝🚌⬝ Bus 50 to Lion d'Or
Anthony Chevalièr is a sommelier from Burgundy and he has run Lille's original wine bar since
1997. Not blinkered against wines from outside his own region, he offers an eclectic selection
of tipples and enjoys introducing the grape to a new aficionados – just as he hosts more than
a dozen local wine clubs at the bar, his team of wine experts are keen to introduce the student
clientele to wines as an alternative to the city's ubiquitous beers. From around €3.50 a glass, many
take that first step! Food is not cheap: €15 will buy a plate of nibbles to enjoy under the glass
ceiling, but the full à la carte meal will set you back double, and you'll find oysters, caviar, lobster
and *entrecôtes* on the menu. €€€

BURGER ALL

One of the biggest changes to the fun dining scene since the last edition
of this guide has been the Gallicisation of the humble hamburger. Since
McDonald's has long been regarded by the French as the front line of
American imperialism in Europe, despised by intellectuals and adored by
the masses, France has attempted to lay its own to the market. MacDo (as
it is known colloquially) is everywhere, the branches on Grand' Place and
Gare Flandres with the longest queues in town. Quick Burger, the domestic
rival (find one at Euralille) has long been the fast-food alternative.

However, in recent years, the burger has been deconstructed,
reconstructed and presented as a brasserie classic dish. **Café Leffe** (page 87)
presents a tuna steak in a bap 'n' fries setting that is quite delicious, the
erstwhile estaminet **La Royale** (page 83) features an Italian job, and a stroll
along the ever-evolving beyond-the-station quarters of rue de Paris and rue
Molinel will open your eyes to delicious constant reinvention of the burger
as presentation of quality regional cuisine. By the side of the Gare Flandres,
Holy Cow ⬝S⬝ (*11 rue de Tournai* ♀ *235 H5* ⬝18⬝) serves freshly prepared and
original burgers all afternoon and evening. The **Urban Basilic Café** (pages
84–5) has been running entirely burger-based menus for a decade and has
proven a grand success. Across town, fine *filet* steak is going into the mincer
at the point the guest orders a classic burger, and classic foods from grilled
Mediterranean vegetables to Alsace *choucroute* are being lured between
petit pains and wedges of multigrain *pain rustique*. When Frédéric Parois

CAFE SOCIETY

The dividing line between a bar and a café has blurred over the years. Generally one does a lot more sitting down in the latter and standing around in the former, and bars stay open later – usually until 01.00 or 02.00. You can enjoy a coffee in a bar and a beer in a café, so your choice really depends on where you feel most at home.

Cafés tend to be best for talking, and Lille has its regular venues for philosophising or swapping notes on this week's great read. Bars range from traditional locals to the seriously fashionable spots where your clothes say more about you than your neighbour can spell. For the hottest joints in town see pages 120–1, and don't forget that the coolest hangouts may not be what you expect (the Gastama hostel (page 67) is a great rendezvous). Who would imagine that the essential address in Vieux Lille would be the Café Oz (a pub better known to locals as 'L'Australian')? Find it on the place Louise de Bettignies, at the corner of the rue de Gand and avenue du Peuple Belge. When televised sport is on the agenda you will be amazed at the

took over the site of Julien Descendos' trendy Tentation on the seriously gastronomic rue des Bouchers in Vieux Lille, he opened **L'Adresse** (page 91), a burger bistro presenting top-notch culinary skills between two slices of interesting bread, with intriguing side orders in kilner jars.

Le Comptoir Volant, an itinerant burger van manned by seemingly all-American boys, is not what you think. For a start, the guys behind the diner-check shirts, aprons and preppy demeanour are César Toulemonde and Greg Chaignaud, proprietors of this food truck that serves up classic French know-how and meat preparation skills. Both burgers and *steaks tartares* are served at what the chaps and their team call their *restaurant itinerant*, where the beef, hot or cold, is priced at €7, with sides and drinks under €2. For the cheeseburger, the van staff add proper Swiss AOC Emmental cheese and a slice of bacon with baby spinach leaves to a burger cooked in a port, veal and shallot stock. Monday lunchtimes find the van outside the bike shop at **B'Twin Village** (*4 rue du Professeur Langevin* ⚲ *235 K8*) on the southeast side of Lille, and the rest of the week in Villeneuve d'Ascq and Tourcoing. Call to order or find out where they'll be on 📱 06 23 89 38 32. They are on also Facebook: 🖱 www.facebook.com/comptoirvolant.

Just as America took France's *bœuf hachée* and processed it into fast food, a walk through the menus of Lille today is proof that La Belle France has reclaimed the patty and her sisters from the Styrofoam box and restored her to her throne on a decent plate.

crowds at the English, Irish, Scottish and Welsh pubs across the city: the distinction between Celtic nations blurs somewhat. On the Solfé, there is a shamrock-daubed pub named O'Scotland. But this is, after all, a city with a Chinese restaurant called Amigos!

The cooler the bar, the later it starts to get busy. Thus estaminets and cafés will do a roaring daytime trade and wind down in the early evening, while the party places often unbolt the front door any time from 17.00 to 20.00, with some truly trendy establishments waiting until 22.00 to get started.

You will often find two sets of prices on display. In most cases the lower price applies to drinks served to those standing at, or leaning against, the bar, and the higher for waiter service at a table. In some trendier establishments, the second figure indicates a 10–20% price hike after 22.00 or midnight. In a neighbourhood bar, one orders a drink, enjoys it and pays on leaving. Busier, fashionable hangouts may expect payment at the time of ordering. If all this sounds stressful and complicated, don't worry. Settle down, have a drink and forget about it. There is never any pressure to move on once you have ordered your first tipple. A modest espresso can last an afternoon, if you've a mind to settle down on a comfortable terrace, and a glass of beer may be nursed as long as you like as the evening dissolves past the witching hour. Beers (page 74) come in bottles or on draught (*à la pression*), served usually as a *demi* (25cl) in a tall glass. Each bar seems to have its own name for a larger half-litre measure, but if you fancy something close enough to a pint, ask for a *grande*. Beer is the best-value drink, wine often surprisingly expensive by the glass, and spirits decidedly shocking considering how cheap they can be in supermarkets. Soft drinks, or sodas, include Coca Light (Diet Coke), Orangina and occasionally the local fizzy violet-flavoured lemonade. And don't forget the mineral waters. A refreshing compromise is a lager shandy, known locally as a *panaché*.

BARS, CAFES AND TEA ROOMS

Nurse a coffee for an hour, have a beer with friends, a late-night light snack or mid-afternoon sugar rush. Traditional restaurants are not the answer: time to explore the infinite variety of bars, cafés and *salons de thé* that provide sustenance before, between and beyond mealtimes.

If, instead of a chunky espresso cup with wrapped sugar cube and square of chocolate, you prefer your coffee served in a large disposable cardboard container with a logo on it, then you may welcome the proliferation of American-style coffee chains offering frappe-fresco-latte-mochaccino-type concoctions. A number of these are emerging around the Gare Flandres station, creeping across the Grand' Place and opening up in a former shop near wherever you are staying sometime soon!

▲ Settle down with an espresso at one of Lille's infinite number of cafés (Anna Moores)

BD FUGUE
VL 5 rue Royale 📍 237 G3 ⑫ ☏ 03 20 15 11 47 🕐 10.30–19.00 Tue–Sat & 14.00–19.00 Mon 🚇 Métro 2 to Gare Lille Flandres & line 1 to Rihour, then cross Grand' Place to rue Esquermoise into rue Royale

It had to happen. After the *café philo* and the *café littéraire*, here comes the café comic strip. The French love their BD – *bandes dessinées*, comic-strip artwork and novellas – just as much as the Japanese love theirs, and vast sections of any self-respecting bookshop are devoted to the form. So now comes a café where aficionados may chat and browse over an espresso. A friendly welcome is guaranteed in this bustling corner of the old town. €

BISTROT DE ST SO
Gare St-Saveur, bd Jean-Baptiste Lebas 📍 235 G8 ① ☏ 03 20 32 05 42 🕐 11.30–23.00 Wed & Thu, 11.30–01.00 Fri & Sat, 11.30–21.00 Sun 🚆 Lille Grand Palais 🚇 Métro 2 to Gare Lille Flandres then bus 14 to Lille-Lebas

The bistro-café-bar at the former railway station, arts centre and community hang out (pages 184–5) has a great programme of live music events. Family friendly in the afternoons and a bit of a party vibe in the evenings. Drop by for a coffee or local beer, a snack and a quick fix of popular culture. €

CAFE AUX ARTS
VL 1 pl du Concert 📍 237 H2 ㉑ ☏ 03 20 21 13 22 🚇 Bus 10 from Gare Lille Flandres to Lion d'Or, then follow rue de la Monnaie

Sit on the strip of pavement terrace and watch the comings and goings of the Conservatoire opposite and the rue de la Monnaie to your right. Nothing special, just the traditional cane chairs and smart blue awning you would appreciate after an hour or so sightseeing. Fine for a quick beer and break after the Hospice Comtesse and Vieux Lille window-shopping. €

LE CAFE DE FOY
GP 6–8 pl Rihour 📍 237 H5 ⑳ ☏ 03 20 54 22 91 🚆 Rihour 🚇 Métro 2 to Gare Lille Flandres then line 1 to Rihour

Squeezed between the thrusting elbows of many a visitor-packed bistro and ice cream parlour, Foy is a popular choice for budget-conscious *plat du jour* lunchers, rendezvous-shifting friends or mere people-watchers. Most visitors know the packed terrace, but locals think of the first-floor room where Thursday night conversation goes beyond shopping stories and idle gossip. This is the café philo of the squares. If your French is up to it, take the plunge. €

CAFE LEFFE See page 87.

CAFE LIVRES ⓥ 35 rue des Bouchers ♀ 237 G4 ㉓ ＼03 20 78 17 56 🖥 www.lecafelivres.fr
⓪ closed Mon ⓜ Métro 2 to Gare Lille Flandres & line 1 to Rihour, then pass the tourist office, turn right on to rue de l'Hôpital Militaire & cross pl de l'Arsenal to rue des Bouchers; alternatively, take the Navette Vieux Lille almost full circle & step off at rue des Bouchers
What's not to love about the concept of a secondhand bookshop with a sideline in cake? A great little address amid the cutting-edge eateries and designer food shops of the up-and-coming street on the far side of Vieux Lille. Not a café with books, but a bookshop with coffee, beer and homemade snacks. Better yet, it's the only bookshop I have ever known that actually hosts a summer barbecue. Stays open quite late in the evening so it's a great place to wait for your tardiest friends, since there's never a shortage of reading material (several books in English, German, even Chinese, and some really good vintage travel and food classics), and even better when you do meet up and it's raining

BEYOND FRANCE

Of course, there is a lot more to dining out in Lille than exploring the diverse delights of French cuisine. With a good 500 restaurants in and around the city, you could discover many of the world's great national dishes. However, if you have made the trip to France and to Flanders, the chances are you have come in search of flavours French or Flemish. Thus the main listings and reviews on these pages concentrate on guiding you to the right table. Nonetheless, the multicultural charms of a modern French city are reflected on the plates of Lille, especially in the streets around the Gare Flandres and along the rue Gambetta, place Sébastopol and Wazemmes. Lebanese, Tunisian, Algerian and Moroccan delights are to be found, with countless cafés and restaurants promising couscous, tabbouleh and tagines. Vietnamese and Chinese restaurants too, with the occasional promise of Caribbean flavours, add to the global menu for a Lille night out. Meze from Greece, paella from Spain and the inevitable trattoria or pizzeria on the corner keep the European flags flying in this food-fest of global diversity. The themed weekends of Lille2004 reflected the gastronomic versatility of the city, with many events marrying food, flavours and sounds of other lands. When Lille went all Bollywood for the first Lille3000 fest, Bombaysers de Lille, the city rediscovered its own excellent Indian restaurants. Eastern fusion concepts have begun to take over many traditional sites in the city centre. The rue de Paris, south of rue Molinel, is a hotbed of start-up ethnic eateries: where else would you find a Lebanese pizzeria?

Remember the simple rule when choosing restaurants unlisted in any guidebook: go where the crowds are. Here are just a few recommendations:

outside, for there are battered boxes of Monopoly and Scrabble to play with. It is also designed for people who do not like to rush out of bed in the morning, opening at 11.45 (half an hour later on Sundays). So if you missed breakfast, you can pop in here for a quiche, soup or salad, with a side order of John Grisham in French. Tables and chairs, even squidgy sofas, are scattered between the bookshelves. The Friday summer evening barbecue from 20.00 to 22.30 boasts a selection of meats and salads, and includes a stiff drink for €18. This event mutates into a €15 evening of unlimited *crêpes* and a glass of cider out of season. Friday meals must be booked by Thursday afternoon. Since the kitchen does not keep strict restaurant hours, you may find a welcoming bowl of onion soup mid-afternoon will hit the spot when everywhere else is shut and tide you over until suppertime. A lively programme of events, from jazz nights to book launches and photographic exhibitions, makes this more than a literary muncheria. The only black mark is the mega stack of steps from the street which renders it out of bounds to disabled bibliophiles. A notice in the window during the heady political weeks of late summer 2014 announced 'English and Scottish spoken'.

CAFE OZ ⓥ 33 pl Louise de Bettignies ♀ 237 J2 ㉕ ☎ 03 20 55 15 15 ⓛ 14.00–03.00 daily 🚌 Bus 50 to Lion d'Or

CARIBBEAN
La Canne à Sucre 68 bd Victor Hugo
♀ 238 F5 ⑫ ☎ 03 20 52 29 00

CHINESE
La Perle d'Orient 8 rue du Vieux
Faubourg ♀ 237 K5 ㉒ ☎ 03 20 31 28 18

FUSION
Tiger Wok 🄶🄿 45 rue des Tanneurs
♀ 237 J7 ㉒ ☎ 03 20 14 91 60. Offers an
early evening plate of East–West tapas.

INDIAN
Aux Indes ⓥ 38 rue Thiers ♀ 237 G4 ⑥
☎ 03 20 21 02 66

ITALIAN
La Bottega See page 94.

JAPANESE
Tokyo 55 rue Nationale ♀ 237 G5 ㊀
☎ 03 20 12 98 88

LEBANESE
Flandres Liban 🄶🄿 127 rue des Postes
♀ 238 B5 ⑬ ☎ 03 20 57 28 69
Layalina See page 124.

MOROCCAN
Soleil d'Agadir 5 rue Princesse ♀ 237 G1 ㊁
☎ 03 20 31 49 71

SPANISH
Las Tapas 116 rue Saint-André ♀ 237 G1 ㊂
☎ 03 20 06 96 59

THAI
Le Marché Flottant Ⓜ 38 rue Léon
Gambetta ♀ 238 E1 ⑦ ☎ 03 20 13 07 87
Madame Yum Yum See page 124.

7

Known to the locals as 'L'Australian', this is the Lille band of a national chain of Aussie pubs. Serves nachos, burgers and *croque monsieur* bar snacks to mop up the Fosters, Monteiths, Tooheys and other brews from Down Under. Anglophone students, backpackers and sports fans come to watch the match on TV, others for a seemingly endless happy hour.

COFFEE MAKERS 151 rue de Paris ♀ 238 J7 ㉚ ☎ 09 73 55 93 60 ⏱ until 18.00, closed Sun ☒ Mairie de Lille ▣ Bus Citadine to Molinel-Paris

Step back from the tourist traps if you want a proper cappuccino or latte in Lille, so make a note of this address. On the southern stretch of the rue de Paris below the rue Molinel a teeny-weeny narrow coffee shop crams in tables and chairs and is usually packed with locals who love a really good coffee (even the tap water is purified before being pumped into the machine) and a range of cakes that verges on the anglophile. The busy people of Lille swear by the coffee here, and the welcome is truly convivial. €

ENVIES DE SAISON ㉋ 7 rue de Gand ♀ 237 K2 ㉟ ☎ 03 20 31 13 28 ⏱ 08.00–18.00 Mon–Fri, 10.00–18.00 Sat, closed Sun ▣ Bus 50 to Lion d'Or, then follow rue de Gand

'Mouthwatering' may be a cliché, but 'drool' is not a word I like to use around food. Sandwiches that give a new dimension and purpose to aspirational salivating are served in this healthy little shop where cheeses blend with berries and honeys and herbs, grilled vegetables in toasted rolls taste like forbidden fruits, and salads and pastas in the chill cabinet are even more alluring than the chunks of charcuterie squeezed between slices of wonderful breads. Read the list of fillings chalked up daily to give goosebumps to your taste buds, then agonise over how to spend your €5. Grab a sandwich or order a herbal tea and take it upstairs for a light lunch or energy boost. A good take-away section too, and here's a tip – 20% off all fresh food after 17.00. €

AU FUT ET À MESURE 5 rue Faisan ♀ 236 D6 ⑤ ☎ 03 29 48 20 66 ⌨ www.aufutetamesure.com ⏱ 17.00–03.00 ☒ République–Beaux Arts ▣ Bus Citadine to Nationale, then walk west on rue Nationale, turning left into rue Faisan

▼ Taste the range of local beers, brewed in the bar: blonde, blanche, brune and ambrée (Anna Moores)

This is so cool. No queues at the bar on match days, you can yell at *les bleus* to *allez* from the comfort of your seat and never miss a goal nor a top-up. Sport on the flat screen and beer on tap – literally. Your table has its own beer pump with a smart card so you can serve yourself directly while keeping a weather eye on your 'online' tab. Settle up at the end of the night. Brothers Benoît and Guillaume, with their friend Quentin, transformed an old office 'twixt the Solfé and the rue Nationale into the obligatory wood-and-steel-look student-hangout bar and the place has been an instant hit with the locals.

GASTAMA 109 rue Saint-André ♀237 G1 ☏03 20 06 06 80 📧www.gastama.com
🚇Métro 2 to Gare Flandres then bus 10 to Magasin; alternatively, take the Navette Vieux Lille from pl Rihour
Officially this is the bar for backpackers dossing in comfort at the hostel upstairs. With the exception of L'Australian, this has become a great meeting point for travellers and locals alike. Mojitos and world beers fuel an international youthful buzz.

KHEDIVE ⓖⓟ7 pl Rihour ♀237 H5 ㉒☏03 20 54 37 82 🚉Rihour 🚇Métro 2 to Gare
Lille Flandres then line 1 to Rihour
In these health-conscious times, when smokers are expected to rend their garments and carry a bell, a politically incorrect *terrasse* for those who otherwise might be seen huddling on doorsteps and blocking the entrance to smoke-free railway stations and shopping malls (interestingly, the fug that garlands the portals of these new breathe-right sanctuaries is like a triple espresso shot of nicotine that could flay and slay an asthmatic at 40 paces), an address for those who still like a cigar and sigh for the sight of a humidor. On most café terraces, drinkers and diners may puff with impunity but here, next door to Leffe and in front of the Foy, is a place where tobaccophiles may walk tall and strut. A sign in the window invites visitors to explore a '*Cave aux Cigares*'. Snacks are served from 06.00 until midnight to satisfy the munchies and refuel those

"Your table has its own beer pump with a smart card so you can serve yourself directly."

whose taste buds have been shattered by a life on the weed and tolerant non-smokers alike, who fancy the shot of a refreshing glass of beer and a freshly made sandwich. The closed-in (in winter) terrace attracts a lively mix of students and musicians from the nearby theatres and concert halls, shoppers and strangers, all squeezed around tables cluttered with ashtrays and beer glasses and army recruitment leaflets. Great for the Christmas markets when a big €3.50 glass of mulled wine is better than any scarf for an early evening warm-up. €

MAISON DU MOULIN D'OR (MOREL ET FILS) ⓖⓟ31–33 pl du Théâtre ♀237 H5 ㊻
☏03 20 55 00 10 🚉Rihour 🚇Bus 10 to Lion d'Or then walk along rue des Chats Bossus &
rue de la Clef
A pastel-blue legend of lingerie is reborn in arabica. In 1997, Morel et Fils, purveyors of ribbons, laces and corsetry since 1831, sadly closed the doors of their Maison du Moulin d'Or, surely the prettiest shop in Lille (page 181). Now, with the familiar window displays, a terrace outside the Opéra, stripped floors,

7

grand staircase and much original décor within, it is a welcome and welcoming café-bar, still under the care of a seventh-generation fils of the original Monsieur Morel. Great photographic exhibitions. €

MEERT ⓖⓟ 27 rue Esquermoise ♀ 237 H4 ⑬ ☏ 03 20 57 07 44 🚇 Rihour ⓔ Métro 2 from Gare Lille Flandres to Rihour, then cross Grand' Place to rue Esquermoise

Charles de Gaulle himself would never have dreamt of saying '*Non*' to the celebrated *gaufrette* – or filled waffle – that has graced many a palace and presidential biscuit barrel since this shop started trading in the 1760s. This unassuming house speciality of the chocolate-box quaint pâtisserie is a tiny miracle: a light, feathery, crispy wafer packed with a sugared explosion of flavour. The town's most famous son continued his regular order for the *gaufrettes* all his life, and ate them, so he wrote, 'with great pleasure'. The Belgian royal family gave their warrant to Monsieur Meert in 1849. The pretty cake shop, decorated in 1839 with mirrors, balconies and Arabian Nights exotica, is a feast for the eyes. The tea room behind the shop provides savoury lunchtime snacks and sumptuous afternoon teas, where a selection of cakes and a pot of tea should set you back around €6–12.

LES HALLES

Ⓜ Pl des Halles Centrales, rue Solférino ♀ 236 D7 🚇 République–Beaux Arts ⓔ Bus Citadines to Sacré Cœur, then walk along rue Solférino to pl des Halles Centrales

Wazemmes may be the daytime weekend capital, but another marketplace, the former Les Halles wholesale district straddling the rues Solférino and Masséna, is the centre of nightlife. Part student hangout, part city of singles and part party-animal safari park, the restaurants, bars and pavements are an electrifying life-force on Friday and Saturday nights. The old covered market itself houses a run-down supermarket that still manages to catch some of the party buzz and cheery chaos as people stock up on last-minute supplies for rendezvous with friends in a student bedsit before hitting the bars. Like any city's party zone, a number of bars and restaurants open and close with the frequency of a revolving door, but firm favourites survive each new influx of undergraduate revellers.

Those who care about looking cool may or may not still hang out at the **Café La Plage** where pavement tables are made from old surf boards. Sporty types (read 'rugby club') make noisy alpha-male sounds and pull their own pints at **Au Fût et à Mesure** (pages 118–19). There's something for everyone: choose your taste by the music blaring out and suss out whether the place is full of '80s retro-heads enjoying the sounds and tipples of the decade that taste may have bypassed, but which hair-care products annexed for all time, or home to more modest Brit-retro such as during the happy hour at **The Fridge**. Current taste is for décor that is faux-British-pub style, such as **Atomic**. But the open doors at **Le Solférino** bar spilling out on the corner of rue Masséna are a bright place to start the evening and meet up with friends. Students on a tight budget bring their own atmosphere to

Lemon meringue tarts are creamy delights; the Safari a surprisingly heavy dose of fluffiness for hardcore chocolate addicts only. See also page 104. €

LE PAIN QUOTIDIEN ⊕ 35 pl Rihour ♀ 237 H6 ⚇ ☏ 03 20 42 88 70 🍴 www. lepainquotidien.fr ① 08.15–22.30 daily, closed Mon evening 🚆 Rihour ⊕ Métro 2 to Gare Lille Flandres then line 1 to Rihour

Readers of my *Bradt Guide to Eurostar Cities* will recognise the name and décor of this café from its earlier Brussels incarnations. This cheerful clone of the ideal brunchery pushes the same indulgence buttons as the original. Imagine turning up mid-morning at a country farmhouse, just as the farmer's wife is removing the day's baking from the oven. OK, so no-one wipes floury hands on an apron, but the welcome smells and tastes are the same, whether you want a generous *tartine* of freshly baked bread, butter and apricot jam or a slice of lemon tart. Yummy hot chocolate and coffee take the chill off a December roam around the Christmas market opposite. Snack inexpensively or lavish €15 on a menu charged with huge salads and

the cheap and cheerful mood **Chez Gino**, where a beer is not much more than €2, while those willing to pay for imported Cuban ambience enjoy tequila slammers at **Le Latina Café**. **La Boucherie**, an institution in the quarter since the social dark ages, is a veritable meat-rack – lively dance floor, cruisy cocktail bar and the benchmark of the social scene – the first point of contact for making new friends.

Restaurants, on the other hand, are strictly for old acquaintances. The season's newest crop of dining rooms will provide a perfect hideaway for couples. Do not dismiss the area as merely the haunt of the green and trendy. There are more than a few bars, cafés and restaurants well worth a detour, both around the square and along the rues Gambetta and Puebla. This is one quarter where you should never rely on the printed word for a guarantee of fashion. Trends change fast here, so it really does pay to walk slow and watch where the locals go. Oh, and don't pronounce the full word when referring to Solférino. That is the mark of a stranger or wrinkly. It is Solfé!

Atomic Pub   138 rue Solférino ♀ 236 D7 ❸ ☏ 03 20 40 18 39
Au Fût et à Mesure   5 rue du Faisan ♀ 236 D6 ❺ ☏ 03 20 48 20 66. See pages 118–19.
La Boucherie   32 rue Masséna ♀ 236 E6 ⑰ ☏ 03 20 30 66 06
Café La Plage   122 rue Solférino ♀ 236 D6 ㉖
The Fridge   166 rue Solférino ♀ 238 C1 ⑪ ☏ 03 20 35 15 11
Chez Gino   21 rue Masséna ♀ 236 E6 ㉓ ☏ 03 20 54 45 25
Le Latina Café   42–44 rue Masséna ♀ 236 E7 ㊸ ☏ 03 20 07 14 81
Le Solférino   156–158 rue Solférino ♀ 236 D7 ⑪ ☏ 03 20 57 03 43

sandwiches served at hefty family-sized tables in a wide, airy room dominated by a massive dresser sporting hundreds of jars of tempting preserves. Weekend brunches for €18. New branch opening in Vieux Lille. €

LE PALAIS DE LA BIERE 11 pl Gare ♀ 237 K6 ⑤⑦ ✎ 03 20 06 38 94 🚇 Gare Lille Flandres
⑤ Métro 2 to Gare Lille Flandres – but you might as well walk
Smart, modern, airy and bright bar contrasts with the greasy chips and soggy beer-mat norm of station 'caffs'. Nice place for coffee and croissant between stepping off the Eurostar and walking into town. €

LA PÂTE BRISEE ⑦⑤ 65 rue de la Monnaie ♀ 237 H2 ⑥⑩ ✎ 03 20 74 29 00 🖥 www. restaurant-lapatebriseelille.fr ⑤ Bus 50 to Lion d'Or
Looking for a light lunch in the old town? Then squeeze past the punters queuing at the counter of this cheery pâtisserie across the way from the Hospice Comtesse and find a seat in the cosy red-brick dining room. All the sweet and savoury pastries you could buy to take home are served here on marble-slab tables. I loved a Roquefort tart, but traditional quiche-lovers will find plenty of variations on the theme to savour, chicken and tarragon being something of a 'wow' with the regulars. My source for this was the lady at the next table whose eyes were watering with the effort of not talking with her mouth full, as she dabbed at the lightest pastry crumbs at the southeastern corner of her lips in her eagerness to advise me on my first journey though the menu. The fruit flan I chose for dessert was so nice I clean forgot to make notes, but it blended the sharpness and sweetness of late plums with a texture that melted off my fork. Main courses are under €10 and there is a full menu for €16 including drinks. €

PAUL ⑥⑦ 8–12 rue de Paris ♀ 237 J5 ⑤⑪ ✎ 03 20 8 20 78 🖥 www.paul.fr 🚇 Rihour
⑤ Gare Lille Flandres & line 1 to Rihour, then cross Grand' Place to the Vieille Bourse
Don't bother with breakfast in your hotel: come to Paul for the best breakfast in town. Not the biggest, nor the most varied, but certainly the best. This corner-site bakery opposite the Vieille Bourse is the place to go for fresh croissants, just-baked bread and creamy, piping-hot chocolate first thing in the morning. The breakfast tray served on solid wooden tables against the blue-and-white tiled walls and heavy tapestries of the bread and cake shop is the perfect way to start the day. Find inspiration in the words of wisdom painted on the old wooden beams, or concentrate on the scrumptious homemade jams and crunchy, crusty baguettes. A range of breakfast options at around €2–6. After a long period of confusion, the curving wooden staircase once again leads to the famously bright and airy first-floor restaurant dining room – but no longer part of the bakery. Use the back door to discover dining *chez* Monsieur Jean (pages 104–6) where those who recall the gentle climb to tasteful tables by the windows and washstands in mirrored washrooms can once more enjoy dining with unimpeachable views across the squares. Paul has now spawned scores of satellite bakeries and *viennoiserie* counters across Lille, throughout Paris and beyond, but this old corner shop between the Opéra and the main square remains something special. €

TAMPER ESPRESSO BAR ⑦⑤ 10 rue des Vieux Murs ♀ 237 H2 ⑦⑪ ✎ 03 20 39 28 21
⏰ until 18.00 (17.30 Sun), closed Mon ⑤ Bus 50 to Lion d'Or, then walk up rue de la Monnaie & turn left on to rue Pétérinck

In a city where *crème pâtissière* is practically a lifestyle, who would have expected a modest north-American carrot cake to become a tea-time best seller? Yet the moist and lightly lusciousie slice *chez* Marie-Sophie and Germain was already making newspaper headlines in Lille within a month of the espresso bar opening its doors. Besides the signature indulgence, an €8.50 Sunday brunch is very popular here (booking recommended: two-hour slots from 11.30, 13.30 and 15.30) and coffee and cakes are available anytime. €

TOUS LES JOURS DIMANCHE ⓋⓁ 13 rue Masurel ♀ 237 H3 ⓩⒶ ☏ 03 28 36 05 92
🕓 11.30–18.30 Mon–Sun 🚌 Bus 50 to Lion d'Or, then take rue de la Monnaie, first left to pl Gilleson & cross the *parvis* to rue Masurel
The dinky little streets around the cathedral constantly produce new delights and diversions, and this is a sweetie, an almost eccentric little tearoom and snack bar in a secondhand shop. So, should you really like the plate or the cutlery with your apple tart, the dish that your quiche was cooked in or the cup from which you are supping a mid-afternoon hot chocolate, ask for it to be added to your bill. It may well be for sale, along with the chair and picture above the table. Brunches at €19.50 served in winter months, afternoon snacks from around €5 and other light meals for €15. €

LES TROIS BRASSEURS See page 90.

LE WINDSOR ⒼⓅ 5 rue Jean Roisin ♀ 237 H5 ⓩⒷ ☏ 03 20 57 45 64 🚇 Rihour 🚇 Métro 2
to Gare Lille Flandres then line 1 to Rihour
The bar of the Grand Hôtel Bellevue (pages 58–9) presents the cocktail-hour rendezvous for those who would prefer to wait in discreet comfort surrounded by potted palms and gentle music than sit on the edge of a fountain in a busy square.

AU VIEUX DE LA VIEILLE See page 85.

VEGETARIAN

I am constantly amazed at the European concept of vegetarian. When researching a Paris guide for the meatless and fancy free, I regularly encountered bacon served as standard on the vegetarian special and, on one occasion, a respected airline served all its passengers broccoli quiche – except for the single soul who had requested the vegetarian alternative, which turned out to be roast chicken and salad!

When I first began researching this guide, I struggled to find any exclusively vegetarian restaurants in the city and, apart from linking to specialist publications and websites, I merely nudged readers towards contemporary student-friendly places with a good range of salads. I have to admit to vegans being completely left out in the cold, but for those who eat eggs, the dreary standby of an omelette is always the unimaginative option. Happily, Lille boasts an enviable range of ethnic restaurants (see box, pages 116–17). In my experience, cuisine from eastern Mediterranean, Hindu or

Muslim cultures is often far more likely to include interesting vegetarian options. Since this book first came out, and during my various visits to the city during its regular yearly cycle or reinvention, I have actively sought decent veggie fare in the city and bombarded student groups with calls and emails in my hunt for good addresses. Here are my tips for a hearty spread.

CIRQUE HOSTEL
139 rue des Postes ♀ 238 B5 ✆ 03 62 10 76 86 🖥 http://lecirquehostel. fr 🚇 Wazemmes ⊕ Métro 2 to Gare Lille Flandres & line 1 to Wazemmes, then walk east along rue léna to rue des Postes

Not a vegetarian restaurant, but a pretty fair chance of a tasty meat-free option on the menu here. Fair trade and locally sourced organic lunches in the café-bar of a hostel in Wazemmes. Good soups and quiches. €

LAYALINA
⊕ 14 rue d'Arras ♀ 238 F5 ⑭ ✆ 03 20 42 85 58 ⊕ Bus Citadine from Gare Lille Europe to Douai-Arras, then walk to rue d'Arras

Although this could never be described as a meat-free zone, this unexpected corner of the Mediterranean offers a simply massive spread of vegetarian mezze. Spend around €15. €

MADAME YUM YUM
⊕ 24 rue des Arts ♀ 237 K5 ㊺ 🖥 www.mmeyumyum.com ⏲ closed Mon evening, all day Sun 🚉 Gare Lille Flandres ⊕ 5–10 mins' walk from Gare Flandres to rue des Arts

Thai restaurant between place Lion d'Or in the old town and the boulevard Carnot, behind the Opera House. A €15 'veggie' set lunch (featuring vegetarian spring rolls and Pad Thai) as well as the regular €15–24 lunch menus. Evening is à la carte only and somewhat pricier. €€€

PULP KITCHEN
⊕ 106 rue de l'Hôpital Militaire ♀ 237 G5 ㊾ ✆ 03 28 14 18 59 🖥 www. pulpkitchen.fr ⏲ closed Tue–Thu eves, all day Sun & Mon ⊕ Métro 2 to Gare Lille Flandres & line 1 to Rihour, then walk along rue Roisin & rue de Pas to the Nouveau Siècle building & cross to rue de l'Hôpital Militaire

Healthy eating, gluten- and lactose-free cuisine, so no surprise that there is a vegetarian alternative for everything on the menu in this restaurant that offers both a carnivorous and veggie *plat du jour* (at €13 and €11 respectively). Lunch menus for vegetarians at €15 and €19, evening meals at €20 and €24, with a meaty option for each at an extra €2. €€

Otherwise, find meat-free options at the following:

Envies de Saison Best sandwiches in town. See page 118. €

Les Flam's See page 99. €€

La Patatière Potato with every kind of filling. See pages 108–9. €€

Meatballs Despite the name, there is an option of a falafel alternative to all the various sauces. See page 81. €

Tamper Espresso Bar See pages 122–3. €

Les Trois Brasseurs The brasserie social snack of as many savoury or sweet flams as you can manage. See page 90. €€

Urban Basilic Café See pages 84–5. €€

8

Nightlife and Entertainment

Lille famously boasts that Saturday night always offers a choice of a hundred alternative diversions – and it is no bragging exaggeration. This is a city that knows how to fill the hours of darkness. Quite apart from the diversity of bars and restaurants, from the *intime* and quirky rue de Gand to the city of singles that is rue Solférino, the variety of performances would not disgrace a national capital city. *Sortir*, the listings magazine, is published every Wednesday. Pick up a free copy at your hotel or the tourist office. The local newspaper *La Voix du Nord* also carries comprehensive entertainment information.

THEATRE

The **Théâtre du Nord** on Grand' Place is a very good place to start. For 15 years, the American actor and director Stuart Seide's artistic direction really put this stage on the national cultural agenda. Challenging and fresh approaches to world classics led to ground-breaking productions of Beckett, Molière and of course Shakespeare – a *Romeo and Juliet* turned round the central schism by 90 degrees, presenting the divide as less between Montague and Capulet than between the two generations. In a city where almost half the population is under the age of 25, that certainly created more than a murmur. The theatre's contribution to Lille2004 was a programme featuring four works by Shakespeare while Pinter, Dylan Thomas *et al.* were frequently on the bill.

Seide's successor, Christophe Rauck, is taking the theatre in new directions with the addition of a second playhouse and performing arts school. His inaugural season featured a programme of classics (Racine to Beckett) alongside new works, and a shift towards community theatre, using three performance spaces: a smaller space in Lille alongside the main auditorium and sharing the season with the **Idéal Theatre** in Tourcoing. Besides the official performances, the season included numerous *cafés philo*, meals with authors and playwrights and talks at the theatre's pop-up bookshop an hour before performances.

▲ The symbol of the Sun King above the Théâtre du Nord – a reminder that this was once the home to the Royal Bodyguard (Anna Moores)

Young theatre has its own voice at **Le Grand Bleu**, where programmes are essentially geared to the hip-hop rather than hip-replacement set. Other fringe and new-wave venues include the **Théâtre de la Découverte à la Verrière** and the semi-itinerant **Théâtre des Nuits Blanches**. The **ZEM** is the community theatre of Wazemmes and has a full programme of workshops. Conventional and comfortable family fare is served up at the **Théâtre Sébastopol**. Light comedies that would run on Shaftesbury Avenue, Broadway or the Grands Boulevards play here. The weekend bill may feature such old favourites as *Le Dîner des Cons* ('The Dinner Game') or concerts by TV crooners. International visitors perform at the up-front **Le Prato** and Villeneuve d'Ascq's **Rose des Vents**. During festivals, scores of other spaces, great and small, are called into service. The playhouses of other towns in the conurbation are also worth checking out since most venues are within half an hour of Grand' Place. After all, public transport in the Métropole continues until midnight. Do not dismiss the Maisons Folies (pages 190–3) nor the newer Gare Saint-Sauveur and other recently established venues (pages 187–90). These have exciting and vibrant performance spaces, and have already been bagged by dance companies, musicians and experimental theatre groups. You'll find fringe theatre and comedy at other alternative venues. The **Péniche** (page 128) (although more of a music venue these days) is worth considering.

Theatres often close on Monday, but several offer Sunday matinées. Tickets for many productions may be bought online (🎭 *www.fnac.fr*) or in person from FNAC's box office (page 159). It is customary to tip the usherette between 50c and €1 when being shown to your seat.

🎭 **Le Grand Bleu** 36 av Marx Dormoy
📍 236 A6 📞 03 20 09 88 44 🎭 www. legrandbleu.com 🚇 Bois Blancs Métro 2 to

Bois Blancs, then walk along the avenue.
🎭 **Idéal** 19 rue des Champs, 59200 Tourcoing 📞 03 20 17 93 30 🚇 Free bus from

Lille Opera House 1hr before performances.
🎭 **Le Prato** 6 allée de la Filature 📍 238 F5
📞 03 20 52 71 24 🖥 www.leprato.fr 🚇 Porte
de Douai 🚇 Métro 2 to Porte de Douai, then
turn left into allée de la Filature.
🎭 **La Rose des Vents** Scène Nationale bd
Van Gogh, 59650 Villeneuve d'Ascq 📞 03 20 61
96 96 🖥 www.larose.fr 🚇 Pont de Bois
🚇 Métro 2 to Gare Lille Flandres & line 1 to
Pont de Bois, then walk along rue Vétérans to
bd Van Gogh.
🎭 **Théâtre de la Découverte à la Verrière**
Ⓜ 28 rue Alphonse Mercier 📍 238 C2 📞 03
20 54 96 75 🖥 www.theatre-verriere-
decouverte.org 🕐 closed Mon
🚇 République–Beaux Arts 🚇 Bus 12 from
Gare Lille Flandres to Eglise Sacré Cœur, then
walk along rue Solférino to pl des Halles

Centrales, right on rue des Stations & right to
rue Alphonse Mercier.
🎭 **Théâtre du Nord** Ⓖⓟ 4 pl du Général de
Gaulle 📍 237 H5 📞 03 20 14 24 24 🖥 www.
theatredunord.fr 🚇 Rihour 🚇 Bus 12 from
Gare Lille Flandres to Théâtre.
🎭 **Théâtre Sébastopol** Ⓜ Pl Sébastopol
📍 238 D2 📞 03 20 54 44 50 🖥 www.theatre-
sebastopol.fr 🚇 République–Beaux Arts
🚇 Métro 2 to Gare Lille Flandres & line 1 to
République–Beaux Arts; rue Inkerman leads
to the theatre.
🎭 **Le ZEM Théâtre** Ⓜ 38 rue d'Anvers
📍 238 C2 📞 03 20 54 13 44 🖥 http://
zemtheatre.free.fr 🚇 Gambetta 🚇 Métro 2
to Gare Lille Flandres then line 1 to Gambetta;
walk up rue de Flandre & rue d'Anvers is the
5th turning on your left.

CABARET AND CASINO

For years, showbiz glamour and comedy were an essential part of Lille
nightlife. As served with a flourish and a flounce at the late lamented Les Folies
de Paris, where *La Cage Aux Folles* met Hollywood with the biggest cross-
dressing floor show north of the capital – a pancake-pasted flurry of feathers,
sequins and star lookalikes. Customers would be entertained, mocked and
teased in camp patois by the revue's outrageous director Claude Thomas, then
be transported to a world where every Celine, Marlene or Liza was a boy,
and a stripping Michael Jackson was revealed to be a Y-chromosome-free
zone. While no self-respecting Parisian is likely to admit to visiting the Paris
cabarets, you would always find locals at the Folies. When the Folies closed
for the last time, it seemed as though ostrich feathers were forever lost to
Flanders. Now, however, the *royaume* of the showgirl is set for a revival with a
new cabaret on the site and the advent, across town, of the recent casino with
the (as yet unfulfilled) promise of floor shows.

AU BONHEUR DES DAMES 61 rue Achille Pinteaux, 59136 Wavrin 📞 03 20 58 55 53
🖥 www.aubonheurdesdames.fr 🚇 Métro 2 to Gare Lille Flandres, then overground train to
Wavrin & it's a 20min walk from the station; alternatively, you can drive or take a taxi for
the 20km journey from Lille
Full Monty-style evenings are provided Au Bonheur des Dames, some way out of town, for
those who like their hen nights scented with squeals and baby oil. A celebration of depilated
masculinity, from the sunbed to the stage, it is a hit with office-party crowds who admire

8

men who can still walk the walk after waxing the boxer line. More popular apparently than its predecessor in Lille itself, where the hunks lost a certain credibility by doubling as drag queens and dressing as Madonna before getting their more manly kit off for the girls. The most common complaint was that the boys' eyeliner used to detract from the full effect of the thongs, but how things have changed. An ad recruiting the 2009 vintage exhibitionists for the venue read: *'Nous recrutons pour les weekends deux strip teasers, profil 18/25 ans, corps sportif et gueule d'ange. Envoyez votre candidature avec plusieurs photos. . .'*. Real angels don't wear mascara, not in this century. Menus €35 (for those who like their chicken on a plate) to €60 (for girls with a champagne lifestyle who prefer their beef hot and peppery).

CASINO BARRIERE DE LILLE 777 bis Pont de Flandres 235 J5 03 28 14 45 00
www.lucienbarriere.com Gare Lille Europe Lift or escalator to bd Turin & walk along the boulevard to Pont de Flandres
The spanking new casino-hotel has a purpose-built showroom theatre for 1,200 diners, a range of theme bars and a snack bar as well as the principal restaurant. The casino spreads itself across 40,000 square metres of the city, which may not sound much, but works out at four hectares for living high on the hog in smart suits while betting the farm on evens. The showroom has not yet set up a regular year-round cabaret, but seasonal musical shows do feature on the programme a few days in each month (a jukebox rock and roll show ran over several weekends in autumn 2014), there's a strong season of concerts by French recording artists, and occasional touring plays visit for one-night stands. The casino website or tourist office will have up-to-date listings each month. If the very notion of a casino conjures promises of full James Bond role-play, you may be only slightly disappointed, since while ties are appreciated on gentlemen, they are no longer *de rigueur*. Full evening dress may be out, but smart and stylish is still essential to get you through the door, thus trainers and T-shirts have no place even in a modern casino. If the old Folies punters make it through the door, we may yet see the dry martini being replaced by a *chuche mourette*, shaken not stirred! Even poker fantasies are PC: no smoking in the gaming rooms or show rooms, although stressed-out gamblers may adjourn to a dedicated fug-filled room for a wheeze, cough and ciggie break before returning to the tables. Not all casino employees work as croupiers or bouncers – the venue has its own resident addiction counsellor.

LA PENICHE Av Cuvier (Opposite Champ de Mars) 236 D2 03 20 57 14 40 www.lapeniche-lille.com Bus 12 from Gare Lille Europe to Champ de Mars
What began as a floating piano bar on the Deûle Is now something of a cult café-théâtre/music venue. Live rap, rock and indie groups, sometimes alternative comedy, and an eclectic range of entertainment – see videos of previous shows and updates on three months' worth of programming on the website. Admission prices for shows vary, but are usually around €10. The previous formula of a set menu has been relaxed and you can dine from €20–25 or just have a drink at the bar.

LE PRESTIGE PALACE 52 av du Peuple Belge 237 J2 03 20 30 93 46 www.leprestigepalace.com 19.30 Thu–Sat, 12.30 Tue–Thu & Sun, closed Aug Métro 2 to Gare Lille Flandres & bus 10 to Lion d'Or, then cross pl Louise de Bettignies & turn left

The *Cage Aux Folles*-style anarchy of the transvestite revue that once held court here is gone. In its place is the traditional pancake-and-feathers revue that has been a staple entertainment ever since Hollywood invented France. Showgirls with their curves factored to the max, with sequins and plumes glistening and shimmering at every wiggle and strut, and hugely amplified voices sing in time to the teeth and tinsel being flashed on the stage. No-one leaves without seeing a can-can! If you are going to stage a floor show, then trust an old stager to do it properly. Thierry Fééry was the original director, producer and mastermind behind the Prestige Palace, no stranger to Lille's entertainment scene, having been a former artistic director of the Théâtre Sébastopol across town. Not only that, but he arrived on the avenue du Peuple Belge having produced shows for Belgium's second-greatest export to France, the actress and singer Annie Cordy. A couple of years ago he handed over the reins to another stalwart of the local cabaret scene, Patrick Lavigne (who also runs a lavish feather-and-flouncerie in Calais). The show room is a big restaurant with all tables facing the stage. Dinner and show €75–95, midweek lunch and show €55. Reservation essential.

CINEMA

Le 7ème art thrives in and around Lille. June sees Lille hosting an international Independent Film Festival. One out-of-town multiplex, Kinépolis at Lomme, boasts 23 screens. However, you will not need to leave the centre of Lille, unless you wish to catch a festival screening of an obscure classic at Le Fresnoy in Tourcoing (pages 202–3), since everything else will be available around the pedestrian shopping streets surrounding rue de Béthune. The main selection is that offered at the 14-screen Ciné Cité UGC. Just along the pavement, the six *salles* of the Majestic specialise in original-language versions of international flicks, with subtitles rather than the dubbed versions screened elsewhere. Artier yet are the preferences at the Métropole near the station. For a truly art-house experience, head to the cultural quarter beyond the boulevard de la Liberté. The new Gare Saint-Sauveur complex has its own 208-seat cinema.

Nevertheless, the coolest place to go to the flicks has to be l'Hybride, an old garage down by the Parc Lebas, where you can flop with friends on old comfy sofas and enjoy an eclectic programme that is as likely to feature obscure eastern European offerings, or even an early Buster Keaton or a late technicolor Hitchcock. First time you visit, pay an extra euro for temporary membership of the cinema, which, after a shaky financial gestation, is now run as a members' club. The venue also hosts the annual animation and short film festivals. Remember, though, that Le Fresnoy in Tourcoing is a must for cineastes, and easily reached by métro.

In addition to press listings and reviews in *Sortir*, a free guide is produced by the mainstream picture palaces of Lille, distributed in cinemas and tourist offices. Budget tip: midweek morning screenings, at 11.00, are often half price.

Ciné Cité UGC 40 rue de Béthune
237 H6 08 92 70 00 00 www.ugc.fr
Rihour Métro 2 to Gare Lille Flandres &
line 1 to Rihour, then rue de la Vieille Comédie
leads to rue de Béthune adults €10.10,
under-18s €7.30, under-14s €4.

**Le Fresnoy Studio National des Arts
Contemporains** 22 rue du Fresnoy, 59202
Tourcoing 03 20 28 38 00 www.lefresnoy.
net Alsace Métro 2 to Alsace, then walk
south on bd d'Armentières & turn right on to
rue du Capitaine Aubert into rue du Fresnoy
adults €5, students/seniors €4.50, under-
14s €3.

Gare Saint-Sauveur See pages 184–5.

L'Hybride 18 rue Gosselet 238 G5
03 20 88 24 66 www.lhybride.org

Mairie de Lille Métro 2 to Mairie de
Lille then bus 14 to Jeanne d'Arc €4
(membership €1).

Le Majestic 54–56 rue de Béthune
237 H7 03 20 54 08 96 www.
lemajesticlille.com Rihour Métro 2 to
Gare Lille Flandres then line 1 to Rihour; rue de
la Vieille Comédie leads to rue de Béthune
adults €9.10, students/seniors €6.50,
under-14s €4.

Le Métropole 26 rue des Ponts de
Comines 237 J6 08 92 68 00 73 www.
lemétropole.com Gare Lille Flandres Av
le Corbusier & right into rue Faidherbe, left on
to rue des Ponts de Comines adults €9.10,
students/seniors €6.50, under-14s €4.

MUSIC AND DANCE

For me, nothing comes close to the experience of the Sunday evening tango in the courtyard of the Vieille Bourse (pages 178–9), but for those who like their music provided by professionals, the city is home to some world-class venues.

LIVE MUSIC The **Orchestre National de Lille** is housed in the big, round Nouveau Siècle building to the side of Grand' Place. Surrounded by restaurants, the building might easily be dismissed by diners as just another office block and underground car park. But nothing is ever quite what it seems in Lille; as I realised on my first visit to the car park when I noticed that signs for motorists were disconcertingly, albeit politically correctly, translated into Braille. Full orchestral programmes alternate with chamber concerts. The all-too-rare, occasional Sunday-morning recitals have always been firm favourites with locals. Nonetheless, other treats abound on other dates. Open rehearsals are fascinating and free to watch – check the ONL website for details – and there is a superb season of pre-concert talks. The orchestra's director, Jean-Claude Casadesus, woos international soloists to his concerts with lunch at local fish restaurants. Concerts are not limited to the Nouveau Siècle hall. The musicians play at many other venues around the region, as well as numerous prestigious international events. Programme details are posted on the orchestra's website.

The **Conservatoire** behind the place des Concerts market in the old town is more than a music school; it's a lovely little concert venue for morning or afternoon Brahms or Mozart and unexpected concerts of new and classic works.

For a harder edge, rock is obviously at home in a district of 100,000 youngsters. Six thousand people a night can raise the roof at the **Zenith Arena**; smaller crowds pack the **Biplan**, the essential rendezvous of Wazemmes, **Le Splendid** (a former cinema) and **La Malterie**. Tickets for major events may be obtained through FNAC (page 159). The **Aeronef** venue high above Euralille is a typical Lille curiosity. Originally an underground organisation for disaffected youth, the club moved to its new high-rise home among the banks and financial institutions of the business district when it was offered the venue by the city. Multinational corporations pitched in with generous grants, and the kids were left to organise their own fun. So much so that when a band offended public morals with their sexually explicit antics on stage, organisers, expecting a mass withdrawal of funding or legal action, were merely sent a memo from the authorities.

Regular concerts and recitals are held at the various churches in central Lille and all venues are open during the year's many music festivals. June itself sees the **Lille Piano Festival**, and May brings accordion players from many lands to an annual ten-day festival in Wazemmes. Programmes for all these events are available at the tourist office.

Tourcoing hosts its own autumn jazz festival, with fringe events spilling over the Belgian border. Despite no longer having a major dedicated jazz

LES PANTHERES DE LILLE

Dressed in leopard-print and no strangers to the red carpet and the paparazzi, '*Les Femmes Panthères*' ('The Panther Women') are Lille's good luck charms. If mother and daughter Pascaline and Esmeralda are spotted at the opening night of a festival or play, if they are to be seen mingling at the private view of an exhibition, or should they turn up at a film premiere, the event will be a success.

When Galeries Lafayette opened its flagship department store in Lille, they received an A-list invite. They were there for the inauguration of Lille2004 and the launch of La Piscine museum in Roubaix. Canny Hollywood directors even fly them to the Croisette for the Cannes Film Festival, where A-listers clamour to be photographed with the duo (Whoopie Goldberg caused a traffic jam when she leapt out of her limo to greet the ladies). Les Panthères have been spreading their unique brand of camp stardust for several decades now. Rumours abound as to how the Spanish mother and daughter duo came to northern France (they live in Armentières). Are they American or Russian spies, underground film stars, or erstwhile exotic models? No-one really wants to know the answer. They are as inscrutable and legendary a part of the city's heritage as its mythical founders.

venue, good jazz may be enjoyed in Lille for much of the year. Events such as the **Jazz en Nord** festival (🕯 *www.jazzenord.com*), which runs across the wider metropolitan area from September until June, are staged in halls as varied as the Conservatoire and the Casino.

Whatever your musical taste, whatever the year, cancel sleep on 21 June. **National Music Day**, created by former culture minister Jack Lang (since then a *député* for Boulogne), is an amazing occasion. Free concerts are held everywhere – in villages, towns and cities – and Lille manages to upstage most of the country with performances in public spaces, matched by live entertainment inside and outside almost every restaurant, café and bar in town. If you can get a table anywhere, keep ordering food and drink as the performances continue through the evening and into the night. If not, just keep on moving from street to street as swing blends into rap and baroque into rock.

Lille3000 seasons always bring exciting music events to unexpected venues, from Bollywood sounds in the inaugural programme to music from central Europe in the XXL fest of 2009. And don't forget that the Gare Saint-Sauveur (pages 184–5), not far from the club district, adapts to festivals and has a thriving music venue in its bistro. The Maisons Folies are always worth checking out as well (pages 190–3), as is the modular Grand Sud concert venue.

Aeronef Euralille 📍 235 H5 ☎ 03 28 38 50 50 🕯 www.aeronef-spectacles.com 🚈 Gare Lille Europe or Gare Lille Flandres 🚌 Av le Corbusier to av Willy Brandt, look for the signs, then scale the outside of the tower block.

Le Biplan 19 rue Colbert 📍 236 A6 ☎ 03 20 12 91 11 🕯 www.lebiplan.org 🚈 Gambetta 🚌 Bus Citadine from Gare Lille Flandres to Colbert.

Bel Ouvrage 4 parvis Saint Michel 📍 238 E4 ☎ 03 20 57 73 56 🕓 17.30–02.00 Mon–Sat, closed Aug 🚈 République–Beaux Arts 🚌 Bus Citadine to Douai-Arras, walk up rue Solférino to parvis Saint Michel. Arrive after 23.00 to get the feel of the place. Very friendly bar, interesting exhibitions & live music.

Conservatoire de Lille 🚎 Rue Alphonse Colas 📍 237 J2 ☎ 03 28 38 77 50 🚈 Métro 2 to Gare Lille Flandres then bus 50 to Palais de Justice.

La Malterie 42 rue Kuhlmann 📍 238 B5 ☎ 03 20 15 13 21 🕯 www.lamalterie.com 🚈 Porte des Postes 🚌 Bus Citadine to Condé.

Orchestre National de Lille 🚇 Nouveau Siècle, 30 pl Mendès France 📍 237 G5 ☎ 03 20 12 82 40 🕯 www.onlille.com 🚈 Rihour 🚌 Bus 12 from Gare Lille Flandres to de Gaulle.

Le Splendid 1 pl du Mont de Terre 📍 235 K8 ☎ 03 20 56 46 16 🚈 Hellemmes 🚌 Métro 2 to Lille Grand Palais, then bus 18 to pl du Mont de Terre in the Hellemmes quarter.

Stade Pierre Mauroy 261 bd de Tournai, 59650 Villeneuve d'Ascq ☎ 03 20 59 40 00 🚈 4 Cantons 🚌 Métro 2 to Gare Lille Flandres then line 1 to 4 Cantons; follow signposts to stadium. The new sports stadium doubles as a major concert venue.

Zenith 🚉 Lille Grand Palais, 1 bd des Cités Unies 📍 235 J7 ☎ 03 20 14 15 16 🚈 Lille Grand Palais 🚌 Métro 2 to Lille Grand Palais then follow signs.

BALLET Another nationally acclaimed company is the **Ballet du Nord**, now under the direction of Olivier Dubois, famously listed as one of the world's 25 greatest living dancers. Performing all over Europe, the company is based in Roubaix, with three principal performance spaces: the Grand Studio, the **Colisée** at Roubaix, a large theatre equally as popular with the world of rock as of dance (where Jacques Brel gave one of his final performances) and the **Condition Publique** (pages 200–1). Ballet also features on the programme of the Opéra de Lille and touring companies bring popular productions of *The Nutcracker* and *Swan Lake* to the Théâtre Sébastopol (page 127).

Ballet du Nord Grand Studio, 33 rue de l'Epeule, 59100 Roubaix ↘ 03 20 24 66 66 🖥 www.balletdunord.fr 🚊 Gare Jean Lebas 🚇 Métro 2 to Carliers, then walk down rue de L'Alouette.

Le Colisée Rue de l'Epeule, 59100 Roubaix ↘ 03 20 24 07 07 🖥 www.coliseeroubaix.com

🚊 Gare Jean Lebas 🚇 Métro 2 to Carliers, then walk down rue de L'Alouette.

La Condition Publique 14 pl du Général Faidherbe, 59100 Roubaix ↘ 03 28 33 57 57 🖥 www.laconditionpublique.com 🚊 Eurotéléport 🚇 Métro 2 to Eurotéléport.

OPERA Opera returned to the city centre thanks to the reopening of the **Opéra de Lille** just a decade ago. Inspired by the Paris opera house, the elegant bars and salons can match the stage for opulence and theatricality. With soloists and choirs mixed and matched from the leading companies of Europe, the season here is among the Continent's best bargains. Just before the place closed for renovation, a production of *Eugène Onegin* boasted a chorus imported from St Petersburg and tickets from under €30. The new regime lived up to its promise to trump all that had gone before, with daring seasons presenting little-known works and lesser-known composers such as Jean-Philippe Rameau alongside intelligent and original stagings of well-known classics, bringing together emerging young performers on stage with exciting mentors in the pit and the rehearsal rooms. A triumphant co-production (with the Brussels opera) of *Rigoletto*, with a witty beach-hut design, showcased some of the most exciting new musical talent around and sold out almost instantly. A delicious new production of Mozart's rarely performed *La Finta Giardiniera* won word-of-mouth acclaim to make it as popular as a *Figaro* or *Don Giovanni*. The opera house also opened itself up as a home to dance, with premières of new works and visits by ballet legends. The first season alone brought Bill T Jones and William Forsythe with the Frankfurt Ballet company. The stunning foyer, glittering with opulence and sheer dazzling style, hosts weekly recitals and performances on Wednesday evenings at 18.00. Balconies and vast windows offer breathtaking views over the city, and the extraordinary rehearsal studio spaces in the attics have access to amazing terraces looking out over the new and the old towns.

As if that were not enough, the district has a second opera venue: the **Atelier Lyrique** in Tourcoing produces studio versions of contemporary and classic works. A cycle of all the Mozart-da Ponte comic operas shared the honours between the main house in Lille and this intimate space at Tourcoing.

Atelier Lyrique 82 bd Gambetta, 59200 Tourcoing ☏ 03 20 70 66 66 🖳 www.atelierlyriquedetourcoing.fr 🚊 Carliers 🚇 Métro 2 to Carliers.

Opéra de Lille 📍 Pl du Théâtre 📍 237 J5 ☏ 03 20 38 40 40 🖳 www.opera-lille.fr 🚊 Rihour 🚌 Bus 12 from Gare Lille Flandres to Théâtre.

CLUBS

Traditionally there have been only two rules to remember when setting out for a night's clubbing in Lille. First, stay in the bars until late, since no-one, but nobody, is seen in a club before well past midnight, however early the doors officially swing open. Secondly, if you really want to party on down, you go to Belgium. Move directly to Belgium, do not pass Go (pages 138–9).

Although the hardened merrymaker continues to make the cross-border trip to Brussels and other Belgian towns, and London's latest venues will be always be on the main weekend agenda for the continental Eurostar set, the second tenet is perhaps a little unfair these days. Lille's smaller clubs are pretty cool and great for letting the evening spill into the night and flow towards the dawn. And, with super venues such as Magazine Club luring the major club players in Lille, the days of forcing a designated driver to Brussels, Pecq and Tournai are numbered. The night scene in the city is pretty much an attitude-free zone of tolerance with fewer of the rigid barriers between crowds that one finds in Paris and London, yet manages to avoid the sorry air of piteous compromise found in many French provincial cities.

I AM SAM, SAM I AM

If a barman or a bouncer asks you 'C'est qui, Sam?' ('Who is Sam?), he simply wants to know which of you is the designated driver – who will remain sober when the rest of the party hits the bottle! Sam is the star of a TV and film cartoon campaign to promote sensible drinking when out on the town. The mini-films show Sam getting the girl, not having a hangover and generally being everyone's respected best mate. Check them out on the website (🖳 www.ckisam.fr) or on his Instagram, Facebook and YouTube pages. So, if you are not drinking alcohol with your meal, in the bar or at the club, the answer to the question 'C'est qui, Sam?' is 'C'est moi!'

▲ In Lille, bars stay open late as no-one is seen dead in a club before midnight (Anna Moores)

A legacy of the Lille3000 project (pages 188–9) has been the emergence of new semi-permanent and even pop-up venues. Le TriPostal (page 190) in particular hosts regular late parties.

Of course, it pays to choose a nightspot best suited to your age, musical tastes or sexuality. So do check out the *Ch'ti* guide at your hotel reception or online at 🖥 www.lechti.com for the views of the student community on which are the current clubs and bars to bless with your company. Listen to the word on the streets around Les Halles (pages 120–1) or find a stylish bar in Vieux Lille or student dive anywhere and pick up flyers for clubs. At the tourist office, the *Autour de Minuit* listings guide has the low-down on where to spend the midnight hour – thanks to the journalists at *La Voix du Nord*.

Admission is often free midweek. Where door charges are made, this often includes the cost of a first drink. Drinks usually cost around double or treble the price charged in bars.

☆ **El Diablo** 8 rue de Wazemmes 📍 238 F5 🖥 www.eldiablo.fr 🕐 20.00–01.00 Mon–Wed, 20.00–02.00 Thu, 20.00–04.00 Fri–Sat, 20.00–24.00 Sun 🚌 Porte d'Arras 🚌 Bus Citadine to Douai-Arras & walk up rue d'Arras, then turn left just before the Maison Folie. A new & popular venue for dancing to live bands. Eclectic programme from ska & jazz to rock & roll.

☆ **La Folie Douce** 6 rue Gosselet 📍 238 G5 📞 03 20 52 97 98 🕐 21.00–04.00 Thu–Sat 🚇 République–Beaux Arts 🚇 Métro 2 to Gare Lille Flandres, changing to line 1 to République–Beaux Arts, then take rue Gaulthier de Châtillon to rue Jeanne d'Arc to rue Gosselet. New name for a long-standing venue for the post-student crowd. Where men with unforgivable eyes break their promises & girls whose lips are wishes pretend to believe, a riper crowd orders shorts from the bar & sips, talks & dances 'til late with the younger punters. The club formerly known as Dukes

Nightlife and Entertainment   CLUBS   8

proudly advertises itself as the venue for mid-20s to mid-40s.

☆ **Golden Wave** 7 rue des Arts ♀ 237 K5 ⓘ 23.00–06.00 daily ⊠ Gare Lille Flandres. No need to take the Eurostar to London for the nightspots of Camden Town. Goth or heavy metal & traditional club scene in this lively arty venue. Great theme nights & no real age bar, so hardcore clubbers who remember the sounds from first time round can share the floor with the inevitable student-core clientele. Happy hour is 23.00–01.00.

☆ **Gotha VIP** Ⓜ 53 rue Gambetta ♀ 238 E1 ☎ 03 20 30 16 16 ⓘ 20.00–07.00 daily ⊠ République–Beaux Arts ⊜ Métro 2 to Gare Lille Flandres changing to line 1 to République–Beaux Arts, then walk along rue Gambetta & the club is on your left. Previously Le Flib & Le Theatro, every new wave of students knows the venue by another name. Hit the floor or check out the crowd from the mezzanine vantage point. Contemporary mainstream club sounds. Arrive after midnight, leave at dawn, crash at a friend's place then go for brunch at the Gospel Café opposite.

☆ **Magazine Club** 84 rue de Trevisé ♀ 238 F5 🖳 www.magazineclub.fr ⓘ 23.00–07.00 Fri–Sat ⊠ Porte de Valenciennes ⊜ Walk to Gare Lille Flandres & take the night bus to Trevisé. One of the most popular of the new arrivals on the scene can be credited with stemming the party flow across the borders. For around 5 years, this bare industrial space on the edge of town has lured the best DJs from Brussels, Paris, London, Amsterdam, Berlin & beyond to Lille. Serious clubbers from Beijing to New York

know the address & the weekend & bank holiday eve nights of electro & indie sounds attract crowds from the party capitals on the European high-speed rail network.

☆ **Network Café** 15 rue Faisan ♀ 236 D6 ☎ 03 20 40 04 91 🖳 www.networkcafe.fr ⓘ 22.30–dawn Tue–Sun ⊠ République–Beaux Arts ⊜ Métro 2 to Gare Lille Flandres changing to line 1 to République–Beaux Arts, then walk along bd de la Liberté & turn left on to rue Puebla leading to rue Faisan. Come early on a Sun for salsa class (from 19.00) or from 21.30 on Thur for a taste of rock & roll. Otherwise, 20- & 30-somethings hit the floor for house sounds at the weekend or ease back into real life with R&B from midnight on Sun.

☆ **Le Smile** 3 rue Ernest Deconynck ♀ 236 E7 ☎ 03 20 57 04 16 🖳 www.smileclub-lille. com ⓘ 23.00–07.00 daily ⊠ République–Beaux Arts ⊜ Métro 2 to Gare Lille Flandres changing to line 1 to République–Beaux Arts, then take rue Gambetta to Solférino & bear right to the rue Deconynck. One of the biggest venues in central Lille, this address is almost an institution, & has a very loyal following with the college crowds – becoming a virtual HQ for scores of new arrivals each freshers' season. Back in the noughties, this was the legendary Snooker Palace Café where Yvette was den mother to a generation of youngsters away from home. Now, with its 3 bars and 3 dance floors, the venue manages to welcome a wider range of clubbers. The under-25s hang out on the ground floor at street level where contemporary sounds are spun. A '70s-themed first-floor venue attracts the 20s to 40s, while the top storey is generally mixed.

GAY LISTINGS

Lille's gay and lesbian community is far less ghettoised than in other cities. Most gay bars stock a free map-guide listing other gay and gay-friendly establishments in town and across the region.

TO XXXX OR NOT TO XXXX

Lille's appointment as European Capital of Culture for 2004 surely reflected the city's total commitment to the arts. A commitment that is found in the most surprising quarters. Some years ago, when a local theatre staged its acclaimed production of *Hamlet*, support came from radio stations, bookshops and even the porno sector. To tie in with the conventional production and a screening of Kenneth Branagh's movie version, a sex shop in the back streets near the station promoted its hardcore video adaptation that gave the lie to the perceived wisdom that there are few female parts in Shakespeare and featured a quantity of natural shocks that flesh is heir to and several consummations devoutly to be wish'd.

For current offerings, check out the sex shops on rue des Jardins, rue de Roubaix and rue Ponts de Comines.

☆ **Coming Out** 11 rue de Gand ♀ 237 K2
☎ 03 62 52 04 61 ⏱ 17.00–24.00 Mon–Thu, 17.00–01.00 Fri & Sun, 17.00–02.00 Sat
🚇 Métro 2 to Gare Lille Flandres then bus 10 to Lion d'Or. Newish gay bar has attracted a loyal crowd since the demise of the quarter's longer-established venues. Thursday night brings a DJ to the bar, & every night promises new & imaginative cocktails scrawled on the blackboard.

☆ **Le Liquium** 71 rue Jeanne d'Arc ♀ 238 F5
⏱ 15.00–24.00 Mon–Thu, 15.00–01.00 Fri, 15.00–02.00 Sat 🚋 Mairie de Lille 🚇 Métro 2 to Mairie de Lille then bus 14 to Jeanne d'Arc. Laid-back bar that considers itself 'non-straight' rather than gay or lesbian! All welcome.

☆ **Le Privilège** 🚋 2 rue Royale ♀ 237 G3
☎ 03 20 21 12 19 ⏱ 15.00–03.00 daily
🚇 Métro 2 to Gare Lille Flandres then line 1 to Rihour, cross Grand' Place to rue Esquermoise & on to rue Royale. A handful of small rooms for chilling out with friends. Welcoming bar staff & manageable prices for a late-night last drink within an easy walk of the Grand' Place. A small dance floor gets the boys on their feet when the varying music

policy veers towards the anthemic. Predominantly gay. Original theme nights such as the 'soirée messaging' where you may text your fellow barflies before starting a conversation.

☆ **S Club** 28 rue de Wazemmes ♀ 238 F5
🖥 www.s-gayclub.com ⏱ 23.00–07.00 Fri–Sat 🚋 Porte d'Arras. House DJ Storm works the decks at the newest weekend dance venue for a young, gay party-'til-dawn crowd.

☆ **Le Sébasto** 47 rue Inkerman ♀ 238 E2
☎ 03 20 54 96 32 🚋 République–Beaux Arts
🚇 Métro 2 to Gare Lille Flandres & line 1 to République–Beaux Arts, then cross the pl de la République to rue Inkerman. Non-scene, non-judgemental, non-cruising but a gay & gay-friendly neighbourhood bar close to the Palais des Beaux-Arts & the Solfé.

☆ **La Suite** 32 pl Louise de Bettignies
♀ 237 J3 ☎ 03 20 42 10 60 ⏱ 23.00–dawn Mon–Sat 🚇 Métro 2 to Gare Lille Flandres then bus 10 to Lion d'Or. This laid-back but lively club with a vaulted-cellar bar has been adapting to Lille's generally straight party scene for years. Gay tea dance on the first Sunday afternoon of the month.

Nightlife and Entertainment   GAY LISTINGS

8

THE MORNING AFTER

If you are really lucky or truly blessed then, fortified with a sturdy breakfast at Paul (page 122), you might cross Grand' Place in time for a second cup of coffee at the Nouveau Siècle concert hall (pages 130–2). Occasional Sunday morning chamber concerts offer an ideal programme of music to face the world by. The only tough challenge for those who have made the most of their Saturday night is finding the correct doorway in a 360° building when they are pie-eyed! You may also find a mid-morning performance at the Conservatoire (page 132). Otherwise, hope for a gospel brunch at the Gospel Café (page 80) or check in advance with the tourist office for other concerts around town and budget your hangover accordingly. If you need more than a spiritual detox, then the Turkish bath spa at the **Maison Folie Wazemmes** (page 191) could well prove your salvation.

☆ **La Tchouka** 80 rue de Barthélémy Delespau ♀ 238 D5 ☎ 03 20 14 37 50 🖥 www. tchoukaclub.org ⏰ 23.00–06.00 Fri–Sat 🚇 Wazemmes 🚈 Métro 2 to Gare Lille Flandres, changing to line 1 to Wazemmes, then rue des Postes leads to rue de Barthélémy Delespau. You may have known this as Le Tunnel. The name has changed, the décor has got camper (Barbie dolls, condoms & confetti) but the party atmosphere remains the same. House sounds, vodka cocktails & a mixed gay & straight crowd in their 20s & 30s.

☆ **Vice Versa** 🆅🅻 3 rue de la Barre ♀ 237 G3 ☎ 03 20 54 93 46 ⏰ 11.00–03.00 Mon–Fri, 14.00–03.00 Sat, 16.00–03.00 Sun 🚈 Métro 2 to Gare Lille Flandres then line 1 to Rihour & take the Navette Vieux Lille to rue de la Barre. Popular with the gay crowd as much as with straight punters, this is cool without being cold. Friendly staff, happening sounds & a good mix of stylish punters make this a good halfway house for meeting up & debating 'where next?'

LEAVE THE COUNTRY

When the bars in old Lille wind down, the punters break for the border as the fun continues across national frontiers. The Belgian city of Tournai is within the Lille Métropole district and nearby Pecq is the party animal's natural habitat with Le Pulse Café (the new name for the former house music legend Le Bush Club) wooing the Lille bar crowd in the small hours. For many years, Le Disco Bus collected Lille's serious *transfrontière* boppers with crowds waiting outside Gare Flandres for all points Belgian. Now, the designated driver earns the gratitude of as many as can squeeze into a secondhand Renault Clio.

The fun is not just for motorists. Just as Lille provides entertainment for the millions of people who live within an hour of the city, plenty of others exit aboard the high-speed trains which run in both directions. Once upon a time the weekend was an excuse for local teenagers to hop aboard the party trains to Amsterdam. These days, members of the speedily mobile social set use the fast trains to party in their capital city of choice. Brussels is the most popular cross-border break and most clubbing travellers aim for Fuse, which is within walking distance of the Eurostar terminal, as well as countless other bars and clubs. Allow around 35 minutes by TGV, Thalys or Eurostar from Lille Europe.

The last Eurostar to London is a favourite for clubbers heading for cool Britannia. Saturday sees Lillois day trippers heading to the West End for matinées of musicals and – since the local branch of the British store closed down – shopping at Marks & Spencer.

France provides other lures. Paris is packed with clubbing, theatrical and gastronomic excuses for spending the evening away from home. In summer, the direct rail link from Lille to Disneyland is popular with the young, free and childless in search of the American dream during the late-night opening season. Since Marne La Vallée after midnight has little to offer, these superannuated *mousquetaires* tend to hit the nightclubs of Pigalle and the Bastille, having checked Parisian listings on the English-language website www.timeout.com/paris, then chill out at the after-parties in the capital before taking the return train home after lunch on Sunday.

To be truly daring, take a TGV to Marseille, Montpellier, Lyon, Nice, Nantes or Bordeaux. But you might not get home in time for breakfast!

☆ **Le Fuse** 28 rue Blaes, 1000 Brussels
+32 2511 97 89 www.fuse.be

☆ **Pulse Café** Chaussée de Tournai, 18 RN50, 7743 Esquelmes–Pecq + 32 472 84 25 20 www.newpulse.be

8

LILLE ONLINE

For additional online content, articles, photos and more on Lille, why not visit www.bradtguides.com/lille.

Cheesemaker to kings, queens, presidents and the locals,
Lille's backstreets welcome foraging foodies (Laurence Phillips)

9

Shopping

There are four main shopping areas in Lille, and each one needs to be explored and exploited to the max. For sheer chic, absolute style and total magic, **Vieux Lille** has to be visited. Even if you have no money, it is worth pressing your nose against a window and inhaling the wealth. The second you step away from the squares of the town centre and take to the cobbles of the old town, the shops shriek class. And they drop names the way a starlet drips diamonds. Chanel, Kenzo and co. come into sharp focus within the first 50 metres. If you are an old hand at Lille shopping, you'll know that the antique dealers cluster around the roads just north of **Grand' Place**, but you might not have spotted the latest trends. Tableware is huge right now and Baccarat and Villeroy & Boch have their own *vitrines* in town (try rues de la Bourse and Esquermoise for that sort of thing). **Rue Basse**, long-time poor relation to the other streets looping around Notre Dame de la Treille, is being colonised by stylish new shopkeepers. Décor and furnishings are well worth the browsing, and the fun is in finding ever more antique dealers with tiny shops groaning under the weight of chandeliers and hiding Drouot bronze *animaliers*, intricate marquetry and lovely Lalique glassware. The **place aux Oignons** and its tributaries, **rue aux Vieux Murs** and the variously spelled **rue Pétérinck** (sometimes Pétérynck), are a hive of good taste and creativity. Find wedding dresses made with antique fabrics, artists' studios, delicious specialist food shops and some amazing tableware in the galleries and *ateliers* tucked away behind the cathedral.

If proof were needed that Lille has the heart and passion of the Mediterranean, it may be found in a simple calendar. In recent years, and to raise money for charity, the male shopkeepers of Vieux Lille have presented themselves to their patrons (albeit via the camera lens) in all their rugged nakedness. No coy hiding behind flower arrangements à la WI: here the proud masculinity of rippling commerce is draped around historic buildings, noble statuary and the grandeur of the opera house. Making the headlines when they first posed shirtless for the millennium, by the 2003 edition the boys' flaunting had become more flagrant and they were dubbed by the press the *Ch'tippendales*!

Wherever a shop closes down, the chances are that within weeks yet another e-cigarette shop will pop up in its place. E-ciggies are huge in Lille, and on every corner you'll find somewhere offering strawberry- or coffee-flavoured refills for your sonic screwdriver mouthpiece. Some boutiques on the edge of the classy districts have designer carved pipes that look to have been inspired by Sidney Paget's illustrations of Sherlock Holmes. **Vaporama** (♀ 237 J3) on place des Patiniers is living proof that *tabacs*, humidors, *fumoirs* and snuff shops are so *hier* – I saw a rosewood e-pipe on sale for €119!

From **Grand' Place** (♀ 237 H5), the shopping possibilities fan out in all directions. Where Vieux Lille meets the squares are rows of extravagant footwear boutiques, while budget shoes, wedding gowns and books may be found along the rue Faidherbe stretching to the stations. The rue Nationale, with its banks and Printemps department store, has respected boutiques, while the pedestrian zone sprawling out towards the place République is shoppers' city. The rues Béthune, Neuve, Paris and Tanneurs, with all their spurs and back-doubles, boast all the major high-street names, and plenty more besides. Galeries Lafayette has been the big star arrival of recent seasons. Meanwhile, H&M brings shoppers out into the sunlight while C&A provides the initial attraction to the **Tanneurs** mall (♀ 237 H7) within the charmed quarter. This precinct and other galleries link an impressive area from rue Molinel to Grand' Place itself. As shopping centres go, the Tanneurs is a manageable and undaunting size, its big attraction for me the clusters of very comfy armchairs for much needed mid-spree recuperation. There is something remarkably decadent and exhibitionist about relaxing in soft furnishings in a public thoroughfare: a little like clothed nudism for the clinically coy. For those who can ignore the garish neon artwork/mission statement suspended above the chairs, it is practically a haven. Another rainy-day option featuring some of the same shops and more is the fabulous **Euralille** complex (♀ 235 H4; page 163), dominating the landscape between the two railway stations and a draw in its own right.

In a district best known for the Sunday market at Wazemmes, **rue Gambetta** is worth knowing about, if only for its Sunday opening hours, a boon for weekenders wanting to spend before travelling home. It is also the very cheapest side of town. Find mini-supermarkets for last-minute bottles of mineral water and hotel-room snacking. Kitschest of cheapo clothing from the Kilo Shop at number 25 (♀ 238 E1) and loads of bazaars selling everything under the sun. Les Aubanes (♀ 238 A2) is a Sunday morning favourite at number 298. Here you will find clothes, saucepans, household goods, toys and games from last year's mail-order catalogues: La Redoute uses this store to offload surplus stock, great for a budget Christmas list. There are literally hundreds of shops, boutiques, stores and stalls to discover in Lille. I have suggested a mere 60 or so that my friends and I like to visit. Follow your nose, your eyes, and trust in your budget and willpower!

True bargain hunters should take the tram or métro out to Roubaix, home of serious savings. The twin giants of factory-outlet shopping have long wooed visitors away from Lille, charmed by the prospects of designer labels at 30–70% off high-street prices. If you are planning to go to Roubaix, don't just visit the shops. As a cultural centre in its own right, make a day of it (pages 198–201).

OPENING HOURS

Unless otherwise stated, shops usually open during the following hours:

Vieux Lille & the City Centre ⏲ 14.00–19.00 Mon, 10.00–19.00 Tue–Sat, closed all day Sun. Smaller shops often close for lunch between 12.00 & 14.00.
Euralille ⏲ 10.00–21.00 Mon–Sat, closed Sun; Carrefour ⏲ 09.00–22.00; restaurants 10.00–24.00.
Les Tanneurs ⏲ 08.30–19.45 Mon–Sat, closed Sun. Monoprix ⏲ 08.30–20.30.
Rue Gambetta ⏲ 14.00–19.00 Mon, 10.00–19.00 Tue–Sat, 09.00–13.00 Sun.

ACCESSORIES

BENJAMIN ⓖⓟ 45 rue de Béthune ⚲ 237 H7 ☏ 03 20 54 69 67 🚇 Rihour ⓔⓧ Métro 2 to Gare Lille Flandres & line 1 to Rihour, then rue de la Vieille Comédie leads to rue de Béthune
Hats, gloves, brollies and finishing touches for any outfit; Benjamin has been accessorising Lille's best-dressed set since 1926.

LA DROGUERIE See page 148.

SHERILEY 94 rue Saint-André ⚲ 237 G1 ☏ 03 20 14 00 37 ⓔⓧ Métro 2 to Gare Lille Flandres, then bus 10 to Conservatoire
Big-name handbags and luggage at real discount prices. Worth the extra couple of hundred metres of cobbles in Jimmy Choos to accessorise.

BOOKS

LE BATEAU LIVRE ⓜ 154 rue Gambetta ⚲ 238 C2 ☏ 03 20 78 16 30 ⏲ 10.00–13.00 & 14.00–19.00 Tue–Sat, closed Sun & Mon 🚇 République–Beaux Arts ⓔⓧ Gare Lille Flandres & line 1 to République–Beaux Arts, then cross the square & walk along rue Gambetta; the shop is on your right, shortly after passing rue Masséna
Even if your own French is rusty, your kids could become proficient if you take them home a children's book in French. Most bookshops in town have a juvenile section, but this *librairie* is strictly for the under-16s and is a temple to the joy of reading. Ask the staff what they would recommend. Perhaps an original *Babar* story, or even a translation of *Harry Potter*. Think how cool your kids would be considered if they could drop the French for muggles and Hogwarts into the playground conversation (*moldus* and *Poudlard*, by the way).

CAFE LIVRES See pages 116–17.

FNAC See page 159.

LE FURET DU NORD ⓖⓟ Pl du Général de Gaulle ♀ 237 H5 ☎ 03 20 78 43 43 ⏰ 09.30–19.30 Mon–Sat 🚇 Rihour ⓔ Métro 2 to Gare Lille Flandres then line 1 to Rihour
France's largest bookshop, an institution on Grand'Place, has a respectable international section and good ground-floor travel department. A must for bibliophiles.

GODON ⓥⓛ 16 rue Masurel ♀ 237 F3 ☎ 03 20 31 56 19 ⓔ Bus 50 to Lion d'Or, & follow rue Chats Bossus to rue Basse, then 2nd right on to rue Masurel
Antiquarian bookseller, for that first edition you always dreamt of owning.

RELAY The nationwide station news and book chain. Bestsellers and local maps.

VIEILLE BOURSE See pages 183–4.

VO 53 rue Molinel ♀ 237 J7 ☎ 03 20 14 33 96 ⏰ 12.00–19.00 Tue–Sat, closed Sun & Mon
🚇 Gare Lille Flandres ⓔ Métro or walk to Gare Lille Flandres then turn left along rue de Tournai
The international bookshop of Lille for English, German and Italian books, untranslated, just as the author imagined 'em. Browsers welcome; you can even enjoy coffee or juice in store. Now in big new premises on the rue Molinel.

CLOTHES

FASHION
Constance le Gonidec 1 rue Basse, 59181 Steenwerck ☎ 03 28 43 35 65
🖥 www.constancelegonidec.fr ⓔ 32km drive or taxi ride out of town!
She has now moved out of town from her original showroom just off rue de la Monnaie, but since I have had lovely emails from readers thanking me for introducing them to this fab designer in previous editions of the guide, who am I to come between a bride and her dreams. The rues Faidherbe and Molinel in Lille proper may yet have plenty of wedding dresses for the freshly affianced, but should you intend to swoon on the threshold of a whole new life, and be caught by anything of Darcy grade or above, then you really need to blush prettily in one of Constance le Gonidec's simply exquisite made-to-measure gowns. Each one a work of art and a joy to behold. Visit by appointment only for this is not a shop, but a workshop where the breathtaking creations are conjured to order and inspiration. Simply stunning outfits.

Cool Cat ⓖⓟ 56 rue de Béthune ♀ 237 G7 ☎ 03 20 38 33 83 🖥 www.coolcat.nl
🚇 Rihour ⓔ Métro 2 to Gare Lille Flandres then line 1 to Rihour & walk down rue de la Vieille Comédie to rue de Béthune
The Dutch line in don't-care-casual for students and clubbers comes to Lille with enough loud

Take the métro down to the end of Line 1 and step off CHR B-Calmette, then follow your innate sense of style to the rue du Faubourg des Postes, aka the Faubourg of Fab. This **Faubourg des Modes** is the alternative fashion district, as launched in 2007 by designer Agnès b. More than a dozen workshops along the street are home to a new generation of designers selling direct from their studios to the public, cutting out middlemen, catwalks and fashion shows.

music pumped out through a good sound system, and plasma screens to keep the right crowd browsing and the wrong crowd at bay. Whatever-wear for a generation.

La Griffe ⓥ 27 rue de la Barre ⑨ 237 H3 ☏ 03 20 57 47 20 ⓣ 14.30–19.00 Mon, 13.00–19.00 Tue & Thu–Sat, closed Wed ⚉ Rihour ⊕ Métro 2 to Lille Flandres, then line 1 to Rihour & take the Navette Vieux Lille to rue de la Barre
Secondhand clothes and shoes from the Continent's leading fashion houses. Everything is in good condition and costs about a third of the original retail price.

Loding 13 rue Lepelletier ⑨ 237 H4 ☏ 03 20 40 08 47 ⚉ Rihour ⊕ Métro 2 to Gare Lille Flandres & line 1 to Rihour, then cross Grand' Place & walk through the Alcide arch towards rue Lepelletier
Happy Father's Day, or just welcome to your new moneyed lifestyle. Classy menswear – shoes, shirts, cuff-links and cashmere sweaters, plus classic gentlemen's club colours and décor. Reeks of tradition, but dates back to the late 1990s.

Miss Sixty 12 rue de la Clef ⑨ 237 J4 ☏ 03 20 21 04 66 ⊕ Bus 50 to Lion d'Or
Where a Bardot pout still trumps a Cyrus twerk, here you'll find street smarts that are fun without being outrageous. I first noticed the windows here back in 2009 when even the dungarees were cute (the choice was then between the baby-doll-nightie style and a floppy-belted hot pant version). Five years on, faded jeans and printed T-shirts look as though they were cut to be worn with Gallic insouciance, playfully retro with a contemporary attitude. The popular name in mail-order style has its Lille shopfront at the edge of the old town by the reality of boulevard Carnot.

Nathalie Chaize 43 rue Basse ⑨ 237 H4 ☏ 03 20 51 27 17 🖥 www.nathaliechaize.com
⊕ Métro 2 to Gare Lille Flandres, then cross the squares to rue Esquermoise & turn right on to rue Basse
One-time architect, all-time fashion designer, darling of the Paris art set, hands-on creator of posh frocks and luscious lingerie, Chaize is one of the characters of the French fashion scene. Her annual collections, presented on Paris catwalks by film stars, are on sale in her new boutique in the old town.

Nenette de Lille ⓥ 43 rue de la Monnaie ♀ 237 J3 ✆ 03 20 06 00 81 ⏰ Sun
mornings, closed Mon ⊞ Bus 50 to Lion d'Or

Co-ordinate your shoes with your teapot and your frocks with your crocks: from fashion to soft furnishings. Clothes, housewares and everything you need for a co-ordinated lifestyle. This boutique does not close for lunch.

Poppy Milton 90 rue Esquermoise ♀ 237 G4 ✆ 03 20 12 98 14 ⊞ Métro 2 to Gare Lille Flandres, then cross the squares to rue Esquermoise

In a quarter where English tea shops sprout up on street corners, it was inevitable that the arrival of this corner shop in girlie pink would be met with press phrases such as 'so British' and 'Notting Hill'. Brit Miss wear and accessories.

La 7ème Compagnie ⒼⓅ 11 rue Jean Sans Peur ♀ 237 G6 ✆ 03 20 54 39 63
⏰ 10.00–12.00 and 14.00–19.00 Tue–Sat 🚇 République–Beaux Arts ⊞ Métro 2 to Gare Lille Flandres, changing to line 1 to République–Beaux Arts, then walk north on bd de la Liberté to junction with rue Jean Sans Peur

Epaulettes, camouflage and good strong fabric. Outfits with a military look from practical combats and standard army-surplus clubwear to costume items such as British Guardsman's uniforms.

BARGAINS
La Griffe See page 145.

Tati 12–14 rue Faidherbe ♀ 237 J5 ✆ 03 20 74 00 00 🖥 www.tati.fr ⏰ 09.30–19.00 Mon–Sat 🚇 Gare Lille Flandres ⊞ Walk along av le Corbusier & right on to rue Faidherbe

Oh, how the mighty have fallen. Once a string of stores along the top of rue Faidherbe, just one store remains with a fraction of what we used to know, now that the street has been colonised by pharmacies and chain restaurants. Mikhail Gorbachev was once late for a meeting of world leaders because his wife, the radiant Raisa, she of the cover-girl style, had fallen for the charms of the main Parisian branch of Tati. This institution is France's bargain basement and, even in well-mannered Lille, the niceties have been known to be abandoned in the scrum for a pair of trousers for the price of a coffee, a skirt for the cost of a sandwich or an entire wedding trousseau for less than €75. It sells everything from jewellery to beachwear, dinner jackets to posing pouches, terracotta candlesticks to pillowcases. Since Kylie Minogue sported an outfit inspired by Tati's trademark pink gingham, and Hockney iconised the pattern, the well-to-do have been known to venture through the doors even without their Hermès headscarves and dark glasses. So what if 90% of the stuff is ghastly, and the cheapest wedding dress so polyester rich it could raise enough static electricity to discipline the naughtiest pageboy at a single touch? Who cares? Cotton T-shirts are cotton T-shirts and the kids will grow out of the €5 jeans long before the seams surrender. Anyone who has found angora and cashmere hidden behind the naffest velour cardies is hooked for life. I've found €3 corduroy slippers a godsend when staying in a cheap hotel, and on the one occasion that I discovered dubious signs of life in the bedsheets at a student hall of residence in Lille, I invested in a full set of linen, pillows and duvet in order to bed down on the floor – and paid Tati just €20 for the privilege. If you have over-shopped elsewhere, find extra luggage at knockdown prices; if you've left the camera at home, buy a disposable one here for next to nothing; and if you've decided to consummate the love of your life, pick up a pack of Tati's gingham-wrapped condoms (just ignore the disconcerting name, 'Soft Life').

FACTORY OUTLETS
McArthurGlen Mail de Lannoy, 59100 Roubaix ☎03 28 33 36 00
🖰 www.mcarthurglen.fr ⏰ 10.00–19.00 Mon–Sat 🚉 Eurotéléport ⊞ Métro 2 to Eurotéléport, or tram to Roubaix
Confirming Roubaix's status as the home of bargain designer shopping, this open-air mall above the main métro station is an avenue of 52 outlet stores. Mostly French high-street names, the international firms offering permanent discounts of 30–70% on regular prices include Adidas, Reebok, Blanc Bleu, Cacherel and Carven. Even Disney's upmarket label Donaldson may be found here, featuring hacking jackets and tweeds with the most discreet Mickey Mouse buttons.

L'Usine 228 av Alfred Motte, 59100 Roubaix ☎03 20 83 16 20 🖰 www.lusine.fr ⏰ 10.00–19.00 Mon–Sat ⊞ Métro 2 to Epeule Montesquieu then bus 25 to Les Hauts Champs
Not as neatly laid out as McArthurGlen, but this is where it all began 20 years ago, and where four million French and Belgian shoppers each year choose to eke out their euros. Three storeys of a former factory, stuffed with linens, clothes and shoes at ludicrously low prices. Since Roubaix is the capital of France's mail-order industry, with Les Trois Suisses and La Redoute both based here, when new catalogues are published, old stock has to be sold off as swiftly as possible. End-of-range goods, factory seconds, everything from footwear to table linen at prices to raise the most plucked eyebrow. A children's playground, choice of restaurants and even a hairdressing salon on the premises for those planning to make a day of it, walking from room to room to pick up Etam, Lacoste, Nike, Dior, YSL, Wrangler and Levi products at well under half the shop price.

XXL
Capelstore Ⓥ 89 rue de la Monnaie 📍237 H2 ☎03 20 57 48 17 ⏰ closed Mon
🚉 Rihour ⊞ Bus 50 to Lion d'Or
Bienvenue chez Monsieur XXL. Suits and casual menswear for the taller or wider chap. It has now left its rather old-fashioned premises along rue Nationale for a more cutting edge, if smaller, boutique.

Je m'Aime en Ronde Ⓜ 318–320 rue Gambetta 📍238 A2 ☎03 20 54 50 82 🖰 www.jemaimeenronde.com 🚉 Gambetta ⊞ Métro 2 to Gare Lille Flandres, then line 1 to Gambetta, walk along rue de Flandre, turn left into rue de la Paix d'Utrecht and into rue Gambetta
Big girls don't cry, they dress up in pretty things, from frilly undies to wafty, summery picnicky outfits. French couture for all. Stylish eye-catching outfits from size 16 to 30 and beyond. Just ask Hélène Coquerelle and her team of *vendeuses* and you will positively strut out of the store looking a million euros and turning heads all the way to the Eurostar home. Flaunt it, flirt in it and carry it off. Don't forget that the shop is open Sunday morning too.

Yokaéli Ⓥ 55 rue de la Barre 📍237 F3 ☎03 20 22 00 48 🖰 http://yokaeli-grandestailles.blogspot.fr 🚉 Rihour ⊞ Métro 2 to Lille Flandres & line 1 to Rihour, then take the Navette Vieux Lille to rue de la Barre

Shopping CLOTHES

9

If you are fed up with fashion designers whose inspiration falters if stretched beyond a size 6, then learn to love the couturier Lindsay Grison. Her outfits are celebrated in this boutique/workshop on the edge of Vieux Lille. Find original, bold and confident clothes in a genuinely comfortable fit, as worn by plus-size celebs.

COSMETICS AND PERFUME

SAGA ⊕ **3 rue Neuve** ♀ **237 H5** ✎ **03 20 39 25 60** 🖥 **www.sagacosmetic.com** 🚋 **Rihour**
Métro 2 to Gare Lille Flandres then line 1 to Rihour, walk to the corner of Grand' Place & right on to rue Neuve
Pharmacies and department stores have a traditional grip on the cosmetics market in France. Even baby soap bought at the chemist may belie the no-more-tears promise when it comes to the price tag. Supermarkets have nudged prices down at the popular end of the scale, but for the big names in make-up, the province of the hyper-plucked eyebrowed cosmetic technician in a white lab coat has remained pretty impregnable – at least until 1999 when the first cut-price retailer elbowed its way into the high street. It has been a slow revolution: Saga has but 13 stores nationwide, and the latest has now opened its doors in Lille. Not all the great marques may be found here but Revlon, Schwartzkopf and Balmain are on the shelves, with low price tags.

SEPHORA ⊕ **7 pl du Général de Gaulle** ♀ **237 H5** ✎ **03 28 36 11 90** 🖥 **www.sephora.fr**
🚋 **Rihour** **Métro 2 to Gare Lille Flandres then line 1 to Rihour; the shop is on the corner of Grand' Place**
National cosmetic chain retailer, now with a branch on Grand' Place. The shop is open until 19.00. A second shop, in the Euralille complex (page 163) remains open an hour later.

SOAPEO **18 rue des Bouchers** ♀ **237 G4** m **07 78 55 33 46** 🖥 **www.soapeo.fr** 🚋 **Rihour**
Métro 2 to Lille Flandres, then line 1 to Rihour & take the Navette Vieux Lille to rue des Bouchers
If your smellies are for behind closed bathroom doors, then pop into Lille's soap shop. As befitting its location in the new foodie quarter, find bath bombs and genuine cakes of soap in the shapes of *petits fours*, cupcakes, *macarons* and fruit tarts. Otherwise stimulate the senses with oils, salts and bubble baths. You may even go for the full Cleopatra beauty regime, since the shop stocks a range of products for those who like to bathe in ass's milk.

CRAFTS

ATELIER DE LA SORCIERE VERTE See page 158.

LA DROGUERIE **50 rue Basse** ♀ **237 G4** ✎ **03 20 55 36 80** **Métro 2 to Gare Lille Flandres & line 1 to Rihour, then walk across the squares, up rue Esquermoise & turn right on to rue Basse**
If you're looking to accessorise or to tart up an old frock found in a flea market then come here, where fabrics, silks, wools and jars of buttons and beads are stacked along the walls in a Bohemian dressmaker's delight.

DAUMY

LILLE3000

Since its term as European Capital of Culture in 2004, Lille has hosted a major international festival every couple of years, reinventing the streets for each season of Lille3000. Rue Faidherbe is always up for a makeover, from a permanent parade of elephants to illuminating the skies in an arcade of lights.

149

HISTORY AND ARCHITECTURE

Lille may be known for the traditional Flemish gables of the old town, but there is so much more to see than just cobbles. From Gothic churches and Art Deco shopfronts to the futurescape beyond Euralille's glass towers, the streets are a gallery of style from across the centuries.

MOREL & FILS

1 The Porte de Paris, overlooked by the Hôtel de Ville. 2 The neo-Flemish Chamber of Commerce. 3 Modern art outside Gare Lille Europe. 4 Morel et Fils. 5 The Voix du Nord building. 6 & 7 Art Deco and Art Nouveau shopfronts. 8 Eglise St Maurice. 9 Homage to the Resistance heroes at the Monument aux Fusillées. 10 Holocaust victims remembered in Notre Dame's church doors.

BEYOND THE CITY

Fifteem minutes by tram or half an hour by métro, a wealth of world-class art collections and museums are waiting to be discovered just outside Lille.

1 Roubaix's Museum of Art and Industry is housed in an Art Deco swimming pool. **2** La Condition Publique, one of the region's Maisons Folies. **3** Lens is home to the brand new Louvre museum – the only branch outside Paris. **4** LaM in Villeneuve d'Ascq.

GRAPHIGRO 71 rue de Paris ♀ 237 J7 ☏ 03 20 74 44 99 www.graphigro-lille.fr
🚊 Gare Lille Flandres Métro 2 to Gare Lille Flandres, then left into rue de Priez; at the
foot of rue Faidherbe walk around the church to rue de Paris
Now that the craft shop in Euralille has been replaced by yet another homeware outlet, come here
for good art supplies.

FLORISTS

D'AUTRES FLEURS 92 rue de Paris ♀ 237 J6 ☏ 03 20 57 45 40 ⊙ 10.00–13.00 & 14.30–
19.00, closed Mon 🚊 Gare Lille Flandres Métro 2 to Gare Lille Flandres, then left into rue
de Priez; at the foot of rue Faidherbe walk around the church to rue de Paris
Martine Desmettre's lovely little florist shop has more than a hint of the Edwardian about it, with
fin du siècle tea services and cherubim among the flowers.

DES FLEURS PAR JEAN LOUIS 1–3 pl des Patiniers ♀ 237 J3 ☏ 03 20 06 07 08
🚊 Gare Lille Flandres Bus 50 to Lion d'Or & walk back down pl des Patiniers
Vieux Lille is decorated with stylish artisanal florists whose teeny *echoppes* are garlanded
with blossom and leaves, hidden behind climbers and foliage and fronted with trestles
containing miniature pewter pots and pails with hyacinths and micro-topiary. But Jean
Louis is ideal for those whose grasp of the language of flowers is ungrammatical and whose
fashion sense does not quite have the cutting edge of secateurs. If you do not know this year's
essential colours nor the design of the home to which you've been invited, then trust in this
master florist, whose blooms and blossoms are exclusively white, with only the occasional
splash of cream or magnolia.

POMME CANNELLE 5 rue du Curé Saint-Etienne ♀ 237 H4 ☏ 03 20 06 83 06
⊙ 14.00–19.00 Mon, 10.00–19.00 Tue–Sat, closed Sun 🚊 Rihour Métro 2 to Gare Lille
Flandres & line 1 to Rihour, then cross the squares, walk under the Alcide arch & turn left
I love this tiny little florist shop. Dinky and dainty terracotta pots of perfect miniature rose bushes
from €4.50, or unusual and exotic plants manicured to perfection.

ULTRA VIOLET 19 rue Lepelletier ♀ 237 H4 ☏ 03 20 06 00 15 🚊 Rihour Métro 2
to Gare Lille Flandres & line 1 to Rihour, then cross the squares & walk under the Alcide arch
towards rue Lepelletier
This place looks rather like a cave thanks to the tangle of roots and branches along the ceiling. Pick
up imaginative table arrangements, mixing fruits, plants, mosses and twigs.

FOOD AND WINE

THE DAILY BREAD
Chez L'Ami des Arts Maison Brésard 44 rue Négrier ♀ 237 G1 ☏ 03 28 36 90
58 ⊙ 07.00–13.30 & 15.00–19.45 Mon–Sat, 07.00–13.30 & 17.00–19.45 Sun Métro 2
to Gare Lille Flandres then bus 10 to Conservatoire, then walk along rue Négrier

A modest little chain of bread shops, for nice buttery croissants and good crusty loaves. Other branches at 28 rue des Postes and 38 place Cormontaigne.

Paul See page 122.

Silence Ça Cuit 26 rue Manuel ♀ 238 C3 ✎ 03 20 51 53 87 🖱 www.silencecacuit.com
🕐 07.30–19.30 Mon–Sat 🚋 Gambetta 🚇 Métro 2 to Gare Lille Flandres & line 1 to Gambetta, then walk the length of rue Manuel

At last a worthy alternative to the ubiquitous Paul. Just when it seemed that all the last quirky corner-shop bakeries were inevitably branded with the logo that lights your route before you even step on the Eurostar in London, a new kid on the block begins his own tradition. Well, new to this block perhaps, but no stranger to Lille. Marc Lelieur runs half a dozen well-known eateries in the heart of town, from the Chicorée and La Paix to Le Square and La Baignoire, and is also the driving force behind the Hotel Kanaï (pages 62–3). This block is way across town: just around the corner and then another turn or two from Sébastopol is the imposing bakery with the air of a venue. Flags around the building declare *maman's* eternal answer to her hungry children, with the signature statement 'Pain by Marc' scrawled across the doorway. Samples of bread laid out for the tasting, *viennoiseries* and delicious pastries displayed as though at an art gallery to whet the appetite. Find service with a brisk, efficient smile at the counter in front of the grand working kitchen. Hygiene rules, and cash transactions (coins at any rate) are handled by a dinky little change machine, while the vendeuse slips your purchase into a neat paper bag. Delicious chocky *crème pâtissière*, and to wash down your *pain au raisin*, stick with the produce of the vine. Some cracking Bordeaux and Champagnes are sold at the bread counter – from a St Estèphe for under €10 to some fizz at around €25.

THE FOOD
L'Abbaye des Saveurs 🍷 13 rue des Vieux Murs ♀ 237 H2 ✎ 03 28 07 70 06
🖱 www.abbaye-des-saveurs.fr 🕐 10.00–19.30 Tue–Sat, 10.00–14.30 Sun 🚌 Bus 50 to Lion d'Or, and from rue de la Monnaie turn left into rue Pétérinck

For true beer lovers this is the place to find artisanal beers from across Flanders, *bières sans frontières*, with superb ranges of the best of Belgium to complement around two dozen local breweries represented on the shelves, available by the bottle or the barrel. Franck and Anthony, the faces of L'Abbaye des Saveurs, are both passionate about local produce and this is reflected in the range of meats, sweets and local delicacies from jars of *potjevleesch* to rounds of cheeses. Most items are supplied directly from the farmers, and shop staff will advise on which producers open their farms to visitors, should you fancy a day in the country. If you are planning a party in Lille, then rent a beer pump from the shop.

L'Arrière Pays 47 rue Basse ♀ 237 H4 ✎ 03 20 13 80 07 🚇 Métro 2 to Gare Lille Flandres and line 1 to Rihour, then cross the squares to walk up rue Esquermoise & turn right into rue Basse

A grocery shop selling incredible and wonderful preserves, oils and pâtés in little bottles and jars. The place doubles as a restaurant and *salon de thé* (page 76).

Benoit ⓋⓁ 77 rue de la Monnaie ♀ 237 H2 ☏ 03 20 31 69 03 ⏱ 09.30–19.30 Tue–Sat, 09.00–13.30 Sun 🚌 Bus 50 to Lion d'Or
Belgium's Neuhaus and Leonidas have high-profile counters in Lille, but forsake them in favour of a taste of the domestic product. The famous chocolate shop of Lille has over 50 varieties of chocolates and truffles to tempt the sweet tooth.

Bio c'Bon ⓋⓁ 35 rue de la Monnaie ♀ 237 J3 ☏ 03 28 53 62 63 ⏱ 10.00–20.00 Mon–Sat, 10.00–13.00 Sun 🚌 Bus 50 to Lion d'Or
Organic supermarket with weigh-and-pay nuts, dried fruits and pulses – as well as food for vegetarians.

Bottega ⒼⓅ 8b rue Pétérinck ♀ 237 H2 ☏ 03 20 21 16 85 🖥 www.la-bottega.com
🚌 Bus 50 to Lion d'Or, & from rue de la Monnaie turn left into rue Pétérinck
Everything Italian, from espresso machines to beautifully crafted Venetian carnival masks, pasta and pesto, coffee and Tuscan olive oil – a celebration of *la dolce vita* at the table in the heart of Vieux Lille. This is the place to find the ingredients used by the very best Italian restaurants in the city (see pages 93–4). If the Latin smile behind the counter looks familiar, but you cannot quite place it, perhaps you do not recognise its wearer with his clothes on. Gilberto Annunzio has been known to display his Latin credentials on the celebrated Vieux Lille calendar (page 141).

Chocolat Passion ⒼⓅ 67 rue Nationale ♀ 237 G5 ☏ 03 20 54 74 42 🖥 www.chocolatpassion.com 🚇 Rihour 🚇 Métro 2 to Gare Lille Flandres & line 1 to Rihour, then walk up rue Roisin & turn left on to rue Nationale

▼ Lille has a lot to offer those with a sweet tooth (Anna Moores)

Good for last-minute pressies, if a little souvenirish. Among the serious chocolate boxes are 'novelty' items such as edible mobile phones and supersized euro coins. You can buy a gift for €5.

La Comtesse du Barry ⓖⓟ 21 rue Esquermoise ♀ 237 H4 ☏ 03 20 54 00 43
⏱ 14.00–19.30 Mon, 09.30–19.30 Tue–Sat 🚊 Rihour 🚇 Métro 2 to Gare Lille Flandres & line 1 to Rihour, then cross Grand' Place to rue Esquermoise

Pâtés in jars and tins of preserved delicacies from across France, but mostly from the farmyards of the southwest. Foie gras, smoked salmon, prepared terrines and cold platters for lunch, or gift-wrapped as savoury presents.

Delassic Frères 11 pl des Patiniers ♀ 237 J3 ☏ 03 28 52 32 88 📱 www.fromage-delassic.fr ⏱ 12.00–14.00 & 19.00–22.00 Tue–Fri, 12.00–17.00 Sat, closed Sun & Mon
🚌 Bus 50 to Lion d'Or & walk back down pl des Patiniers

Lille's first cheese bar (page 111) is the latest address for picking up that special something for rounding off a meal to remember. Choose your cheese by animal (goat, ewe or cow), by strength, or even by family (creamy, smelly, hard, etc). Described as a *crémerie* and *bar à fromages*, you can climb the stairs to a first-floor dining room and have a meal of cheese or just dither in the teeny shop on the petticoats of the historic centre.

Ferme en Ville 15 pl Mendès France ♀ 237 G4 ☏ 03 20 55 42 53 🚊 Rihour 🚇 Métro 2 to Gare Lille Flandres then line 1 to Rihour, then take rue Roisin into rue de Pas & pl Mendès France

Farm animals in the centre of the city do not stop the traffic. The Lillois are used to Grand' Place being transformed into agricultural plots, just as frequently as it becomes a ballroom or a Christmas grotto. But the static cow that stands outside 15 pl Mendès France is something of a permanent fixture, the little local landmark that tells passers-by that the city has a genuine farm shop in its midst. If you miss market day, then rely on Aurélie and Gladys to sell you the freshest leeks and endives, fine strings of ripe garlic, jars of farmyard pâtés and all other creamery, charcuterie, market-garden or farmhouse-table produce to perk up your picnic.

A l'Huîtrière See page 100–1.

Pâtisserie Meert See page 104. When closed on a Monday, find the famous waffles at Printemps department store (pages 162–3).

Philippe Olivier 3 rue du Curé Saint-Etienne ♀ 237 G4 ☏ 03 20 74 96 99 ⏱ 14.30–19.30 Mon, 10.00–12.30 & 14.30–19.30 Tue, 10.00–19.30 Wed–Sat 🚊 Rihour 🚇 Métro 2 to Gare Lille Flandres & line 1 to Rihour, then walk across the squares, under the Alcide arch & turn left

Maître Olivier is one of the country's grand masters of cheese. His main store in Boulogne supplies the Elysée Palace, the Vatican and the White House. Buy a Camembert marinated in calvados or try a local Flanders speciality such as a Mont des Cats. There's another branch in Lens, if you are going out of town to visit the new Louvre.

THE WINES AND BEERS
L'Abbaye des Saveurs   See page 154.

La Cave du Parvis St Maurice   98 rue de Paris ♀ 237 J7 ☎ 03 20 13 76 68 ☒ Gare
Lille Flandres ⊕ Av le Corbusier to Gare Lille Flandres, then left on to rue de Priez; at the
foot of rue Faidherbe, walk around the church to rue de Paris
This treasure stands in the shade of the St Maurice church on rue de Paris. Come here for wines,
wine accessories and lots of wine wisdom. This knowledge and insight is dispensed to even the
most casual of browsers, but by the figurative magnum to those who book for the special *soirée
découverte et dégustation* tutored tasting sessions. You may buy a place at one of these evenings as
a gift. Don't be misled by the modest shopfront. As the sign in the window explains, 'our window
may be small, but our cellar is huge', and there are around 17,000 labels to be discovered here.

Au Gré du Vin   See page 111.

Les Vins d'Aurélien   5 rue Jean Sans Peur ♀ 237 G6 ☎ 03 20 64 36 63 🖰 www.
lesvinsdaurelien.fr ☒ Rihour ⊕ Métro 2 to Gare Lille Flandres then line 1 to Rihour, then
follow rue du Palais Rihour, turn left on rue de l'Hôpital Militaire & right to rue Jean Sans
Peur
Around 1,000 wines collected over eight years in what might become the Lille wine-lover's Diagon
Alley. Aurélien himself, *caviste* and infectious enthusiast, has the air of a bearded Harry Potter as he
shares a total love and appreciation of the wines of France and beyond. He knows the people and
stories behind each bottle, from the great traditional houses to the *chais* of exciting new *vignerons*.
Shell out €40 for one of his themed tasting events (discover the Languedoc, Bordeaux versus
Burgundy, etc) or just chat about *la bouteille juste* for your next dinner party.

Les Vins Gourmands   33 rue Esquermoise ♀ 237 H4 ☎ 03 20 30 12 20 ☒ Rihour
⊕ Métro 2 to Gare Lille Flandres & line 1 to Rihour, then cross the square to rue
Esquermoise
Since Annie-Paule gave up her fabulous boutique shop around the corner and across the way, I've
been seeking another shop where one's every purchase is a lesson. This will do nicely. Well-read and
open-minded staff know not only their French *cépages* and vintages, but have a good knowledge of
the wider world. So when talking of the picnic or dinner party you have in mind, do not be surprised
to be offered a New Zealand white or South African red as well as a Burgundy and a Côtes du Rhône.

Silence Ça Cuit   See page 154.

GIFTS

ARTISANAT MONASTIQUE   ⓥ Parvis Notre Dame de la Treille, pl Gilleson ♀ 237 H3
☎ 03 20 55 22 19 ⏲ 14.00–18.30 Mon, 09.30–18.30 Tue–Sat ⊕ Bus 50 to Lion d'Or then
walk from rue de la Monnaie to the cathedral
Religious and liturgical gifts, from monastic-themed accessories to devotional items.

ATELIER DE LA SORCIERE VERTE Ⓥ 19 rue de la Clef ♀ 237 J4 ☏ 03 20 12 07 06
🖰 www.latelierdelasorciereverte.fr 🚌 Av le Corbusier & right into rue Faidherbe; walk behind the opera house to rue de la Clef

The good green witch sells lovely stationery, elegant nibs and inks for calligraphers, smart and elegant diaries and calligraphy papers.

NATURE ET DECOUVERTES Euralille ♀ 235 H4 ☏ 03 20 78 01 00 🖰 www.natureetdecouvertes.com 🚆 Lille Europe 🚌 Cross parvis Mitterand to Centre Euralille

A fabulous calming oasis in any shopping centre (there is another branch in the Galerie Grand' Place), where ecologically responsible shoppers can browse in a state of relaxation occasioned by the headphones playing sounds of nature and rainwater and cups of freshly infused herbal tea. Wooden toys, ramblers' accessories, books, gifts and a range of eclectic wonders. I love the store's suggestion of the perfect present to mark the birth of a child: an acorn and planter so that a tree grows with the new life.

NENETTE DE LILLE See page 146.

HOME

CAMILLE STOPIN Ⓥ 14 pl Louise de Bettignies ♀ 237 J3 ☏ 03 20 55 39 02 🖰 www.stopin.fr ⏰ 09.00–12.00 & 14.30–19.00 Mon–Fri (appointments are preferred) 🚌 Bus 50 to Lion d'Or

For something rather special, this family of cabinet-makers has served Lille's stylish householders since 1860. Father-and-son craftsmen work on restoring and creating some choice pieces of furniture. The family has been called upon by France's museums to restore some of the nation's premier pieces of furniture. Should you find a battered *escritoire* or *armoire* at the Braderie or the flea market, this is the place to take your antiques. If you've brought the car, push the boat out.

GUILLAUME MOISSON Ⓥ 3 rue Pétérinck ♀ 237 H2 ☏ 03 20 15 08 99 ⏰ 09.30–12.00 & 14.00–18.30 Tue–Sat 🚌 Bus 50 to Lion d'Or, & from rue de la Monnaie turn left on to rue Pétérinck

When I first discovered this gallery it was known as the Atelier Un Vrai Semblance, the go-to place for a Rembrandt on a budget. In those days, people in the know would drop in to Guillaume Moisson's studio to see if he could run them up a quick Rubens or come up with a nice Cézanne for the spare bedroom. Moisson earned his living making copies of great artworks from the world's leading galleries. After a successful first career recreating greatness as a scenic artist for the theatre, he set up this little studio, between the rue de la Monnaie and the cathedral, where he produced copies of Caravaggios on demand for a four-figure sum (reproduction Monets from perhaps a little less). Commissions usually take three months. Of course, he is a talented artist in his own right and those who asked would be invited to visit his private gallery. Nowadays the Picassos are no longer in the frame, and you can pop round to consider a Moisson original for your home, without a trace of faux-vism or impression of impressionism.

LA PUCE A L'OREILLE ⓥ 10 pl Louise de Bettignies ♀ 237 J3 ☎ 03 28 36 28 28
🖥 www.la-puce.com 🚍 Bus 50 to Lion d'Or

A mix of the genuine antique, reconditioned, worn-out and repro at this quaint interiors specialist. Sturdy and stylish wooden furniture, imaginative décor ideas and some luxurious linens within this highly browsable old building.

MISSMAP 21 rue Basse ♀ 237 H4 ☎ 03 20 21 19 80 🖥 www.missmap.eu 🚍 Bus 50 to Lion d'Or, then follow rue Chats Bossus to rue Basse

Turn your address into an artwork at this thrillingly original gallery. I first encountered the concept when the Missmap Store held an exhibition at a local festival. Once I came to terms that this was not an emporium devoted to the works of E F Benson, I was seduced by the idea and the reality of digitised maps, aerial photography, vintage images of your own address or favourite places manipulated in styles from cod-Warhol to Day-Glo. Choose from composite images or grand tableaux, triptychs or military-style posters. All may be printed and mounted as card light-boxes, on perspex or even weather-resistant metal. Prices start at under €30. Buy off the peg or commission your individual design and have it delivered.

HOME ENTERTAINMENT/MUSIC

For musical instruments, go to place Vieux Marché au Chevaux off place Béthune (🚇 *République–Beaux Arts*) where several small shops sell keyboards, accordions, woodwind and brass instruments. Serious guitar collectors should visit Cosmik Guitar (♀ 238 C2) nearby at 63 rue Jean Sans Peur.

CARREFOUR 🖸 Euralille ♀ 235 H4 ☎ 03 20 15 56 00 ⏰ 09.00–22.00 Mon–Sat 🚉 Gare Lille Europe 🚍 Opposite the station

The hypermarket at Euralille has a good department selling electrical goods, CDs and computer accessories. Their own-brand products often come with a two-year warranty. See also page 162.

FNAC 🖸 20 rue Saint-Nicolas ♀ 237 H6 ⏰ 10.00–19.30 Mon–Sat 🚉 Rihour 🚍 Métro 2 to Gare Lille & line 1 to Rihour, then on Grand'Place, walk through La Voix du Nord building

Hi-fi and photographic equipment and accessories, books, discs and videos at the nation's favourite chain store and box office. A self-service gift-wrapping desk is located near the cashiers.

O'CD 🖸 21 rue des Tanneurs ♀ 237 H6 ☎ 03 20 40 04 62 🖥 www.ocd.net ⏰ 14.00–19.30 Mon, 10.00–19.30 Tue–Sat, 15.00–19.30 Sun 🚉 Rihour 🚍 Métro 2 to Gare Lille Flandres & line 1 to Rihour, then rue de la Vieille Comédie leads to rue des Tanneurs

Secondhand CDs and DVDs bought and sold daily. Priced at €2–13, and guaranteed to be good quality, all discs may be heard before you buy, thanks to rows of headphones around the shop.

URBAN MUSIC 🖸 30 rue Saint-Nicolas ♀ 237 H6 ☎ 03 20 63 90 83 🚉 Rihour
🚍 Métro 2 to Gare Lille then line 1 to Rihour; at the corner of Grand'Place turn right on to rue Neuve then left to rue Saint-Nicolas – it's the shop is just along from FNAC

Strictly vinyl, from Motown to club sounds. A proper record shop for those whose ears are strictly analogue. Cheekily (or cannily) located next to the mainstream music shop FNAC.

JEWELLERY

LE PAGE ⓖ 6–10 rue de la Bourse ♀ 237 H5 ☎ 03 20 12 04 04 ⓒ 14.00–19.00 Mon, 10.00–12.30 & 14.00–19.00 Tue–Fri, 10.00–19.00 Sat, closed Mon in Jul & Aug 🚇 Rihour
ⓔ **Walk past the opera house to rue de la Bourse**
A jewel box of a shop, the ornate façade is always one of the treats of the town when the Christmas lights are switched on. Upstaging even the building are the watches and trinkets from Gucci, Chanel and Rolex.

MARKETS

BRADERIE See page 12.

PLACE DU CONCERT ⓥ Pl du Concert ♀ 237 H1 ⓒ 07.00–14.00 Wed, Fri & Sun
ⓔ **Bus 50 to Lion d'Or then follow rue de la Monnaie to the marketplace**
Chic, low-key and a treat in the centre of the old town. None of the bustle of Wazemmes, but quality goods, and walking distance from some fine restaurants, most of which are not averse to sourcing the dish of the day from these very stalls.

▼ The late summer Braderie is heaven for antique and bargain hunters, but fleamarkets and collectors' fairs are held all year round (Anna Moores)

SEBASTOPOL Ⓜ Pl Sébastopol ♀ 238 D2 ⓘ 07.00–14.00 Wed & Sat 🚉 République–Beaux Arts Ⓔ Métro 2 to Gare Lille Flandres, then line 1 to République–Beaux Arts; walk along rue Inkerman to the market square

In the shadow of the extravagantly overdesigned theatre come cheery local traders with mainly a food market. Don't forget that chicory (known in France as *endive*) is the pepperiest and crunchiest accompaniment to any picnic. Dubbed *les perles du Nord*, they are the stars of the fruit and veg stalls. I have found some stylish jewellery here on occasions and friends swear by the bag stalls as excellent value.

VIEILLE BOURSE See pages 183–4.

WAZEMMES MARKET Ⓜ Pl de la Nouvelle Aventure ♀ 238 A3 ⓘ Sun morning; covered produce market from 06.00 until late afternoon Tue–Sun 🚉 Gambetta Ⓔ Métro 2 to Gare Lille Flandres & line 1 to Gambetta, then cross the rue du Marché & walk around the church to pl de la Nouvelle Aventure

Emerge from Gambetta métro station and prepare for all your senses to be ravaged. Surrender to the pulse of the city and simply follow the crowds past puppies and chickens, rabbits and budgerigars. Around the church of St Pierre and St Paul swims the tide of humanity, past antiques, bric-a-brac and junk, past piles of clothing. Into the place de la Nouvelle Aventure the adventure continues, past mounds of gloriously plump fresh chicory, rose-red radishes and tear-blushed artichokes from the market gardens of Artois and Flanders, past puppets and playthings, smart coats and swimwear; shop doorways flung open on a Sunday; past promises of 'Special prices just for you Monsieur, Madame, only today from my cousin in Africa'. Into the red-brick market hall itself: past fresh North Sea fish on the slab and crates of seafood; past cheeses from the region and beyond; past exotic sausages and pristine plucked poultry. Through the hall to the flower market: past carnations and lilies; past spring blooms or Christmas wreaths.

From café doorways hear the sound of the accordion playing. An old man on a bicycle offers bunches of herbs from his panniers to passers-by and a younger biker steps off his Harley to try on a new leather jacket for €70. Backs are slapped, hands are shaken, noses are tapped and deals are struck. As the church bells toll for mass, traders' cries mingle with the sound of a barrel organ. At the back of a lorry blocking the rue des Sarrazins, gleaming saucepans are offered at never-to-be repeated prices, and in the midst of the whirlpool of the market square a salesman demonstrates his miracle wonder-broom or incredible, magical vegetable-slicing machine.

On street corners, enormous rotisseries drip the juices from turning chickens on to trays of roast potatoes and vegetables, the scent of a traditional Sunday lunch competing with the more exotic aromas from the enormous drums of couscous and paella as a French market merges into the multi-ethnic North African souk. Follow your nose and keep your hand on your wallet. All in all, Wazemmes on a Sunday morning is an unforgettable experience for bargain hunters and browsers alike.

PHARMACIES/CHEMISTS

See pages 26–7.

SUPERMARKETS/DEPARTMENT STORES

Most of the supermarkets have smaller city, métro or market versions in commercial shopping streets. So find Monop' (a mini Monoprix) on rue Faidherbe and place Béthune, and a teeny Carrefour on rue Tournai at the side of Gare Flandres. They even turn up on the narrow streets of Vieux Lille.

CARREFOUR Euralille ♀ 235 H4 ✎ 03 20 15 56 00 ⏲ 09.00–22.00 Mon–Sat ⛫ Gare Lille Europe 🚌 Opposite the station

This massive hypermarket is the ideal place for stocking up before catching the train home (except on Sunday). The branch is so vast, staff use roller skates to whizz between checkouts and aisles. Look out for the logo featuring a belfry and a heart. This denotes local products, and the store sells a good selection of ales and prepared foods from the region and a large range of fresh halal meats. For free parking in the Euralille car park, get your ticket stamped at the checkout.

MATCH Halles Centrales, 97 rue Solférino ♀ 236 D7 ✎ 03 20 57 71 45 📧 www.supermarchesmatch.fr ⏲ 08.30–21.00 Mon–Sat, 09.00–12.30 Sun ⛫ République–Beaux Arts 🚌 Bus Citadine to Sacré Cœur then walk down rue Solférino

The best ever setting for a supermarket, the old iron and glass structure of Lille's former wholesale food market in the heart of the party district. An in-store bakery producing decent breads all day long (buy loaves hot from the oven, or cooler and sliced to order) plus a fair range of general groceries – including a good variety of gluten- and sugar-free options. Students may sign up for a 10% discount on their shopping.

MONOPRIX 🚇 Les Tanneurs shopping centre, 80 rue Paris ♀ 237 H7 ✎ 03 28 82 92 20 ⏲ 08.30–20.30 Mon–Sat ⛫ Gare Lille Flandres 🚌 Bus Citadine to Molinel-Paris

Since moving from its larger home on rue Molinel, this modest supermarket has proved some solace to the town-centre workers who still mourn the passing of the Marks & Spencer food hall up the road. Good grocery section on the lower level, even a kosher counter. Upstairs, find a limited range of clothes and household wares.

GALERIES LAFAYETTE 🚇 31 rue de Béthune ♀ 237 H6 ✎ 03 20 14 76 50 ⏲ 10.00–22.00 Mon–Thu, 10.00–21.00 Fri–Sat ⛫ Rihour 🚌 Métro 2 to Gare Lille Flandres & line 1 to Rihour, then walk down rue de la Vieille Comédie & turn left on to rue des Fossés to rue de Béthune

The long-awaited validation of Lille as a key destination for the fashion-conscious, France's premier department store opened its largest branch outside Paris here in the heart of the pedestrian zone with a glitzy launch party in 2007. A cinematic sweep of frontage among the movie houses of the rue de Bethune. All you'd expect from the A-listers' emporium, plus a branch of the Zeïn Spa (page 191).

PRINTEMPS 🚇 41–45 rue Nationale ♀ 237 H5 ✎ 03 20 63 62 00 ⏲ 09.30–19.30 Tue–Thu & Sat, 09.30–20.00 Fri ⛫ Rihour 🚌 Métro 2 to Gare Lille Flandres then line 1 to Rihour; the rear entrance to the store is behind Palais Rihour

A branch of the famous Parisian department store. Fashion, classy luggage and decent tableware. Car park beneath the store.

UNDER ONE ROOF

EURALILLE Av le Corbusier ♀ 235 H4 ☎ 03 20 14 52 20 (Euralille), 03 28 38 50 50 (Aeronef) 🚆 Gare Lille Europe or Gare Lille Flandres ⊕ Cross the parvis François Mitterand

Between the two railway stations, Euralille is one of France's biggest shopping centres. With new floors, lighting and a general make-over set for early 2015, the mall of malls remains a key player in Lille. Hardcore consumers may squeak with excitement at the massive Carrefour hypermarket and specialist shops such as the temple to new-age consumerism, Nature et Découvertes (page 158). Personally, I mourn the passing of the pet superstore that once advertised the special offer '15 caged birds for the price of 12', either the zenith or nadir of promotional hype. Exhibitions and displays in the centre have ranged from tableaux of zebra and rhino on loan from the Natural History Museum to a free circus with high wires and trapeze acts above the heads of bemused shoppers. The mall is more than merely 140 shops spread over two storeys of consumerism: office units, hotel rooms and serviced short-stay apartments hide behind the smoked glass. Even the once-underground nightclub L'Aeronef is now to be found several levels above ground in the Euralille complex, with its programme of cutting-edge rock music and bad-taste film festivals. Together with Christian de Portzampac's 'ski-boot' Tour Crédit Lyonnais balanced over Lille Europe station and Rem Koolhaas's own Grand Palais exhibition centre and concert venue, Euralille is testament to Koolhaas's concept of 21st-century living, Lille's remarkable civic optimism and Mayor Mauroy's belief in the Eurostar dream. Before the glass gambling palace was built just behind the complex, an interim 'temporary' casino was housed here: fine dining, floor shows and roulette within a barcode bleep of the family supermarket shop. Between Gare Europe and Euralille, the parvis François Mitterand has been colonised by the microscooter and rollerblade fraternity. A statue of President Mitterand waves passengers on their high-speed way, a gigantic bunch of tulips is a cheery legacy of Lille2004 and the recently ripened Parc Matisse offers a comfortable walk towards Vieux Lille.

▼ Consumerism under one roof – the Euralille shopping mall shares its home with hotels, apartments and nightclubs (Anna Moores)

163

Louis Cordonnier's neo-Flemish belfry at the Chamber of Commerce marks the border between old and new Lille (Production Perig/S)

10

Walking Tour

This favourite walk takes in the 'best of…' and provides the perfect appetiser to a weekend of self-indulgence. Straight from the Eurostar station, it meanders through the three central squares, along the cobbles of the historic old town, and finishes amid the wide open spaces of the largest park and woodlands in the city centre.

It also brings you within a lip's smack of the most delicious little food stores in town, so bring a basket and shop for a picnic (following our suggestions on pages 153–6) to round off the hike and build up your energies for the return walk to your hotel. Another gastronomic subtext of my preferred stroll is that it takes you past many of the best restaurants in town, so you can always press your nose to a window and check out the menus for later!

Although the circuit is perfectly manageable within an hour for those who prefer a brisk constitutional, I would recommend that you allow two to three hours and take your time. Every other shop window is a digression in waiting and so many of the old buildings deserve a more leisurely appreciation.

Note: If you would rather not start at the station, you could always pick up the trail at the place du Théâtre.

THE WALK *Map, pages 234–5*

From the Gare Lille Europe, step down to the parvis François Mitterand, with its giant tulips. To your right is the **Parc Matisse** (page 195) and the **Porte de Roubaix** (pages 182–3); to your left is **Euralille** (page 163). Head towards the Gare Lille Flandres and perhaps check out an exhibition at **Le TriPostal** (page 190). At the place de la Gare, bear right along the rue Faidherbe towards the place du Théâtre, the belfry and the opera house (page 181).

Step inside the **Vieille Bourse** (pages 183–4) and savour the timeless atmosphere of this unique enclave, then come out on to the place du Général de Gaulle, or **Grand' Place** (pages 177–80). This is the central square of Lille and its many façades reflect the varied and dazzling history of the city. Spot the gilded suns atop public buildings, symbol of Louis XIV, and admire the central fountain and **La Déesse** (page 177).

Pass the archway inscribed with the name of the Brasserie Alcide, and instead follow rue de la Bourse, with its 17th-century houses adorned with images of innocence and corruption, to the rue de la Grande Chaussée. Follow the pointing arm above the first shopfront to direct you along the cobbled street lined with designer names, where d'Artagnan once lived (page 10) in the house that is now La Botte Chantilly shoe shop, and pause at the spectacular Art Deco mosaic shopfront of A l'Huîtrière (pages 100–1). Step inside just to admire the décor and peek in the restaurant (you could double back along rue Basse to visit the original site of the restaurant before it moved to its present location in 1928 if you have time). Follow the rue des Chats Bossus to the place du Lion d'Or and walk down to 29 place Louise de Bettignies to admire the Baroque façade of the Demeure Gilles de la Boë. You could always trot down towards the rue de Gand for some menu fantasising, but there is still plenty to see back in the oldest street in town.

So, turn back to place du Lion d'Or and walk along Lille's first commercial centre, the rue de la Monnaie, with original shop signs above the doors denoting early merchants' trades. Stop off at the **Musée de l'Hospice Comtesse** (pages 171–2) and turn left into rue Pétérinck, where 18th-century weavers' houses have now become very fashionable artists' studios, boutiques and eateries. This road leads to the place aux Oignons (page 141), which may seem an appropriate name in light of the many small delicatessens in the area but is actually a corrupt spelling of the word *donjon* (dungeon). For here was the keep of the original fortress on the marshland that was the city's birthplace.

Having explored all the treats on offer in place aux Oignons and its tributaries, take the little alleyway that leads to place Gilleson, and climb the steps to the side entrance to **Notre Dame de la Treille** (pages 186–7). Walk through the magnificent church and leave by the brand new doors. Turn left into rue du Cirque, stopping at any of the little art and antique shops that take your fancy. Turn right into rue Basse and take a sharp left into rue Lepelletier, at the tiny little bakery with the leaded-glass windows reading 'A Notre Dame de la Treille'. This is now a branch of the ubiquitous Paul (page 122), and if you have not already succumbed to the gastronomic temptations on the walk thus far, grab a pastry or some bread to sustain you for the rest of the trek!

By now you may have got hopelessly lost thanks to the sirens of so many boutiques and antique shops nudging into your peripheral vision and the fact that none of these streets follows any geometric rules. But if you are sticking closely to the map, you should be able to take the first turning on the right, the rue du Curé Saint-Etienne, to lead you to rue Esquermoise (and the further enticement of Meert's tea rooms!).

▲ Hidden behind shopfronts on rue de la Monnaie is a glimpse of old Flanders: the Musée de l'Hospice Comtesse (Anna Moores)

Just across the rue Esquermoise is the rue Saint-Etienne, a narrow street that takes you past the town's major Renaissance façade, the restaurant Le Compostelle (page 97).

At the place Mendès France with the undistinguished circular Nouveau Siècle building (pages 132–3), turn sharp left into rue de Pas, crossing the bustling rue Nationale into rue Roisin. This leads you to the place Rihour (pages 180–1) and the tourist office and remains of the ducal **Palais Rihour** (page 176). Worth a dawdle if brasserie-menu browsing or enjoying the stalls at the Christmas market; otherwise continue past the palace along the rue du Palais Rihour and turn right on the rue de l'Hôpital Militaire.

Cross over the rue Nationale once more and turn left along the thoroughfare until you come to the square Foch with its statue of the **P'tit Quinquin** (page 183). Walk through the recently smartened-up gardens, where you may appreciate other statues including a bust of Maréchal Foch or the saucier Suzanne at her bath! Keep on walking through the leafy squares (the next garden is called square du Tilleul) until the road opens up to the canal basin, and stroll along the quai du Wault admiring swans until you come out by the square Daubenton. Look across at the charming and elegant **Jardin Vauban** (page 194), with its puppet theatre and manicured pathways. But opposite you, across the pont de la Citadelle, is the **Bois de Boulogne** (pages 193–4), a perfect place to relax with a picnic.

Equestrian statue of local hero General Louis Faidherbe was deemed too large for place République, so it looks on from the sidelines of place Richebé (skyfish/S)

11

Museums and Sightseeing

PRICES AND OPENING HOURS

Most museums now charge admission and prices listed below are for the full adult rate. You will usually find discounted rates for children, seniors, students, etc. Entry is free at many museums for holders of the Lille City Pass (page 48) with unlimited public transport in the metropolitan area. Many places do not charge for admission during the first Sunday of the month. Prices shown are usually for the permanent collection with a supplement sometimes charged for special temporary exhibitions (check websites for details). National museums close on Tuesdays and local museums shut on Mondays. See *Chapter 12* for details of the excellent collections located just a bus, métro, train or tram ride out of town. In May, some museums will stay open until midnight or beyond on the Nuit des Musées (page 15).

Check **opening hours** given in this guide carefully. Since no hours are set in stone, before setting out on a dedicated mission to any one specific museum or restaurant, always phone ahead just to be sure.

THE UNMISSABLES

PALAIS DES BEAUX-ARTS Fine Arts Museum; pl de la République ♀ 238 F2 ＼ 03 20 06 78 00 🖰 www.pba-lille.fr ① 14.00–18.00 Mon, 10.00–18.00 Fri, 10.00–19.00 Wed–Thu & Sat–Sun, closed Tue & public holidays 🚋 République–Beaux Arts ⊛ Métro 2 to Gare Lille Flandres, changing to line 1 to République–Beaux Arts ⬡ €7 (discounts for under-25s), but free admission on the 1st Sun of the month; free access to atrium

For years, in a modest office tucked away behind the magnificent splendour of the museum, the original curator (now retired) Arnaud Brejon de Lavergnée pondered over the Palais des Beaux-Arts's many treasures. France's second museum after the Louvre has Goyas and Rubens, Picassos, Lautrecs and Monets, but the greatest treasure of them all was Arnaud Brejon de Lavergnée himself, self-effacing overlord of the museum's reinvention. The passions of this modest and unassuming art lover are as much a part of this fabulous palace as the rich red walls, the floppy chairs, and the catalogue of some of the world's greatest artworks. During the renovations, Monsieur Brejon de Lavergnée could be seen at the station platform, clutching bubble-wrapped masterpieces to his chest as he personally escorted the Palais's jewels to be restored at the National Gallery in London. Until the day in 1997 that President Chirac inaugurated the new museum, every picture, every frame and every detail came under his exacting scrutiny. Monsieur Brejon has since handed over the reins to Alain Tapié, who in turn passed on the responsibility to current curator Bruno Girveau, but he long continued leading privileged visitors around the museum. On the eve of a legendary Rubens exhibition, I left my allotted tour group to tag along behind the master as Monsieur Brejon laid bare the genius of the artist to a privileged party including Prince Jean of France aka Duke of Orleans, banker, philosopher, MBA, erstwhile footballer and current Dauphin and pretender to the throne.

The breathtaking art collection was brought to Lille on the orders of Napoleon, who stripped the walls of palaces and private galleries throughout his European empire, from Italy to the Low Countries. The plan paid off: what had been a pleasure for the cultured

> "What had been a pleasure for a cultured few is now a cherished symbol of civic pride."

few is now a cherished symbol of civic pride, and was the triumph that awoke the world to the news that Lille had achieved greatness.

Today's visitors take one of the twin grand staircases adorned with leaded windows heralding the *arts et métiers* of Lille to the first floor, where room after room offers French, Flemish and European masterpieces from the 17th to the 19th centuries. Highlights include Rubens's *Descente de la Croix*, an entire room devoted to Jordaens, and a succession of high-ceilinged galleries housing the works of Van Dyck, Corot and Delacroix with Watteau, *père et fils*, the collection's first curators. Best of all is the celebrated pair of Goyas, *Les Jeunes* and *Les Vieilles*, the former a timeless portrayal of a teenage crush, as relevant to the SMS texting generation as to its own time, and the latter a cruelly satirical dissection of old age: crones at one with their malevolence. With so many riches, it is easy to overlook the corridor devoted to the Impressionists. Make time for Monet, Van Gogh, Renoir and Sisley, not to mention Lautrec and Rodin's *Burghers of Calais*.

Back on the ground floor, the sculpture gallery includes the best of 19th-century classical statuary, some imperial, some disturbing. A good halfway refreshment point for your visit, the collection leads to the rear courtyard and the modern architects' remarkable prism comprising the glass-fronted administration block and a sheet of water that turns the grey skies of the north into pure natural light to illuminate the basement galleries.

▲ The Palais des Beaux-Arts is home to some of the world's finest art (Nord Tourism)

The underground rooms should not be missed. The Renaissance room includes Donatello's bas-relief *Festin d'Herod*, and many sketches by Raphaël. It also houses 19 of Vauban's detailed models of his fortified towns – among them Lille and Calais – frozen in time and space between sheets of glass in an otherwise blacked-out exhibition of the landscape of 18th-century France and Flanders.

The catalogue of treasures on every floor could never leave anybody feeling short-changed. In his day, anyone lucky enough to come across Monsieur Brejon de Lavergnée escorting his guests around the gallery, his infectious enthusiasm drawing total strangers to his enlightening discourse on a favourite painting, well, that was a bonus beyond price. The bright and airy foyer is open to the public as a meeting place or coffee stop – admission free.

LOUVRE-LENS (See pages 210–12) Well worth the train journey to visit the only Louvre outside Paris, an amazing 21st-century museum in its own right.

MUSEE DE L'HOSPICE COMTESSE 32 rue de la Monnaie 237 J2 03 28 36 84 00 14.00–18.00 Mon, 10.00–12.30 & 14.00–18.00 Wed–Sun, closed holidays Bus 50 to Lion d'Or €3.50; joint tickets also available with Palais des Beaux-Arts
I love the stillness of the old hospital ward, with its boatbuilder-vaulted ceiling. This most tranquil of sanctuaries is a season apart, even from the rest of the historic quarter. Tucked away behind the shops and archways of the oldest street in town, the former 13th-century hospital captures the life and talents of another Lille in another time. The city's benefactress Jeanne de Constantinople, Countess of Flanders, built the hospice for the needy in

11

1237, a charitable gesture that has echoed down the centuries in a city that nurtures the ideals of civic responsibilities. After all, the celebrated annual Braderie (page 12) was born of a sense of *noblesse oblige*, when servants were granted the right to sell their masters' clothes in these very streets. Once both a hospital and a convent, the site has been restored as a museum of local arts and crafts. Outside is a medicinal herb garden; inside, find an eclectic collection of carved furniture, rare musical instruments, domestic tableaux and wooden panels adorned with paintings of local children. The art collection includes paintings by Flemish and northern French masters, among them Louis and François Watteau, as well as tapestries by Lille's famous weaver Guillaume Werniers. The kitchen is typically decorated with the traditional blue-and-white tiles of the Low Countries, and vestiges of the original murals can be seen in the 17th-century convent chapel. The chapel, the 15th-century ward and other buildings around the central courtyard are favourite locations for informal concerts and intimate musical recitals. Guided tours are available at no extra charge most afternoons.

LA PISCINE (See pages 198–200) A truly remarkable building that very nearly upstages Roubaix's remarkable art collection.

LAM (See pages 204–5) Picasso, Braque, Modigliani and much, much more – well worth the métro ride out of town.

MUSEUMS AND GALLERIES

MUSEE DE L'ART RELIGIEUX See page 187. Within the Cathédrale Notre Dame de la Treille.

MUSEE DES CANONNIERS SEDENTAIRES DE LILLE 44 rue des Canonniers 📍 235 H3 📞 03 20 55 58 90 🖱 http://museedescanonniers.wix.com/lille 🕐 14.00–17.00 Mon–Sat, closed holidays (1st 3 weeks of Aug & 15 Dec–2 Feb) 🚇 Gare Lille Flandres 🚶 Walk through the Parc Matisse & pass through the Porte de Roubaix to rue de Roubaix, then turn right into rue des Canonniers & 2nd right into rue des Urbanistes 🎟 €5
It is fitting that a garrison town should have a museum of military hardware, and over 3,000 weapons, documents and maps from 1777 to 1945 are on display in the former Urbanistes convent. The stars of the show are the magnificent cannons, most notably the Gribeauval – the Big Bertha of its day. Despite the postal address, the public entrance is in rue des Urbanistes.

MUSEE D'HISTOIRE NATURELLE ET DE GEOLOGIE Natural History and Geology Museum; 19 rue de Bruxelles 📍 238 G5 📞 03 28 55 30 80 🕐 9.30–17.00 Mon & Wed–Fri, 10.00–18.00 Sat & Sun, closed Tue 🚇 République–Beaux Arts 🚇 Métro 2 to Gare Lille Flandres then bus 14 to Jeanne d'Arc 🎟 €3.50; free midweek & 1st Sun of the month

This is among my favourite time warps, more for the rooms themselves than the collections. I always feel as though I have entered a Victorian draper's shop that does a nice line in sabre-toothed tigers. A typical 19th-century museum, with its glass cases, iron walkways and spiral staircases, this very old-fashioned throwback to the days of hands-off musty scholarship is an oddity in a city that prides itself on cutting-edge exhibitions. There is something comfortingly nostalgic about the place, with its whale skeletons suspended from the ceiling, irresistibly camp tableaux of stuffed birds and animals and studiously catalogued trays of geological specimens and fossils.

MUSEE DE L'HOSPICE COMTESSE See pages 171–2.

MAISON DE L'ARCHITECTURE ET DE LA VILLE Urban Architecture Centre; pl François Mitterrand 📍 235 H4 📞 03 20 14 61 15 💻 www.mav-npdc.com 🕐 10.00–12.30 & 14.00–17.00 Tue–Thu, 11.00–18.00 Sat (exhibition & festival dates vary) 🚉 Gare Lille Europe 🚇 Leave the Eurostar, cross the piazza below the station & the entrance is under the viaduct 💶 free

Legacy of the 2004 festivities, this gallery devoted to urban architecture is sited slap bang in the heart of the Euralille district, underneath – and almost propping up – the concrete viaduct that is the avenue le Corbusier. Not merely a showcase for town planning, the venue plays a key role in city festivals and hosts workshops and talks on architecture past and present across the region. Slightly more offbeat are the special dinners when chefs and architects work together to illustrate design concepts on a plate.

MAISON NATALE DU GENERAL DE GAULLE Général de Gaulle's birthplace; 9 rue Princesse 📍 237 G1 📞 03 28 38 12 05 💻 www.maison-natale-de-gaulle.org 🕐 10.00–12.00 & 14.00–17.00 Wed–Sat, 13.30–17.00 Sun, closed holidays 🚇 Métro 2 to Gare Lille Flandres then bus 10 to Magasin, then take rue Saint-André to rue Princesse 💶 €6

War hero, statesman and Europe's most celebrated Anglo-sceptic, Charles de Gaulle was born here, in his grandmother's house, on 22 November 1890, opposite the Eglise St André where the once and future president was baptised. See his christening robes in the museum. The exhibition tells the story of the first president of the Fifth Republic with lesser-known tales from his early life, and documents his refusal to accept Marshal Pétain's 1940 truce with Nazi Germany, then rallying the Free French army with his historic broadcast from London that same year. Dramatic episodes are well illustrated, with the very Citroën DS in which the president was travelling outside Paris when he survived an assassin's bullet. Last admission is one hour before the museum closes. The Navette Vieux Lille passes close by, otherwise it's a long walk on the cobbles to the far side of the quarter.

PALAIS DES BEAUX-ARTS See pages 169–71.

BY APPOINTMENT There are several other museums in Lille that may be visited by appointment or during special exhibitions.

Musée de l'Institut Pasteur 24 bd Louis XIV ♀ 235 H8 ☏ 03 20 87 72 42 ⌘ Lille Grand Palais 🚇 Métro 2 to Lille Grand Palais then walk along bd Vaillant & turn right on to bd Louis XIV 🕿 individual tour €7, group tour €10

Life and work of Louis Pasteur and his successors.

Maison de la Photographie 18 rue Frémy ♀ 235 K6 ☏ 03 20 05 29 29 ⌘ Fives 🚇 Métro 2 to Gare Lille Flandres & line 1 to Fives, then take bus 13 or walk to Legrand & rue Frémy

Occasional photographic exhibitions featuring original work by local artists.

SITES AND MONUMENTS

CITADELLE Av du 43ème Régiment d'Infanterie ♀ 236 B1 ⓜ 08 91 56 20 04 (€0.225/ min, tourist office) 🚇 Bus 12 to Champ de Mars 🕿 €7 (advance reservation essential, guided tours only on selected dates in summer)

A town in its own right, France's Queen of Citadels was the greatest fortress of the reign of Louis XIV. When the Sun King commissioned the great military architect Sébastien Le Prestre de Vauban to protect his kingdom with a ring of 100 fortified towns, this imposing and impenetrable, pentagonal, star-shaped Citadelle was hailed as the masterpiece of the world's finest military engineer. Built by 400 men in just three years using 16 million newly baked bricks, the garrison opened in 1670 as home to 1,200 soldiers. Three hundred years on, it remains the nucleus of the modern army with 1,000 French soldiers and foreign legionnaires stationed here.

In April, 14 of the 28 northern fortresses hold an open day; otherwise the public are permitted to tour the site only on summer Sunday guided tours. Visitors are expected to behave themselves. When a couple of schoolchildren sat on the parade-ground rostrum, the young soldier of the 43ème Régiment accompanying our group was confined to barracks, a sharp reminder that this is no museum, but a working garrison. Its five-sided design is as effective a security measure today as it was in the 17th century – and is said to have inspired the US Pentagon. Soil banks the ramparts to absorb artillery shells, and the main walls are 4m thick. The principal entrance, the Porte Royale, was built at an angle to the drawbridge to avoid direct hits. This gateway, facing the old quarter of Lille, was a major strategic and symbolic feature with regal motifs and Latin mottos representing the king himself. In the centre of the pentagonal parade ground is a ship's mast, a reminder that the fortress was built along the banks of a river and was originally protected by the navy. The soldiers stationed here today still wear naval badges. Around the parade ground are the renovated barracks, arsenal, chapel and officers' quarters. The king, a regular visitor, appointed Vauban as the first governor of the Citadelle. His successor, Charles, Comte d'Artagnan (best known as hero of Dumas's *Three Musketeers*), died in 1673. The original governor's residence is no more, but traces may still be found in the chapel of the gubernatorial doorway. Vauban's original models for the fortified towns of the north are displayed at the Palais des Beaux-Arts (pages 169–71). The rest of the Vauban collection is housed at Les Invalides in Paris.

LA DEESSE See page 177.

L'HERMITAGE GANTOIS See page 59 for more on this restored historic building.

HOTEL DE VILLE Town Hall; pl Roger Salengro ♀ 235 G7 ☏ 03 20 49 50 00 🚇 Mairie de Lille ⬤ Métro 2 to Mairie de Lille
Although the Christmas Ferris wheel on Grand' Place offers the best view in town, there is a summer alternative. From April to September (check with the tourist office first), take a detour from the main historic and shopping quarters and climb to the top of the 104m belfry of the town hall (a lift takes you most of the way). Completed in 1932, the tower crowned Emile Dubuisson's striking Hôtel de Ville, which replaced the original Gothic Palais Rihour building with a ferro-concrete tribute to the gabled houses of Flanders. More than merely a nice place to enjoy a pleasant view, in 1950 the top of the tower became the first regional television studio, Télé-Lille. Holding up the tower are the figures of giants Lydéric and Phinaert, the Romulus and Remus or Sirius Black and Voldemort of Lille. Lydéric was raised by wild deer and a hermit after his family was killed by the tyrant Phinaert. On 15 June 605, the two fought: Lydéric was the victor and he founded the town. The history of Lille is told in a huge comic-strip fresco inside the building, painted by the Icelandic artist Erro. The building was constructed over the ruins of the original working-class quarter of St-Sauveur where, in the long-demolished bar, La Liberté, local wood-turner Pierre Degeyter composed and played the music for Eugène Pottier's socialist anthem *L'Internationale* for the very first time in 1888. The address is named for Roger Salengro, another of Lille's native socialist mayors and government minister between the wars. He had been taken prisoner of war in 1915 after being captured attempting to rescue a colleague's body from no man's land. However, his war record and patriotism were called into question during a malicious slur campaign by his political enemies on the far right, and he was eventually hounded and consequently committed suicide in 1936. Before the Théâtre du Nord opened on Grand' Place, the building had been known as the Salle Salengro.

11

MAISON COILLOT 14 rue Fleurus ♀ 238 E4 ⌂ République–Beaux Arts ⊜ Métro 2 to Gare Lille Flandres changing to line 1 to République–Beaux Arts, then take rue Nicolas Leblanc to pl Lebon on to rue Fleurus

An unexpected flourish of Art Nouveau in a quiet residential street off the place Lebon. All the houses around the Church of St Michel are identical. All but one, that is. If 14 rue Fleurus looks more like a Paris métro station than a private home, then thanks are due to its original owner, Monsieur Coillot, a ceramics maker who commissioned Hector Guimard to redesign his house. Guimard's celebrated flourishes, dark green swirls and horticultural sweeps are the hallmark of the capital's subway system. His reinvention of the domestic townhouse is no less flamboyant, using Coillot's own ceramics alongside cast iron and volcanic rock. These remarkable windows, balconies, gables and even a suggestion of a pagoda on the roof are worth a modest detour when trekking between local museums for, although still a private address, the house was so designed that the interiors appear open to the street.

PALAIS RIHOUR ⊕ Pl Rihour ♀ 237 G6 ⊙ by appointment with tourist office ⌂ Rihour ⊜ Métro 2 to Gare Lille Flandres then line 1 to Rihour

To most people this old building behind the monumental war memorial was merely a rather quaint tourist office. I've even heard some visitors dismiss the Gothic arches and mullioned windows as a Victorian folly. Heresy. Cross the threshold and you are standing in the remains of a ducal palace, seat of power in Lille for over 450 years and boasting an A-list guest list that has included England's Henry VIII and France's Louis XV. The original Palais Rihour was built by Philippe le Bon, Duke of Burgundy, when he moved the court to the city in 1453. His son Charles le Téméraire completed the palace 20 years later. It was through the Burgundian line that Lille passed to the Hapsburgs when Marie de Bourgogne married Maximilien of Austria in 1474. When Philip IV of Spain sold the palace to the city in the 17th century, it began a new life as the town hall and continued to serve the community until ravaged by fire in 1916. The stairwell and chapels, among the finest surviving examples of flamboyant Gothic architecture in town, could hardly house a city's local government, so a new Hôtel de Ville was built in the St-Sauveur district (page 6). The ground-floor guards' chapel served, until 2014, as the city's main tourist office. Climb the winding stairs to the upper chapel to admire the trefoil windows and vaulted ceiling. Burgundian coats of arms adorn the walls, and a real sense of the original palace remains. Now that the tourist office has moved across the road, the question of public access to the Palais Rihour is still under discussion. However, exhibitions and concerts sometimes held here are the perfect opportunity to sneak a peek at an often overlooked monument. Do take time to admire the beautifully restored glass of the sacristy.

PLACE DU GENERAL DE GAULLE ⓖⓟ ♀ 237 H5 🚉 Rihour 🚇 Métro 2 to Gare Lille Flandres then line 1 to Rihour

Named after Lille's most famous son, but known to everyone simply as the Grand' Place, the main square is the very heartbeat of the city. Almost pedestrianised, although a serpentine trail of traffic slithers slowly and safely along two sides, this is a veritable forum where shoppers break their day, friends plot an evening and revellers celebrate the night.

The essential rendezvous is the central fountain around the column of the **Déesse**, the goddess and symbol of the spirit of the city. The statue commemorates the bravery of the townsfolk, withstanding the siege of Lille by 35,000 Austrian soldiers in 1792. The original idea, mooted the day after the victory, was to build a monument by melting down all royal statues (the Revolution was at its height and Marie Antoinette had not yet been executed). Enthusiasm waned, but eventually the Déesse was cast by Théophile Bra, with the intention of placing her atop his Arc de Triomphe in Paris. That plan too was abandoned, and the goddess returned to Lille, standing for three years in place Rihour before moving to Charles Benvignat's column on Grand' Place in 1845. Her crown represents Lille's ramparts, her right hand ever ready to fire another cannon, her left pointing to a plaque inscribed with the brave words of Mayor André's rebuttal of Austria's demands. Tongues soon began to wag, since from upper windows locals noted the goddess's uncanny resemblance to Mme Bigodanel, the 54-year-old wife of the then mayor. It seems her fuller figure had not gone unnoticed by the artist.

Under her watchful gaze, students hold their protest rallies, bands play on Gay Pride Weekend and the city's tame giants parade during the Fêtes de Lille. Grand' Place has a habit of dressing for every occasion: most famously as a Christmas grotto in December and January when, surrounded by Cinderella candelabra, a huge Ferris wheel swings sensation seekers into the skies to take in the panorama of gables and belfries from a swaying cradle high above the cobblestones. The wheel turns from mid-morning until well past midnight. Sometimes the cobbles are covered with plants, lawns and box hedges as the city gardeners decide to transform the square into a park. Perhaps the whole area will become a farmyard, with rows of market-garden cabbages in front of the theatre, and a herd of cows grazing contentedly outside McDonald's. On one memorable visit, thousands of screaming fans turned out for a free pop concert on a sultry summer's night, and obliging students on rooftops sprayed the crowd from mineral water bottles.

Around the square, look out for carved and gilded images of the sun, symbol of King Louis XIV, whose royal bodyguard lived in the Grande Garde, a splendid galleried building that today houses the Théâtre du Nord. Alongside the theatre is the striking frontage of the home of *La Voix du Nord*, once a wartime Resistance news-sheet and now the regional daily newspaper. Dominating the square, its tiered roof is topped out by three

11

TRIUMPH OF A LATIN NIGHT

It was a Sunday evening, summer had already surrendered to the anticlimactic half-season prologue to autumn and Lille lay between excuses. A rare weekend with no festival, no season, no theatre. To cap it all, as I glided upwards from the métro to a subdued place Rihour, it was raining. Not heavily, just the lightest drizzle of a mild evening on the cusp of equinox. Yet, I was contemplating a sulk.

Just when I thought that Lille held no more teasing for me, I looked up and stared across the empty squares.

Those yellow, syrupy pools of light that slipped from glistening gables to bright washed cobbles lured me across the place du Général de Gaulle towards the inexcusably beautiful Vieille Bourse. The sounds of music filtered through: echoing cracked shellac tones of a long-forgotten afternoon crooner at 78rpm and from Renaissance arched doorways escaped the unmistakable Latin sound of the tango.

Long shadows sliced the glow from the cloisters and I prowled around the building, looking for an open door. From the place du Théâtre I stepped up and through the entrance to the Vieille Bourse, Lille's timeless Rialto for bibliophiles and chess players, where usually the most physical effort comes from the holding to the light of the slightly foxed uncut pages of a 19th-century novella, or the flourished taking of a queen's bishop by a cannily primed pawn.

Before me was movement, the seductive synchronicity of backs arching in tandem, toes pointing forward then sliding up close-pressed calves, waists pulled, shoulders shrugged, and eyes locked in concentrated complicity. But this was no geriatric *thé-dansant*, nor a choreographed show dance. This was Lille taking its weekend rites as a right to the last second of liberty. In a city defined by youth this was, in fact, a genteel coup of measured effusion, *sagesse* and experience over unrefined *jeunesse* and exuberance.

In the squares outside, the weather dictated the sprit. Within, the soul triumphed over the elements. Generations swept across the courtyard, defying the rain and convention. The will was for a Latin night and, enclosed by red brick, white stone and a garland of gables framing the evening sky, a Latin night triumphed.

All along the cloisters around the dance floor stood students with bicycles, and as yet uninitiated couples soon to learn from a generation who knew (from the tango) the potent supremacy of prized promise over instant gratification.

As the gramophone played, so the ages merged. Just as a record from over half a century ago was boosted through digital speakers, so groomed grey heads led where tight designer-encased buttocks and thighs followed. Age and social status played second fiddle to the imperative pulse of the accordion. Where dinner jacket took to the floor with a yellow cardie, a classic little black dress and the partiest, stripiest cocktail stilettos followed the lead of a jumper and jeans.

A great bearded bear of a working man in a heavy, plaid woodsman's shirt lumbered rhythmically and steadily through each stride and turn of the dance, while his whisper-waisted partner, hair a pre-Raphaelite tumble of curls, neatly picked her way around his strides, turning his bulk into gallantry. Behind them banker-brown brogues stepped from caution to promise, lured into seductive swirls by sharp white Vogues.

A well-upholstered Juno clasped a tiny lad to her embonpoint, as they danced, cheek to breast, his eyes peering through the shade of her formidable protection to follow her feet, defining determined arcs through shiny puddles. And on the far side of the Bourse, sharp, bright tailor's eyes peered expertly through wire-rimmed spectacles as a veteran of the dance floor continued nimbly to foot it across the courtyard, his younger companion knees bent, raised, swept and strutted in coy assertion of confident complicity in this ritual courtship.

Shoddy trainers kicked off and toes treading rainwater, the most timid of onlookers would allow himself to be lead across the flagstones floor by a lady of means, experience and purpose. Other discarded pumps and boots lay safely dry behind pillars as barefoot bohemia joined the measured maelstrom, delicately turning and tripping through the puddles.

Ahead and among these shifting couplings, a sweeper picked his way through the swirl with his broom pushing the rainwater away from the participants, every thrust of his broom an unconscious echo of the discipline of the dance all around.

Of course, the city had been dancing long before the rain shower beckoned me across the squares to discover yet another of its secrets. And the modest ball continued until the lights in the Bourse were switched off at 22.00, to a genteel round of applause, an announcement of the following week's rendezvous, the promise of dance classes for novices and the *bonbon* reward of one last dance under the stars of a freshly rinsed clean indigo sky before bedtime.

And I headed back to the métro having learnt the happy lesson never to take this city for granted.

Tango at the Vieille Bourse is held on Sunday evenings in summer (Jul–Sep). Check with the tourist office or go to 🖳 *http://souslesmarronniers.blogspot.fr.*

11

golden Graces, symbolising the regional provinces of Artois, Flanders and Hainaut. Continental Europe's biggest bookshop, the Furet du Nord, boasts half a million volumes in stock, and is spread over eight storeys on different levels served by a complicated arrangement of lifts, staircases and walkways. Across the square, linking Grand' Place with place du Théâtre, is the stunning Vieille Bourse. The gateway to Vieux Lille is the archway bearing the name of the Brasserie Alcide. Brasseries, bars and cafés abound, the square and its arteries liberally sprinkled with tables for alfresco dining and people-watching.

PLACE PHILIPPE LEBON ♀ 238 E4 🚆 République–Beaux Arts Ⓜ Métro 2 to Gare Lille Flandres changing to line 1 to République–Beaux Arts, then take rue Nicolas Leblanc to pl Lebon

This intersection of the rue Solférino boasts the kitschest statue in town. On the edge of the original university district, this is a lavish homage to Louis Pasteur, first dean of the science faculty. As the microbiologist who first discovered that germs cause disease and the pioneer of pasteurisation, the great man is shown surrounded by grateful mothers offering their babies aloft. And you thought science could not be camp. This is a cult classic. Totally fab. Across the square is the Romanesque-Byzantine church of St Michel surrounded by identikit townhouses. The Maison Coillot (page 176) is on rue Fleurus. Walking south, Solférino leads to an equestrian statue of Joan of Arc. To the north are the Théâtre Sébastopol and Les Halles (pages 120–1).

PLACE RIHOUR ♀ 237 H5 🚆 Rihour Ⓜ Métro 2 to Gare Lille Flandres then line 1 to Rihour

Place de Gaulle trickles into place Rihour, home of the Palais Rihour (page 176) and tourist office, by way of a row of restaurants, cafés and bars where late-night revellers adjourn for an onion-soup breakfast in the small hours. A massive war memorial dominates the square, and is the scene of civic remembrance services on Armistice Day. Some rather disturbing coloured lighting illuminates the fountain that rinses the glass pyramid above the métro station. The result varies from fairground garish to an effect not unlike spilt hospital custard. In winter, a Christmas market of wooden chalets sells hot mulled wine and handmade gifts. The rue de la Vieille Comédie is named after Voltaire's visit to Lille in 1741 for the *première* of his play *Mohamet*. Arrive at the end of the morning to see a monochrome line of committed smokers in front of the métro pyramid. Waiters and *maîtres d'hôtel* in black (whether T-shirts or formal wear), chefs in whites, each with both hands fully occupied in service industry multitasking: texting and smoking at the same time. Restaurant professionals smoke proper cigarettes – no e-cigarettes for them, the electro-plastic is for terrace diners. As the body clock strikes a quarter to the house the *confrérie de la cloppe* disperses to the bistros and brasseries of the quarter and all are ready for the first punters when the belfry chimes midday.

PLACE DU THEATRE ♀ 237 J5 🚉 Rihour ⊂🚈⊃ Métro 2 to Gare Lille Flandres and line 1 to Rihour, then walk along the rue des Mannaliers past the Vieille Bourse (pages 183–4); behind the Vieille Bourse, and looking down towards the old station, is the place du Théâtre. Only pedestrianised as part of the city's millennium renovations, this is the junction of Lille ancient and modern. Spot the iron arm hanging above the junction of rue de la Bourse and rue de la Grande Chaussée pointing visitors to Vieux Lille. The two most striking buildings on the square are surprisingly new, dating from the 20th century: the Neoclassical opera house, with its monumental sculptures of Apollo and the Muses, and the splendid 76m neo-Flemish belfry of the imposing Chambre de Commerce et d'Industrie – both built by Louis Cordonnier.

The Chamber of Commerce building is home to a magnificent hall, used for civic and corporate events, but until now rarely seen by the public (except during heritage weekend – see page 15). Rumours abound that with the business and administrative affairs of the city now managed in the shiny new southeastern quarters of Lille, Cordonnier's masterpiece may become the latest grand building to be reborn as a cultural venue open to one and all. Answers may come during the Lille3000 season in 2015–16.

The Opéra's lavish restored interiors are even more dazzling than ever. Inspired by the Palais Garnier in Paris, the Opéra de Lille has always been a place to be seen, and its programme usually features both classics and new works with an international cast of principals (page 133). Opposite is the Rang de Beauregard, an extraordinarily ornate terrace of 14 three-storey houses and shops constructed in 1687 to complement the Vieille Bourse, and lovingly restored. Look closely at the elegant shopfronts: still embedded in the walls are cannonballs from the siege of 1792. The favourite façade and interior is found *chez* Morel et Fils, purveyors of legendary lingerie from days of yore until the millennium. Today, the vintage mannequins welcome guests to the emporium's reincarnation as a charming café, Maison du Moulin D'Or (page 119).

PORTE DE GAND ⟨VL⟩ ♀ 235 H1 🚉 Rue de Gand ⊂🚈⊃ Bus 50 to Lion D'Or, then cross pl Louise de Bettignies & walk the length of the rue de Gand The last remaining fortified entrance to Vieux Lille stands astride the rue de Gand, looking down over the cobbles and menus of this fashionable dining area. From the old town, admire the coloured patterns in the brickwork above the archways. The windows at the top belong to a restaurant, Les Ramparts (pages 109–10). From the other side, the Porte de Gand can be seen as part of some serious defensive walls. The original perimeter was strengthened twice in the 17th century, the porte and ramparts built in 1621

Museums and Sightseeing **SITES AND MONUMENTS**

11

▲ The Porte de Paris is Lille's Arc de Triomphe (Production Perig/S)

by the Spanish authorities against the French, and an extra line of defence added by Vauban against everybody else. Between the two walls are gardens that can be seen from the restaurant terrace in summer when diners may sit at tables on the ramparts. Since the winding road leading from the gate still serves a working barracks, the rue de Gand has serviced the many appetites of young soldiers since long before the restaurants arrived on the scene. Pools of lamplight under the trees beneath the city walls continue to offer late-night comforts à la Lili Marlène.

PORTE DE PARIS Pl Simon Volant ♀ 238 H3 ☒ Lille Grand Palais ⊕ Métro 2 to Lille Grand Palais, & take rue des Déportés past the Hôtel de Ville

On the traffic roundabout named after the porte's architect stands the greatest of the three remaining city gates. Unlike the portes des Roubaix and Gand, this is an unashamed piece of monumental triumphalism, a lavish declaration of the might and majesty of Louis XIV and celebration of Lille's embrace into the Kingdom of France. Unveiled in 1692, this *arc de triomphe* has an image of the king himself surrounded by angels and cherubim. Columns frame niches holding classical images of war and power, Hercules and Mars paying tribute to France's own Sun King. Originally the gateway rose above the town's fortifications. The walls were torn down in 1858 to make way for boulevards, and the rest of the district of St-Sauveur was demolished in the slum-clearance programmes of the 1920s. A small landscaped garden replaces the moat, once spanned by a drawbridge, and the baroque arch itself is as imposing as ever. Impress your new friends with the trivial nugget that the gateway was not dubbed the Porte de Paris until the Revolution. Despite its regal statuary, it was originally called the Porte des Malades ('Sick People's Gate') because it led to the hospital!

PORTE DE ROUBAIX Parc Matisse or rue de Roubaix ♀ 235 H3 ☒ Gare Lille Europe ⊕ From the station enter the park and follow the footpath to the city walls

From the rue de Roubaix, this nearly neglected old gateway long presented a rather sorry and run-down appearance, and most passers-by simply pass it by. Yet this is the door that saved a city. The Parc Matisse offers a far more appropriate perspective from which to view this remnant of the old fortifications. Here the crenellations and drawbridge channels may be seen to best advantage, and you can imagine the moment in 1792 when the door was slammed in the face of the Austrian duke of Saxe-Teschen and his army of 35,000 men. If the two smaller archways seem to give the gate an air of a triumphal arch, blame it on the commuters. The side walls were opened up in the 19th century for a long-forgotten tramway to the suburbs. The gateway took a belated bow with architectural Botox and celebratory illumination as part of Lille2004.

P'TIT QUINQUIN Sq Foch, rue Nationale ♀ 237 F5 🚇 Rihour 🚌 Bus Citadine to Nationale

This is the statue to a lullaby that won the heart of a town (page xvii): the sentimental patois melodrama of a poor lacemaker whose child would not stop crying. Le P'tit Quinquin was composed in 1852 by town-hall clerk Alexandre Desrousseaux, and was soon adopted as a bedtime ballad by every mother in town. When the composer died in 1892 it was adapted as his funeral march, and the town commissioned Eugène Deplechin to build a memorial to the songwriter. The statue of Desrousseaux's working-class Madonna and Child is as unashamed a manipulator of the heartstrings as the song itself. If you would like to hear the tune, make your way to the place du Théâtre, where the bells of the clocktower chime the lullaby every day at noon.

VIEILLE BOURSE 🚌 Pl du Général de Gaulle ♀ 237 H5 🕐 Tue–Sun 🚇 Rihour 🚇 Métro 2 to Gare Lille Flandres then line 1 to Rihour

Exquisite and unmissable, the most beautiful building in town has been restored to its original Flemish-Renaissance brilliance. The greatest legacy of the Spanish occupation of the city was this jewel box of a Bourse de Commerce merchants' exchange between the two main squares. In fact, the Bourse comprises 24 individual 17th-century houses ranged around a cloistered courtyard. Although at first glance the houses, with their ground-floor shops, may seem identical, the intricate carvings and mouldings on each façade are unique, thanks to the skills of builder Julien Destrez who worked on the project from 1652 to 1653. Destrez had already won a distinguished reputation as a carpenter and sculptor, and he dressed his masterpiece with ornate flourishes of masks and garlands on the outer walls. Lions of Flanders adorn the four doorways into the courtyard, which is itself decked with floral and fruit motifs. Today, above the symbols of the original guilds that once traded here, is a discreet row of contemporary logos representing the private enterprises sponsoring the restoration. As the sun rises over Lille, it catches the gilded belltower on the roof and radiates

11

GARE SAINT-SAUVEUR

Bd Jean-Baptiste Lebas ♀ 235 G8 ✎ 03 28 52 30 00 ⏰ 11.00–19.00 Wed
🚉 Lille Grand Palais 🚇 Métro 2 to Gare Lille Flandres then bus 14 to
Lille-Lebas 🎫 free

The legacy of Lille3000's 2009 Europe XXL season is beyond question the
reinvention of an old railway station and goods yard between the city
centre and the residential Moulins quarter. Instead of demolishing the site
and imposing yet another office block or sports stadium on the landscape,
the city opted to inspire a new community straddling the 19th and 21st
centuries. More than merely another arts centre, the Gare Saint-Sauveur,
opposite the new Parc Lebas (itself the fruit of a previous Lille3000 event
– see pages 188–9), at the foot of the great thoroughfares of Liberté and
Solférino, is a grand space designed for living. With the original railway
tracks still embedded in the ground and the distinctive thick, red walls of the
industrial revolution, some 21ha of land cordoned off for generations from
the people of Lille was handed over, parcelled and portioned by architects
Franklin Azzi. The two striking station buildings are linked by a south-
facing terrace for lazy summer days and nights. One hall is now a cinema
and brasserie, the exposed timbers and revitalised brickwork framing more
modern concepts of interior design. The other space has been left empty,
the blank canvas a grand exhibition centre, performance area, theatre or
concert hall that is ripe and ready for constant reinvention. There is even a
'hotel' called the Europa where subterranean-themed rooms (with industrial

golden beams across the Grand' Place. Step inside the contemplative cloister
to find a charming weekday market selling antiquarian books under the gaze
of busts of local pioneers of science and literature. A sanctuary from summer
sun and winter winds alike, people come here to sit and read or play chess
from mid-morning until early evening. Sunday evening in summer finds the
old walls echoing to the sound of the tango (pages 178–9).

CHURCHES

EGLISE STE CATHERINE 🚊 Pl Jean-Jacques Louchard ♀ 237 F3 ✎ 03 20 55 45 92
⏰ 14.30–17.00 (16.30 in winter) Sat, 14.30–16.00 1st & 3rd Sun, & 2nd & 4th Thu 🚉 Rihour
🚇 Métro 2 to Gare Lille Flandres and bus 10 to Danel, then west along rue Négrier to rue
Ste Cathérine 🎫 free

Out-of-towners rarely discover this 13th-century church. Yet until work started
on Notre Dame de la Treille, this was home to the town's precious statue of the
Virgin Mary (page 187). Rubens's *Martyrdom of Sainte Cathérine*, now in the
Palais des Beaux-Arts (pages 169–71), hung here for years, and many striking

art) may be rented for 30 or 60 minutes at a time. The bistro at the St So, as the site is known to the locals (pronounced 'sanso'), is an essential venue for chilling out with friends or catching live music during the afternoon or evening. Reservations advised for performances. See page 115.

The social anarchy of festival fever allowed the inaugural season a free-flow feel. A visitor might set up a table or pitch a tent on the site, or hang out at the book exchange café, where paperbacks were dropped and picked up by strangers. A huge wall was erected in summer 2009 for visitors to scrawl their thoughts and, across the site, the Braderie tradition of anarchic free trade was celebrated as anyone who wished might set up stall to sell their attic trove and rummage through a neighbour's unwanted treasure. You could nip out for a coffee and a mooch and end up invited to an alfresco dinner party with strangers.

Five years on and the site has become an essential part of the community. In spring 2014 the entire population was invited to the station to pick up a planter box, compost and bulbs to cultivate at home in gardens or on balconies. A few months later, the boxes were returned in full bloom and laid out in intricate patterns to cover the Grand'Place in a carpet of flowers: a massive garden project for the city landscaped by the people.

At this long-forgotten railway station at the far end of the boulevard of respectability and best behaviour, Lille's twin passions of art and hospitality are consummated over coffee, a beer, a good book, a song and a bargain.

works by lesser-known artists may still be seen in the spacious and bright interior. The altar is graced by some excellent artworks including adoration of the shepherds and images inspired by Leonardo's *Last Supper*. Over the centuries the parish church of the rural suburb of Faubourg de Weppes expanded to become a traditional Flemish *hallekerque* (page 186). Its three spacious naves were probably saved from demolition during the Revolution when the building was called into service as a barn, returning to the Catholic Church in 1797. By then it had lost the ornate iron partition grilles and other elaborate furnishings. Other splendid items remain, from the carved choir stalls to the beautifully painted pillars, and Ste Cathérine has at last won historic monument listing status.

EGLISE STE MARIE MADELEINE Rue du Pont Neuf ☎ 03 20 74 46 83 ⏰ 14.00–18.00 Mon & Fri, 15.00–18.00 Sun, closed mid-Jul–mid-Aug 🚌 Bus 50 to Palais de Justice

One of the most exciting concepts of Lille2004 was the project that lured some of the world's leading cinematographers to illuminate and interpret the interior of this deconsecrated church. Peter Greenaway, Miwa Yanagi, Chiharu Shiota, Emir Kusturica and Erwin Redl have each designed their

▲ The 19th-century Cathédrale Notre Dame was finally completed in 1999 (Anna Moores)

own two-month reinterpretation of the building, which reintroduced Lille to one of its forgotten treasures. The unassuming flat frontage belies the magnificence within, notably the dome, so painstakingly restored in the 18th century. Now reclaimed as an exhibition venue.

EGLISE ST MAURICE GP Parvis St Maurice, rue de Paris ♀ 237 J6 ↘ 03 20 06 07 21
⏱ 13.15–18.00 Mon, 10.15–12.15 & 13.15–18.00 Tue–Sat, 15.30–20.00 Sun (guided visits (French) Sun 15.00–17.00; telephone for English & signed tours) 🚉 Gare Lille Flandres
🚇 Métro 2 to Gare Lille Flandres, then turn left on to rue de Priez at the foot of rue Faidherbe
The first of the sudden surprises that make Lille so special. Unless you decide to take a short cut from the station to the pedestrian shopping streets, you might never see this magnificent 15th-century church, its gleaming white stone façades restored to pristine condition – at the cost of many a summer night's sleep to neighbours within earshot of the sandblasting. Built on marshland, it has five high naves to distribute its weight equally across a wide area, in a style known as Hallekerque Flamande – literally 'Flemish Market Church' – after the airy market hall-style interior. Yet another unsung art collection may be viewed here, even if many original treasures have since found their way into the Palais des Beaux-Arts. The dramatic stained-glass windows of *The Passion* were inspired by the heroic 19th-century style of Ingres. Summer Sunday organ recitals are worth catching, as are the occasional Saturday night concerts by local musicians.

NOTRE DAME DE LA TREILLE V2 Pl Gilleson ♀ 237 J3 ↘ 03 20 55 28 72 ⏱ 10.00–12.00 & 14.00–18.30 Mon–Wed & Fri–Sat, 10.00–18.30 Thu, Sun: respect service times;

For most of the last century, Lille was a city with three-quarters of a cathedral. Notre Dame de la Treille had not only a fine Gothic chapel and apse, but also the largest expanse of corrugated iron in northern Europe. For, although the foundation stone had been laid in 1854 and the bulk of the edifice completed by the turn of the 19th century, work during the 20th century finally ground to a halt when the money ran out in 1947. What should have been the great front entrance was hastily boarded up. By 1999, in the golden age of accountancy, funding had finally been found and Lille was able to unveil its cathedral. From the outside, architect P L Carlier's designs are very much of the age of the out-of-town shopping mall: B&Q perpendicular. But inside, it is quite a different story: imposing yet welcoming, a delicate blend of light and shade. The new rose window by Kijno produces a powerful effect within, and the remarkable doors created by sculptor and Holocaust survivor George Jeanclos, representing a barbed-wire vine of human suffering and dignity, are quite magnificent. The cathedral stands on the Îlot Comtesse, site of the former château of the counts of Flanders, and the surrounding streets follow the line of the old fortifications, with traces of a moat still visible. A Museum of Religious Art in the crypt opens on weekend afternoons from 14.30 to 19.00, housing 200 works of art and historic objects, including the original statue of Notre Dame de la Treille, dating from 1270. Regular free guided visits.

OTHER ARTS AND CULTURAL VENUES

A tradition of reclamation and reinvention, renaissance and revival with a dash of pure *chutzpah* has led to an exciting programme that has seen old and abandoned buildings being called into service as arts and cultural venues. Inspired by the original Maisons Folies concept (pages 190–1) during Lille2004, it is largely sponsored, nurtured and mentored by the Lille3000 team.

Besides the original Maisons Folies, Lille2004 opened up many overlooked or forgotten buildings to the public. Three in particular were taken very much to the hearts of the Lillois and their visitors. The Eglise Ste Marie Madeleine (page 185–6) continues to stage occasional exhibitions after its stunning debut. The remarkable horticultural hall, the Palais Rameau on boulevard Vauban (page 194), has had a habit of stepping out of retirement time and again, should occasion demand it. Unfortunately, a shameful lack of ongoing care has made its public outings pretty rare nowadays. Check with the tourist office for exhibitions. It may be run-down, but it is an essential diversion for anyone with a soul. And, the more people who ask to see it, the greater support for the lobby actively campaigning for the restoration of one of northern France's most delightful buildings.

11

LILLE3000

After the remarkable success of Lille's reign as European Capital of Culture in 2004 (page xvii), with the world's imaginative and creative talents reinventing every corner of the city from churches to squares, when abandoned factories and forgotten buildings were reborn as cultural and community centres, and even the skies were transformed into works of art (who could forget the inverted forest suspended above the place de l'Opéra?), the decision was taken to continue the magic long after the European baton was passed to other host cities.

Thus, the same core team was itself reborn as **Lille3000** (℡ *03 28 52 30 00* 🖥 *www.lille3000.eu*), an infinite arts season of biennial festivals and intermittent treats. They kept hold of such commandeered buildings as **Le TriPostal** (page 190) and the **Maisons Folies** (pages 190–3) and breathed new life into other sites, including the railway good yards at **Saint-Sauveur** (pages 184–5). The first flamboyant flourish was the Bombaysers season in 2006–07, where the city was a glorious Bollywood extravaganza, with rue Faidherbe lined with triumphant elephants through the winter. Then came Europe XXL in 2009, a celebration of central and eastern Europe, and two years later the city evoked scenes of pure fantasy in an international celebration of the imagination.

You may have had to turn more than a hundred pages before reading this, but in so many of the previous and following chapters the legacy of those Lille3000 seasons lives on in public spaces and parks, new galleries and performance venues whose working lives continue far beyond the original time-stamped programme.

Between official festivals, each attracting one or two million new visitors to programmes of art exhibitions, performances, parades and deliciously

The major surprise star of the City of Culture season was the old postal sorting office by the railway tracks that served as cultural HQ and itinerant exhibition centre and party venue. **Le TriPostal** (page 190) stands between the Gare Lille Flandres and Euralille shopping centre. Lille3000 manages to stage events here even when there is no official festival, so you should check out the place whenever you find yourself in Lille.

The **Gare Saint-Sauveur** (pages 184–5) was the most recent slice of railway real estate to be appropriated by the city. Rumour has it that the ornate **Chambre de Commerce** on place du Théâtre (page 181) will be the next classic building to be made over to the public.

LE GRAND SUD Rue de l'Europe ♀ 238 F5 ℡ 03 20 88 89 90 🚏 Porte des Postes
🚇 Métro 2 to Port des Postes then bus 11 to Verne & walk up rue Garrau to the park

This is a new modular and versatile building in the upcoming southern overblown public gestures – such as massive soup banquets to feed a city or teeny restaurants hidden inside giant art installations – the Lille3000 brand, with its slogan '*Le Voyage Continue*' ('The journey goes on'), attaches itself to some fantastic mini cultural seasons. This has included bringing gems from the Saatchi Gallery collection to Lille during a 2010 celebration of the Silk Route, to inviting the entire population of the city to landscape Lille's Grand' Place with home-grown plants and flowers in 2014. The cusp of winter 2015 saw another micro-festival, Secret Passions, opening up the traditionally private collections of the secretive and reclusive art collectors of Flanders. Millionaire industrialists and wealthy families in this corner of northern Europe have long had their own remarkable collections and, for three months, Lille3000 shared these treasures at Le TriPostal.

The fourth major cultural festival since Lille2004 runs from 26 September 2015 until early 2016 and honours the phenomenon for which Lille3000 may itself share the credit. Entitled Renaissance, the event is no regurgitation of the 16th-century European artistic and intellectual rebirth, but a proud celebration of the early 21st century, which may claim to be the greatest ever resurgence, emergence and merging of global cultures. Looking to diverse inspirations from Rio to Detroit, Eindhoven to Phnom Penh and Seoul, the festival will feature its trademark parades and world-class exhibitions, the metamorphoses of public and private spaces, celebrations of food and writing, and a surfeit of performance and debate.

As ever, news and programme information will trickle from the festival's website and from the Lille Tourist Office. Le TriPostal will serve as box office and rendezvous.

quarter of Lille. Between the existing green spaces of the Jardin des Plantes, the Cimetière du Sud and the Parc de l'Aventure, this is a venue that could be staging an international rock concert one night and your best friend's 35th birthday the next. Less of an arts/exhibition centre than other new addresses, this is essentially a community space and locals can book the site for family functions.

LA MALTERIE 42 rue Kuhlmann ◊ 238 B5 ◊ 03 20 15 13 21 ◊ www.lamalterie.com
◊ Porte des Postes ◊ Bus Citadine to Condé
Like Rita in Roubaix (page 201) this is a vast, multi-storey industrial building on the edge of the city, now colonised by a community of artists in residence. Much of the building is given over to individual studios, where artists working in all media are commissioned to work on Lille3000 projects or follow private passions. Much of the exhibition space and time

11

at the Gare St-Sauveur in 2014 originated here. The ground floor includes a concert venue with an eclectic programme of events throughout the year, and a versatile exhibition space. Upstairs find the artists' canteen, top-floor dance studios and even darkrooms for traditional photography.

LE TRIPOSTAL   Av Willy Brandt ♀ 235 H4 ☏ 03 20 14 47 60 ▥ Gare Lille Flandres ◷ Take the av le Corbusier viaduct to Euralille & cross to av Willy Brandt
The enduring legacy of Lille2004 was the renaissance of a tired postal sorting office at the side of the Gare Lille Flandres. The harsh state-owned railway and postal service architecture lent anonymity to the site that allowed it to be reinvented with each phase of the festival. Attracting around a quarter of a million visitors in its first season, the potential of this industrial warehouse-style shell with its mail cages and three 2,000m² galleries was irresistible. Martine Aubry, charismatic mayor and all-round superwoman, wrested Le TriPostal from its landlords to allow it to remain open for five more years. It is still going strong more than a decade since. Shows in its first year included futuristic robots, Buckingham Palace reinvented as a council estate, and a sensual tickling machine. Since then it has highlighted gems from private collections, even a Saatchi retrospective. A key venue (and box office) for Lille3000 festivals, it also hosts special events during non-festival months and years, and is often a venue for clubbing and social events.

MAISONS FOLIES

'Folly' is too frivolous a word since, in reviving abandoned or forgotten buildings, this audacious project has breathed new life into many a community: exciting spaces able to adapt to the imagination of each quarter. The longest-lasting legacy of the 2004 Capital of Culture is the fabulous scheme that created a dozen permanent arts centres in Lille and across the region into Belgium. Transforming abandoned buildings and creating entire new community spaces, the Maisons Folies are at once a celebration of the past, an indulgence for the present and a magnificent gift to future generations. Former industrial, military and religious buildings become galleries, theatres, nightclubs, party venues and recording studios, with artists in residence, gardens in the sky and libraries. Named for the architectural follies that were the bricks-and-mortar whims of the wealthy aristocrats of the *ancien régime* and industrial *nouveaux riches*, these projects should revive and inspire local communities and entertain their visitors for years, even decades, to come. Unlike Marie Antoinette's model farm and other mini-châteaux and fairy-tale boathouses, the Maisons Folies belong to the people: kitchens and dining rooms, where local people can prepare and serve their own meals; gardens for those who want to get their hands dirty; libraries with books in many languages; not to mention the opportunity for local children to meet and work with artists living on site.

Folies came of age with Lille2004, a focus for the diverse communities of the 21st century. The project has evolved comfortably over its first half-decade. The sites, once forbidden to their communities, have become so much a part of everyday life that their involvement in all activities and occasions is a given. Lille3000 sets out its diary across these venues with ease, so that festival time is not contained within strict city limits, but is carried across into the wider community, generating a previously unimaginable sense of involvement.

LILLE

Maison Folie Wazemmes Usine Leclercq, 70 rue des Sarrazins ♀ 238 A3 ⬑ 03 20 31 47 80 ⬛ http://mfwazemmes.lille.fr ⬛ Gambetta ⬛ Métro 2 to Gare Lille Flandres & line 1 to Wazemmes, then walk west along rue d'Iéna & take the 4th turning on your right, rue d'Austerlitz

A 19th-century textile factory which finally closed its doors in 1990 is reinvented with a stunning yet sympathetic building alongside the original structure, a brand new, undulating, red-brick road and public square in the vibrant Wazemmes district. Indoor and outdoor spaces, conceived by the architect Lars Spuybroek, are thrilling, eye-catching and versatile. Alongside studios, exhibition hall and urban orchard is a well-judged theatre space. The Folie is set to become a permanent home to many local arts and performance groups. However, to the locals its allure is far more practical. They wanted a Turkish bath, so the architect created a luxurious sauna and steam complex incorporating the warm red-brick vaulting with some beautiful tiling and interior design. The Zeïn Oriental Spa is open to women 11.00–21.00 (Mon, Wed, Thu and Sat) and 11.00–18.00 (Tue and Fri), to men 18.00–21.00 (Tue and Fri), and is mixed for families on market day, Sunday, 11.00–21.00.

Maison Folie des Moulins 47–49 rue d'Arras ♀ 238 G5 ⬑ 03 28 52 20 04 ⬛ http://mfmoulins.lille.fr ⬛ Porte d'Arras ⬛ Métro 1 to Porte d'Arras and walk along the rue d'Arras

This former brewery, an abandoned site of brick and copper, is set to become the very heart of the Moulins district, which already has a thriving arts scene (the Prato Theatre and Univers Cinema are both within a short walk). An imposing 140m^2 exhibition hall doubles as a theatrical rehearsal space, and the recording studios open out into a weekend nightclub dedicated to contemporary sounds. Two interior courtyards will host open-air performances and the building's original function is reflected in a new bar-brasserie on site.

Maison Folie Beaulieu Pl Beaulieu, quartier de la Délivrance, 59160 Lomme ♀ 236 A6 ⬑ 03 20 22 93 66 ⬛ Maison des Enfants ⬛ Métro 2 to Bourg then bus to Délivrance

The newest of Lille's Maisons Folies opened its doors during the 2009 Lille3000 season and has proved a great success, enjoying a close association with local theatre companies and the Centre Régional des Arts du Cirque.

11

Maison Folie Lambersart Le Colysée, av du Colysée, 59130 Lambersart
☎ 03 20 08 44 44 ⊠ Bois Blancs ⊜ Métro 2 to Bois Blancs & follow signposts through the park

Technically belonging to the commune of Lambersart but, since it is just across the river from Lille proper, it counts as a city venue. Originally known as the Maison de la Plaine, it is an open-space folie by the waterside, where Vauban once built a fortress, and where locals once came to dance by the banks of the Deûle. Thus, the architects conceived the house of the future and set it in a meadow, where once again people may come to take in the air. The project soon evolved into Le Colysée with an art gallery and two 40-cover restaurants on site. A rarity in Lille, there's free parking here too.

ARRAS
Hôtel de Guines Rue des Jongleurs, 62000 ☎ 03 21 71 66 17
Next to the Musée des Beaux Arts in the St Vaast Abbey, a grand 18th-century private house has two wings embracing an enclosed courtyard. Its grand façade had already been listed as a national monument before the Maisons Folies project was launched. The stylish rooms are perfect artists' salons for many a cultural rendezvous, and experts from the nearby theatre have helped create performance areas for concerts and cabarets.

MAUBEUGE
Les Cantuaines La Porte de Mons, pl Vauban, 59600 ☎ 03 27 62 11 93
This is an artists' retreat within a former convent on the site of a 16th-century hospice at La Porte de Mons, the last great town gate to be constructed for Louis XIV by Vauban. Seven cells near the chapel have been converted into studios for artists in residence. The gardens will host exhibitions and performances, and the grand gateway itself, long-time home to the local tourist office, has been converted into a brasserie and art gallery.

MONS-EN-BAROEUL
Fort de Mons Rue de Normandie, 59700 ☎ 03 20 61 78 90
This place thrills me as a performance space: brick and sky crying out for open-air theatre and screaming with potential. An elegant 19th-century moated fortress with three paved courtyards, rather than the traditional central parade ground, now houses a cinema, restaurant and library, with exhibition halls and music and dance venues within the fortified walls.

ROUBAIX
La Condition Publique See pages 200–1.

TOURCOING
L'Hospice d'Havré See page 204.

VILLENEUVE D'ASCQ
La Ferme d'en Haut See page 206.

BELGIUM
Courtrai
Lille sur l'Isle L'Isle Buda, 9 Budastraat, 8500 ⟍ (+32) 056 51 81 00
On an island on the River Lys, warehouses and cloisters become theatres and museums. The Limelight Centre for Contemporary Arts boasts a cinema, restaurant and galleries, and even the river itself becomes an exhibition space with floating billboards presenting art on the waters.

Mons
Les Arbalestriers 8 rue des Arbalestriers, 7000 ⟍ (+32) 065 39 98 01
Outside, an open-air summer theatre; within, a café-concert, *médiathèque*, exhibition hall and auditorium. And so a former school in the heart of the town becomes the cultural crossroads of Mons, working with theatre companies across the French border in Maubeuge. For more on the 2015 European Capital of Culture, see Bradt's *Mons: A European Capital of Culture* (pages 222–3).

Tournai
Seminaire de Choiseul 11 rue des Soeurs de Charité, 7500 ⟍ (+32) 069 44 38 82
The original 13th-century church of Ste Marguerite was mostly destroyed by fire and rebuilt in 1760 in the style of a Neoclassical temple. An earlier 16th-century tower remains and is a landmark in the centre of the Belgian town. As a Maison Folie, the church hosts visiting exhibitions, stage concerts and creative workshops and is at the heart of local fairs, markets and carnivals.

PARKS AND GARDENS

Lille boasts 350ha of green spaces within the city limits, and the wider region stretches out into open country (see page 204 for the lakes and hilly walks of the nature reserve at Villeneuve d'Ascq). Even if you do not have time to head to the sand dunes by Dunkerque or the farmland beyond the city, enjoy a breath of fresh air within a few minutes of your next urban adventure.

BOIS DE BOULOGNE Av Mathias Delobel ♀ 236 B3 ⟍ (zoo) 03 28 52 07 00 ⏲ zoo Apr–Oct 09.00–17.30 Mon–Fri, 10.00–17.00 Sat–Sun & holidays; Nov–Mar 10.00–17.00 Mon–Fri, 09.00–18.30 Sat–Sun & holidays; closed 2nd Sun in Dec & Feb 🚌 Bus 12 to Champ de Mars
The countryside comes to town where panthers prowl, joggers run and families take the air. Neatly tied up in a loop of the River Deûle's canals are 50 hectares of greenery, picturesque towpaths and an island filled with monkeys. Home to the famous fortress (pages 174–5), the Bois de Boulogne

11

is where the city loosens its tie on weekends and holidays. Children love the zoo, free to all, with its Ile des Singes ('Monkey Island') and contented rhinos and zebras. There is also a playground for dodgems, side-shows and candyfloss moments (page 43). Outside the zoo is a cobbled pathway that forms part of the arduous Paris–Roubaix cycle race, known colloquially as 'The Hell of the North'. Fitness fanatics pace themselves running around the former moat, following the signposted route between the ramparts and the willow trees. You can always tell the soldiers and foreign legionnaires by their blue tracksuits. Lovers wander into the woods, while more decorous strollers prefer the esplanade, landscaped in 1675 by Vauban himself, or the Champ de Mars where funfairs pitch their tents during school holidays. If all seems carefree and inconsequential, take a moment to pause by the Monument aux Fusillées on square Daubenton at the edge of the Bois. Félix Desruelle's memorial pays tribute to those Lillois members of the French Resistance shot by the Nazis against the walls of the Citadelle.

JARDIN VAUBAN Bd Vauban ♀ 236 C4 ☻ Bus 12 to Champ de Mars

A delightful 19th-century park, often overshadowed by the large lush expanses of the Bois de Boulogne across the River Deûle, this is a pretty confection of dainty flower-beds, waterfalls, lawns and grottos, landscaped in 1865 by Paris's chief gardener, the aptly named Barillet Deschamps. Poets' Corner contains memorials to writers and musicians, and a monument to Charles de Gaulle stands at the square Daubenton entrance. Locals visit the immaculate miniature orchard to meet the present-day gardeners who are always willing to give advice and tips on growing fruit and vegetables at home. The most famous corner of the park is the puppet theatre in Monsieur Rameau's Goat House, where every Sunday and Wednesday Jacques le Lillois performs for local children (page 43). This Chalet aux Chèvres was one of Charles Rameau's many eccentric legacies to the town. He was a noted horticulturist who gave Lille the splendid Palais Rameau (♀ 236 C5) at the junction of rue Solférino and bd Vauban, a vast horticultural hall that has doubled as a circus and performing-arts venue. In need of renovation, the hall is nonetheless a gem of its time and type. These munificent bequests were given freely on the condition that his grave at the Cimetière du Sud (♀ 238 F5) is always marked by a bed of potatoes, a tomato plant, strawberries, a vine, rosebush and dahlias.

JARDIN DES PLANTES Rue du Jardin des Plantes ♀ 238 G5 ☏ 03 28 36 13 50 ⊙ park Apr–Sep 07.30–21.00 daily & Oct–Mar 08.30–18.30, greenhouses 09.00–12.00 & 13.30–17.00 ⊞ Porte de Douai or Porte d'Arras ☻ Métro 2 to Porte de Douai, then follow the rue Carrel south & turn right on the rue Cap Michel towards the park

Waterfalls and tropical greenhouses, rare plants and trees from many lands, all to be found just a little too far south for most visitors to bother with. Yet just below the ring-road is one of the most romantic escapes in the city, where many a troth has been plighted at the top level of the conservatory, or in the cooling summer shade of the *orangerie*. Botanists are not the only visitors to feel their pulses quickening when they wander through the lovingly maintained gardens. Sense the sultry south in the most unlikely corner of northern France.

PARC JEAN-BAPTISTE LEBAS Bd Jean-Baptiste Lebas ♀ 238 H4 ☞ Métro 2 to Gare Lille Flandres then bus 14 to Lille-Lebas

Proof that Lille does not need an international title to come up with fresh projects, this conversion of a car park into a haven of greenery was 2005's gift from the city to its residents and guests, opening midway through the year. Where the Porte de Paris and bd de la Liberté come to their natural conclusions, the tarmac is laid to lawns and century-old chestnut trees augmented by more than 12 dozen new lindens in 3ha of unexpected city-centre garden. Naturally there are nice chairs and lamps, with of course a *bouledrome* for the grown-ups and a children's play area too, and all wrapped in high railings with monumental gateways to the various boulevards back into town, and to the Gare Saint-Sauveur (pages 184–5) by the railway tracks.

PARC HENRI MATISSE Euralille ♀ 235 H3 ⊠ Gare Lille Europe ☞ Step out of the station & it is right there!

Part of another grand project within a grand project (the wish to create a green belt around the old city walls), the Parc Matisse was chosen to be one of the installation-art sites of Lille2004. Happily, this newest of city parks has ripened and weathered itself to sit well in the urban landscape. Spindly saplings are now emerging as adolescent trees, lawns mellowing to meadow, wild flowers sitting comfortably against centuries-old walls as a foreground to the futuristic glass empire of Lille Europe that rises from the gardens. Popular with picnickers as much as with those looking for a short cut through the Porte de Roubaix (pages 182–3), the park has come of age and proven itself as a treasured haven. You can tell it works – even office workers hold hands as they stroll through its eight green hectares.

PARC BARBIEUX See page 201.

JARDIN DES GEANTS Rue du Ballon ♀ 235 J2 ⊙ 09.00–sunset (latest 21.00) ⊠ Gare Lille Europe ☞ Take the lift to street level; behind the Crown Plaza above the station turn left to rue du Faubourg de Roubaix then right on rue du Ballon & follow signs

Lille's newest park is by the Cimetière de l'Est between the Eurostar station and the Madeleine district. To be honest it is really more of a conceptual art installation than a stroll through nature. Leafy lanes, waving bamboo and water features are threaded with eccentric modern sculptures of giant chairs and faces in metal and willow.

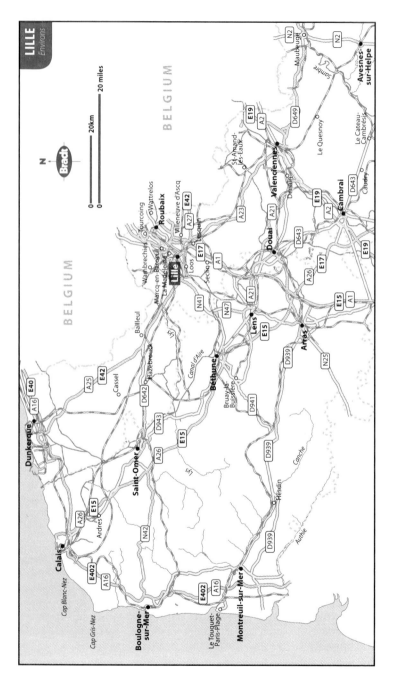

N

Bradt

0 ___ 20km
0 ___ 20 miles

BELGIUM

BELGIUM

Dunkerque
E40
A16
E42
A25
Cassel
Bailleul
Hazebrouck
D642
E15
D943
A26
Saint-Omer
N42
A26
E15
Ardres
Calais
E402
A16
Cap Blanc-Nez
Cap Gris-Nez
Boulogne-sur-Mer
E402
A16
Montreuil-sur-Mer
Le Touquet-Paris-Plage
D939
Authie
D939
Hesdin
Canche
D939
D941
Bruay-la-Buissière
Béthune
Canal d'Aire
Lys
Lys
D941
N25
D939
Arras
A21
E15
A1
Lens
E15
N47
N41
Wambrechies
Marcq-en-Barœul
La Madeleine
Lille
Loos
Seclin
Sechin
A1
E17
Lesquin
A27
E42
Villeneuve d'Ascq
A23
Roubaix
Tourcoing
Wattrelos
Douai
A21
D643
E17
A26
E19
A2
E19
Cambrai
D643
Caudry
D643
E19
E15
A1
Valenciennes
Denain
St-Amand-les-Eaux
E19
A2
Le Quesnoy
Le Cateau-Cambrésis
Sambre
Maubeuge
N2
Avesnes-sur-Helpe
N2

12

Beyond the City

Pretty gardens of the Parc Barbieux and Disney-quaint houses line the roads on the half-hour tram route to the two major satellite towns of **Tourcoing** and **Roubaix**. These days, the extended métro cuts journey times in half, blurring the boundaries between the city of Lille and the other towns that make up Lille Métropole. The metropolitan population is over a million, and the artistic honours of the conurbation are now shared fairly around Lille's immediate neighbours. So the Ballet du Nord performs at the huge Colisée theatre in Roubaix, and the Atelier Lyrique at Tourcoing stages intimate productions of favourites from Mozart to Bernstein. Tourcoing has its annual jazz festival, while Roubaix holds an open-air art market. **Villeneuve d'Ascq** may now be a university centre and home to one of the leading modern art collections in northern

"The elephant in the room is Lens, home to the spectacular new Louvre museum."

Europe, but the area was once famous for its windmills and watermills. Lille's tourist office has information on events in all the surrounding towns within the metropolitan area and offers plenty of seasonal alternatives to conventional public transport – canal boats and vintage trams among them.

The elephant in the room is the neighbouring town of **Lens**, home to the spectacular new Louvre Museum. In case you wonder why there are no high-profile transport and PR links to one of the region's most important attractions, you need to understand local politics. While Lille is the capital of the département of the Nord, Lens is just across the county line, in the neighbouring département of Pas de Calais, and in France, anywhere beyond a local political border may as well be in another time zone. So, despite the fact that Lens is close enough to be a virtual suburb of Lille, it is not on the local transport map, meaning you'll have to find your own way there (page 209).

Wherever you roam, remember to dial 32 65 from any phone in France and you will be put through to the local tourist information centre (French and English spoken), be it a village, town or city.

For more information on any of the towns, villages and sites away from the Lille Metropolitan area, visit the new Maison du Tourisme (page 16) where staff from the regional tourist office can advise on places to stay and attractions.

ROUBAIX

The town of a thousand chimneys evolved from the 15th to the 19th centuries, as Roubaix developed its textile industry. Originally a useful sideline for farmers in winter, the manufacture of fabric and clothes created a boom town during the industrial revolution, its wealth matched only by its social conscience. A succession of enlightened civic and business leaders saw the town pioneering crèches, social housing, family allowance benefits, allotments and hospitals for the workers. Meanwhile, the town fathers accumulated an incredible collection of sample books, fabrics, fashion designs and ephemera: a comprehensive catalogue of styles from the ancient Egyptians to the 20th century. This archive is now displayed to best effect at La Piscine (below), alongside the private art collections of the entrepreneurs who owned the original mills. The only Ingres in town (even Lille's Palais des Beaux-Arts cannot claim one of these), Picassos and works of local artists Cogghe and Weerts are to be seen there. The exhibits' original home was destroyed in World War II: however, architect Jean-Paul Philippon has reinvented one of the great buildings of Roubaix's heyday to provide a worthy successor, within the one place in town where citizens of all classes would mingle as equals. For years before the Maisons Folies project breathed new life into abandoned factories and sites, Roubaix was reinventing its architecture to serve future generations.

TOURIST INFORMATION As well as visiting the Roubaix Tourist Office (*12 pl de la Liberté* \ *03 20 65 31 90* ☎ *www.roubaixtourisme.com* ⏱ *09.30–18.00 Mon–Sat, closed Sun*), you can also download the free ZeVisit app to any smart device, featuring a guided tour to the town and its museums (page 35).

WHAT TO SEE AND DO
La Piscine – Musée d'Art et d'Industrie Art & Industry Museum; 23 rue de l'Espérance \ 03 20 69 23 60 ☎ www.roubaix-lapiscine.com ⏱ 11.00–18.00 Tue–Thu, 11.00–20.00 Fri, 13.00–18.00 Sat–Sun 🚋 Gare Jean Lebas 🚇 Métro 2 to Gare Jean Lebas, then walk down av Jean Lebas & turn right to rue des Champs & left on to rue de l'Espérance 🎟 €5.50

The sun also rises at the former municipal swimming pool: a dramatic stained-glass window radiates stylised sunbeams over this most ambitious project. With the Palais des Beaux-Arts in Lille, this is one of the musts of the area. An exciting, eclectic and always stimulating collection housed in a building that is itself the town's greatest art treasure of them all. Albert Baert's Art Deco swimming pool is listed as the finest example of the genre in the land. Even when I was picking my way through the site, ten years after it had been abandoned and as work was beginning on its renaissance, the building still had the power to thrill. Restored and reinvented as a combination art gallery and sensual archive of textiles, it takes the breath away. The original floors and walls are impressive enough, but the form and shape of the place is a ravishing assault on the senses.

It is built in the fashion of a Cistercian abbey, around a central courtyard, once a rose garden, now a *jardin des plantes* reflecting the textile industry (flax, mulberry and the like having played their roles in Roubaix's past). To one side is the magnificent vaulted swimming pool, to the other the municipal bathhouse, where some of the tiled bathrooms remain. The rest of the wings house the art collection.

And what a collection it is, with Bonnard, Dufy and Gallé among the big-name draws. Most dating from the end of the 19th and the first half of the 20th century, the artworks provide a forensic examination of the lives and people of Roubaix. Originally housed in the textile college across the way, the museum grew from a collection of fabrics from the textile factories to include works of art accumulated and acquired by the industrialist families of the town. Some of these works show remarkable glimpses into the lives of the town's working men and women. Others are deliciously camp: Shaw's middle-class morality, with allegorical images of high ideals. I love the whore rising above her surroundings, the rose symbol of her baser trade being replaced by the lily of purity as she rejects sin in favour of redemption. Some offer a more perceptive grasp of reality: the initially enchanting idyll of children playing in a field takes on a grimmer aspect when you notice the eldest little girl burying her dolls, as factory chimneys beckon her beyond ambrosia to an adult life of toil. Social politics merge with artistic merit in a gallery devoted to the emancipation of women through art. A wry evocation of the *Mona Lisa* shows a modern woman of learning; Camille Claudel's evocative bust of a child was a challenge to Rodin, her mentor and former lover, to acknowledge the paternity of her own daughter.

As you wander through the galleries, the occasional sound of splashing and shrieking within the unmistakable acoustic of swimming baths leads you to the heart of the museum, the pool itself. The witty sound effect is even more effective in situ. A sheet of water still runs almost the length of the Olympic baths, fed by the fountain head of Neptune at the end of the dazzling mosaic basin. This continues to reflect brilliant-coloured glass sunrise and sunset windows at each end of the building. Catch your breath and then walk along the boardwalks lined with 19th- and 20th-century sculpture. These, like Cogghe and Weerts' paintings in earlier galleries, reflect the social history of the town. Some are worthy religious icons, others starkly socialist interpretations of the dignity of the working man. A massive Moorish arch in Sèvres porcelain dominates the room, and along each side of the pool are ranged tiers of original shower and changing cubicles. Glazed to protect their exhibits, these are now treasure houses, including a remarkable range of ceramics by Picasso. On upper levels the textile collection brings gowns and underwear, accessories and shoes of bygone ages. The *tissuthèque* is an archive of thousands of years of material patterns, from ancient Egypt to the present day. Around the museum, filing-cabinet drawers of fabrics allow visitors to plunge their hands into a sensory wonderland of the soft and silky, matted and furred.

Take time to reflect on the day with a cool drink in the restaurant or on its terrace, run by Meert of Lille (pages 120–1), flicking through an art book from the excellent museum shop.

Manufacture des Flandres
Jacquard Museum; 25 rue de la Prudence ✆ 03 20 65 31 90 🖥 www.manufacturedesflandres.fr ◷ 14.00–18.00 Tue–Sun, closed Mon, holidays & 3 weeks in Aug; guided visits 14.00, 15.00, 16.00 & 17.00 🚃 Roubaix 🚋 Tram or métro 2 to Roubaix–Eurotéléport, then bus 15 or 16 to Fraternité 💶 €6

A loom with a view on the history of the weaving industry at this working museum that explains the story of mass production of textiles. See looms, from the original hand-operated contraptions, through the growth of the Jacquard machines, to contemporary computer-operated systems. The museum is a great place to shop for faux-medieval wall hangings, arts and crafts tableware and contemporary scatter cushions.

Maison Folie – La Condition Publique
Pl Faidherbe ✆ 03 28 33 57 57 🖥 www. laconditionpublique.com ◷ 12.30–18.30 Tue–Sat 🚋 Métro 2 to Roubaix–Eurotéléport then bus L4 to Condition Publique 💶 free

I have loved this Maison Folie (page 190) ever since it was still just a construction site, when I visited the work in progress over a decade ago. A magnificent building, irresistibly reminiscent of a Victorian railway station without the trains, this was the place where wool, and occasionally silks too, would come to be treated and packed. In recent years it has hosted many a local festival and concert, its cobbled driveway between the two vast warehouses giving it a sense of a town within a town. One original aspect of the original building is the eccentric sloping lawn on the glass roofs. In order to provide a constant year-round temperature, the glazed roof was turfed over and workers would often lie down and doze on this incidental meadow in the sky. Indoors, discover the exhibition halls, arts space and facilities of the Maisons Folies projects, a grand estaminet and local heritage centre. Visit in December for the traditional Braderie de l'Art, a cross between a make-over and a flea market. People sell their old junk and artists use the bric-a-brac to make original artworks which they then sell off for anything between €1 and €300.

Chez Rita 49 rue Daubenton ☎ 03 20 26 22 88 🛏 www.chezrita.fr ⏱ 17.00–22.00 Thu (shop), phone for other opening times 🚊 Gare Jean Lebas 🚇 Métro 2 to Gare Jean Lebas then bus Cit-R to bd Metz

Is it a biscuit or is it art? Once upon a time, the Rita waffle factory closed down. Since the family who ran the business wanted to leave something to the local community that had served the company so well for so many years, they handed over the factory building to a community of artists, who now work, rest and play in the nooks and crannies, workshops and loading bays. Every corner has been converted into an individual's creative space, with easels, divans, installation art and canvases personalising each artist's studio. With superb Art Deco etched glass, wide industrial doorways and a romantic roof where invited guests might sit to watch a sunset, the building has a personality to rival any of the artworks on display and on sale. Some lunchtimes, the artists open their estaminet bar and café, where modestly priced pâté, salads and locally brewed ale are always on the menu. The Thursday evening *librairie* is a co-operative affair shop selling books, CDs, artworks, etc.

Le Parc Barbieux Av Jean Jaurès 🚇 Tram (towards Roubaix) to Parc Barbieux

The Tourcoing and Roubaix trams run alongside this prettiest of gardens where, for generations, middle-class families have pushed prams and strolled away the hours of sunny Sunday afternoons. Delightful flower-beds, some rare trees and hidden statuary punctuate the manicured lawns. You may be forgiven for imagining that these long narrow strips of colour might have been laid out to complement the tramway. In fact they were created in the 18th century by Georges Aumont, a Parisian landscape gardener, on a site earmarked for development as a canal.

McArthurGlen Mail de Lannoy. See page 147.

L'Usine 228 av Alfred Motte. See page 147.

SECLIN

The reason tourists might venture from Lille to the unassuming town of Seclin is probably the private museum devoted to Napoleon (page 202). But while you are here, enjoy a typical town of le Nord. If you have time, visit the Notre Dame Hospital founded by the great Marguerite de Flandres with its 13th-century architecture and fine garden. Like the town's monumental cemetery archway and 13th-century Collégiale Saint Piat, the hospital is listed in the register of historic monuments. However, the main attraction is the world-class carillon in the belltower, a peal of 42 church bells weighing in at over seven tonnes and said to be among the finest in Europe. The bells have a fine repertoire of folk tunes. On the quarter-hour, they play *Le Roi Dagobert*, at half past *Mandoline d'Oisueau*, and at quarter to the hour *J'ai du Bon Tabac*. But arrive in time for the chimes on the hour – the classic Lille lullaby *Le P'tit Quinquin* (page 183). Like many other towns in the region, Seclin has a totemic giant. Here, Marguerite de Flandres is paraded through the streets during June's herring festival. There is a tourist information office on 70 Roger Bouvry (☎ *03 20 90 12 12* 🖳 *www.seclin-tourisme.com*).

WHAT TO SEE AND DO
Domaine Mandarine Napoléon 204 rue de Burgault ☎ 03 20 32 54 93
🖳 www.domainenapoleon.com ⏰ 10.00–17.00 Mon–Fri, closed w/ends 🚇 Métro 2 to Lille Porte des Postes, then bus 55 to Burgault

A hit with readers of my Bradt guides, thanks to the *chambre d'hôte* in the old manor house (page 57), this is worth a visit even if you are not planning on spending the night in imperial splendour. Ten minutes outside town at exit 19 of the A1 is the new home of the Mandarine Napoléon distillery. The liqueur, a firm favourite of the short man with big ideas, so we are told, is actually a Belgian tipple, but the distillery has now moved its operations across the border to this wonderfully restored farm with arboretum and butterfly gardens. Visitors may tour the distillery and a superb private collection of memorabilia of the great military man himself. George Fourcroy, head of the drinks company and descendant of the creator of the original recipe, personally created the Napoléon Bonaparte Museum with artefacts spanning 28 years, from the legend's rise to political power to his death. From letters and uniforms to the bronze death mask, the collection is well displayed in a specially designed showroom. The complex also houses banqueting suites for weddings and conferences. An area is set aside for private games of *pétanque* and a tasting lounge and gift shop cater to museum visitors.

TOURCOING

In a region famous for its belltowers, Tourcoing, renowned as a centre of the arts ancient and modern, makes space for a museum of bell-ringing, as well as some excellent art exhibitions. There is a tourist information office at 9 rue de Tournai (☎ *03 20 26 89 30* 🖳 *www.tourcoing-tourisme.com* ⏰ *09.30–12.30 & 13.30–18.30 Mon–Sat, closed Sun*).

WHAT TO SEE AND DO
Le Fresnoy Studio National des Arts Contemporains 22 rue du Fresnoy
☎ 03 20 28 38 00 🖳 www.lefresnoy.net 🚆 Alsace 🚇 Métro 2 to Alsace; walk south on bd

d'Armentières then right to rue du Capitaine Aubert on to rue du Fresnoy 🎬 cinema €5, exhibitions €4 (exhibition hours vary)

The arts centre and college on the site of an old bowling alley, dance hall and fleapit cinema has a lively programme of exhibitions and film screenings, but any event is easily upstaged by the building itself and the vision of architect Tschumi. Le Fresnoy is perhaps the only building ever to have been designed to pander to human nature. Its charm lies in the 'in-between', a magical hinterland between two roofs. Tschumi decided to retain the original shells of the 1905 movie theatre and hall and create a footpath between the old tiles and the futuristic canopy of the modern centre. And so it is that students, locals and visitors alike can wander hand in hand around the chimney-stacks on a network of suspended metal gantries and steps. One path leads to a dead end behind a sloping roof. 'Why?' I asked. The answer was simple: 'The architect said that young people need somewhere to, you know, to kiss!' On summer nights they may hold hands as well, since the design also incorporates a mini-grandstand for watching old movies projected on to the tiles. Films are also screened in the art centre's two small cinemas. During Lille2004, Le Fresnoy twinned itself with the home and studio of film-making legend Jean-Luc Godard and ran live feeds of the master's works in progress. As a college concentrating on audio-visual arts, it was way ahead of its time, being one of the first establishments for students of the techniques that now dominate the crossover between museums and the internet.

MUba Eugène Leroy 2 rue Paul Doumer ☎03 20 28 91 60 🖥www.muba-tourcoing. fr ⏰ 13.30–18.00 Wed–Mon 🚉Tourcoing Centre 🚊Tram or métro to Tourcoing Centre, then walk Rue Leclerc to rue Paul Doumer 🎬 €5

It was inevitable. No museum worth its place in the modern world can live without an acronym. Just as the Musée d'Art Moderne (pages 204–5) is now the LaM, so the Musée des Beaux Arts has become the MUba. Of course, another reason for the rechristening was a mega donation in 2009 of the works and archives of local artist Eugène Leroy. In order to keep the artist's complete *œuvre* intact, his sons presented the town with around 200 paintings, drawings and sculptures by Leroy as well as a vast collection of works by other artists. Apart from this bonus collection, there is plenty to enjoy from the original museum. Eclectic, imaginative and never less than stimulating, Tourcoing's art collection has long spanned the artistic spectrum from Brueghelesque Flemish works to the Cubists, and the archives are regularly ransacked by the curator to keep exhibitions fresh and nicely incongruous. So find a Rembrandt next to some local artist's portrait of a much-loved grandmother or discover a Picasso between a couple of mundane still lives. My favourite painting is the deliciously grand portrait of *Mlle Croisette en Costume d'Amazon*, a prim and proper bourgeois equestrian pose with more than a hint of passion beneath the unseen corsetry. The pictures are housed in elegant galleries dating from

Beyond the City   TOURCOING

12

the 1930s. If the pick-and-mix nature of the museum appeals to you, cast your eye over the front of the nearby **Maison du Collectionneur** (*3 sq Winston Churchill*), an architectural buffet of a house whose original owner wanted to combine as many styles as possible in one building.

Maison Folie – L'Hospice d'Havré   Rue d'Havré 〢 03 59 63 43 53 ⏲ 13.30–18.00 Wed–Mon, closed Tue and holidays ⊜ Métro 2 to Tourcoing Centre; follow rue de Tournai to turn right on to rue Havré

Known locally as Notre Dame des Anges, this former monastery and poorhouse has retained all of its original buildings, and its various wings and cloister are a living record of styles from Lille baroque to Louis XIV's 18th-century influences. The chapel, gardens, hospice and baths now house an exhibition hall, artists' workshops, concert hall, restaurant and comic-strip centre in its new incarnation as Tourcoing's Maison Folie (pages 190–2). The blend of historical monument and free-for-all accessibility is rather exciting and, like so many of the Maisons Folies, lends a supercharge to the most modest occasion. The chapel gives chamber music a deserved home in a town better known for jazz. Guided tours on the first Sunday of each month (except August) at 11.00.

Musée du Carillon   11 rue de Tournai 〢 03 59 63 43 43 ⏲ May–Oct 15.00–18.00 Sun 🚉 Tourcoing Centre ⊜ Tram or métro 1 to Tourcoing Centre, then cross pl République

Not only does this bell-ringing museum include some 62 bells weighing more than six tonnes, but the bell-ringer's cabin offers the best view of the town!

VILLENEUVE D'ASCQ

Renowned as home to Lille's university campus and boasting a vast shopping mall, it might be easy to forget that there is a strong rural heritage to be explored in this bustling satellite. Just outside the centre is the museum of windmills, a fascinating and unexpected little treat, as is the farming Musée du Terroir. Get outdoors at the Parc Urbain and use your field glasses at the Héron nature reserve with its lake and forested artificial hillside that welcomes 200, mostly migratory, types of bird. The tourist office has walking maps to some 30km of country footpaths, over 155,000ha of open spaces and six lakes. There is a tourist information centre (*Château-de-Flers, Chemin du Chat Botté* 〢 03 20 43 55 75).

WHAT TO SEE AND DO
LaM Musée d'Art Moderne   1 allée du Musée 〢 03 20 19 68 88 🖥 www.musee-lam.fr ⏲ 10.00–18.00 Tue–Sun, closed 1 Jan, 1 May & 25 Dec ⊜ Métro 2 to Gare Lille Flandres then line 1 to Pont de Bois, then bus L4 to LaM, & follow the footpath into the park 🍽 €7

▲ LaM is home to works from some of the most influential artists of the last century (loic4467/Flickr)

Discover the greatest artists of the 20th century in the galleries and gardens of this unexpected cultural park in Villeneuve d'Ascq, Lille's university campus suburb. Renamed the 'LaM' for its grand reopening after a major expansion programme, the light and unassuming brick building that was once known merely as the Modern Art Museum makes no attempt to upstage the top-notch collection that it houses. A comprehensive tour through the most influential painters of each of the key artistic movements of the past 100 years includes half a dozen Picassos, Braque's *Maisons et Arbres*, works by Rouault, Léger, Klee, Miró and Masson, and some renowned canvases by Modigliani, including his *Nu Assis à la Chemise*. The bulk of the museum's wealth comes from generous bequests to the community from the private collections of Roger Dutilleul, and Jean and Geneviève Masurel. The Fauvist and Cubist rooms are most popular, but post-war artists are equally well represented through more recent acquisitions. Temporary exhibitions vary in style and quality. If you are lucky you may spot an engaging new genius. Of course, you may have to wade through more than a few luminaries of the post-talent movement to find it. As you step between eras, huge plate-glass windows look out on the lawns where locals walk their dogs, ride their microscooters and kick footballs between installation sculptures, including Picasso's *Femme aux Bras Ecartés* and Alexander Calder's *Southern Cross*. The park opens an hour earlier and closes an hour later than the museum. Jewellery and other objects by local artists are sold in the museum shop, and the café and restaurant on site provide plenty of opportunity to continue the 'Yes, but is it art?' debates. Download a free app from the App Store or GooglePlay to carry your own guide to the museum on your smartphone or tablet.

Forum des Sciences Centre François Mitterand Science Museum & Planetarium; 1 pl Hôtel de Ville ☎03 59 73 96 00 🖳 www.forumdepartementaldessciences.fr
🕒 10.00–17.30 Tue–Fri, 14.00–18.30 Sat, Sun & holidays, hours may differ during French

Beyond the City   VILLENEUVE D'ASCQ

12

school holidays, closed Mon, 1 Jan, 1 May & 25 Dec 🏛 Hôtel de Ville 🚇 Métro 2 to Gare Lille Flandres then line 1 to Hôtel de Ville 😊 €5–10 depending on which attractions you visit, free admission 1st Sun of the month

See Lille's night sky by day at the planetarium. You will probably not want to take the trip to Villeneuve d'Ascq simply to see the planetarium but, if you are travelling with children, this science centre makes an enjoyable diversion and bargaining counter for buying your own time at the modern art museum. The entertaining and informative shows (some in English) range from speculation as to life on Mars to the history of time itself. All presentations begin with a simulation of the Lille sky at dusk. A splashy, hands-on activity centre appeals to little ones, and adults will like the thought-provoking temporary exhibitions.

Maison Folie – La Ferme d'en Haut 268 rue Jules Guesde, Flers Bourg
✆ 03 20 61 01 46 🚇 Métro 2 to Lille Flandres then line 1 to Pont-de-Bois followed by bus 41 to Château

The Upper Farm of the former Château de Flers (which is itself home of the tourist office and archaeological museum) is a typical red-brick and white-stone building of the region. In its Maison Folie incarnation (pages 190–3), farming heritage can be explored in an experimental kitchen, and many dance, drama or cabaret performances may well be accompanied by a meal in the performance space. I visited the place in its very early days and found an exhibition of circuses. The town has a long love affair with the big top and even involves acrobats and performers in its work with children with disabilities and learning difficulties. As I was browsing the fascinating displays, and discovering a charming and unsung aspect of the local community, I could hear jazz musicians preparing for a performance later the same day.

Musée de Plein Air Open-Air Museum; 143 rue Colbert ✆ 03 20 63 11 25
🖥 www.museedepleinair-asso.org 🚇 Métro 2 to Gare Lille Flandres & line 1 to Pont-de-Bois, then bus 13 to Masséna; 10-min walk is signposted

This open-air museum is in fact a preserved rural hamlet with architecture and traditional skills on display.

Musée du Souvenir Museum of Remembrance; 77 rue Mangain ✆ 03 20 91 87 57
🖥 www.shvam.com P 14.30–17.30 Sun (also Tue, Wed, Thu in Jul & Aug) 🚇 Métro 2 to Gare Lille Flandres then line 1 to Pont de Bois, then bus 13 to Masséna & 10-min walk is signposted

If you come to Villeneuve d'Ascq on a Sunday, find time to pay your respects to the memory of the victims of the Ascq Massacre, on Palm Sunday 1944. When local members of the Resistance blew up a train on the Tournai–Lille railway line, even though no-one was injured, an SS convoy from the Russian front rounded up every man in the little community of Ascq. Some were shot in their homes, others taken to this site to be executed. In total, 86 died in the massacre, some as young as 15 years old. This simple museum has the usual wartime posters, but far more poignant are the clusters of personal effects of the victims that make the tragedy horribly personal. In the 1960s, when the area was swallowed up by the expanding city of Lille, it was decided to rename the district as Villeneuve d'Ascq in tribute to those who died.

WAMBRECHIES

This is one of the nine towns making up the Val de Deûle that follows the serpentine river out of the city centre. A 1906 vintage tram runs every 15 minutes along the canal bank between Wambrechies and Marquette on Sundays and public holidays between April and September, 14.30–19.00. Passengers may join the tram at Vent de Bise in Wambrechies or rue de la Deûle in Marquette. Pay €4.50 return fare and sit on authentic wooden benches, as refurbished in 1926. You may buy a combined tram ticket taking in the ride and admission to the doll museum for only €8 (🖱 *amitram.asso. fr*). Nevertheless, most people come to Wambrechies for the hiking routes along the riverbanks. There is information at the Office de Tourisme Val de Deûle (*Fondation Ledoux, 21 pl du Général de Gaulle, 58119 Wambrechies* ℡ *03 28 38 84 21* ⏰ *09.30–12.30 & 14.00–17.30 Tue–Fri, 10.00–12.30 Sat, mid-Apr–mid-Oct 14.30–18.30 Sun*).

WHAT TO SEE AND DO
Distillerie Claeyssens 1 rue de la Distillerie ℡ 03 20 14 91 91 🖱 www.wambrechies. com ⏰ tours 09.30–12.30 & 13.30–17.30, closed during holidays 🚌 Bus Citadine to

Beyond the City   **WAMBRECHIES**

12

République–Beaux Arts then line 1 to Wambrechies Mairie; from rue 11 Nov 1918 take rue Leclerc to rue de la Distillerie 🛏 €6.30 (reservation essential)

There is nothing high-tech about this distillery that has been making *genièvre* gin from junipers for the past 200 years. The original wooden equipment still sifts seeds, mills flour and heats, cools and distils the spirit, just as it did in Napoleonic times, when the waterways of the Deûle brought grain from Belgium after an edict banned the use of French crops. The hour-long tour is an anecdote-filled meander through a past that can hold its own in the present. An opportunity to taste the robust tipple follows the tour and a shop sells not only the *genièvre* itself, but two rather special by-products: beer made during the fermenting process, and a single malt of Highland quality. You may also combine the distillery tour with a canal trip from Lille on Claeyssens's private barge.

Musée de la Poupée et du Jouet Ancien Doll & Antique Toy Museum;
Château de Robersart ✆03 20 39 69 28 🖱 www.musee-du-jouet-ancien.com 🕐 14.00–18.00 Sun, Wed & school holidays, closed 25 Dec & 1 Jan 🚌 Bus Citadine to République–Beaux Arts then line 1 to Wambrechies Mairie 🛏 €4

At last, they tie the knot. The wedding of Barbie and Ken is a glittering occasion, the guest list itself reads like a who's who of Barbie. There's Beach Barbie, Beautician Barbie, Trolley Dolly Barbie and, for all I know, Feng Shui Consultant Dietician Barbie, in the biggest gathering of big hair on plastic heads since *Dynasty* slipped off the TV listings pages. The nuptial tableau featuring scores of versions of the doll from each year of her long career is staged in a model of a Gothic cathedral, and is typical of the imaginative displays at this charming museum of childhood. The setting of the museum itself is something of a happy ever after, housed in the family château of Juliette, the last countess of Robersart. Two galleries feature dolls and toys from every era. Among the most interesting items in the permanent display are miniature fashion outfits made to patterns printed in the leading women's magazines of the last century.

BEYOND THE METROPOLE

The Maisons Folies network stretches far beyond Lille Métropole, even across the border into Belgium. So if you have a day to spare for exploring, check out the list on pages 191–3. This is a land rich in shared history, with Henry V's Agincourt around 100km away (visit the battle museum built to resemble a row of English bowmen – I was the token Shakespeare-loving Brit on the French selection committee that chose the design), Henry VIII's Field of the Cloth of Gold on the road back to the ferry in Calais and the mustering station for Napoleon's putative invasion of Britain outside Boulogne. And, of course, Flanders fields lie all around you.

LENS A decade ago, the town of Lens was known for just two things: sports and unemployment. An internationally known sports stadium, Stade de la Licorne, home to the Racing Club de Lens football team (better known as Sang et Or after their red and gold colours) and a legacy of abandoned coal mines and slag-heaps. Today, this is a happy town with pride in its newest acquisition and its role as an essential stop on any cultural tour of northern Europe. Just a half-hour drive or 40-minute train ride from Lille, Lens is the home of the newest galleries of the world's most famous museum, the Louvre, and the rest of the town basks in the glory, with restaurants and shops to greet the day trippers. There are market stalls every Tuesday and Thursday morning on place du Cantin, Philippe Olivier (page 156) has a cheese shop at 39 rue René Lanoy and master *chocolatier* Jean-Claude Jeanson sells some of his signature sweets at the museum (notably his lavender-flavoured chocolate pyramids), but his main counter for *bonbons* and cakes is at 42 place Jean Jaurès. Of course, football and rugby fans still come to Lens on match days. However, those who wish to keep their relationships intact may still soak up the atmosphere in the streets, but watch the match on three TV screens while chomping on traditional local cuisine at the restaurant l'Ardoise on route de Béthune.

Getting there and away Several trains per hour leave Gare Lille Flandres for Lens. The quickest direct trains do the journey in 39 minutes; slower services take around 50 minutes. Fares are around €8.50 each way, and a free shuttle bus links the station to the museum. Disabled travellers should contact Accès Plus (page 30) for assistance; many local trains on the route are wheelchair accessible, as is the shuttle bus.

Tourist information Information is available at the Tourist Office (03 21 67 66 66 www.tourisme-lenslievin.fr), and you can also download the ZeVisit app for your smartphone or tablet (page 35) for a free guided tour of Lens.

What to see and do
Gare de Lens Don't rush from the train to the museum shuttle bus. First, take a moment or two to walk the length of the platform and discover the station itself. Here you will find art to reach out to your senses and history to chill your soul.

The station building itself is a listed monument, a stunning 1926 Art Deco creation by railway architect Urbain Cassan, commissioned to design a *gare* to reflect the importance of the *bassin minier* mining community after the original station, and much of the town itself, was destroyed in World War I. Inspired by the work of the miners, Cassan envisaged an 80m-long low horizontal building to reflect the tunnels of the mines, and the 23m-high clocktower evokes the structure of a mine shaft. Constructed in the new-wonder material of reinforced concrete, the station has worn far better than many better-known

Beyond the City **BEYOND THE METROPOLE**

12

structures. A simple lozenge-style frieze décor for the façade is echoed in the stunning ironwork on the windows designed and forged by artist Edgar Brandt. Step into the ticket hall to admire the mosaics, also inspired by the life of the miners of Lens, created by the cubist Auguste Labouret, whose glass works and mosaics adorn some of Paris's finest churches and department stores.

As well as the subterranean motif, the serpentine nature of the building also reflects the reality of the seemingly infinite railway trucks that shuttled coal through the goods yards to the rest of the country. However, the rails have a more sinister history as a modest plaque on the platform wall reveals. Sixty years before 9/11 entered global consciousness, the date was etched into the lives of the people of Lens.

At 04.00 on 11 September 1942, police raided homes across Lens. Altogether, 317 men, women and children were rounded up and taken to the platform at the Gare de Lens and loaded on to trucks, heading to a Nazi camp across the Belgian border in Malines. In vain, the head of the local Jewish community wrote to the *départemental Préfet* (the most senior French official in the area) in Arras, pleading for the life of children born in France, such as six-year-old Denise and Jacques, aged five, as well as for those parents and grandparents who had fled persecution in 19th-century Poland and found sanctuary in Lens. His letter arrived with 700 fellow inmates from Malines after the victims of the *rafle de Lens*, who had already arrived at Auschwitz. All the children named in the letter perished in the gas chambers and, around a week after posting the letter to Arras, the author was arrested at his home (on the ironically named rue Emile Zola) and taken with 15 of his neighbours to the same station and the same fate. Before the war, there were 991 Jews living and working in the mining towns, 467 of which were sent to the camps. Only 18 returned.

Musée du Louvre-Lens 99 rue Paul Bert ☏ 03 21 18 62 62 🖳 www.louvrelens.fr ① museum 10.00–18.00 Wed–Mon (Sep–Jun 10.00–22.00 first Fri of the month); park summer 07.00–21.00, winter 08.00–19.00 ⊕ SNCF train from Gare Lille Flandres, then free shuttle bus to museum; if driving, follow signs for car parks & walk through park to museum (disabled guests may use the designated drop-off point by the entrance) ⛟ free until the end of 2015, exhibition €9

Just as Lille can thank François Mitterand for wooing Eurostar to the city, so Lens owes President Chirac a drink for sending it one of the world's most renowned museums. It was Chirac's final campaign against France's Paris-centric approach to the arts (although this had not been a problem for him when he was mayor of the capital). He decided that the Paris museums needed to reach out to the regions, so the Centre Pompidou went to Metz in the east and the Louvre was thrown to the north. The major towns of the Nord-Pas de Calais region fought for the prize, but the outside candidate won, since Lens was the only major town in a region with almost 50 major museums that didn't have a decent gallery of its own.

Since the location of the new museum is a major part of the nation's industrial heritage, the Japanese architects of the project created a park from a former coal mine with a meandering line of low-level glass and aluminium buildings, their walls reflecting the northern skies and landscape where pit-heads once dominated the skyline. The brief was to showcase, not upstage, both art and landscape, rather than to create an architectural statement. While the original industrial buildings are but a memory, two slag-heaps remain on the horizon and there are plans to include a model of the original mine within the museum.

This is the region's most subtle reinvention of the mining heritage. Nearby the pit buildings at **Lewarde** are a heritage centre and museum of mining, and **Noeux-les-Mines** converted its slag-heaps into artificial ski slopes and launched the year-round winter-sports resort **Loisinord**.

What has been created at Lens is a virtual time machine of art. This unique museum for our time has unrivalled access to the stores and archives of the parent museum in Paris, where just a tiny fraction of the national collection would ever see the light of day. Now, in a versatile new space, the art of the whole world may be seen in a timeline that takes us from the marvels of the ancient world to living memory; from anonymous heroic statuary to the framed and signed dignity of the likes of Raphael and Ingres.

The principal wing of the museum is a vast 120m walk through the centuries, stepping around sculptures, canvases, artefacts and legacies from every generation. A five-year exhibition running until 2017, the Gallery des Temps (Time Gallery), has a timeline on the walls to provide the visitor with a global view of cultures: the art of the East and Arab worlds to the left and Western creativity on the right. Similarities, rather than differences, strike the visitor, as an oriental portrait of a prince hangs but a glance away from a European portrait of power, painted within the space of a generation at a distance of many thousands of miles. The timeline also reveals the gentle evolution of familiar art, as painters left the studio for the great outdoors, then swapped the sharp eye of the recorder for the misty spirit of impressionism. Rather than divide the collection into movements and styles, this 3,000m²-experience was designed as an opportunity to wander among the exhibits, and the massive hall allows visitors the space to enjoy and appreciate the art and creativity around them. In busy periods, admission may occasionally be postponed in order not to crowd the gallery. The collection evolves, with the most famous initial exhibit (Delacroix's *Liberty Leading the People*) now safely home in Paris, making way for other treasures to travel north.

Occasionally, artworks become the backdrop for the performing arts, so do check the website for details of occasional concerts and other events in the exhibition halls as well as in the purpose-built theatre space. In December 2014, as a temporary exhibition on the animals of the ancient Egyptians

12

opened in the galleries, so a ballet of Camille Saint-Saëns' *Carnival of the Animals* was staged in the building.

A variety of alternative spaces emerge through the free-flow experience. Since the purpose of the project was to bring the treasures of the Louvre to fresh audiences, even the 'stacks' are no dusty archives. Underground is a mezzanine gallery with virtual lecture booths for studying specific works and a glass wall looks down on the art stores. There's also a restoration studio so visitors can observe experts reviving paintings and statues. Another bubble in the *médiathèque* stages thrice-weekly lectures with curators and experts inviting the public to explore just one item from the collection in great detail.

Picnic in the grounds, snack on a €10 lunch at the cafeteria or sip a drink outside on the terrace. You could also cross the gardens to the museum's own restaurant, l'**Atelier de Marc Meurin** (📧 *www.atelierdemarcmeurin.fr* ⏰ *12.00–18.00 Wed–Mon, 14.30–18.00 Tue*). Just as the Nausicaä in Boulogne chose Michelin-starred chef Tony Lestienne to run the food side of things, here Marc Meurin, bearer of two Michelin stars (and patron of Monsieur Jean in Lille – see pages 104–6), offers a €25–32 set menu of simple local ingredients treated with the utmost respect.

ARRAS When you visit the Maison Folie (page 192), do explore the rest of this stunning town. Incredibly, the 17th- and 18th-century squares are not the real thing, but recreated faithfully from the original architects' plans rescued from the rubble when the town was razed in two wars. Climb the belfry for views, and descend into the bowels of the town to see the remarkable network of underground passages that links the cellars of the old houses and was commandeered by the Allies in World War I as a command post. Railways ran under the city to the front line. Don't miss the unforgettable Canadian memorial and trenches at Vimy Ridge. There a is tourist information office in the Hôtel de Ville (*Pl des Héroes* ✆ *03 21 51 26 95* 📧 *www.explorearras.com* ⏰ *Oct–Apr 10.00–12.00 & 14.00–18.00 Mon, 09.00–12.00 & 14.00–18.00 Tue–Sat, 10.00–12.30 & 14.30–18.30 Sun; May–Sep 09.00–18.30 Mon–Sat, 10.00–13.00 & 14.30–18.30 Sun*).

BOULOGNE-SUR-MER The delightful port with its old town perched on the hill is as charming as ever. Visit the **Château Museum** (*Château Comtal, Rue de Bernet* ✆ *03 21 10 02 20* ⏰ *closed Tue*) and walk the ramparts. By the port, **Nausicaä** (*Centre National de la Mer, Boulevard Sainte Beuve* ✆ *03 21 30 98 98*), an interactive museum of the sea with sharks and sea lions, is a fascinating day out in its own right and an ardent exponent of green issues. There is a tourist information office on boulevard Sainte Beuve (✆ *03 21 10 88 10* 📧 *www. tourisme-boulognesurmer.com winter* ⏰ *10.30–12.30 & 14.00–17.30 Mon–Sat; summer 10.00–12.30 & 13.45 –18.00 Mon–Sat, 10.30–12.00 & 14.30–17.00 Sun (weekday lunch hrs Jul & Aug)*.

CALAIS The Channel port best known for booze cruisers may not be as quaint as its neighbours, but take time to explore. The **Musée des Beaux-Arts et de la Dentelle** (*25 rue Richelieu* ✎ *03 21 46 48 40* ○ *closed Tue*), with arts and fashion exhibits, was a major player in Lille2004. Other sights include a war museum in a bunker, the lighthouse and many fine restaurants. Tourist information is available at 12 boulevard Georges Clemenceau (✎ *03 21 96 62 40* ☷ *www.calais-cotedopale.com* ○ *Sep–Apr 10.00–18.00 Mon–Fri, 10.00–17.00 Sat; May–Aug 10.00–18.00 Mon–Sat, 10.00–17.00 Sun*).

CASSEL The true spirit of Flanders, with windmills and estaminets. Delightful gardens to visit. The tourist office is at 20 Grand Place (✎ *03 28 40 52 55* ☷ *www.cassel-horizons.com* ○ *09.30–12.00 & 13.30–17.30 Tue–Fri, 09.00–12.00 Sat*). ZeVisit guided tour app is also available (page 35).

LE CATEAU-CAMBRESIS Birthplace of Henri Matisse: visit the fabulously restored museum devoted to the artist and his works (*Palais Fénelon* ✎ *03 59 73 38 00* ○ *closed Tue*). Tourist information office is on 9 place Commandant Richez (✎ *03 27 84 10 94* ☷ *www.tourisme-lecateau.fr* ○ *09.30–12.30 & 14.00–18.00 Mon & Wed–Sat*).

DUNKERQUE The port of privateers and adventure has museums of fine arts, maritime heritage and piracy. Tourist information office can be found on rue de l'Amiral Ronarch (✎ *03 28 66 79 21* ☷ *www.dunkerque-tourisme.fr* ○ *Sep–Jun 10.00-12.30 & 14.00–18.30 Mon–Fri, 10.00–18.30 Sat; Jul–Aug 10.00–18.30 Mon–Sat, 10.00–12.00 & 14.00–16.00 Sun*).

MARCQ-EN-BAROEUL For generations this was Lille's Sunday in the country, the racecourse proving a magnet for the working man planning a flutter on the horses on his day off. One attraction is the **Septentrion gallery** (*Chemin des Coulons* ✎ *03 20 46 35 80* ☷ *www.galerieseptentrion.com* ○ *closed Mon*) a contemporary art space that shares its name with a local gastronomic restaurant, housed in a magnificent building in its 24-hectare park. This is also home to the **Château du Vert Bois** (*Chemin des Coulons* ✎ *03 20 46 26 37* ☷ *www.fondationseptentrion.fr*), a 16th-century chateau with its charming grounds, and a museum of telecommunications. The château estate actually straddles the border with the neighbouring commune of Bondues and its museum devoted to the **French Résistance** (*av du Général de Gaulle* ✎ *03 20 28 88 32* ○ *14.00–16.30 Tue–Fri*), which, although small, is important in the homeland of Charles de Gaulle (page 173). The tourist office is at 5 place du Général de Gaulle (✎ *03 20 72 60 87*).

SAINT-OMER Head here for the **Musée Sandelin** (*Rue Carnot* ✎ *03 21 38 00 94* ○ *closed Mon & Tue*) to see how a table should be laid; for **Arc**

International (*132 av du Général de Gaulle* ✆ *03 21 12 74 74* 🖱 *www. visiteverreriearc.com*), better known as Crystal d'Arques, Europe's greatest glass-making empire (factory visits may include boat trips and always shopping opportunities); and for the fabulous Marais Audemarois's hidden world of floating market gardens, the chicory and wildlife, explored by canoe or tour boat from the café-restaurant **Le Bon Accueil** at Salperwick. But, most importantly, visit Saint-Omer for **La Coupole** (*rue Clabaux* ✆ *03 21 12 27 27* 🖱 *www.lacoupole-france.com*), a Nazi V2 bunker just out of town, housing twin museums of life in occupied France and the space race. Do also take time out to visit the aerodrome. The Royal Flying Corps was based here during the Great War and you will find a rarity – an RAF memorial away from British soil. Tourist information can be found at 4 rue Lion d'Or (✆ *03 21 98 08 51* 🖱 *www.tourisme-saintomer.com* 🕐 *summer 09.00–18.00 Mon–Sat, 10.00–13.00 Sun; winter 09.00–12.30 & 14.00–17.30 Mon–Sat*).

WATTRELOS Party on, dudes. This is where the northern passion for good times beats its heart. March has the annual Salon des Artistes, April brings the great parade of giants and September boasts Les Berlouffes, France's second biggest flea market on the weekend after the Braderie of Lille itself. The art of fun is explored in the **Musée des Arts Populaires et Traditions** (*96 rue François-Mériaux* ✆ *03 20 81 59 50* 🕐 *09.00–12.00 & 14.00–18.00 Tue–Sat, 15.00–18.00 Sun*), a museum of daily life and traditions housed in a former farm building. There is a tourist office (✆ *03 20 75 85 86* 🖱 *www. ville-wattrelos.fr*).

HIKING AND BIKING

If you've a yen for the great outdoors, rather than simply site-hopping on four wheels, then leave the city behind and explore the countryside of the Nord département. The Comité Départemental de Tourisme (CDT) (page 16) publishes imaginative hiking and biking itineraries for exploring the trails of buccaneers, bandits and garlic smokers. Walk the Flanders Opal Coast in the path of legendary corsair and buccaneer Jean Bart; ride the frontiers where smugglers once toted their contraband between Belgium and France; enjoy the intimate and welcoming country estaminet bars in the front rooms of village houses; or simply head out into the natural and regional parks within reasonable reach of Lille.

Two English-language packs for walkers and cyclists have been created by the CDT Nord and offer practical and easy-to-use trails, with plenty of information on sites and diversions *en route*, as well as recommended IGN maps. The packs may be downloaded free of charge from 🖱 www.tourisme-nord.com or obtained directly from the tourist office on ✆ 03 20 57 59 59.

The Flanders of recent memory, the fields where poppies grow beneath the crosses, is to be found in small hamlets and the grander memorials of Vimy Ridge and the Mennen Gate. An essential drive by car, since so many of these monuments and cemeteries are close to the city. For visitors without their own car, a coach tour leaves the Tourist Office every Saturday from June until mid-December at 13.00 (⤫ *03 59 57 94 00* ⏚ *en.lilletourism.com/beyond-lille.html* ⬚ *€44*). An English-speaking guide explains the *lieux de mémoires en route* to Ypres in Belgium, taking in the vast Tyne Cot Commonwealth Cemetery and Essex Farm, inspiration of John McCrae's immortal poem, *In Flanders Fields*.

Essential companions for any such tour would be the Bradt guides, *World War I Battlefields* and *Cross-Channel France* (page 222).

Pack One suggests 30 excellent walks in the area, ranging from coastal hikes through the sand dunes to trails highlighting more gastronomic traditions, such as the *genièvre* gin distilleries (pages 207–8) and the Hainaut village of Arleux, famous for its smoked garlic soup. A waymarked 12km monastic trail is useful for building up an appetite, since it takes in the greatly appreciated Trappist sidelines of brewing and cheese-making, as well as the windmills and ornate altarpieces! Trails through the Avesnois regional natural park combine the beauty of nature with the opportunity to learn traditional skills of earlier times, such as glassblowing.

The second pack has 22 trails for all-terrain bikers. Like the hikers' guide, it features a range of treats, from Paris–Roubaix cobbled circuits within Lille Métropole to the smugglers and estaminets trail through Flanders, along the cat-and-mouse footsteps of customs officers and their prey as well as excursions through the wetlands of the Scarpe-Escaut regional park and the hideaway habitats of wild deer.

For those who want more, **Randofamili**, a new, free interactive app for your smartphone or tablet, has 80 suggested walks and itineraries with maps, GPS links, videos, games and audio guides. Buy from the App Store or GooglePlay, or visit ⏚ www.randofamili.com.

You can post your comments and recommendations, and read the latest feedback and updates from other readers, online at ⏚ www.bradtupdates.com/lille.

Beyond the City HIKING AND BIKING

12

Language

The principal language of Lille is, of course, French but, with its historical and geographical history, the Flemish side of the city is comfortable speaking Dutch. After all, until Eurostar awakened Britain to this gem on its doorstep, virtually every visitor came from Belgium. The Flemish for Lille is Rijsel, by the way.

The locals have their own patois, *Ch'ti*, a variation of the Picard argot spoken across northern France. You will rarely come across an entire conversation in the northern tongue; however, local cabarets aimed at domestic rather than visiting audiences will feature a smattering of phrases, and should you hang around a genuine estaminet you may well pick up some words that would baffle a Parisian! If you fancy trying your hand at a few words, do so in the comfort of your own home with an online dictionary (such as 🖳 www.freelang.com/dictionnaire/chti.html). But don't worry if you don't get it. Local variants on language the world over, from rhyming slang to Yiddish, are designed for local communities. Outsiders are meant to be baffled! And you will probably have to let playground and street slang pass you by. Verlan (from *l'envers*) is popular 'back slang' (try *beur* for *arabe*), and is the most commonly spoken.

Around Wazemmes market you may well be able to hear Arabic, so a few choice words and phrases from your wider travels may stand you in good stead.

FRENCH

The French are in general better mannered than their anglophone friends and neighbours, and simple courtesies are a way of life, with the lack of them making a negative impression.

The simple greetings '*Bonjour*' ('Good day') or '*Bonsoir*' ('Good evening') are essentials. Use this as much as possible. Even in a doctor's waiting room, a general '*Bonjour*' to the assembled company is expected.

When a shopkeeper says '*Bonne journée*' or '*Bonne soirée*', that is the equivalent of the American salutation 'Have a nice day!'

Traditionally, one should use the courtesy titles *Monsieur* (Sir) or *Madame* (Madam) when speaking to strangers. Nowadays one should always refer to an adult woman as *Madame*, whether or not she sports a wedding ring. 'Ms' does not exist in France. In fact in 2013, *Mademoiselle* was formerly dropped as a title on official forms. Oh, and courtesy applies to waiters as well: it is considered plain rude to snap the fingers and yell '*garçon*'. Restaurant staff in France are considered professionals: many will have studied for years from the age of 14 in order to perfect their art.

Shake hands whenever humanly possible. The French love doing it. The kissing on both cheeks business has its own rules that remain practically Masonic. Between men in the north it is rarely done except 'twixt father and son or heads of state who hate each other, but if a woman is being introduced or encountered on a social basis (at a dinner party perhaps), the brushing of proffered cheeks is the thing to do. Usually twice, although between friends this may become three pecks, and within families four times is not unknown. (I have finally worked out the rules for cheek air-kissing: once = rude, twice = polite, thrice = friendly, four times = familial, five times = foreplay.)

Shake hands on entering a room, meeting someone for the first time in the day and on ending a conversation. The only exception would be at a urinal or during an autopsy. However, I've found hands extended my way in an abattoir. To refuse would have gone down as well as a discussion on the many uses of tofu.

Then comes the heady question of pronouns, the second person in particular. In school we learn that *tu* and *toi* are the familiar version of 'you', with *vous* being the more formal usage. Of course there are no hard and fast rules, but I strongly recommend using *vous* to start any conversation and be guided by the local as to how you should continue.

There are, of course exceptions. These days young people – and Lille is a student town – tend towards *tutoyer* (ie: use *toi*) as a matter of course, and in trendy or gay bars the informal form is the norm, rather as the words 'love', 'darling' or 'mate' might be bandied in a British pub. Rule of thumb: always use *vous* when talking to someone of a different generation.

Remember your p's and q's. *S'il vous plaît* and *merci* cost nothing and should be bandied about at every opportunity.

A1

USEFUL PHRASES In Lille, you will find that English is pretty widely spoken. A huge percentage of the population is involved with further education. The city's international business community and canny shopkeepers can handle most conversations in your native tongue. However, it is always appreciated when visitors make at least a modest attempt to speak the local language. So the following words should be used – even if you bashfully return to English after the initial contact:

Bonjour/bonsoir	Good day/good evening
Au revoir	Goodbye
Bonne nuit	Good night
Merci	Thank you
S'il vous plaît	Please
Oui	Yes
Non	No
Comment allez-vous?/Ça va?	How are you?
Très bien, merci	Very well, thank you
Au secours!	Help!
Aidez-moi!	Help me!

Only once you have memorised thus far may you learn the following phrase:

Parlez-vous anglais? Do you speak English?

However, if you can remember that, then surely the following nuggets cannot be too difficult to deliver:

Je ne comprends pas	I don't understand
Parlez moins vite, s'il vous plaît	Speak a little slower, please
Je ne sais pas	I don't know
Je suis anglais/écossais/gallois/ irlandais/américain/canadien/ australien*	I am English/Scottish/Welsh/ Irish/American/Canadian/ Australian
Avez vous une chambre avec deux lits/ avec un grand lit?	Have you a twin/double room?
Avec baignoire/douche	With bath/shower
Veuillez me réveiller à huit heures?	Could you wake me at 08.00?
Où est…?	Where is…?
Où?	Where?
Comment?	How?
Quand?	When?
Pourquoi?	Why?
Je voudrais…	I would like…
Combien?	How much?
Bon marché	Cheap
Cher/chère	Expensive
L'addition, s'il vous plaît	The bill, please
Je suis végétarien(ne)	I am vegetarian
Je suis malade	I am ill

* The examples given are in the masculine; women should add an 'e' (or 'ne') to each national adjective.

If you are still reading this chapter, the chances are your French grammar is pretty rusty and you want to know which words are masculine (using *le* or *un*) and which feminine (*la* or *une*). Well, I hate to break it to you, but you are hardly going to squeeze in a decent education between the top of this page and the index, so allow me, in my unorthodox way, to suggest an extremely useful compromise: learn essential nouns, use gestures, smile and remember to say *merci* (that sound you just heard was Mrs Stockton, my third-form French mistress… fainting).

USEFUL NOUNS

beer	*une bière*	station)	*la station*
	(see page 114)	money	*l'argent*
bread	*le pain*	motorway	*l'autoroute*
breakfast	*le petit déjeuner*	park	*un parc*
bus	*un car*	passport	*un passeport*
bus station	*la gare routière*	petrol	*l'essence*
car	*une voiture*	postcard	*une carte postale*
chemist	*la pharmacie*	soup	*potage, consommé,*
condom	*le préservatif*		*soupe, bouillon*
credit card	*la carte de crédit*	stamp	*un timbre*
dinner	*le dîner*	station	*la gare (train), la*
doctor	*le médecin*		*station (subway)*
fish	*le poisson*	telephone	*le téléphone*
hospital	*l'hôpital*	ticket	*le billet/ticket*
letter	*une lettre*	toilet	*les toilettes/WC*
luggage	*les bagages*		(pronounced
lunch	*le déjeuner*		doob-levay-say)
meat	*la viande*	town	*la ville*
menu	*la carte*	train	*le train*
métro station (but		water (mineral)	*l'eau (minérale)*
NOT railway		wine	*le vin*

DAYS AND MONTHS

Monday	*lundi*	Friday	*vendredi*
Tuesday	*mardi*	Saturday	*samedi*
Wednesday	*mercredi*	Sunday	*dimanche*
Thursday	*jeudi*		

January	*janvier*	June	*juin*
February	*février*	July	*juillet*
March	*mars*	August	*août*
April	*avril*	September	*septembre*
May	*mai*	October	*octobre*

A1

November	*novembre*	evening	*le soir*
December	*décembre*	night	*la nuit*
day	*le jour*	today	*aujourd'hui*
morning	*le matin*	yesterday	*hier*
noon	*midi*	tomorrow	*demain*
afternoon	*l'après-midi*		

NUMBERS

1	*un/une*	19	*dix-neuf*
2	*deux*	20	*vingt*
3	*trois*	30	*trente*
4	*quatre*	40	*quarante*
5	*cinq*	50	*cinquante*
6	*six*	60	*soixante*
7	*sept*	70	*soixante-dix*
8	*huit*		(except for
9	*neuf*		Belgians who
10	*dix*		say *septante*)
11	*onze*	80	*quatre-vingt*
12	*douze*	90	*quatre-vingt-dix*
13	*treize*		(except for
14	*quatorze*		Belgians who
15	*quinze*		say *nonante*)
16	*seize*	100	*cent*
17	*dix-sept*	1,000	*mille*
18	*dix-huit*		

Note: During sporting fixtures between the UK and France, I adopt Australian or Canadian nationality and accent if outnumbered on public transport.

Further Information

ESSENTIALS

Lille Tourist Office 🖱 www.lilletourism.com

ENTERTAINMENT

A range of daily freesheet newspapers, handed out at métro stations and especially around Gare Lille Flandres, are aimed at local commuters and have up-to-date listings and reviews. Also check out the day's *La Voix du Nord* at your hotel (page 38).*Sortir* magazine, a weekly entertainment listings magazine, is published on Wednesdays and is available from the tourist office (free), hotels and bars. *Autour de Minuit* nightlife guide is free from the tourist office. *Going Out* is a local leisure/lifestyle magazine mixing Hollywood interviews with features on Lille's bar and restaurant scene.

LOCAL TRANSPORT

🖱 www.transpole.fr

🖱 www.voyages-sncf.com

🖱 www.eurostar.com

🖱 www.ter-sncf.com (for local trains)

TRAVELLERS WITH LIMITED MOBILITY

See *Chapter 3*. Always worth keeping to hand in France is the *Michelin Red Guide* (£17.99 or €24) which now features a wheelchair symbol indicating hotels and restaurants with sensible facilities/access for disabled visitors. The free guide *Handi-Tourisme*, with listings of hotels and attractions, is also available from the CDT Nord (page 16).

GAY LILLE

A free guide and map listing all gay venues in the region is available from bars, clubs and other gay establishments in the city (pages 136–7).

MODERN LILLE

A book of photographs by Jean-Pierre Duplan and Eric Le Brun, *Lille, Voyage en Métropole* (Ravet-Anceau), features six essays by leading French journalists on life in modern Lille. Available from bookshops in and around the city.

MAPS

The Michelin *Regional Map 511* covers the Nord-Pas de Calais region and the larger-scale *Local 302* features greater Lille (including the Belgian towns). Online route-finders can be found at ⏼ www.viamichelin.com and ⏼ www.mappy.fr.

OTHER BRADT GUIDES

Cross-Channel France: Nord-Pas De Calais: The Land Beyond The Ports. John Ruler (2010). Bradt Travel Guides. John Ruler takes visitors to sample Vieux Bologne, the smelliest cheese in the world, and to climb the hill at Cassel, up (and down) which the Grand Old Duke of York marched his 10,000 men. He leads them to Agincourt, site of Henry V's famous battle (and where yours truly was the token Shakespeare-loving Brit on the Lille-based French selection committee that chose the design of the museum), and takes in more recent history from the trenches of World War I to the World War II beaches of Dunkirk. The guide also reveals where visitors can shop for cut-price goods; where they can cycle, walk and ride horses; how to enjoy the Festival of the Giants; and which are the top seaside resorts for children.

World War I Battlefields: A Travel Guide to the Western Front. John Ruler & Emma Thomson (2014). Bradt Travel Guides. Essential companion for touring the memorial sites and towns on both sides of the border.

Flanders: Northern Belgium. Emma Thomson (2012). Bradt Travel Guides. Most people think they have Flanders figured out: beer, chocolate and the EU are the standard tag lines. However, dig beneath the surface and you will discover a region of quirk and style. Author Emma Thomson introduces travellers not only to the World Heritage Sites of Brussels's Grand Place or Bruges's romantic canals, but also to snug spots like the bewitched village of Laarne and Geraardsbergen, the real home of Manneken-Pis.

Mons: A European Capital Of Culture. Antony Mason (2014). Bradt Travel Guides. This is the first dedicated English-language guidebook to Mons, a European Capital of Culture for 2015 and a town itching to be discovered.

Cobbled streets rise on a twisty medieval grid to its beautiful central square, and then on up to a crescendo at the 17th-century belfry, one of the town's four UNESCO World Heritage Sites. Historic, pretty and manageably compact, it is the perfect short-stay destination.

Lest We Forget: memorial to the dead of the two World Wars at the side of Palais Rihour (Anna Moores)

AVX LILLOIS
SOLDATS · CIVILS
LA CITE A ELEVE CE MONVMENT AFIN
DE RAPPELER AV COVRS DES SIECLES
L'HEROISME ET LES SOVFFRANCES DE
SES ENFANTS MORTS POVR LA PAIX
1914 · 1918   1939 · 1945

Index

Page numbers in **bold** indicate major entries; those in *italics* indicate maps and those in red indicate photos.

Pastel façades and cobblestones in
Vieux Lille (Production Perig/S)

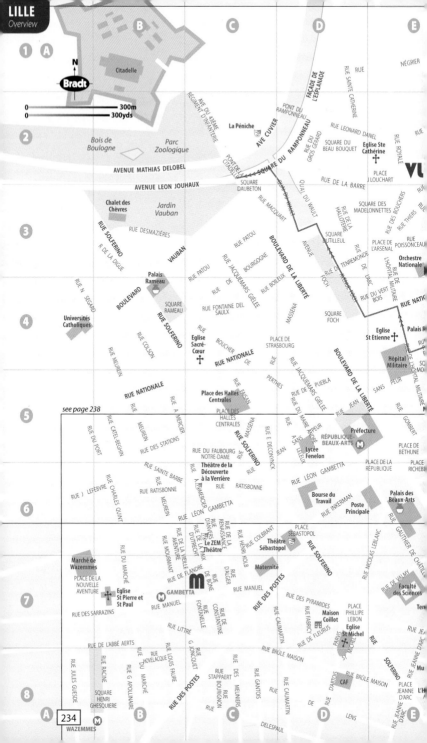

N

Bradt

300m
300yds

Citadelle

Bois de
Boulogne

Parc
Zoologique

La Péniche

AVE CUVIER

FAÇADE DE
L'ESPLANADE

RUE SAINTE CATHERINE

RUE

RUE

NÉGRIER

PONT DU
RAMPONNEAU

RUE DU
GROS GÉRARD

SQUARE DU
BEAU BOUQUET

RUE LEONARD DANEL

Eglise Ste
Catherine

PLACE
U LOUCHART

RUE ROYALE

VL

SQUARE DU RAMPONNEAU

AVENUE MATHIAS DELOBEL

AVENUE LEON JOUHAUX

PONT DE LA
CITADELLE

AVE DU 43ÈME
RÉGIMENT D'INFANTERIE

SQUARE
DAUBETON

RUE DE LA BARRE

QUAI DU WAULT

RUE DE LA BARRE

RUE MACQUART

RUE DE LA
HALLOTERIE

SQUARE DES
MADELONNETTES

RUE DES BOUCHERS

RUE THIERS

RUE

Chalet des
Chèvres

Jardin
Vauban

RUE DESMAZIÈRES

RUE
SOLFERINO

R DE LA DIGUE

VAUBAN

RUE PATOU

RUE PATOU

BOULEVARD DE LA LIBERTÉ

AVENUE

SQUARE
BUTILLEUL

PLACE DE
L'ARSENAL

PLACE DE
POISSONCEAU

RUE N SEGARD

Palais
Rameau

BOULEVARD

SQUARE
RAMEAU

RUE SOLFERINO

RUE JACQUEMARS GIÉLÉE

RUE PATOU

RUE DE
BOURGOGNE

RUE BOILEUX

FOCH

RUE DE TENREMONDE

RUE DE
L'HÔPITAL MILITAIRE

Orchestre
Nationale

RUE
DE L'ARC

RUE DU VERT
BOIS

RUE NATIO

Universités
Catholiques

RUE COLSON

RUE MEUREN

RUE FONTAINE DEL
SAULX

RUE
Eglise
Sacré-
Cœur

RUE NATIONALE

BOUCHER

DE

MASSENA

PLACE DE
STRASBOURG

RUE

SQUARE
FOCH

Eglise
St Etienne

Hôpital
Militaire

BOULEVARD DE LA LIBERTÉ

RUE

Palais R

RUE DE L'HÔPITAL MILITAIRE

RUE NATIONALE

see page 238

RUE DU PORT

RUE CATEL-BEGHIN

RUE A MERCIER

MEUREN

RUE DES STATIONS

RUE DU FAUBOURG
NOTRE-DAME

Place des Halles
Centrales

PLACE DES
HALLES
CENTRALES

RUE FAIDAN

RUE MASSENA

RUE SOLFERINO

RUE E DECONYNCK

JEAN

RUE A SANS

RUE DU MAIRE
PEUR

RUE JACQUEMARS GIÉLÉE

RUE DE LA PUEBLA

PERTHES

JEAN

RUE

RUE A SANS
PEUR

LÉLEIX

RÉPUBLIQUE-
BEAUX-ARTS

Préfecture

PLACE DE
BÉTHUNE

GOMBERT

RUE

Théâtre de la
Découverte
à la Verrière

RUE SAINTE BARBE

RUE RATISBONNE

RUE A MERCIER

RUE MEUREN

RUE RATISBONNE

RUE
RATISBONNE

Lycée
Fenelon

RUE LÉON GAMBETTA

PLACE DE LA
RÉPUBLIQUE

PLACE
RICHEB

RUE J LEFEBVRE

RUE CHARLES QUINT

RUE LÉON GAMBETTA

Bourse du
Travail

RUE INKERMAN

Poste
Principale

Palais des
Beaux-Arts

RUE

RUE DE LA
RENAISSANCE

RUE DE LA VIEILLE
AVENTURE

RUE D'ANVERS

RUE DE LA PAIX

RUE D'UTRECHT

RUE DE
FLANDRE

RUE HENRI KOLB

RUE COLBRANT

PLACE
SÉBASTOPOL

Théâtre
Sébastopol

RUE SOLFERINO

RUE NICOLAS LEBLANC

RUE GAUTHIER DE CHÂTIL

Le ZEM
Théâtre

RUE MOURMANT

RUE DU MARCHÉ

RUE D'ALGER

RUE DE BOVE

Maternité

RUE MANUEL

RUE DES POSTES

RUE DE VALMY

Faculté
des Sciences

Tem

Marché de
Wazemmes

PLACE DE LA
NOUVELLE
AVENTURE

Eglise
St Pierre et
St Paul

GAMBETTA

RUE MANUEL

RUE FONTENELLE

RUE DE
CONSTANTINE

RUE DES PYRAMIDES

RUE FABRICY

PARIS

Maison
Coillot

PLACE
PHILLIPE
LEBON

Eglise
St Michel

RUE JEA

RUE DES SARRAZINS

RUE DE L'ABBÉ AERTS

RUE LITTRÉ

RUE RACINE

RUE HOVELACQUE

RUE DU MARCHÉ

RUE G APOLLINAIRE

RUE LOUIS FAURE

RUE DES POSTES

G JONCQUET

RUE STAPPAERT

RUE DES
MEUNIERS

RUE DE FLEURUS

RUE CAUMARTIN

RUE BRÛLE MAISON

RUE
ST
MICHEL

RUE BRÛLE MAISON

RUE D'ARTOIS

SOLFERINO

RUE JEANNE D'ARC

Mu

RUE JULES GUESDE

SQUARE
HENRI
GHESQUIERE

RUE BOURIGNON

RUE GANTOIS

RUE CAUMARTIN

DE

RUE

CAF

PLACE
JEANNE
D'ARC

L'H

RUE JEANNE D'ARC

234

WAZEMMES

DELESPAUL

LENS

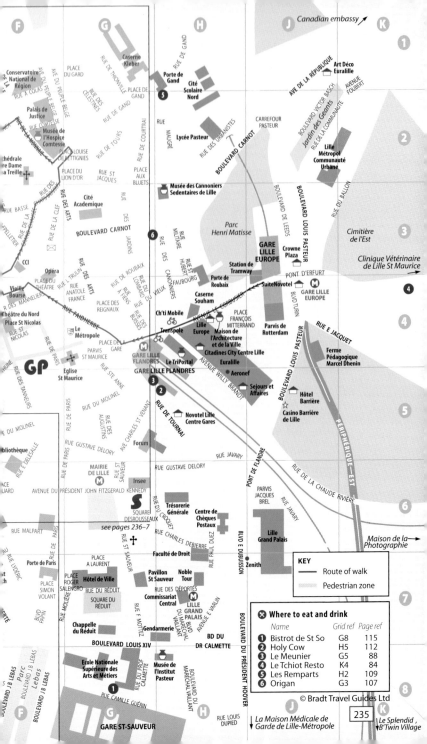

KEY

— Route of walk

Pedestrian zone

⊗ Where to eat and drink

Name	Grid ref	Page ref
❶ Bistrot de St So	G8	115
❷ Holy Cow	H5	112
❸ Le Meunier	G5	88
❹ Le Tchiot Resto	K4	84
❺ Les Remparts	H2	109
❻ Origan	G3	107

© Bradt Travel Guides Ltd

235

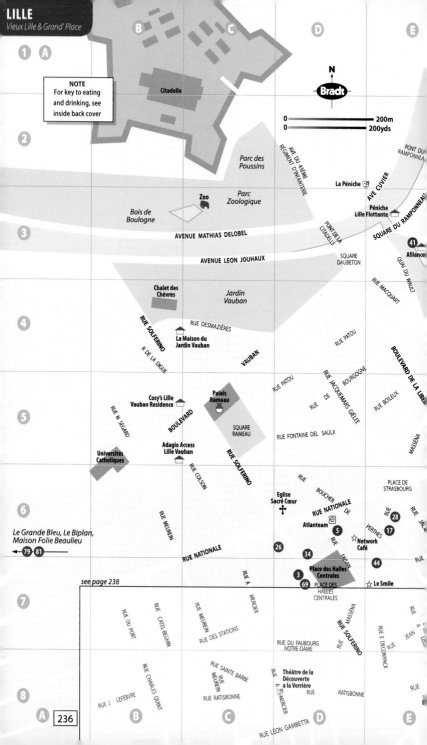

LILLE
Vieux Lille & Grand' Place

A

B

C

D

E

1

2

3

4

5

6

7

8

NOTE
For key to eating and drinking, see inside back cover

Citadelle

N

Bradt

0   200m
0   200yds

Parc des Poussins

AVE DU 43ÈME RÉGIMENT D'INFANTERIE

La Péniche

PONT DU RAMPONNEAU

AVE CUVIER

Zoo

Parc Zoologique

Péniche Lille Flottante

Bois de Boulogne

AVENUE MATHIAS DELOBEL

PONT DE LA CITADELLE

SQUARE DU RAMPONNEAU

QUAI DU WAULT

AVENUE LEON JOUHAUX

SQUARE DAUBETON

41

Alliance

RUE MACQUART

Chalet des Chèvres

Jardin Vauban

RUE DESMAZIÈRES

RUE SOLFERINO

La Maison du Jardin Vauban

BOULEVARD DE LA LIBER

R DE LA DIGUE

VAUBAN

RUE PATOU

RUE PATOU

RUE JACQUEMARS GIÉLÉE

RUE DE BOURGOGNE

RUE BOILEUX

Cosy's Lille Vauban Residence

Palais Rameau

RUE N SÉGARD

BOULEVARD

SQUARE RAMEAU

RUE FONTAINE DEL SAULX

MASSENA

Universités Catholiques

Adagio Access Lille Vauban

RUE SOLFERINO

RUE COLSON

RUE

PLACE DE STRASBOURG

RUE MEUREIN

Eglise Sacré Cœur ✝

RUE BOUCHER DE

RUE NATIONALE

RUE

28

PERTHES

17

RUE JA

Le Grande Bleu, Le Biplan, Maison Folie Beaulieu

◄ 79 81

Atlanteam

5

Network Café

26

34

RUE FAÇAN

44

RUE

RUE NATIONALE

3

Place des Halles Centrales

see page 238

RUE A

69

PLACE DES HALLES CENTRALES

☆ Le Smile

MERCIER

RUE DU PORT

RUE CATEL-BEGHIN

RUE MEUREIN

RUE DES STATIONS

RUE DU FAUBOURG NOTRE-DAME

RUE MASSENA

RUE SOLFERINO

RUE E DECONINCKX

RUE JEAN A

RUE

RUE CHARLES QUINT

RUE SAINTE BARBE

RUE MEUREIN

Théâtre de la Découverte a la Verrière

RUE

RATISBONNE

RUE

RUE J LEFÈBVRE

RUE RATISBONNE

RUE LÉON GAMBETTA

A

B

C

D

E

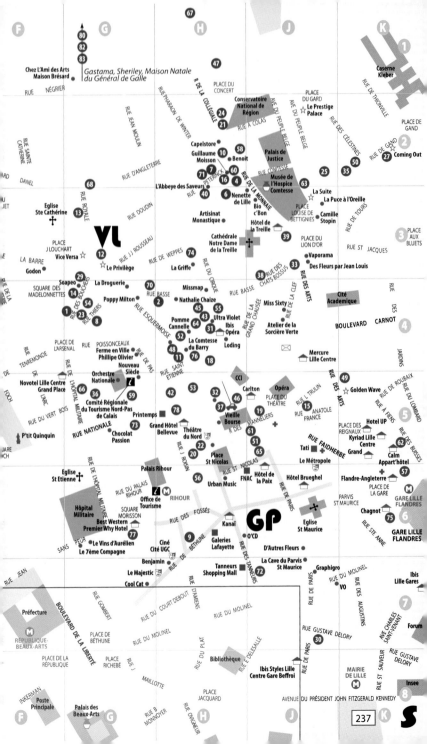

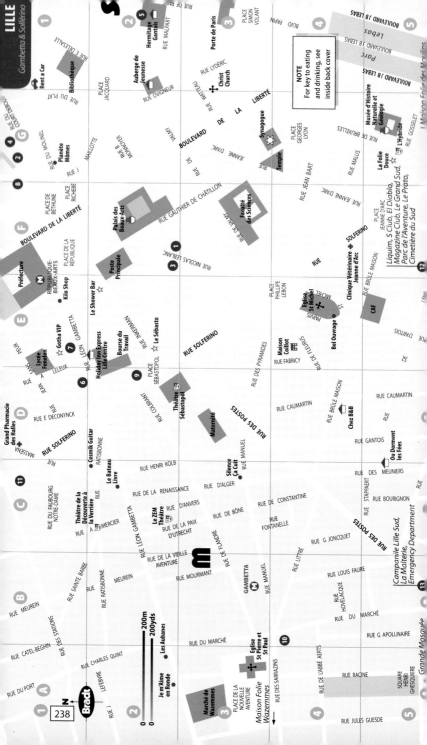

KEY

Métro (VAL)
Line 1
Line 2

Tram
⊸◦⊷ incl. underground section

Other routes

© 2013 UrbanRail.Net (R. Schwandl)

Bradt

CH Dron **2**
Bourgogne
Pont de Neuville
Phalempins
Mouscron, Gent
Colbert
Tourcoing-
T Centre
Tourcoing
Victoire
Tourcoing-
Sébastopol
Pont Hydraulique
Carliers
Ma Campagne
Mercure
Faidherbe
Alsace
Trois Suisses
Comines
Gare-Jean-Lebas
Roubaix
Triez
Roubaix-
Grand Place
Grand Cottignies
Croix-
L'Allumette
R Roubaix
Eurotéléport
Cartelot
Roubaix-
Charles de Gaulle
Alfred Mongy
Épeule-
Montesquieu
Jean Moulin
Château Rouge
Croix-
Wasquehal
Hôpital Victor Provo
Cerisaie
Centre d'Affaires
Croix
Marquette
Mairie
Parc Barbieux
La Madeleine
Pont de
Croix Centre
Calais,
London
St André
Le Quesne Wasquehal
Foch
Wasquehal-
Hôtel de Ville
Bol d'Air
Croisé Laroche
Le Sart
Villa Cavrois
Clemenceau
La
Hippodrome
Terrasse
Planche
La Marque
Brossolette
Buisson
Épinoy
2 St Philibert
Acacias
Mitterie
St Maur
Wasquehal-
Jean-Jaurès
Bourg
Maison
Botanique
Pavé de Lille
des Enfants
Pont Supérieur
Romarin
St Maurice
Lomme Lambersart
Pellevoisin
Les Près
R **T**
Lille Gare Europe
Canteleu
Mons
Gare Lille Flandres
Sarts
Fort de Mons
Bois Blancs
Rihour
Mairie
Port de Lille
République
de Mons
Beaux Arts
Mairie
Caulier
Cormontaigne
de Lille
Gambetta
Lille
Fives
Montebello
Grand Palais
Marbrerie
Wazemmes
Porte de
Porte des Postes
Valenciennes
Lezennes
Porte
Porte
Hellemmes
d'Arras
de Douai
Lezennes
Pont de Bos
Lille CHR
Hellemmes
Loos-lez-Lille
Annappes
Ascq
Tournai
Porte de Douai
Mont de Terre
CHR Oscar Lambret
Villeneuve d'Ascq-
Hôtel de Ville
Triolo
CHR B-Calmette **1**
Ronchin
Cité Scientifique
Lens, Béthune
Douai, Lens
Quatre Cantons **1**
Valenciennes,
Orchies
Valenciennes,
Paris, Bruxelles

40 Years of
Pioneering Publishing

ALONG ANCIENT WAYS
IN PERU AND BOLIVIA

HILARY
AND
GEORGE
BRADT

TRAVEL PIONEERS
40
FOR OVER 40 YEARS

Bradt...take the road less travelled